THE
COWBOY
LEGEND

THE WEST SERIES

Aritha van Herk, Series Editor

ISSN 1922-6519 (Print) ISSN 1925-587X (Online)

This series focuses on creative non-fiction that explores our sense of place in the West - how we define ourselves as Westerners and what impact we have on the world around us. Essays, biographies, memoirs, and insights into Western Canadian life and experience are highlighted.

No. 1 · Looking Back: Canadian Women's Prairie Memoirs and Intersections of Culture, History, and Identity **S. Leigh Matthews**

No. 2 · Catch the Gleam: Mount Royal, From College to University, 1910–2009 **Donald N. Baker**

No. 3 · Always an Adventure: An Autobiography **Hugh A. Dempsey**

No. 4 · Promoters, Planters, and Pioneers: The Course and Context of Belgian Settlement in Western Canada **Cornelius J. Jaenen**

No. 5 · Happyland: A History of the "Dirty Thirties" in Saskatchewan, 1914–1937 **Curtis R. McManus**

No. 6 · My Name is Lola **Lola Rozsa, as told to and written by Susie Sparks**

No. 7 · The Cowboy Legend: Owen Wister's Virginian and the Canadian-American Frontier **John Jennings**

No. 8 · Sharon Pollock: First Woman of Canadian Theatre **Edited by Donna Coates**

UNIVERSITY OF CALGARY
Press

THE COWBOY LEGEND

Owen Wister's Virginian and the Canadian-American Frontier

JOHN JENNINGS

© 2015 John Jennings

University of Calgary Press
2500 University Drive NW
Calgary, Alberta
Canada T2N 1N4
www.uofcpress.com

This book is available as an ebook which is licensed under a Creative Commons license. The publisher should be contacted for any commercial use which falls outside the terms of that license.

LIBRARY AND ARCHIVES CANADA CATALOGUING IN PUBLICATION

Jennings, John, 1941-, author
    The cowboy legend : Owen Wister's Virginian and the Canadian-American frontier / John Jennings.

(The west ; 7)
Includes bibliographical references and index.
Issued in print and electronic formats.
ISBN 978-1-55238-528-9 (paperback).–ISBN 978-1-55238-529-6 (pdf).
–ISBN 978-1-55238-752-8 (epub).–ISBN 978-1-55238-753-5 (mobi)

    1. Johnson, Everett, 1860-1946. 2. Cowboys–West (U.S.)–Social life and customs. 3. Cowboys–Alberta–Social life and customs. 4. Frontier and pioneer life–West (U.S.)–History. 5. Frontier and pioneer life–Alberta–History. 6. Wister, Owen, 1860-1938. Virginian. 7. Cowboys in literature. 8. Cowboys in popular culture. I. Title. II. Series: West series (Calgary, Alta.) ; 7

F596.J46 2015   978   C2015-904842-7
                                                                                       C2015-904843-5

The University of Calgary Press acknowledges the support of the Government of Alberta through the Alberta Media Fund for our publications. We acknowledge the financial support of the Government of Canada through the Canada Book Fund for our publishing activities. We acknowledge the financial support of the Canada Council for the Arts for our publishing program.

Printed and bound in Canada by Friesens
This book is printed on 57lb Rolland Enviro 100 paper

Cover design, page design, and typesetting by Melina Cusano

To Jean Johnson

CONTENTS

Acknowledgments	ix
Preface	xi
Prologue: A Synopsis of *The Virginian*	xviii
Introduction	1
1: Beginnings (1860–74)	31
2: The Black Hills (1875–76)	45
3: Bill Cody (1876–78)	61
4: Wyoming (1878–88)	89
5: Owen Wister and Wyoming (1885)	153
6: Alberta (1888–1904)	195
7: The Book (1891–1904)	267
8: Afterword (1904–1946)	313
Notes	337
Bibliography	371
Index	403

Acknowledgments

This book is dedicated to Jean Johnson. Her manuscript of her father-in-law's life, deposited in the Glenbow Archives, is the basis for this book. I also owe a large debt to her daughter Donna Butters for all her help over the years. Donna's sons, Erik and Lamont, read the manuscript and provided important information.

All historians of the Canadian West are very fortunate to have the Glenbow Archives and Library. It is a fabulous resource, as are the people who work there. I would especially like to thank Hugh Dempsey and Sheilagh Jameson for sharing their vast knowledge of the early western Canadian frontier, first when I was working on my doctoral thesis on the early Mounted Police and Native relations and, later, as I was researching the history of the early Alberta range. I would also like to thank Doug Cass, a former student of mine at the University of Calgary, and now Director, Library and Archives, at the Glenbow Museum, for all his help over the years.

This book required research in a number of archives in both eastern and western United States: the American Heritage Center at the University of Wyoming; the Buffalo Bill Center of the West in Cody, Wyoming; the Library of Congress; the Houghton Library at Harvard University; the Historical Society of Pennsylvania in Philadelphia; the Historical Society of New Hampshire in Concord; and the Remington Museum in Ogdensburg, New York. Without exception, the staff of these institutions were generous with their time and often bombarded me with extra material that they thought might prove useful.

A number of individuals were also very generous with their knowledge. In Wyoming, Bill Henry, the grandson of Mike Henry, the model for

Wister's Judge Henry, put aside a busy day to show me around the ranching country of Wyoming and to provide me with useful material. In the ranching community of Johnson County, Wyoming, and in its urban centre, Buffalo, I met many people with an extensive knowledge of early Wyoming history and a refreshing openness to share it with me.

I have been very fortunate in receiving generous advice from historians of the Alberta ranching frontier, starting with Lewis G. Thomas, the dean of Alberta ranching history; Simon Evans, who read an early version of the manuscript and gave me much invaluable advice and detailed suggestions; David Breen, whose work on the Alberta ranching frontier is the starting point for any work in the area; Donald Smith, one of Canada's foremost experts in the field of Native history; Ted Chamberlin, whose broad knowledge and fresh insights into both the history and the literature of the early West were exceedingly useful; Rod Macleod, the foremost historian of the Mounted Police and early law in Alberta; and my great friend Max Foran, who stood up with me when I was married in the little log church in Millarville in the heart of Alberta ranching country. Max is equally ferocious in his pursuit of history and on the squash court!

I was very fortunate in having editorial advice from Ramsay Derry, with his great breadth of literary knowledge, and from Peter Enman at the University of Calgary Press, who was a delight to work with. Donna Livingstone, former Director of the University of Calgary Press and now President and CEO of the Glenbow Museum, was very helpful in the early stages of this book.

And, finally, to my wife Nicola, a very special thanks for your unwavering encouragement, your keen eye for mistakes, and discerning ear for the English language. This book owes much to you.

Preface

The cowboy is, arguably, America's foremost folk figure. The creation of this most American of folk heroes began quite suddenly with the publication of Owen Wister's novel *The Virginian* in 1902. The romantic cowboy that Wister created launched a deluge of cowboy literature that firmly placed the cowboy at the forefront of American popular culture. It is the main contention of this book that Wister's Virginian was based on Everett Johnson, a cowboy from Virginia, who lived on the cattle frontiers of Wyoming and Alberta during their most exciting and decisive times.

Sidney Freifeld, in his delightful *Undiplomatic Notes: Tales from the Canadian Foreign Service*, recounts an incident in 1967 when he was part of Canada's delegation to the United Nations during one of the most tense moments in that institution's history – the Six-Day War in the Middle East. Canada was then a member of the Security Council and the Cold War was at its height. In the midst of round-the-clock negotiations, an old boyhood friend from Ottawa who happened to be in New York asked Freifeld for a tour of the UN. The friend in question was Lorne Greene, fresh from the set of Bonanza, the most popular western TV show of the time. Greene starred as Ben Cartwright, the patriarch of the Ponderosa Ranch. Bonanza was a Sunday night institution across North America.

On Greene's arrival at the UN, one of the most fraught debates in the history of the UN almost ground to a halt. Translators became distracted; delegation members began to leave their seats to climb the stairs to the gallery for autographs. At lunch in the delegates' dining room, heads of state were shunted aside for Freifeld and his guest.

Then, in the corridor on the way to the delegates' lounge, they met the Soviet Ambassador, Nicolai Federenko, and the Soviet Foreign Minister, Andrei Gromyko. As Gromyko stood bemused, Federenko greeted Greene with outstretched arms, "My distinguished representative from Ponderosa, my dear Ambassador Cartwright from Bonanza, I want you to know that for years you have been one of my own family. You are with us after dinner in our family living room in Moscow. You are with us in our living room in New York. You are one of our very own. You must autograph something for my children."[1] Before departing, he urged Greene to visit him in Moscow.

Fast forward several decades to June 4, 1989, the day that the first free election in Poland since the Second World War resulted in the overwhelming renunciation of Polish communism and a victory for Solidarity, the Polish union movement. Solidarity's campaign poster perfectly captured the mood that started the unravelling of communism, the Cold War, and the Soviet Empire: a picture of Gary Cooper, the sheriff in the famous western film *High Noon*, symbolizing the day of reckoning for Dodge City East!

It all started with Wister. Before Owen Wister's publication of *The Virginian* in 1902, the image of the cowboy was essentially one drawn from the dime novel – a rough, violent one-dimensional drifter – or the stage cowboy variety found in Buffalo Bill Cody's Wild West show. Wister's novel transformed, almost overnight, this image of the cowboy.

This book sets out to do three things. First, its purpose is to tell Everett Johnson's story. His life is interesting in its own right. He was witness to a fascinating period in the development of the American, and later Canadian, western frontiers. His story, as he told it to his daughter-in-law, is worth recording for all the people, places, and events he touched – the Texas cattle trails, Deadwood at the height of its gold frenzy, Buffalo Bill Cody, Wild Bill Hickok, Wyatt Earp, Wyoming and Alberta in their early frontier days, Butch Cassidy, and Johnson's best man when he married in Alberta, Harry Longabaugh – otherwise known as the Sundance Kid. The list goes on. But what gives Everett Johnson's story its special importance is his connection with the emergence of the cowboy legend, the most powerful legend yet produced by America. It is the contention of this book that Johnson was the initial and most important inspiration for the creation of Owen Wister's cowboy, the Virginian. Wister, with his two accomplices, Frederic Remington and Theodore Roosevelt, literally created the popular image of the cowboy. The alchemy performed by these three is both fascinating and, in places, quite unexpected. Together they manufactured a myth that has been extraordinarily powerful and lasting.

Third, Everett Johnson spent a significant time on both the Wyoming and Alberta ranching frontiers. His life on those frontiers gives the historian an unusually good chance to compare them. Comparative history is often like weighing apples and oranges. It is not often that the historian – through the lens of one individual's life – is able to study two frontiers at almost the same stage of evolution. As well, a comparative study of these frontiers says much about the political and cultural underpinnings of the societies that produced them. A major argument of this book will be that, although the two western cattle frontiers were remarkably similar in many ways, the very different legal institutions, in both criminal and land law, caused them to develop in very different ways.

Law is at the very heart of a society. Despite the great similarities between the frontiers of Wyoming and Alberta – the geography, the day-to-day life of the cowboy, the shared equestrian culture, and the dynamics of the cattle business – the one thing that set the two frontiers apart was the law. Not only was there a clear difference in the way the law functioned on either side of the line, but that difference was the most important factor distinguishing the two frontiers. Johnson's life on these two ranching frontiers offers an ideal opportunity not only to study the repercussions of the two very different legal systems in Wyoming and Alberta but also to look at the wider picture. Law, as it evolved in the two countries, is arguably the feature that most differentiates Canada from the United States, both then and now.

Here is a double-edged sword. Legal institutions and customs were brought to the frontier from the East in both Canada and the United States. In Canada, the law that came west was imposed on the Canadian West by the federal government in the form of the Mounted Police, and was little changed by the frontier. In the United States, what is often thought of as uniquely western law was first brought to the frontier by easterners, the legacy of the Revolution and the Mexican and Civil wars. Easterners also brought to the West the legacy of a fierce belief in populist local self-determination. (Billy the Kid was more a product of inner-city New York than of New Mexico.) The American West, in turn, shaped the law, giving it a distinct flavour of western romance, energy, impatience, and lack of deference. In a fascinating transformation, the West gave back to the nation a legacy of law based on the mythology of the frontier and a romantic vision of the handgun. From this mythology came the justification of vigilantism as a positive force, despite its use, for example, as a tool for racial intimidation by the Ku Klux Klan. This devotion to vigilantism has had a profound influence on American society into the twenty-first century.

* * * * *

I barely remember Everett Johnson. I was only five when he died in 1946. He was then eighty-six and had been, for some time, a patient of my father's in Calgary. Little could he imagine that the small boy who was allowed, as a very special treat, to stay up past his bedtime to listen to his memories would someday be writing his story.

This book is very special to me. I grew up steeped in the aura of Ed Johnson and the West that he represented. He was a frequent visitor to our house, and his wonderful stories of the early West undoubtedly influenced my choosing history as a profession. He had that carefully honed gift, now almost a lost art, of spinning out an interminable story, which drew in the listener irresistibly. And then the punchline, which turned the story on its head. I can remember my parents just looking at each other and bursting out laughing as they remembered one of his tales.

Ed Johnson was introduced to my parents by Jack Reid, the son of Bill Reid, one of Johnson's great friends from Wyoming days, who had been a key figure in the Wagon Box Fight in 1867. Jack Reid, after a fascinating career – the only one I know of – as a lawman on both sides of the border, settled down to farm near Calgary. He later became a renowned gunsmith. He met my father through rifle competitions and the two became fast friends. I mention this because it was only as a result of this friendship with the son of Bill Reid that Johnson let down his reserve with my parents and told them about some of his early experiences. Ordinarily, he was almost painfully reticent.

Over the years, the links between our families grew. Johnson's son, Laurie, was a very fine horseman and one of Alberta's best polo players. At a time, in my teens, when most of my waking hours in the summer were devoted to thoughts of horses and training and playing polo ponies, Laurie Johnson was very generous with his advice. Laurie's wife, Jean, was also a very fine horsewoman – and polo player. She used to tell a marvellous story of her women's polo team, composed of Alberta ranching women, which travelled to New York to play a women's team in the 1930s. They planned to show these New York women a thing or two about riding and polo and then sell them their ranch-bred ponies. Instead, they were thoroughly trounced and couldn't sell their horses, returning home with a new respect for the toughness and economic canniness of New York women.

And I have known Laurie and Jean's daughter, Donna Butters, for many years. Her parents' horsemanship and love of horses were certainly passed on to her. We have competed together for many years in horse shows and cross-country jumping events.

I have also spent many special hours on the Butters' ranch in the Ghost Valley, one of the most spectacular ranching areas in Alberta. The family is still carrying on the ranching tradition there, which began with Everett Johnson. As I write, the smell of their log ranch house is vivid in my mind.

Only Johnson's family and a few others know the story that is told here. Over the years, his daughter-in-law, Jean, put together his story as he told it to her. I have tried to stay as close as possible to that story, but I have also added considerable material because Johnson's life touched so many fascinating and important moments in western history. Since he was on two very different cattle frontiers – Wyoming and Alberta – which developed almost at the same time, his life gives the historian an ideal chance to compare these two areas, especially regarding the institutions and customs that shaped and coloured life on these frontiers.

I have also added many details concerning the lives of a few of the more colourful characters that Johnson knew. The original manuscript is frustratingly tight-lipped regarding people such as Bill Cody and Harry Longabaugh (the Sundance Kid). At times, I have worried that I have strayed too far from my subject. Originally, I had planned simply to edit Jean Johnson's manuscript, which resides in the Glenbow Archives in Calgary, Alberta. But the deeper I got into the subject, the more I realized that the events that Johnson witnessed were just too important to skim over. His story transcends personal biography.

I have also worried, of course, about the credibility of his recollections. I have very little proof that Johnson's story is true. Normally this would not matter. Many cowboys have recounted their lives without any proof and have still been published by reputable publishers. However, this story obviously demands more evidence because of the link with Wister and the claim that Johnson was the original inspiration for the character of the Virginian.

During my years of research on Johnson and Wister – in Alberta and Wyoming – and on the trail of Wister at the Library of Congress, the Pennsylvania Historical Society, the Houghton Library at Harvard, St. Paul's School near Concord, New Hampshire, and at the Remington Museum in Ogdensburg, New York, I have had many disappointments in not being able to prove some of the important claims of this story. Once Johnson got to Alberta, his story is easy to verify. By then he was important. But before that, it is almost impossible to prove that he even existed. He was a minor player in most of the events that he witnessed, and thus his presence was not recorded. Also, he was living in the American West at a time when the recording of events was spotty at best. Newspapers were just coming into existence, few records were being kept; most of the people who were shaping events in the West were far too busy or too illiterate to record what was happening.

As I researched this story, I realized, after exhaustive detective work, that certain claims in the manuscript could not be verified. Quite simply, I have almost no physical proof that Owen Wister ever laid eyes on Johnson. Nor have I any proof that some of the events in *The Virginian* were based on Johnson's life. For instance, a great deal of time was spent trying to track down the man that Johnson claimed to have killed in a gunfight in Buffalo, Wyoming, the man that Wister would transform into the villain Trampas. Newspapers were no use whatever; at the time of the gunfight in the 1880s, the Buffalo newspapers were just beginning in a haphazard way. Court records were no better. In 1895, Clear Creek, which runs through the middle of Buffalo, flooded and destroyed all the records at Buffalo City Hall. Finally, I was sent to a Buffalo funeral home, where the coroner's records for the period were kept. When I explained my mission, the owner of the funeral home just shook his head and told me that I was wasting my time. If the fight was considered fair, then there was probably no inquest, and thus no record. He told me that he could show me a number of unmarked graves from that period; they just dug them in, no questions asked. The *Billings Gazette*, in an article on early days (August 20, 1965), reported that there were fifty-two unmarked graves at Buffalo from the early days and no records of who those people might be. I was no more successful in proving a link with Bill Cody or Nat Boswell. The records surrounding both men's lives were depressingly casual.

On the other hand, I was able to find considerable material that filled in much of the background for the events discussed here. One of the great satisfactions of being a historian is to talk to people who can still remember interesting bits from the old days; their generosity and enthusiasm make historical sleuthing a delight.

I particularly remember one rancher in the Powder River country of Wyoming who was able to tell me a lot about the Powder River Cattle Company. Somehow, we got onto the subject of rattlesnakes, and I admitted that I had a near phobia of snakes. I made the mistake of telling him that, as I was sleuthing about, my solution to the problem was to sing very loudly to scare them away. He gave me one of those long western looks and said, "Singin' to rattlers don't do much good, you know. They got no ears. They don't hear worth a shit."

Despite the lack of hard evidence for some of the claims in Johnson's manuscript, I never lost faith in his truthfulness. On occasion, I thought his memory might have been playing him tricks, such as having Wyatt Earp in Deadwood in 1876 when almost every source had him in Dodge City and the standard books on Deadwood made no mention of him. But nowhere did I find that he had said something that was clearly untrue. For instance, I finally did find Wyatt Earp in Deadwood, in the firewood business!

My obsession was to prove the link with Wister. This I was able to do only in a tenuous way. But, again, after exhaustive research, I was unable to find anything that disproved his story or indicated that the Virginian was clearly someone else. In every case where Johnson indicated that Wister based *The Virginian* on his life, I could find no convincing evidence to the contrary, either in Wister's papers or in Wyoming archives.

And, finally, through all my research into the Wister connection, I was encouraged by one fact. Soon after the publication of *The Virginian*, Wister sent Johnson a copy, inscribed "To the hero from the author." Unfortunately, that one piece of proof, together with some letters from Wister, was destroyed in a fire. But I have no doubt whatsoever that they existed. Both my parents told me that they had seen the book and its inscription.

Johnson was not just an old-timer with an active imagination. He did not go around making claims about himself; he told his story only to his family and a few close friends. It was his old friends from Wyoming who made the claims for him. He was the real thing.

There is one great sadness in the writing of this book. Jean Johnson died in the spring of 1992, before she could see the completed manuscript. This book is for her. Though I have tampered considerably with her original manuscript, this book rests on her years of patient work. My efforts are dedicated to her memory.

When I try to give my students in western history a picture of frontier women, Jean is my model. She would have bristled if someone had called her a feminist, but in her quiet way, she was as determined and outspoken as the best of them. She was one of that breed of women that made the West. She could ride with any man and loved the ranching country with a passion. She could come back from an all-day cattle drive and ten minutes later be serving an elegant tea with grace and wit. She was widely admired for her gentleness, toughness, and subtle humour; she is greatly missed.

Prologue: A Synopsis of The Virginian

To understand the chapters dealing with Wister's novel, a basic outline of the story or a quick refreshing of the plot will be helpful. *The Virginian* is essentially a stringing together of episodes depicting cowboy life and manners that is intended to portray Wister's central theme: the cowboy as the true American. The western frontier will save America from becoming over-civilized, effete, and decadent.

The novel begins with Wister, the narrator, leaving the newly constructed railway at Medicine Bow, a real "no-account" little town in southern Wyoming, midway between Laramie and Rawlins. Here Wister is met by Judge Henry's trusted man, the Virginian, for the journey by buckboard to the ranch, where Wister is to spend the summer. Throughout the novel, the hero is never given a name. He is always just the Virginian. Thus, a certain mystery surrounds the Virginian, and Wister creates an air of authenticity by recounting events through his own eyes.

Wister's first sight of the Virginian is a glimpse of him roping with great skill. Wister describes his hero as a tall, dark-haired Southerner, in his mid-twenties, gentle of speech, "a slim giant, more beautiful than pictures."

Wister immediately introduces the reader to the atmosphere of Wyoming in a card game at Medicine Bow. Wister and the Virginian have to stay the night in Medicine Bow before setting out for the ranch, 260 miles to the north. The Virginian decides to fill the evening with a game of poker, and Wister notices that he prepares for the game by taking his pistol from its holster and shoving it between his overalls and shirt. (A number of famous "shootists" preferred this method of quick draw.)

Charles M. Russell illustration for the 1911 edition of *The Virginian*. All the illustrations in the synopsis are by Russell.

In conversation over cards, it comes out that the Virginian has recently been in Arizona and now works for Judge Henry's Sunk Creek Ranch. As the game progresses, it comes to the Virginian's turn to bet. As he hesitates, the dealer, a man named Trampas, says with impatience, "Your bet, you Son-of-a- —."

> *The Virginian's pistol came out, and his hand lay on the table, holding it unaimed. And with a voice as gentle as ever, the voice that almost sounded like a caress ... "When you call me that, smile."*

Trampas backs down from the challenge, but from this instant the final showdown between the two is set. And into western literature enters one of its most famous phrases.

In the squalid little town of Medicine Bow, beds are at a premium and in such circumstances, it was usual for travellers to share a bed. The Virginian's good friend Steve enters into a bet with the Virginian that he can't get a bed to himself. This bet sets the scene for the first example of the Virginian's wicked genius. In this incident Wister demonstrates both the unique flavour of western devilment and his superb capture of western language. The Virginian is to share a bed with a travelling salesman – a "drummer." As an expectant crowd gathers at the bedroom door, the Virginian undresses and prepares to get into bed with the salesman.

> Many listeners had now gathered at the door.... We made a large company, and I felt that trembling sensation which is common when the cap of a camera is about to be removed upon a group.
> "I should think" said the drummer's voice, "that you'd feel your gun and knife clean through that pillow."
> "I do," responded the Virginian.
> "I should think you'd put them on a chair and be comfortable."
> "I'd be uncomfortable then."
> "Used to the feel of them, I suppose."
> "That's it. Used to the feel of them. I would miss them, and that would make me wakeful."
> "Well, good night."
> "Good night. If I get to talkin' and tossin', or what not, you'll understand you're to –"
> "Yes, I'll wake you."
> "No, don't yu' for God's sake."
> "Not?"

"Don't yu' touch me."

"What'll I do?"

"Roll away quick to your side. It don't last but a minute." The Virginian spoke with a reassuring drawl.

Upon this there fell a brief silence, and I heard the drummer clear his throat once or twice.

"It's merely the nightmare I suppose?" he said after a throat clearing.

"Lord, yes. That's all. And don't happen twice a year. Was you thinking it was fits?"

"Oh, no. I just wanted to know. I've been told before that it was not safe for a person to be waked suddenly that way out of a nightmare."

"Yes, I have heard of that too. But it never harms me any. I don't want you to run risks."

"Me?"

"Oh, it'll be all right now that yu' know how it is." The Virginian's drawl was full of reassurance.

There was a second pause, after which the drummer said:-

"Tell me again how it is."

The Virginian answered very drowsily: "Oh, just don't let your arm or your laig touch me if I go to jumpin' around. I'm dreamin' of Indians when I do that. And if anything touches me then, I'm liable to grab my knife right in my sleep."

"Oh, I understand," said the drummer, clearing his throat. "Yes."

Steve was whispering delighted oaths to himself, and in his joy applying to the Virginian one unprintable name after another.

We listened again, but no further words came. Listening very hard, I could half make out the progress of heavy breathing, and a restless turning I could clearly detect. This was the wretched drummer. He was waiting. He did not wait long. Again there was a light creak, and after that a light step. He was not even going to put his boots on in the fatal neighbourhood of the dreamer. By a happy thought, Medicine Bow formed into two lines, making an avenue from the door. And then, the commercial traveller forgot his Consumption Killer. He fell heavily over it. Immediately from the bed the Virginian gave forth a dreadful howl.

And then everything happened at once; and how shall mere words narrate it? The door burst open, and out flew the commercial traveller in his stockings. One hand held a lump of coat and trousers

THE COWBOY LEGEND

> with suspenders dangling, his boots were clutched in the other. The sight of us stopped his flight short. He gazed, the boots fell from his hand; and at his profane explosion, Medicine Bow set up a united, unearthly noise and began to play Virginia reel with him. The other occupants of the beds had already sprung out of them, clothed chiefly with their pistols, and ready for war.
> "What is it?" they demanded. "What is it?"
> "Why, I reckon it's drinks on Steve," said the Virginian from his bed. And he gave the first broad grin that I had seen from him.

The next morning Wister and the Virginian set off for the ranch, and Wister describes the landscape of Wyoming which so bewitched him. He also comments on the Virginian's cultivated politeness toward him, and the "bar of his cold and perfect civility." Two important themes have been introduced: the rhapsodic beauty of Wyoming and the proud reticence of the Southerner.

Wister arrives at Judge Henry's ranch and almost immediately earns the title "tenderfoot" for his ability to become entirely lost shortly after breakfast. So Judge Henry decides to have the Virginian look after him, much to the Virginian's humiliation. However, the Virginian bears the situation in courteous silence. At this stage in the story, Wister sets himself up as the rather pathetic and effete Easterner, a perfect foil for the many superior qualities of his untutored but innately gentlemanly Southerner – the natural aristocrat.

Molly Wood, the schoolmarm, now enters the story. She traces direct descent from Molly Stark, the wife of General John Stark of Revolutionary War fame, a fact of central importance to the story. Her family has come on hard times with the closing of the mills, so she decided to apply for the teaching position at Bear Creek. On reaching Wyoming, she takes a stagecoach driven by a man somewhat the worse for drink. This condition results in the stage becoming bogged down at a river crossing. As the stage careens, a tall rider suddenly appears and sweeps her from the stage. After setting her down, he disappears just as abruptly, leaving Molly somewhat shaken, and also intrigued!

They do not meet again until the Swinton brothers' barbeque at their Goose Egg Ranch on Bear Creek. There is much speculation among the cowboys about the new teacher; which one of them might be successful in seeking her favour? In the midst of this speculation, Trampas makes a comment about her that verges on the lewd and impugns her reputation.

> They laughed loudly at the blackguard picture which he drew; and the laugh stopped short, for the Virginian stood over Trampas.
> "You can rise up now, and tell them you lie."
> Trampas replied, "I thought you claimed you and her wasn't acquainted."
> "Stand on your laigs, you polecat, and say you're a liar."
> Trampas's hand moved behind him.
> "Quit that, or I'll break your neck."
> Trampas looked in the Virginian's [eye] and slowly rose. "I didn't mean —" he began, and paused, his face poisonously bloated.

Again, Trampas has been very publicly humiliated.

It is at this barbeque that the famous baby swapping takes place, an event claimed by various locales across the West. As Lin McLean and the Virginian are chatting at the whisky barrel, one of the babies in the room adjoining the dance makes a drowsy noise. The idea is born. The Virginian, abetted by Lin, proceeds to his diabolical scheme.

> "If they look so awful alike in the heavenly garden," the Southerner continued, "I'd just hate to be the folks who has the cuttin' out o' the general herd..." This soon led to an intricate process of exchange.... Mr McLean had been staring at the Virginian puzzled. Then, with a joyful yelp of enlightenment, he sprang to abet him.
> Meanwhile the parents went on dancing and the occasional cries of their progeny did not reach them.

The barbeque ends, the parents gather their offspring and depart for their distant ranches. It is only some time later that the monstrous scheme is realized and the distraught and murderous parents descend on the Goose Egg to retrieve their rightful offspring. Lin McLean has departed at sunup, and there is some thought of pursuit, but the Virginian owns up in such a charming way that he somehow avoids lynching by the collected mothers. There is evidence in the Wister papers that he first heard the baby-swapping story in Texas, but there are strong claims in Wyoming as well. Such a story would circulate up and down the cattle trails with considerable speed, soon to be claimed and magnified by sundry communities.

There now ensues one of the main themes of the story – the untutored Southerner's campaign to capture the heart of the reluctant Vermont lady of distinguished background. Several themes now become clear: the coming together of North and South in the aftermath of the Civil War and the

Prologue: A Synopsis of The Virginian

overcoming of eastern gentility by the natural aristocracy of the western cowboy. Except there is a falseness in this theme because it is impossible to imagine any of the other cowboys that Wister portrays in *The Virginian*, or in any of his other western stories, triumphing over Molly's reluctance. It is really the gentle manners of the Tidewater Southerner, coupled with his iron code of behaviour, that finally wins her over. Molly doesn't fall for cowboys as a class; she falls for one very particular cowboy who is not at all typical.

The Virginian becomes the acting foreman of the ranch. In this role he is sent east with a consignment of cattle for Chicago. By chance, Wister, on his way west, meets the Virginian in Omaha and agrees to go back to Wyoming with him and the six hands from the Sunk Creek Ranch who make up his crew. One of them is Trampas, who tries to undermine the Virginian's authority by luring the six off to the gold diggings near Rawhide.

Somehow, the Virginian has to assert his authority over Trampas. He cannot order him to return to the ranch; he must somehow best him in a more subtle way. What follows is the frog story, based on the delicacy of frogs' legs à la Delmonico, which takes up four chapters. It is a classic example of the western tall tale, which is spun out interminably, until the sudden twist at the end, usually at some easterner's expense. But Wister's genius is to make Trampas, the westerner, the butt of the story, while a group of easterners listen in disbelief that a westerner could be sucked in by such a story. The Virginian piles one improbable detail on another in a way that seems quite natural: herding bull frogs into a separate pasture; the diabolical subterfuge of pretending to wander into a new field of anecdote, to be brought back to the main story by his audience; the frog herd breaking through the fence due to a pelican attack; frog trains tearing across Arizona through to New York; and finally, the frog market killed by revenge and disease.

> "Disease?" asks Trampas.
>
> "Just killed 'em. Delmonico and Saynt Augustine wiped frawgs off the slate of fashion. Not a banker in Fifth Avenue'll touch one now if another banker's around watchin' him. And if ever yu' see a man that hides his feet an' won't take off his socks in company, he has worked in them Tulare swamps an' got the disease. Catch him wadin' and yu'll find he's webfooted. Frawgs are dead, Trampas, and so are you."
>
> "Rise up, liars, and salute your king!" yelled Scipio.

Trampas is thoroughly humiliated, once again, by the Virginian, and the mutineers return to the ranch.

On returning to Judge Henry's ranch, the Virginian is made foreman and now moves into his own house, just as a visiting preacher appears on the scene unannounced. Dr. McBride is pompous, overbearing, and utterly without humour. And because there are other visitors at the ranch, the Judge asks the Virginian to give Dr. McBride a bed in the spare bedroom where Wister is sleeping. Thus, Wister, our narrator, is able to provide the details of the aftermath of Dr. McBride's mind-numbing sermon to the cowboys. Dr. McBride announces that he is going to spend the week at the ranch; the cowboys of the Sunk Creek outfit deserve his undivided attention! His opening sermon: *"There is no hope in any of you."* And then he invited them all to glorify the Creator of this scheme. His message to the cowboys: *"They were altogether become filthy."*

The Virginian regards Dr. McBride throughout his sermon with a "cream-like propriety." Then, after Dr. McBride is comfortably asleep, Wister hears the door open and the Virginian waking the good doctor.

> *"I feel like my spirit was going to bear witness. I feel like I might get an enlightening...."*

After a period of earnest conversation, all is quiet, but just as the preacher is getting back to sleep:

> *"Excuse me, seh. The enemy is winning on me. I'm feeling less inward opposition to sin."*

Again, a long period of hushed conversation. The reverend doctor is nicely back to sleep when, again, Wister hears the Virginian's feet padding across the floor.

> *"I'm afeared to be alone. I'm afeared. I'm losin' my desire afteh the sincere milk of the Word ... I'm afeared! I'm afeared! Sin has quit being bitter in my belly."*

Then, as the grey light of dawn enters the room,

> *"I'll worry through the day somehow without yu.' And to-night you can turn your wolf loose on me again."* Once more it was no use. *My face was deep in the pillow, but I made sounds as of a hen who*

has laid an egg. It broke on the doctor with a total instantaneous smash, quite like an egg. He tried to speak calmly. "This is a disgrace, an infamous disgrace."... I cried into my pillow, and wondered if the Doctor would come and kill me.

The doctor packs and leaves the ranch early that morning in high indignation.

The next incident in the book is completely without humour. While in Wyoming, Wister had witnessed an incident of unspeakable cruelty to a horse. He had done nothing about it and it preyed on his conscience. His way of resolving his cowardice was to have the Virginian mete out his terrible justice on Balaam, the horse abuser.

In the story, the Virginian happens to be at Balaam's ranch to collect two horses belonging to Judge Henry that Balaam has borrowed, when Shorty rides up on his pet horse Pedro. Shorty is down on his luck; Balaam realizes this and seizes the opportunity to buy Pedro, a very superior little cowpony. Poor Shorty, who has been led astray by Trampas, sells his beloved horse with the promise that he can buy him back when he is flush. Then the Virginian and Balaam set off for the Judge's ranch with the Judge's two half-wild horses in tow. The two horses try to escape and Balaam flies into a rage, which he takes out on poor Pedro. Soon Pedro is completely played out, wringing wet and bleeding from the mouth.

> *Pedro too tried to go forward – Suddenly he* [Balaam] *was at work at something.... For a few moments, it had no meaning to the Virginian as he watched. Then his mind grasped the horror, too late. Even with his cry of execration and the tiger spring that he gave to stop Balaam, the monstrosity was wrought. Pedro sank motionless, his head lolling flat on the earth. Balaam was jammed beneath him.*
>
> *Then vengeance like a blast struck Balaam. The Virginian hurled him to the ground, lifted and hurled him again, lifted him and beat his face and struck his jaw.... He fended his eyes as best he could against these sledge-hammer blows of justice. He felt for his pistol. His arm was caught and wrenched backward, and crushed and doubled. He seemed to hear his own bones, and set up a hideous screaming of hate and pain.*
>
> *Vengeance had come and gone. The man and the horse were motionless. Around them silence seemed to gather like a witness.*
>
> *"If you are dead," said the Virginian, "I am glad of it."*

Prologue: A Synopsis of The Virginian

But Balaam soon recovers enough to help the Virginian herd the two horses toward the Sunk Creek Ranch. When they get into the high country, the Judge's two horses become even more spooked and take off into the bush, with the Virginian in hot pursuit. It is then that Pedro, who is being led by Balaam, alerts him to the danger. They are being trailed by renegade Indians, and it is their presence that has spooked the horses. Pedro bolts across a stream, and, in an effort to make him turn back, Balaam shoots to turn him and, by mistake, breaks his leg. Balaam is forced to put him out of his misery. Pedro has saved his life and now lies mutilated and dead. Balaam decides to leave the Virginian to his own devices and heads for home.

Meanwhile, Molly has decided to run away from her heart. She realizes that she doesn't have the strength to refuse the Virginian, but can't face her family's accusations that a Stark would marry beneath herself. So she resigns her teaching post, writes a letter of farewell to the Virginian, and packs for home, with the words of her next-door neighbour, Mrs. Taylor, ringing in her ears, "*Since the roughness looks bigger than the diamond, you had better go back to Vermont. I expect you'll find better grammar there deary.*" With Mrs. Taylor's rebuke burning, Molly saddles her horse and rides off to settle her jangling emotions. On the trail, she finds the Virginian's horse Monte and, close by, the Virginian, badly wounded from an Indian ambush. With great difficulty, she gets him on Monte and leads him back to Bear Creek and her cabin.

More dead than alive, and in a state of delirium, the Virginian mutters about Trampas and then shouts, "*No Steve, it ain't so, Steve, I have lied for you.*" These words mean nothing to Molly, but introduce the next important section of the book: the lynching of the Virginian's good friend Steve, who has become a cattle rustler.

Then, later, on the way to recovery, the Virginian receives Molly's letter telling him that she is leaving permanently for Vermont. He realizes that she is running away from him and the roughness of the West. He confronts her and says,

> "Once I thought love must surely be enough. And I thought I could make you love me, you could learn me to be less – less – more your kind...." At last he looked at her again. "This is no country for a lady. Will yu' forget and forgive the bothering I have done."
> "Oh!" cried Molly. "Oh!"... "But," said Molly – "but I – you ought – please try to keep me happy!" And sinking by his chair, she hid her face on his knees.

Not with words, not even with meeting eyes, did the two plight their troth.

When the Virginian has fully recovered under Molly's care, he leaves her with the ominous observation that the cattle thieves are growing more audacious. He has arranged to meet Wister for some hunting in the Wind River country. But when Wister arrives – a few days early – he realizes that he is not expected yet, or wanted. He finds himself in the middle of the lynching of two rustlers by a party of cowboys led by the Virginian. One of the two to be lynched is Steve. And it is shortly implied that two other rustlers have escaped – Shorty and Trampas. On the morning of the lynching, the rustlers and the vigilantes engage in easy, fraternal conversation. Both sides know the game – and the consequences. It transpires that the two have been caught because of Shorty's carelessness with a fire. Wister stresses that Steve "died game," saying goodbye to all the vigilantes – except the Virginian, who is extremely upset by his friend's snub.

Wister and the Virginian, both of them much shaken, depart for some hunting, but soon realize they are following the tracks of two men and one horse. Next dawn they are awakened by something spooking their horses. Somewhat later, they hear a distant shot. They continue to follow the tracks and come upon a very recent camp and a very dead Shorty, shot from behind. The implication is clear. Trampas and Shorty realized that they were being followed; Trampas knew that they could not evade a posse with only one horse. So, exit Shorty!

By the campfire Wister finds the newspaper that he had given to Steve before he was lynched. Trampas and Shorty had obviously come upon the scene or had been watching and had taken the newspaper, probably to light a fire. In the margin Steve had written in pencil,

> "Good-by Jeff. I could not have spoken to you without playing the baby."
> "Who's Jeff?" I asked.
> "Steve used to call me Jeff because I was Southern. I reckon nobody else ever did."

When word reaches Molly of the lynching, she is, understandably, extremely upset, enough that it is feared that she might call off her engagement. So Judge Henry is recruited by Mrs. Taylor to persuade her of the necessity of vigilante law on a raw frontier. Coming from a federal judge, the justification for vigilante law does make Molly reluctantly reconsider her view and, at last, concede that there is a difference between lynching in Wyoming and the terrible barbarity of the public torture and lynching of Blacks in the South.

Despite her lingering misgivings, the date for the wedding is set. By this point, it has become clear that she is no longer the Virginian's superior, despite all his untutored ways.

> *Her better birth and schooling that had once been weapons to keep him at his distance ... had given way before the onset of the natural man himself. She knew her cowboy lover, for all he lacked, to be more than ever she could be, with all that she had.*

Molly and the Virginian ride into town for the wedding, to be met by three of the Virginian's good friends. They warn him that Trampas is in town and on the prod, full of liquor and bravado.

> *It had come to that point where there was no way out, save only the ancient, eternal way between man and man. It is only the great mediocrity that goes to law in these personal matters.*

The Virginian goes for a pre-wedding drink with his friends.

> *Suddenly Trampas was among them, courageous with whisky.... Others struggled with Trampas, and his bullet smashed the ceiling before they could drag the pistol from him.... "Your friends have saved your life" he rang out, with obscene epithets. "I'll give you til sundown to leave town."*
> *"Trampas," spoke the Virginian, "I don't want trouble with you."*
> *"He has never wanted it," Trampas sneered to the bystanders. "He has been dodging it five years. But I've got him corralled."*

The Virginian goes to the hotel storeroom to get his gun.

> *[The pistol] according to his wont when going into risk, he shoved between his trousers and his shirt in front.*

Then he goes to the hotel to tell Molly why he has to face Trampas. He explains that he did everything possible to make Trampas back down from his threats. Still, Molly asks him to come away. Everyone knows he is not a coward. The Virginian replies that this is his home, his life:

> *"If folks come to think I was a coward – ... I could not hold my head up again among enemies or friends."*

Molly makes her New England argument: *"There is a higher courage than fear of outside opinion."*

> *"Can't you see how it must be about a man?" "I cannot," she answered.... "If you do this there cannot be a to-morrow for you and me."*
>
> *Suddenly his hand closed hard. "Good-by, then," he said. And then before his desire could break him down... he was gone, and she was alone.... And next – it seemed a moment and it seemed an eternity – she heard in the distance a shot, and then two shots.*

Trampas has had second thoughts. After five years, it has all come to this. He has made his challenge publicly and can't go back on it. He had thought of trying to ambush the Virginian, but realized it had gone too far for that. He is now forced into a showdown of his own making.

The Virginian positions himself out on the street with his three friends behind him to cover his back.

> *A wind seemed to blow his sleeve off his arm and he replied to it, and saw Trampas pitch forward. He saw Trampas raise his arm from the ground and fall again, and lie there this time, still.*
>
> *"I expect that's all," he said aloud.... "If anyone wants me about this," he said, "I will be at the hotel." "Who'll want you?" said Scipio. "Three of us saw his gun out." And he vented his admiration. "You were that cool! That quick!"*
>
> *The Virginian walked to the hotel, and stood on the threshold of his sweetheart's room. She had heard his step, and was upon her feet. Her lips were parted, and her eyes fixed on him, nor did she move, or speak.*
>
> *"Yu' have to know it," he said. "I have killed Trampas."*
>
> *"Oh, thank God!" she said; and he found her in his arms. Long they embraced without speaking, and what they whispered then with their kisses, matters not.*
>
> *Thus did her New England conscience battle to the end, and, in the end, capitulate to love. And the next day, with the bishop's blessing, and Mrs. Taylor's broadest smile, and the ring on her finger, the Virginian departed with his bride into the mountains.*

After the wedding, the Virginian and Molly leave Buffalo and ride up into the mountains, to a very special place that the Virginian selected long ago

– a magical island – where they spend a month before departing for the East to make the rounds of Molly's family at Bennington.

Bennington is disappointed. Instead of a cowboy with a six-gun at his hip, it got a man in an understated and beautifully tailored suit, whose conversation was fit to come inside the house. Finally, they visit Molly's great-aunt at Dunbarton. She is the first of Molly's relations to really understand the Virginian. She shows him the portrait of General Stark, and says, *"There he is…. New Hampshire was full of fine young men in those days. But nowadays most of them have gone away to seek their fortunes in the West."*

The Virginian talks to her of Wyoming's future, about the end of the free grass era, and about the good land he has chosen close to coal deposits and the railway. The great-aunt sends Molly to bed and stays up talking to the Virginian and showing him her special things. *"We, too, had something to do with making our country."*

The book ends with the great-aunt's endorsement and with the Virginian telling her his dreams for the future of Wyoming and the West. Molly and the Virginian return to Wyoming and to Judge Henry's wedding present – a partnership in his ranch. The book ends with a vision of the new West and the Virginian's and Molly's place in it as people of substance surrounded by family.

No solitary horseman riding off into the sunset!

Introduction: *America's Gun Culture and the Vigilante Tradition*

Before embarking on the particulars of Everett Johnson's life and on Owen Wister's creation of the legendary cowboy figure, some general comments on the nature of law and Native relations on the two frontiers will help to put their actions and thoughts in context. Of special interest in the discussion of frontier American law is the emergence of vigilantism. It became a powerful force, to such an extent that the institution has had a profound and malign effect on modern America.

Both Johnson's life and Wister's novel were deeply influenced by western law or – more to the point – the absence of law. Vigilantism was an important part of Johnson's life in Wyoming and was one of the main themes of Wister's novel, which lay the ground for hundreds, if not thousands, of other western cowboy novels, movies, and TV shows. In fact, the latest book on American vigilantism begins with a discussion of Judge Henry's argument in favour of vigilantism in *The Virginian*.[1] This conception of the cowboy, which Wister initiated, has become the most powerful mythology, thus far, in American popular culture. And Wister's cowboy hero without a gun at his belt would be a very different and diminished figure. The allure of the gun became a central feature of the American frontier and, too, of the literary cowboy that Wister invented. One of the most powerful images in American literature is that of the Virginian, with his hand resting on his pistol as he stares down the villain Trampas during a card game and says, "When you call me that, *smile*." Words said almost as a caress, but with lethal intent. Today, no other industrialized country idolizes firearms as does America. Nor does any other advanced country come remotely close to America's level of gun ownership and gun violence. There is a direct connection between America's gun-soaked westward movement and America's current firearms crisis, which both fascinates and repels the rest of the industrialized world.

Vigilantism, originally an eastern institution, acquired a gloss of respectability on the western frontier that it had nowhere else.[2] Nor did vigilantism die out with the frontier; it entered mainstream American society of the twentieth and twenty-first centuries in a very different form – as a never-ending theme in American literature and film and also in real life. It was the American frontier West that gave vigilantism and American gun culture their respectability and frisson. Witness the number of state laws today that not only condone, but encourage, American citizens to "Stand Your Ground." These laws come straight from the American frontier's dictate that a real man had "No Duty To Retreat" from danger or a slight to his honour. This modern vigilantism, coupled with a semi-crazed gun mystique, has had a very sinister influence on modern America.

The doctrine of "No Duty to Retreat," which evolved on the American frontier, was a direct reversal of the old English common law doctrine which stated that a citizen did, indeed, have a duty to retreat from a threat, unless under extreme provocation. British law was transplanted in Canada essentially unabridged and was brought to the western Canadian frontier by the North-West Mounted Police. As the western Canadian ranching frontier developed and cattle rustling became a very real problem, the Mounties made it very clear that any vigilante action, especially lynching, would be regarded as murder. As a result, western Canada has virtually no history of vigilantism.

When Johnson came to Alberta, he came to a cattle frontier presided over by the North-West Mounted Police and under a different form of land law. Together, these two factors produced a very different frontier. The Mounted Police brought to the Canadian West a brand of law based on British law, and reinforced by the legal beliefs of the losers in the American Revolution – the United Empire Loyalists – many of whom came to Canada with staunch Tory principles that had been repudiated by the Revolution.[3] These Loyalists exercised a double influence. Their voice was removed from the debate as American legal institutions were being shaped. On the other hand, they arrived in Canada as the first "un-Americans." They were determined to help create a conservative counterbalance to the post-Revolutionary American experiment. Loyalist beliefs strengthened existing Imperial law at a crucial period of Canadian legal development. Together, leading

Loyalists and British colonial administrators vowed never to let the popular voice gain control of the law in Canada. There would be no elected judges or lawmen in Canada. Instead, judges would be carefully selected and lawmen appointed from those who believed firmly in an ordered and structured society. Some generations later, the Mounted Police brought these same institutions and beliefs to the Canadian West. In fact, a surprising number of Mounted Police officers were descendants of Loyalists. Almost all the early commissioners came from Loyalist roots, as did a very significant number of officers.[4] Since the officer corps dictated how the law in the field would be applied, it had a uniformity that was not found south of the border, where sheriffs and marshals were allowed a level of individuality and autonomy that was totally absent on the Canadian frontier. This fact alone says much about the difference in the law that Johnson encountered when he crossed the line to make his new home in the ranching country of Alberta.

Because the Mounties were able to keep the white population more or less in line, relations with the Native peoples on the ranching frontier remained relatively benign, until Native people realized the full impact of the reserve system. Johnson came to Alberta during a period of tension with Native groups just as the buffalo vanished – officially exterminated on the Canadian plains by 1879 – and Native people were being compelled to abandon the hunt and take up farming, as they were shunted aside on reserves to make way for white progress.

The rationale for this dispossession was the same in Canada as in the United States. Native peoples must give up their nomadic way of life and become farmers in the interests of progress. The sad fact is that these hunter-gatherer societies, that had nurtured and cherished their homelands for millennia, were dispossessed to make way for the agriculturalists, the real nomads.[5] Americans were known as the "Restless People," continually on the move as they looked for greener fields.

But the European view prevailed, and by the time Johnson arrived in Alberta in the late 1880s, the one western Canadian eruption, the 1885 Rebellion, had been quelled and all the Native peoples of the Canadian plains were now being tutored in the joys of farming. They were kept on their reserves and were allowed to leave only with a pass from the Indian Agent, a measure that was totally illegal and that went against the clear promises of the treaties.[6] The sad truth is that peace with Native people on the western Canadian frontier came about through the suppression of Native rights. Canadians should not, perhaps, be quite so proud of their record of a peaceful frontier. It came at a price. And without the presence of the Mounted

Police, it is hard to imagine that the Canadian West would have been as peaceful as it was.

The average Canadian and American in the West were – and still are – not all that dissimilar. Witness the ease with which either group transplanted itself. Canadians in the West were more orderly largely because of the legal institutions imposed on them, just as the vast majority of the Americans who came north were equally law-abiding once under these institutions. The difference was in the far greater ability of Canadian law to deal effectively with the small minority intent on causing trouble.

There has been plenty of violence in Canadian history, as Kenneth McNaught has pointed out in an important article, "Violence in Canadian History."[7] But very little of that violence has involved guns. The essential difference between Canada and the United States in the late nineteenth century was that in Canada there was a form of gun control and a quick response to violence, especially political violence. Canadian federal governments of all stripes have always argued that violence, and particularly political violence, has no place in Canada. This attitude has been held with equal determination by an English Conservative prime minister in the Winnipeg General Strike in 1919 and by a francophone Liberal prime minister in the FLQ Crisis of 1970. Only after the violence has been quelled does the government stop to consider the cause. The American penchant for violence stems largely from the Revolutionary sanction of civil disobedience and the inability of American law to control the small minority responsible for the vast majority of the crime. As this Revolutionary legacy moved westward over the Appalachians, what law there was took on a new flavour. The ancient English common law doctrine of the "Duty to Retreat" in a situation of threat was turned on its ear.[8] In the American West, territory after territory reversed this edict, on the grounds that a "true man" does not retreat in the face of danger. And it is no surprise that Texas became the strongest defender of the doctrine that it was perfectly legal and justified to take the law into your own hands if threatened. It was only a small step to what became the Code of the West, which dictated that honour was more precious than life, and another small step toward the ideology of vigilantism.[9] In the Canadian West, the Mounted Police upheld the original English doctrine; it was, indeed, the citizen's duty to retreat, except as a last resort. Vigilantism had no place in the Canadian West; lynching would be regarded as murder.

AMERICA'S ACHILLES HEEL

The critical views expressed here about American law, and western frontier law in particular, are not those of a Canadian with an anti-American bias. My mother was an American, as was my father's mother. My mother, over the years, showed me many of the wonderful aspects of her country. The United States, in many ways, is the most extraordinary country on the planet, not just because of its political and economic dynamism, but because of its place in the world of ideas. The three small words "We the People," that introduced the Declaration of Independence, launched the most startling idea of the age, the idea that the people, and not the few at the top, could, and should, steer the destiny of the American democratic "experiment." These words would transform, not just America, but the entire world.[10] Perhaps it is because of all the positive energy unleashed by America, the great optimism about the prospects of humankind in a new setting, and the extreme faith in the ability of individuals to better themselves, once shed of the social and economic shackles of the old world, that one critical element has suffered. Restraints on human behaviour are also a critical part of any functioning society. Perhaps Americans were too caught up in the uplifting rhetoric of the Declaration of Independence, and too inhibited by the powerful doctrine of states' rights, to give proper weight to the conservative principles of law and order. It certainly seems, looking from the outside, that the one great failure of America – its Achilles Heel – has been its weak legal structure.

America's one great failing, emerging from the period of the Revolution and the Constitution, was her fashioning of criminal law. Canada, with the benefit of witnessing first-hand the failings of the American legal system, wisely followed a policy of always keeping "a-hold of nurse, for fear of finding something worse."[11] At Confederation, Canada chose to import British criminal law intact and place it in the hands of the federal government.

Despite all the great qualities and achievements of America, her defective legal system has done terrible harm over time. It is the dark side of the American dream. Although the Declaration of Independence, one of the great triumphs of mankind, marked a major turning point in the world's history, it lacked a conservative counterbalance, and this lack had a malignant influence as the United States expanded westward. The sentiments of duty and service, so fundamental to the working of the law, were singularly absent from the declaration.[12]

As the two nations expanded, this westward movement in the United States was guided by the philosophy of the Northwest Ordinance, which allotted to the local population at an early stage a large degree of self-determination. One of the revolutionary legacies was a strong dislike of authority, whether foreign or congressional. A strong case could be made that a great many of America's shortcomings involved a lack of legal authority at the centre. The strength of states' rights and popular sovereignty were to blame. For instance, the issue of slavery, which was to haunt the United States throughout her history, could not be resolved short of a horrifying civil war because all attempts to soften or eradicate the institution at the federal level were consistently thwarted by the southern states.

In Canada, the opposite tradition took hold. The Canadian Parliament, until a much later stage in territorial development, kept a tight control over all important aspects of western development; the West was kept essentially in the position of a Crown colony. Not until 1888 did the Territorial Council become a Legislative Assembly.[13] All officers of the law were appointed, not elected, and for the critical period of territorial development on the Canadian plains, the Mounted Police, a federal force, held almost total sway. In fact, the Mounties essentially established a police state in the Canadian West; Canadians clearly valued peace and order over human rights and local self-determination.

In the United States, a similar weakness of law at the federal level was a major factor leading to a dismal history of relations with Native peoples. For instance, President Jackson's Indian Removal Act of 1830, a clear policy of ethnic cleansing of Native peoples east of the Mississippi River, which has been called "one of the most morally repugnant movements in American history," saw the Cherokee Nation forced out of Georgia and into exile west of the Mississippi.[14] This situation occurred because of a failure of law. The Supreme Court of the United States under Chief Justice John Marshall ruled both that the Cherokee were subject to the laws of the United States, not Georgia, and that the laws of Georgia relating to the Cherokee were unconstitutional; hence, forced removal of the Cherokee was illegal, unconstitutional, and counter to the treaties with them. Despite this ruling from the highest court in the land, President Jackson, whose sacred duty was to uphold the laws of the United States, stated, "John Marshall has made his decision; let him enforce it now if he can." The flouting of the law by the highest official in the land says much about the American disrespect for the law in the nineteenth century and for the weakness of federal law when opposed by a state like Georgia. At the very least, Jackson showed a blatant contempt for the constitutional principle of the separation of powers between the executive and the judiciary branches of government. No wonder vigilantism gained such strength in this atmosphere. But, as will be seen in chapter 6, there were many in western Canada who closely echoed the sentiments of Jackson's removal policy. However, the Canadian federal government was able to ignore this sort of local sentiment since very little actual power resided in western local opinion.

The embracing of immigrants was one of the great American success stories of the nineteenth century. The Statue of Liberty welcomed the greatest migration in history to America's shores. But the immigrant experience, in many cases, turned sour, not because of racism and intolerance, which were to be expected, but because the laxity of the law allowed vicious racism and religious intolerance to go unchecked. The Irish and Germans, for instance, each escaping their potato famines at mid-century, were terribly persecuted.[15] Or the Chinese, who were allowed to be badly mistreated in successive mining communities up the spine of America, from the gold rush in California to similar strikes in Wyoming and Montana. At Rock Springs, a coal town in Wyoming, twenty-eight Chinese were murdered by Welsh coal miners for not joining a strike, while the Welsh women laughed and clapped as the Chinese were forced to leave under threat of lynching.[16] There were no convictions. Rock Springs was a familiar theme, played over and over as the mining frontier moved from California to Montana. In most cases of anti-Chinese violence the police were completely ineffectual; the army or the militia had to be called in. One scholar has estimated that, between 1852 and 1908, 143 Chinese were murdered in the American West and over 10,000 displaced, usually chased out of town by white mobs.

The great American "pogrom of lynching and ethnic cleansing" in the American West was essentially unrestrained. Jean Pfaelzer and Alexander Saxon have thoroughly documented an epidemic of roundups and mass expulsions, burnings, murders, and lynchings spreading from California to Colorado and on to Wyoming and Montana. The legal response? Essentially none! Or worse; many local politicians rode the atmosphere of race hatred to power.[17]

A similar anti-Chinese incident occurred in Calgary in 1892, which vividly underscores the difference between legal institutions in the American and Canadian Wests. A riot against the Chinese erupted after a cricket game, fuelled by drink and a receptive crowd because a smallpox outbreak had been traced to a Chinese laundry. Sentiment against the Chinese became extremely ugly after nine people became infected and three died. When the quarantined Chinese were released, a riot ensued, the purpose of which was to run the Chinese out of town. As the mob of about two to three hundred formed, the Mayor of Calgary, Alexander Lucas, and the Chief of Police, Tom English, and his constables all decamped Calgary very quickly, leaving a complete void in authority. At this point, the Calgary riot had all the earmarks of a typical western American pogrom. Except for the Mounties! Although the Mounted Police no longer had jurisdiction in the city of Calgary, they decided, reluctantly, to move in and take charge of the deteriorating situation. They quickly gave protection to the Chinese in their barracks and dispersed the mob. Thus ended what could have been a very ugly incident. Instead, western Canadian historians have written off these events as a small footnote only because the intercession of the Mounted Police turned it into a minor farce. If they had not stepped in, the riot of 1892 would certainly have punctured the complacency of western Canadians.[18]

The experiences of Chinese immigrants in North America during the nineteenth century provides another important comparison. Between 1878 and 1886, during a period of intense anti-Chinese sentiment in British Columbia, the BC Supreme Court struck down five provincial BC statutes or municipal bylaws that were anti-Chinese. In four of the five cases, the BC judges cited the Supreme Court of California and the federal circuit courts of California and Oregon.[19] There is a very important issue here. In both Canada and the United States, the protection of minorities is far more likely to come from the federal level of law or government. The striking difference between the two countries at the legal and political level is that Canadian federal law could override local prejudice far more easily than was the case in the United States. There was a remarkable similarity in legal outlook between the members of the BC Supreme Court and their American counterparts. But the American Supreme Court and Federal Circuit Court judges fought an uphill and losing battle against the forces of grassroots democracy and local self-determination.[20]

GUNS AND THE LAW

If there is one area that clearly differentiates Canada from the United States from the nineteenth century to today, it is gun legislation and the attitudes associated with that legislation. Canadians, for instance, simply cannot fathom the popularity and the political power of the National Rifle Association, or the near reverence for the Second Amendment, which supposedly gives Americans the "right to bear arms." It is important here to establish a context for later discussions of gun violence in the West and also to point out the enormous nationwide repercussions of a gun-happy American West.

Guns, both long and short, were part of the essential working tools of the American cowboy. Cowboys on the cattle trails from Texas required handguns on occasion, for instance, if attacked, to turn a stampeding herd, or to deal with rattlesnakes. A handgun and spurs became regular items of American cowboy apparel; without them a cowboy felt naked. And a handgun became a necessity for self-protection in the cattle towns, since these towns were bristling with guns and unfinished business from the Civil War. The prevailing Code of the West dictated that cowboys must answer a besmirching of their honour, and the rough justice of the American frontier dictated that, on the occasion of a shooting, the crucial question was whether the bullet entered from the front or the back. If from the front, the verdict was almost always justifiable self-defence, with no necessity for an inquest. This casual nature of the law in early cattle towns required the carrying of a handgun for protection.

The Canadian frontier was entirely different. The Mounted Police brought with them to the West both liquor prohibition and strict handgun laws. There were, of course, smuggled liquor and lots of guns on the Canadian frontier, but the source of the vast majority of violence on the western American frontier – handguns and liquor in the setting of the ubiquitous saloon – was legislated by the Mounties into a zone of relative safety. The Mounties had the power to shut down drinking establishments if they allowed clients to get drunk. They also relied on the local vagrancy act to cleanse western towns of drifters and troublemakers.

From this frontier period in the American West has also emerged an extreme fascination with firearms. Here, perhaps, lies the most distinguishing feature separating the two frontiers: an American frontier defined by the handgun and its Canadian counterpart with strict gun control.

Over time, Canadians have retained a fascination for American gun culture but also a revulsion for the logical outcome of a population armed to the teeth and determined not to let governments erode their right to possess firearms. Today, the rate of firearm ownership in the United States, especially ownership of handguns, is vastly higher than in any other industrialized country. American murder and incarceration rates follow suit. Canada, on the other hand, has some of the strictest handgun legislation in the world and, as a consequence, much lower gun murder rates.

It is impossible to prove in any statistical way, but it would just seem to be common sense that the romantic image of western frontier firearms, especially handguns, that has bombarded generations of movie and TV viewers accounts for a large part of today's continued American fascination with guns. The combination of a free-flowing availability of handguns on the frontier and the ethic of the right to take the law into one's own hands – the ethic of vigilantism and No Duty to Retreat – have put a unique stamp on the western American frontier. Even accounting for the gross exaggeration of frontier lawlessness and violence found in newspapers of the period, popular literature and, later, movies and TV, there is enough carefully documented American frontier violence to make it stand out from other frontiers, and especially the Canadian frontier.[21]

How violent was the frontier American West? This issue has certainly been a subject of lively debate among historians. Roger McGrath, in his 1984 study *Gunfighters, Highwaymen and Vigilantes: Violence on the Frontier*, has taken a tally. On the side arguing that American frontier violence has been exaggerated, he cited three important historians: Robert Dykstra, Frank Prassel, and Eugene Hollon.[22] For instance, Frank Prassel argued that the westerner "enjoyed greater security in both person and property than did his contemporary in the urban centres of the East."[23] Eugene Hollon pointed out that the frontier was less violent than American society today. Frontier violence was largely urban and only a very small proportion of the population was involved.[24] Newspapers and dime novels, of course, grossly distorted the picture. To this argument that violence was largely an urban rather than a frontier phenomenon, he added that frontier violence was the result, not the cause, of America's violent society.[25] However, these comments say more about the high rate of crime in the East in the nineteenth century and the even higher rate throughout America in the twentieth century than they do about a low rate of crime in the American West. Also, McGrath argued that the three authors' views were based only on actual gun killings and didn't take into account all the woundings or the situations that almost led to violence and killing. There were also a large number of shootouts in which there were no injuries, because the shootists were too drunk to shoot straight.[26]

On the other side of the ledger, McGrath lists himself, Joe B. Franz, Harry Sinclair Drago, Joseph Rosa, Philip Jordan, Richard Slotkin, and Richard Maxwell Brown. McGrath argues that Richard Maxwell Brown's collected studies of violence and vigilantism are the best general studies on the subject.[27] To this list could be added the work of Richard Hofstadter and Michael Wallace on violence.[28] Franz made the important point that the frontier West attracted the rootless and those avoiding responsibility and deference toward an established society, so it is only logical that violence would flourish.[29] Harry Sinclair Drago, in his litany on the range wars, linked cattle rustling to the violence, claiming that it had reached "epidemic proportions."[30] Jordan made the connection between the rise in violence in the 1830s and the advent of Jacksonian democracy, which resulted in the demise of deference in American society.[31] Rosa claimed that an "extraordinary amount of killing" occurred on the western frontier.[32]

Perhaps Richard Maxwell Brown should have the last word. All of the above views are focused solely on the American western frontier. Brown adds a comparative view:

> Comparative studies of the Canadian and American West show that miners prone to violence and vigilantism under the loose, permissive rule of the American federal system became peaceable and law-abiding when they migrated to Canada.[33]

Brown concludes by pointing out that the legacy of America's violent frontier is the "unenviable distinction as the most violent nation among its peer group of the technologically advanced democracies."[34] Brown also stresses that America's history of ethnic, racial, religious, industrial, agrarian, and political violence have contributed greatly to the current general state of violence in America.[35] But, of all these, only frontier violence is filled with the romance of the six-gun and the horse. It is the romantic violence of the frontier and its link with the western code of vigilantism that today sanctions both modern vigilantism and staggering levels of gun violence in the United States.

But western American frontier violence had a more sordid and greed-ridden aspect. Brown sees the staggering level of western violence in the context of what he calls the western "wars of incorporation." Brown coined this term to encompass the elevated levels of western violence in the post–Civil War era, an era of a robber baron mentality in the West unrestricted by conscience or law. Brown's wars of incorporation pitted the conservative forces of commerce, industry, and the railroads against labour and farmers. In the West, these wars matched the army against the Hispanic settlers, the Texans against the Mexicans, Apaches, and Comanches, the big ranchers against the settlers and modest ranchers. Many of the battles were fought out in courtrooms, but many involved vigilante groups on either side of the equation. And into this charged atmosphere stepped the professional gunfighters of popular myth, upward of three hundred of them who were *well-known*, plus many hundreds more of mere local reputation. Many of the local "grassroots" gunmen yearned for national fame so that they, too, could end up as celebrities in the dime novel industry. Gunmen like Wyatt Earp and Bill Hickok were hired by the conservative forces of wealth and power. Billy the Kid represented the other side. Many of these gunmen represented the law, such as it was, and many "social outlaws" like

Butch Cassidy and Sundance Kid claimed to represent the little people. In the absence of effective law, vigilantism blossomed.[36]

VIGILANTISM AND MODERN AMERICA

Vigilantism is a major theme in *The Virginian*. Wister's justification for western vigilantism represented the thinking of a great many of his class (see chapter 5). Certainly Theodore Roosevelt shared his beliefs on the issue. And, according to Johnson, it was a significant part of his life – both the reason he lost the real schoolteacher he was wooing and the reason he left Wyoming for Alberta. Vigilantism bears examination in some detail because not only was it a major force on the western American frontier, but the vigilante ethic of the West continues to have an extraordinarily powerful influence in modern America.

The uniquely American institution of vigilantism emerged first in North Carolina during the Revolution, and then gained considerable strength with the Civil War. Although forms of vigilantism can be traced back many centuries and have been found recently in places like northern Ireland, only in the United States has vigilantism taken on a national character and, in its western frontier form, a decided mystique.[37] Vigilantism arose as a response to a particularly American problem – the absence of effective law, especially in frontier regions.[38] At its height, it became sanctified by both the highest in the land and the lowest sort of lynch mob, from presidents, senators, congressmen, state governors, and judges to illiterate rabble.[39]

Vigilantism and lynchings saw a sharp increase during the Jacksonian period, as did levels of violence. This increase resulted from the shift in this period from a more deferential society to one in which there was a greater emphasis on democracy and self-determination, especially in frontier communities. After the Civil War, in the era of the northern carpetbagger and the Thirteenth, Fourteenth, and Fifteenth amendments to the Constitution, which ended slavery, extended civil rights and equal protection under the law, and gave the right to vote to the newly freed slaves, Southern white society, from top to bottom, embraced vigilantism and lynching as the most effective means of keeping the Black population in line. Certainly, by the end of the nineteenth century, the motives for vigilantism and lynching in the South and West were very different, but they shared one common root. Vigilantism and lynching in the West, except in the California gold fields, had little to do with race, but, in both the old South and the raw West, the fundamental reason for their widespread popularity was a glaring deficiency in, and often a contempt for, the law. And, in both regions, this extra-legal enforcement was condoned from top to bottom of society. The fact that political leaders, from President Roosevelt to the governor and senators of Wyoming, should enthusiastically embrace western vigilantism clearly indicated that western law did not protect the rich. Yet vigilantism was equally embraced at the bottom by the lynch mobs that regularly liberated men from jail, to depart life at the end of a rope. There are complex motives here that warrant deeper study. Vigilantism has often been explained, and excused, by western historians, who point out that it was a temporary expedient on a raw frontier. But this argument falls totally flat when one looks both at the extraordinary breadth of vigilantism in America and its equally remarkable longevity.

The majority of the almost 5,000 lynchings in America since 1892, when Ida Wells-Barnett, a Black woman brave enough to write about the institution and systematically collecting data on it, have occurred in areas that were not remotely a frontier.[40] J. H. Chadbourn's study in 1933 claimed that, between 1889 and 1932, there were 3,753 lynchings in the United States. Obviously there were far more; they only started keeping score in 1889.[41] And, until very recently, the institution had considerable respectability, even in high places. Despite the nearly 200 anti-lynching bills introduced to Congress in the twentieth century, it was not until June 2005 that the American Senate finally passed a bill banning lynching in the United States![42]

The frontier justification for vigilante law is nowhere better expressed than in Wister's novel, in the passage where Judge Henry explains to Molly that the Revolution has given the people the democratic right – and duty – to take back the law if it is seen to be in limp hands (see chapter 5). "We the People" means that the people gave the functioning of the law to certain officials, and if these officials are found to be wanting, then the people have the right to take back the law and make it function properly. The Judge implies that it will be "the better people" who will then be meting out justice. However, the Judge cannot explain how the people are to have the wisdom to make a complex legal system function properly by mob rule. Wister's adulation for vigilantism was essentially upper-class America's justification for the institution; it had strong overtones of the arguments of Theodore Roosevelt and other prominent Americans.

The only problem with the Judge's argument for vigilantism filling a temporary void on the frontier is that it is nonsense. As much as some historians of the American West would like to divorce the lynching of cattle thieves from the hundreds of other more sordid vigilante movements, it is clear from the perspective of the twenty-first century that they were all related. As will be seen later, vigilantism continued and even grew as the frontier period faded. Wyoming, for instance, was already a state when the famous vigilante war, the Johnson County War, broke out. The vigilantism of the various Ku Klux Klan movements flourished in developed communities, as did later urban vigilante movements aimed, for instance, at Catholics, immigrants, or the cleansing of Mormons from eastern communities. As Richard Maxwell Brown has pointed out, from 1767, when vigilantism began, to 1900 when it faded, there may have been as many as five hundred American vigilante movements, accounting for as many as 5,000 killings. A great many of these movements were in the settled East. Only the New England states lack a vigilante tradition.[43]

The glorification of vigilantism still thrives in literature, film, and TV; the adulation for the individual who takes the law into his own hands, in a never-ending morality play, is still a major theme. As Dick Harrison has pointed out in *Unnamed Country: The Struggle for a Canadian Prairie Fiction*, the hero of American fiction is very often a man who embraces individual vigilante law to resolve a situation. John G. Cawelti, in his *Six Gun Mystique*, adds that an important part of the cowboy hero's literary power is the necessity to take the law into his own hands; the authorities are always incompetent. The cowboy hero exudes an aura of good violence, pure like the knights of old.[44] Richard Slotkin, in *Gunfighter Nation*, notes that much of the Virginian's mystique would evaporate if he didn't have a gun at his hip – the enforcer of his Code of Honour – and didn't clearly demonstrate that he would use it. This same theme seems to be played out endlessly in American film and TV. Now the western enforcer has faded, to be replaced by the ultimate vigilante figures, Superman, Batman, and Spiderman. The simplistic message stays the same. They are there to battle evil because the law is inept.

The parallel Canadian literature says much about a difference in outlook between Canadians and Americans. In place of the highly individualistic American hero embracing vigilante virtues, his Canadian counterpart was the very Anglo-Saxon Mountie standing for a somewhat different set of values: devotion to duty, toughness, honesty, perseverance, understatement, a quiet steely authority, and a pronounced chivalry toward women. Above all, this hero must distance himself from an over-civilized effeminacy. For Wister's cowboy, the open range of Wyoming was the testing ground; for the Mountie, it was the wilderness of the Canadian Northwest.

In Harwood Steele's *Spirit-of-Iron*, the heroine, commenting on her Mountie's virtues, says that he was brave, strong, and chivalrous – like a knight of the Round Table.[45] And his red coat "goes to my head like champagne."[46] The women in these Mountie tales were there, very much like the Virginian's Molly, to fall in love with a symbol of Anglo-Saxon manliness. Like the cowboy novelists who followed Wister, the Mountie novelists were also onto a winning theme. Ralph Connor (Charles W. Gordon, a Presbyterian minister) sold over five million copies.[47] There were also over 250 Mountie movies, mostly Hollywood productions, which almost always accentuated the Mountie's Anglo-Saxon virtues by casting him beside a French-Canadian or Métis villain.[48]

In the twenty-first century, there is, perhaps, no stronger evidence of the strong link between western frontier vigilantism and modern American law than Florida's Stand Your Ground law, an almost exact replica of the western frontier's No Duty To Retreat doctrine. In 2012, a Black teenager, Trayvon Martin, was shot and killed by a neighborhood watch volunteer, George Zimmerman, who thought him "real suspicious" because he was wearing a hoodie. Martin was unarmed and merely walking to a convenience store to stock up before a game on TV. He became upset that Zimmerman was following him, so he accosted him and hit him. Thereupon, Zimmerman shot and killed him.

The police questioned Zimmerman and immediately released him because, under Florida's Stand Your Ground law, he had every right to shoot someone he considered a threat. In a situation where it is expected that someone like Martin could be carrying a concealed weapon, there is no requirement under Florida law to prove either imminent danger or a need to use deadly force. It didn't matter that Martin was an unarmed teenager. And, as it was on the frontier, the Florida police can decide whether it was a justifiable case of self-defence.

Florida's Stand Your Ground law is similar to those in twenty other states. Collectively, these laws are a clear indication that vigilante law is still thriving in modern America. Critics call these laws a licence to kill and, since this law was introduced in Florida in 2005, the state's rate of "justifiable homicide' has tripled.[49]

Although public outrage turned this killing into an international incident, Zimmerman was found not guilty. The verdict polarized the nation between those who argued that Trayvon Martin had been lynched and gun activists who said that Zimmerman was merely exercising his Second Amendment rights. But, as the judge's instructions to the jury stated, Zimmerman had "no duty to retreat," and had the right to meet force with force.[50] Subsequently, George Zimmerman has been arrested and charged with several counts of domestic assault and road rage.

The United States is unique in the developed world in having a vivid history of gun violence, an adulation for a western vigilante past, and ludicrously easy means of acquiring guns capable of mass murder. A comparison with some other developed countries shows just how isolated the United States continues to be in its attitudes and policies toward guns, and how fascination and reverence for firearms have set that country very distinctly apart. For a start, the United States leads the world in the rate of civilian gun ownership.[51] The *Economist*, a very sober and careful journal, estimated in 2007 that Americans owned about 240 million guns, one third of which – 80 million – were handguns.[52] Now, only five years later, it is estimated that Americans privately own almost 300 million firearms.[53] Texans alone have over 50 million guns (for a population of 25.5 million!). The United States has three times the per capita gun ownership that Canada has, and fifteen times that of Great Britain.[54] The American fascination for firearms shows no sign of abating. At the Oscars in 2015, the film American Sniper, based on the life of military sniper Chris Kyle, who claimed the most enemy kills in military history, had made more money at the box office than all the other seven nominated films put together. The film was essentially a eulogy of American gun culture. Kyle stated in his other book, *American Gun*, "Perhaps more than any other nation in the world, the history of the United States has been shaped by the gun."[55]

On a per capita comparison, the US handgun murder rate is roughly ten times that of Canada, a country with very strict handgun regulations, and one hundred times that of Britain and Japan![56] In an average year, roughly one hundred thousand Americans are killed or wounded by guns.[57] Since 1965, more than one million Americans have been killed by guns – more than the number of Americans killed in all foreign wars combined during the twentieth century.[58] And it has been estimated that the annual cost of gun violence is in the range of $100 billion![59] The surprising thing is that, despite the above statistics on American gun ownership, only about a third of Americans actually own guns.[60] A survey like this makes it all the more puzzling that the American gun lobby has such power in politics.

Canada has had a very different history of gun ownership and violent use of guns. A Statistics Canada survey of Canadian homicides for a nine-year period between 1974 and 1982 showed clearly that there was an average of 654 homicides a year and, of those, an average of slightly fewer than seventy a year were committed with handguns.[61] Seventy a year for the whole country! Ten percent of total homicides. In 1979, there were sixty homicides with handguns for all of Canada; in that year, there were 900 handgun homicides in New York alone, and over 10,000 handgun homicides for all of the United States – twenty times the Canadian rate per capita.[62]

Canadians possess lots of rifles; they share with Americans a vibrant hunting culture. But handguns are a completely different matter. The combination of tight handgun control and very fierce penalties for armed robbery results in Canadians generally feeling no necessity to arm themselves for self-defence.[63] Handgun control began with the Mounties on the Canadian frontier in 1885 and then was made national seven years later.[64]

Surely, Americans must someday wake up to the fact that they have produced a very violent society, and one that seems to be continuing on that path, largely because, as Hofstadter and Wallace have so clearly argued, Americans have spawned a gun culture without parallel in the world:[65] "Our entertainment and our serious literature are suffused with violence to a notorious degree; it is endemic in our history."[66] And they add that the further America gets from its frontier roots, the stronger its gun culture becomes.[67] There is certainly a direct link to the frontier and to the Revolution and the Civil War. Hofstadter and Wallace rightly point out the paradox of a stable American political system co-existing with a level of crime on a par with the most volatile areas of the world, a fact perhaps best explained by the weakness of the central government in areas of crime prevention and by the diffusion of authority.[68] They also point out the terrible harm that inexact wording can produce. In their view, the Second Amendment, allegedly giving private Americans the right to bear arms, is absolutely not what the framers of the Constitution had in mind. The right was *only* in the context of a "well-regulated militia."[69] On this point, one expert argues that the loose interpretation of the Second Amendment (giving private individuals the unlimited right to possess firearms) "is widely rejected by most legal experts."[70] As Gary Wills observed, the Second Amendment is not commonly understood to apply to hunters. "One does not bear arms against a rabbit."[71]

The vital issue here is the ablative absolute! The framers of the Constitution, who drafted the Second Amendment, were all classically educated and, thus, well-acquainted with Latin. The ablative absolute in Latin is the opening phrase or clause of a sentence, which gives meaning and context to the rest of the sentence. The architects of the Constitution clearly meant the clause "A well-regulated Militia, being necessary to the security of a free State…" to give context and direction to the rest of the amendment. They had just emerged not only from a Revolutionary war but also two centuries of intermittent warfare with New France and her Native allies, during which the colonial militias had been vital to the survival of the American colonies. Here, surely, was the context for the amendment. And, at that time, it was the duty, not the right, of citizens to keep arms for the purpose of protecting their homes, and their colony, from attack. In the notes from the Constitutional Convention of 1787, there is not a single word about individual gun ownership, and over the next two hundred years, when the interpretation of the amendment came to the Supreme Court, the court ruled on four occasions that the Second Amendment did not uphold individual gun ownership. Certainly, two of the foremost historians of the Revolutionary period, Gordon Wood and Bernard Bailyn, argued forcefully that, in the period of the Constitution, it was the duty, not the right, to bear arms.[72] But in 2008, the Supreme Court in Heller vs District of Columbia reversed two centuries of precedent in a close decision (5 to 4), the majority arguing that the issue of the militia was irrelevant. In other words, the first clause of the amendment could just be ignored! The Heller decision extended the right of individuals to bear arms for self-defence.[73]

The political guardian of the Second Amendment's widest interpretation is the National Rifle Association. The NRA began in 1871, but didn't pick up steam until after the assassination of the Kennedys and Martin Luther King Jr., when a serious debate on gun control threatened unrestricted gun ownership. Since then, the NRA has become the principal defender of the right to own all forms of firearms.[74] The NRA spends millions of dollars annually to lobby against any form of gun control. In 1994, under President Clinton, Congress enacted the Federal Assault Rifle Ban, which was to be in effect for ten years. The act prohibited, for civilian use, the manufacture of certain semi-automatic firearms. It expired in 2004.[75] Attempts to renew the act have come to nothing. Although President Obama, before his first election, stated that he wanted to reinstate the assault rifle ban, in his first administration, he did nothing. Although an advocate of gun control, he did not dare confront the NRA; in fact, he signed legislation expanding gun rights. He knew that gun control legislation was an issue that could lose him the presidency.[76] In 1994, the NRA bragged that it had targeted twenty-four politicians in the mid-term elections who had voted for Clinton's gun control measures. Nineteen of them lost their seats.[77] It is thought that the NRA was responsible for Democrats losing fifty seats in the 1994 mid-term elections.[78]

It is perhaps unfair to blame the NRA entirely for America's gun mania, but it is certainly the NRA attitude that is responsible for the seeming complete inability to change American gun laws so that the endless string of gun "massacres" might abate. For a start, US gun legislation, unlike Canada's, is under both state and federal control.

Over the past twenty years, gun rights advocates have won almost every battle and states have passed over one hundred new laws loosening gun restrictions since Obama became president. In 2009, for instance, the Montana legislature passed the Firearms Freedom Act, which made new firearms manufactured in Montana exempt from federal regulation. Seven other states have followed Montana's lead.[79] Even if, by some miracle, the federal government were able to pass new gun control measures, they could still be thwarted at the state level.

There is also the fact, of course, that the American fascination with guns, especially handguns, has made untold millions for Hollywood. First came the Colt .45 of hundreds, if not thousands, of westerns, followed by the Smith & Wesson .44 Magnum of Eastwood's Dirty Harry Callahan character in the 1970s, and then the movie debut in *Die Hard 2* of the Glock, now America's handgun of choice, each handgun in its time eliminating badness in the name of vigilante justice. It is not hard to understand the allure of these celluloid avengers.

Clearly, then, the US media has had an overpowering influence on the public mind, an unsettling fact when linked to vigilantism. How many unstable people, endlessly bombarded with the vigilante theme, have harboured fevered visions of changing the world through their actions? Surely, a perversion of the vigilante attitude lies behind the problem, unique to America in the developed world, that so many presidents and politicians have become targets for vigilante-style assassination. The combination of the vigilante ethic and the saturation of America with easily acquired firearms of mass murder has led to a long succession of such killings or attempted killings by those of paranoid and unstable mind.[80] And who knows how many other attempts may have been thwarted?

This combination has also resulted in an escalating incidence of mass Rambo-style killings throughout the United States. Increasingly, Americans of dubious mental stability are bombarded by an ever-intensifying American media preoccupation with violence and simple-minded vigilante solutions to the ills of society, real or perceived. This vigilantism was originally cloaked in the romantic and democratic trappings of the frontier West. The process by which this ethic spread to the entire nation in the twentieth century would make a fascinating study in media manipulation.

Taking a fifty-year period in America, beginning in the 1960s, it is alarming to realize that these twisted vigilante "massacres" are escalating each decade, with no solution in sight. The first decade of the twenty-first century witnessed more of this madness, unquestionably made worse by the vehemence of the NRA in placing its very considerable influence and money behind its argument that no gun, however absurdly lethal, should be restricted. The *Economist* commented that in the worst peacetime shooting in American history to that date (the Virginia Tech killings in 2007), a 9mm Glock pistol was used, a handgun available only to the police in virtually any other developed country but easily acquired over the counter at thousands of US gun shops.[81] The decade would end with the Fort Hood killings, thirteen killed and twenty-nine wounded.[82]

The second decade of the twenty-first century gives every indication of living up to and exceeding every other. In just the first year and a bit, there were five "massacres."[83] Then, on July 12, 2012, in Aurora, a suburb of Denver, James Eagan Holmes, killed twelve and wounded seventy in a packed movie theatre. The setting for this shooting was the initial midnight screening of the latest Batman movie, *The Dark Knight Rises*.

The most bizarre aspect of this killing spree was that the killer, a twenty-four-year-old medical graduate student at the University of Colorado, had dyed his hair orange, dressed in black combat gear, and called himself the "Joker." His shooting began in a very violent segment of the film, so that many patrons, at first, thought he was part of a publicity stunt. As with so many of these massacres, he carried perfectly legal firearms – a Remington 12-gauge Express Tactical shotgun, a .40-calibre Glock pistol, and a Smith & Wesson M&P 15 (Military and Police) version of the AR-15 semi-automatic assault rifle with a 100-round drum magazine. (Another Glock pistol was found in his car.) The M&P 15 is classified as a hunting rifle![84] According to some of his classmates, Holmes had been threatening to kill people for some time, but he still had no difficulty acquiring his arsenal. An effective background check might well have stopped this awful killing.

Batman is the ultimate vigilante figure, together with Superman and Spiderman. Collectively, they are unique American creations and say much about America's vigilante obsession. Batman films depict the ultimate in mass violence. Surely, there must be a connection between the crazed world of the Joker and the equally crazed little world of the man who left his booby-trapped apartment to go and shoot up the opening night of a movie. Hollywood has a lot to account for, though it did show an unexpected sensitivity in cancelling a movie trailer that was to accompany the Batman film. The movie *Gangster Squad* depicted a scene in which the main characters shoot up a movie theatre with machine guns. Also, it delayed the release of *Batman Incorporated*, in which a female agent, disguised as a teacher, brandishes a handgun in a classroom full of children. There is a lot on the heads of these Hollywood producers who are making fortunes by churning out films of ever-increasing violence, most of them with the simplistic theme of vigilante justice triumphing in the end. Recently, it has been found that the violence in PG (parental guidance) movies has increased alarmingly. The furor over the Batman killings had hardly subsided when one of the worst killings yet hit the cozy little community of Newtown, Connecticut. On December 14, 2012, Adam Lanza, armed with the usual arsenal of deadly weapons, killed twenty children and six staff members of the Sandy Hook Elementary School, after first killing his mother. He then killed himself. Once again, it was a case of an unhinged man having easy access to weapons of mass destruction, in this case his mother's dozen guns. She was a rather extreme gun enthusiast who had taught her son how to shoot her Bushmaster XM 15 semi-automatic rifle, with which he eliminated twenty-seven lives before taking his own.

The murder of so many small children shocked a nation hardened to such killings. As the *Economist* commented, "If America is ever to confront its obsession with guns, that time is now.... If even the slaughter of 20 small children cannot end America's infatuation with guns, nothing will." Well, nothing did. President Obama was very moved by this mass slaughter and vowed that he would make gun control one of his top priorities. He was spectacularly unsuccessful. Despite a poll indicating that 85 percent of Americans favoured background checks on gun purchases and 55 percent supported a ban on assault weapons and high-capacity clips, his efforts were defeated.[85] Once again, the NRA went into high gear to counter the president's attempt to limit semi-automatic rifles with large clips and to initiate meaningful background checks on firearms purchasers. The NRA argued that these checks could lead to a national gun registry, the prelude to confiscation. Obama failed, despite clear evidence that a large majority of Americans backed his proposals.[86] But this outcome was to be expected. According to one newspaper, the Sandy Hook shooting was the sixty-seventh mass school shooting since 1974. The *Globe and Mail's* editorial "Gun Sickness" argued that this sort of issue could not be resolved by legislation; America's gun culture was too thoroughly entrenched.[87] In the wake of Sandy Hook, American gun manufacturers had record sales, as Americans rushed to stock up before possible gun legislation could come into effect. Gun shows did a booming business, especially in the sale of assault rifles.

After allowing the anger over Sandy Hook to subside, the NRA announced its solution to the Sandy Hook killings – more guns! If the teachers had been armed, it argued, the killings would not have happened. The NRA's executive director, Wayne LaPierre, proposed that principals be armed and tutored in the art of killing the bad guys. As well, a special police officer should be placed in every school, the officer's salary to be paid for by cuts to foreign aid.[88] Texas Republican Congressman Louie Gohmert weighed into the debate with the helpful suggestion that, if the elementary school principal at Sandy Hook had been armed with a high-powered rifle, she could have taken the "killer's head off." Gohmert also urged the carrying of concealed weapons in daycares and churches.

Perhaps this is the moment to reflect on what might have been if the president's legislation had passed. The vital question hangs there: Could gun control, at this point in America's history, have any hope of success? To help answer this question, some comparisons are instructive. In 1996 a mass killing similar to that in Sandy Hook happened in Dunblane, Scotland. Thomas Hamilton killed sixteen children and a teacher and then committed suicide. This slaughter led to the Conservative government of John Major bringing in strict gun laws, which were later further tightened by Tony Blair's Labour government. There was a clear political consensus that guns should be restricted. After Dunblane, Britain's murder rate dropped significantly, so that Britain now has one of the lowest murder rates by firearms in the developed world.[89]

In the same year as the Dunblane killings, a killing spree at Port Arthur in Tasmania resulted in thirty-five deaths, the worst firearms killing in Australian history. Within weeks, the Australian government, like Britain, imposed strict gun laws, including a ban on all automatic and semi-automatic rifles and a mandatory buy-back of these illegal weapons. In the eighteen years before the new law, there had been thirteen mass killings in Australia; in the fourteen years since 1996 (to 2010), there has not been a single mass shooting. Also, the murder rate from 1996 to 2006 has dropped by almost 60 percent.[90]

Much the same story applies to South Africa, which had a gun culture very similar to America's. Much stricter gun legislation was imposed in 2004. Between 2004 and 2013, gun-related crimes have dropped 21 percent, while general crime has remained the same.[91] And then there is Japan, where the general population have no guns. There are virtually no gun killings in Japan.

When Canada is added to the debate, it would seem to be very hard to argue against the simple conclusion that stricter gun laws result in significantly lower murder rates. And Canada's murder rate from firearms killings would be much lower if her border were not so porous. In Toronto alone in 2012, the police confiscated 2,000 illegal guns, most of which had been smuggled across the American border.[92] It is estimated that 70 percent of the illegal firearms currently in Canada came from the United States.[93] Gwynne Dyer, an international journalist, has argued that the gun murder rate in the United States is twenty times the average rate in twenty-two of the top industrial countries.[94] Even if Dyer is only approximately accurate, half his estimate would still be a very shocking figure. Dyer concluded that there were two main reasons for this extraordinary murder rate: easy access to guns, an obvious reason, and instant celebrity, which points to a twisted vigilantism and the media's obsession with violence.

There can be no better evidence of the power of western vigilantism on current American society than Sarah Palin's message at a recent NRA convention that violent crime is down and gun ownership is at an all-time high. "So go figure." She is urging all Americans to be their own gun-totin' vigilantes, to go get a gun and stand their ground. Perhaps she hasn't actually read Walter Prescott Webb's *The Great Plains*, but his influence on modern vigilantism of this type is unmistakable.

Webb, the famous historian of the Great Plains frontier, is rightly renowned for his groundbreaking book, which, in 1931, argued that the one-hundredth meridian was the dividing line in America, an institutional fault line that divided East and West. Beyond this line, eastern institutions no longer worked; new institutions were required in a new landscape. Certainly, he was absolutely right in arguing that the 160-acre homestead in arid Wyoming was absurd and did great harm. But Webb also argued that criminal law had to change at the hundredth meridian. It is important to follow his argument in some detail because it, and others like it, have had, in popular form, a large influence on modern America. Webb wrote:

> The West was lawless for two reasons: first, because of the social conditions that obtained there during [the frontier period]; secondly, because the law that was applied there was not made for the conditions that existed and was unsuitable for those conditions. It did not fit the needs of the country, and could not be obeyed.
>
> [Because of the sparse population and lack of established law] Each man had to make his own law because there was no other to make it. He had to defend himself and protect his rights by the force of his personality, courage and skill at arms. All men went armed and moved over vast areas among other armed men. The six-shooter was the final arbiter, a court of last resort, and an executioner. How could a man live in such a milieu and abide by the laws that obtained in the thickly settled portions where the police gave protection and the courts justice. [Thus the reversal of English common law. On the frontier, a real man had no duty to retreat]. Could the plainsman go unarmed in a country where danger was

ever present? Could a man refuse to use those arms where his own life was at stake? Such men ... could not be cowboys or Indian fighters or peace officers or outstanding good citizens.

In the absence of law and in the social conditions that obtained, men worked out an extra-legal code or custom by which they guided their actions. The custom is often called the code of the West. The code demands what [Theodore] Roosevelt called a square deal; it demanded fair play. According to it one must not shoot his adversary in the back, and he must not shoot an unarmed man. In actual practice he must give notice of his intention, albeit the action followed the notice as a lightning stroke.... Thus was justice carried out in a crude but efficient manner, and warning given that in general the code must prevail.

Under the social conditions the taking of human life did not entail the stigma that in more thickly settled regions is associated with it. Men were all equal. Each was his own defender. His survival imposed upon him certain obligations which, if he were a man, he would accept.... Murder was too harsh a word to apply to his performance, a mere incident as it were. But how could an Easterner, surrounded and protected by the conventions, understand such distinctions....

Other forms of lawlessness arose because the law was wholly inapplicable and unsuited to the West.... Land laws were persistently broken in the West, because they were not made for the West and were wholly unsuited to any arid region.[95]

Webb's words are clearly not a lament; he had an extreme admiration for the ways of the West. His famous and powerful arguments are surely right on one count. Land law for the arid West was absurd and caused enormous friction. But, whatever can be argued about Webb's contentions about criminal law, he made it very clear that his argument pertained only to the arid western frontier, west of his fault line. The civilized East was entirely different. What has happened in America is that Webb's arguments for a western frontier code have been dragged east across his line, to be celebrated by Sarah Palin and millions more who think as she does.

Palin's invocation to the NRA convention urged Americans in the twenty-first century to take up the frontier code. She, like Webb, argued that Americans must arm themselves and take the law into their own hands because the law isn't functioning as it ought to. Webb made a strong distinction between law for settled regions and law for a raw frontier. But the power of the Code of the West has transformed America into the only armed industrial nation on the globe. Palin's message to the NRA leads to the logical conclusion of Webb's frontier mantra. "Each man had to make his own law ... by the force of his personality, courage and skill at arms ... the six-shooter was the final arbiter, a court of last resort, and an executioner.... All went armed ... among other armed men.... Men were all equal. Each was his own defender." And finally, and most unsettling, "murder was too harsh a word ... a mere incident as it were.... the taking of human life *did not entail the stigma*" of a settled region. What would he be thinking now about Florida? Would he be appalled or delighted by the western frontier's hold on the country's system of justice?

Canada's western frontier experience makes nonsense of Webb's words. He was not describing a frontier in the abstract. His was a very specific frontier, made lawless for very specific reasons. It is the great tragedy of American society that the western myths were so powerful that a great many Americans of the twenty-first century continue to believe that Webb's frontier virtues can still – or ever did – form a workable blueprint for society. The Canadian frontier experience clearly illustrates that a frontier need not be violent and lawless. Webb was describing not so much a frontier as a general American state of the law in the nineteenth century, which profoundly influenced the development of their frontier. And their frontier law, in turn, had a direct and powerful influence on America's later legal development.

The Canadian western frontier, as well, was strongly influenced in its development by eastern Canadian society, and, in its turn, the Canadian western frontier had a powerful influence on later Canadian legal development. What other country has a police force, born and nurtured in the West, as one of its most important national symbols?

The Canadian West, for a start, has no vigilante tradition. Although Great Britain has had much violence in its past, a vigilante tradition never emerged, and an abhorrence for taking the law into one's own hands spread to her Canadian colonies. The legal institutions and traditions that reached the western Canadian ranching frontier were, in many ways, the opposite of those on the American frontier. For a start, the Canadian British North America (BNA) Act of 1867, which came into effect at Canadian Confederation, very deliberately reversed the legal philosophy of the American Constitution, which gave much of the control over criminal law to the individual states. In Canada, exclusive jurisdiction over criminal law remained with the federal government. Canada's prime minister at the time, Sir John A. Macdonald, stated, "We shall have one body of criminal law.... It is one of the defects of the United States system that each state has or may have a criminal code of its own." Macdonald was referring to the fact that in the United States there were "widely varying standards" between the states, and criminal law policy was divided between Congress and the individual states.[96] In Canada, even though the BNA Act gave the administration of justice to the provinces, all provincial laws relating to crime can be disallowed by the federal minister of justice. Ultimate power over the interpretation of criminal law was vested in the Supreme Court of Canada.

The critical issue for the western Canadian frontier was handgun policy. The first national handgun legislation came in 1892, which mandated that anyone carrying a handgun outside the home or business was obliged to have a certificate from a justice of the peace. But even before that, a special law for the Canadian West was enacted in 1885, in an attempt to keep the Canadian West from copying the lawlessness of the American West. It became necessary to have a permit from the Lieutenant Governor of the Northwest Territories to be in possession of a handgun or a rifle (shotguns were allowed without a permit). Ignoring the law could result in six months in jail.[97] The 1892 legislation also required all gun dealers to keep records of all handguns sold.[98] Even before that, the federal government had reacted swiftly to American gun culture by beginning to introduce a series of legislative controls on firearms.[99] The 1892 national legislation was tightened in 1913 and again in 1933, raising the penalty for carrying a handgun without a permit to a minimum of five years in jail.[100]

Between the two world wars, there was a rising concern in Canada that American pulp fiction and movies portrayed guns in a way that would encourage Canadian youth to copy a violent gun culture. And a majority of Canadians believed that it was the duty of the federal government to control the rise of violence in the atmosphere of the Great Depression.[101] Thus the Bennett government enacted two laws relating to handguns: in 1933, a jail sentence of up to five years for carrying a concealed weapon and, in 1934, a law requiring the registration of all handguns. The Mounted Police, now a national force, was able to develop a national handgun registry.[102] This registry was followed, in 1940, by a comprehensive firearms registry.

Handgun legislation was further tightened in 1969 after the killing of President Kennedy, his brother, and Martin Luther King, and again in 1979, adding a minimum of a year in jail for using a handgun in an offence.[103] In response to the political violence in the United States in the 1960s, the Trudeau government enacted laws banning a number of dangerous weapons and restricting access to firearms by the mentally ill. In 1979, a federal order in council placed the AR-15, America's most popular gun, on the prohibited list.[104]

In the 1970s, the federal Ministry of the Solicitor General asked Martin Friedland, the dean of the University of Toronto law school, to prepare a study on gun control in Canada.[105] Friedland found that, for 1979, the per capita ownership of handguns in the US was ten times that in Canada, but the handgun murder rate in the US was twenty times that of Canada. In that year, there were 10,000 handgun murders in the US and fewer than sixty in Canada. New York, alone, had 900 handgun murders, Detroit, 300, and Boston, seventy-five. That year there were four handgun murders in Toronto. Roughly 50 percent of American murders were carried out with handguns. Friedland concluded that, because of strict handgun legislation in Canada, most Canadians felt no need to have a handgun for protection. But the US was so saturated with handguns that citizens were justified in feeling the need of one for self-defence.[106]

In 1991, the federal legislation put about two hundred types of guns on the restricted and prohibited list and placed limits on the size of magazines. The minimum age to acquire a firearm was raised to eighteen and a month-long waiting period for a gun permit was imposed before an FAC (firearms acquisition certificate) was granted. As well, the applicant had to supply two references.[107] One can just imagine the howls of outrage from the NRA if this sort of legislation had been attempted in the US. But, in Canada, a few years later, a Gallup poll found that 83 percent of Canadians favoured the regulation of all firearms.[108] There were, of course, opponents to this federal regulation because property and civil rights came under provincial jurisdiction. But the Supreme Court ruled unanimously for the federal government. The court dismissed the argument that gun ownership was a right. Instead, it was ruled to be a privilege, and the federal government trumped all with the POGG power argument – peace, order, and good government!

In 1995, the federal government, despite much resistance, passed Bill C-68, making Canada's gun control the toughest in the world. The bill required all firearms to be registered. Failure to comply was a criminal offence. The bill mandated a minimum four years in jail for some offences involving firearms. At first, 70 percent of Canadians supported the bill, but support weakened as it became clear that the management of the gun registry was deeply flawed. Very recently, the Conservative government has rescinded the bill.[109] But, until then, one of the most restrictive legislative regimes of universal gun registration in the world faced across the border a country with the highest level of gun-related violence in the world. Although Bill C-68 has been rescinded, the fact remains that these fierce federal statutes could be made law in the first place with relative ease because, unlike in the US, there was no dispute between political jurisdictions. The federal cabinet system makes it far easier to pass controversial laws, such as this recent gun registry.[110]

There are also no powerful lobby groups such as the NRA, with its nine-storey headquarters in Washington, or a large gun manufacturing industry to exert significant pressure on federal firearms policy. As well, there is far less enthusiasm in Canada for unrestricted firearms and the carrying of handguns. For instance, a national Gallup Poll in 1975 found that 83 percent of Canadians favoured registration of all firearms, while only 67 percent of Americans did so. But the real difference is in an attitude toward handguns. The same poll found that 81 percent of Canadians wanted handguns prohibited, while only 41 percent of Americans favoured a ban on handguns. Actually, the astonishing fact that emerges from the above poll is that, in 1975 at least, two-thirds of Americans wanted firearms to be registered, yet the power of the NRA was able to block any meaningful policy.[111]

An important purpose of this study is to show that frontier law has had a significant influence on the development of the nation today. In the United States, the frontier gun mystique has persisted and blossomed. The frontier vigilante ethic has become a national ethic of an armed citizenry with an almost unlimited individual right to carry guns. In Canada, the Mounted Police, a police force that was created on the plains frontier, evolved into a national police force and, in the process, became one of Canada's foremost national symbols. The policies that the Mounted Police developed on the Canadian plains in the nineteenth century became national policies when the Mounted Police became a national police force in the twentieth century. Today, Canada's legal principles related to crime could not differ more from those of America's gun culture and vigilante ethic. Most Canadians believe that gun control is a core value in society, which differentiates Canadians from Americans. The two nations, in these vital areas, could not be farther apart.

Everett Johnson's life on the ranching frontiers of both Wyoming and Alberta puts in sharp focus the importance of both criminal and land law in the shaping of these two frontiers. Johnson witnessed the development and decline of the ranching frontier in Wyoming during most of the 1880s. He moved to Alberta in the late 1880s to escape the atmosphere of lawlessness on the Wyoming range. Although he had participated in the lynchings of cattle rustlers in Wyoming and had used his gun to deadly effect on a number of occasions, he hated what was becoming of Wyoming and decided to leave this atmosphere of violence for the more docile ranching frontier of Alberta, a frontier made relatively orderly and placid by very different principles of criminal and land law under Mounted Police jurisdiction. These differing legal principles, as will be seen through Johnson's eyes, had a profound influence on the aura of the Alberta range. Johnson's life illuminates the critical importance of law in shaping the development and character of the two ranching frontiers at the height of their existence.

1: Beginnings (1860–74)

Everett Cyril Johnson was a Virginian whose forebears had come to America from Scotland before the American Revolution. His great-grandfather, William Johnson, had arrived in Virginia just in time to fight in the Revolution, finally becoming a captain in the Army of Virginia. Because of his military service, he was given land in Powhaten County. There he married an Irish girl, Elizabeth Hunter, and had two children, Thomas William and Elizabeth Hunter.[1]

Johnson's grandfather, Thomas William Johnson, acquired land in Goochland County, Virginia, and married Sarah Quarles Poindexter, a member of one of Virginia's most prominent families. Although Tom Johnson was a well-educated man, the Poindexter family did not consider him much of a catch and, for a while at least, resisted the marriage.

But Sarah's parents finally relented, Tom and Sarah were married, and they eventually produced seven children. Their third son, George Poindexter, was Everett Johnson's father. George, born in 1830, was named after his great-uncle George Poindexter, who had moved to Mississippi and had been governor of that state from 1820 to 1822. In his youth, George had spent much of his time with an aunt, Patricia Quarles Holliday, whose husband, Alexander Holliday, had been an ambassador to England. Aunt Patricia had a house in Richmond and a plantation called Cherry Grove.

In 1855, George went to Black Hawk, Mississippi, where his eldest brother had opened an academy. There he met and fell in love with Martha Lucretia Foster, whose mother was an Adams. The Fosters and the Adamses, natives of Mathews County, Virginia, had come to Mississippi and established many successful plantations in Carroll County.

Cyril Foster thought that his daughter was too young for marriage and sent her off to Mrs. Young's School for Young Ladies in Vicksburg, but George pursued her there and finally persuaded Martha's parents to give their consent to the marriage, which took place in 1856. George and Martha at first lived on Tom Johnson's plantation near Manassas. Here their daughter, Jessie Foster, was born in 1859 and their son, Everett Cyril, in November 1860.

Life was rather pleasant in this self-contained world of the plantation; slaves did virtually all the work, and almost everything was produced on the plantation itself. Young Ebb, as he was called, was raised by a slave woman who was devoted to him. But he remembered little of this southern life so soon to be shattered.

When the Civil War broke out, Johnson's father, George, fought with the Confederate Army and was wounded at Vicksburg. The first battle of Bull Run was fought over Tom Johnson's land; all that the Johnsons had built was destroyed in that battle. Johnson's mother had to take her children and go over the mountains to Lost Creek in West Virginia, where Sarah Johnson, now a widow, had another plantation.

Several years before he died, Tom Johnson made a trip to Minnesota and was very favourably impressed by what he saw. So he acquired farmland there and placed a German family on it as tenants. After the war, Ebb Johnson's father, thinking that his young family might have a brighter future in the North, moved them to the farm in Minnesota. Although she was now free, the children's mammy refused to be left behind and accompanied the family to their new home. Another person who was to have a profound effect upon young Ebb – his maternal grandmother – also came with them.

The Johnson family travelled by riverboat down the Ohio River and up the Mississippi to a point not far from Lake City, Minnesota, and there they settled on the farm called "Twin Mounds," which was a short distance from the river. A large eight-room house was built, as well as barns, granaries, sheds for machinery, a chicken house, and a smokehouse. They kept horses, cows, turkeys, and chickens, but Ebb's father refused to have pigs on the place. That did not fit with his Tidewater background. They also had a grain field, a hay meadow, a good garden, and a small orchard of apple and plum trees. Two small lakes provided water for the livestock and a place for the children to swim in the summer and skate in the winter. About a quarter of a mile from the house, there was a four-room log cabin for Carson Minke, the German who worked the land. Jessie and Ebb spent much of their time playing with the Minke children, Heinrich and Inger. The children had a great deal of freedom, but they were responsible for certain chores. As well, although at first there was little in the way of schooling, their grandmother made sure that they learned to read.

During the winter evenings, their father read to them from Shakespeare or Sir Walter Scott. Among the other books in that pioneer home, Johnson could remember Dickens, Thackeray, George Eliot, and Roman history and poetry. Jessie read Josephus with her father's help. He gave her a melodeon, and she could play both the piano and the organ by the time she was eleven.

Both children loved animals. They each owned a pony and a calf. Ebb was given a bulldog, an inveterate fighter that he named Cassius M. Clay. When he was ten years old, he was given a shotgun with which he soon began to take a toll on the numerous prairie chickens, quail, and ducks.

The family were briefly Episcopalian until, one Sunday, the minister pounded the pulpit and shouted, "No man who has ever owned a slave will enter the Kingdom of Heaven!" So Johnson's father gathered up his family and left the church. Ebb Johnson never became a churchgoer.

The children heard stories of the Santee Sioux uprising in Minnesota in 1862, in which the Sioux killed many hundreds of settlers. The uprising had resulted from the federal government's neglect of treaty obligations to the Santees due to the impending Civil War. When the Santee complained that the government was starving them, trader Andrew Myrick allegedly responded that if the Sioux were so hungry, "let them eat grass." He was very pleased with his historical allusion until he became the first victim of the outbreak, found scalped and with his mouth stuffed with grass.[2]

Johnson's father joined the western army to fight in the Indian wars, which had again erupted during the Civil War. For this and for the fact that he left the South as soon as the war was over, his brothers never forgave him. To the brothers in Virginia, Minnesota was enemy territory, and the blue uniform was the crowning insult. George felt the estrangement keenly and was quite overcome when, years later, he received a letter from his brother William. Undoubtedly, his father's experiences as an Indian fighter coloured Ebb Johnson's attitudes toward Native people.

Two more children were born at Twin Mounds: a girl, Elizabeth Ann, and a boy, Charles Robert Colfax. With their father away, the children had to become even more self-reliant and resourceful. Ebb became the man of the house, responsible for the horses, cattle, and much of the farm work. He found many excuses to avoid school.

When his father came home on leave, he brought with him buffalo robes, beaded buckskin, and tomahawks and told the children stories of the Sioux, Winnebagos, Crows, and the Chippewas, whom he liked best. He was a cavalry officer and one winter was stationed at Fort Snelling, near Saint

Paul. Johnson's mother, wishing to be near her husband, took Jessie and the two youngest children and moved to Saint Paul for the winter, leaving Ebb, aged ten, at home with his grandmother, his mammy, and a neighbour boy to help with the chores.

The grandmother, whose Virginia accent was even more pronounced than her son's, enthralled young Ebb with stories of Poindexter derring-do. She told him, too, of Meriwether Lewis, who was connected to the family by marriage – of Lewis's expedition with William Clark up the Missouri River and over the Rocky Mountains to the Columbia. She told him of the meeting of these two explorers with John Colter in 1806 and of Colter's incredible journeys alone through Indian Country and of his even more incredible ordeals and escapes. And so, with stories of romance and danger, she fired the boy's imagination and pride in his family. When Johnson's mother came home, Sarah Poindexter Johnson returned to her home at Lost Creek, where she died. And when Johnson left Minnesota for the West, he carried with him only one picture, a little tintype of his grandmother.

* * * * *

When Johnson was twelve, his father left the army and moved the family into Lake City, where, he hoped, the children could attend school regularly. Johnson hated to leave the farm and did not take much to school. But he was not to endure school for long. One day, one of the boys at school called him a dirty rebel. Johnson picked up a piece of broken slate and threw it at the boy, cutting him badly on the face. He knew he was in trouble so he decided to run away from home. This was not a new idea; he and an older boy, Will Furlow, had often talked of going west to seek their fortunes. So one night they rode off, taking with them some food, two blankets, and a gun apiece. There were rumours at the time of gold in Colorado, so they headed in that direction.

They found work at Camp Clark, Nebraska, where they lived in rough quarters with miners, trappers, and stockmen, altogether a wild breed of men. Unfortunately, Will Furlow was hot-tempered and ready to fight at the least provocation. Finally, one night, he got into a gunfight and was killed. His death caused little stir in frontier Nebraska. The shooting was considered a fair fight, so there was no recourse to the law.

With his friend dead, Johnson decided that there was nothing to keep him in Nebraska. Longhorned cattle were now coming into the northern plains, and Johnson had become acquainted with some cowhands who had trailed cattle north from Texas and were returning home. So he decided to accompany them since he had an uncle ranching in Victoria County, not far from San Antonio.

It was not unusual at this time for a boy of twelve to be hired on for such a trip. During the Civil War thousands of young boys fought in the Confederate Army. Boys of twelve were expected to pull their weight. For instance, Charles Goodnight, the famous Texas cattleman, rode bareback from Illinois to Texas when he was only nine years old. Boys grew up fast on the frontier. Johnson hired on as a horse wrangler on that trip and considered himself a man when he reached his uncle's ranch.

Texas, in 1872, was not altogether tamed. According to T. R. Fehrenbach, an expert on the subject, the amount and character of lawlessness in Texas at this time was entirely unprecedented in the United States. "As often as not, justice was private and vengeance was personal."[3] The legacy of the Alamo, the Mexican War, and the Civil War still had an immediacy for Texans in the 1870s, as did their campaign to clear the state of the "Indian menace."

Texas, perhaps more than any other state in the Union, had been conceived in violence and was developed by Anglo-Celtic frontiersmen, the descendants of those who had pushed through the Cumberland Gap and wrested the interior from the Comanche and Apache. They were a tough, stubborn, independent lot who asked for and gave no quarter to Mexican, Comanche, or Yankee. More than all other types put together, they were responsible for advancing the frontier. Johnson would have felt right at home with these people; after all, he was very much of the same breed, though his Tidewater Virginia background undoubtedly distanced him from some of the coarser aspects of the Texas frontier.

It was not long after reaching his uncle's ranch that Johnson was introduced to a typical brand of Texas violence. His uncle somehow got wind of a plot on the part of his Mexican cowboys to kill him. He was in the habit of rising early and going to the bunkhouse to wake the men. This particular morning, he went, gun in hand, and, after waking the men, began to shoot; he killed every Mexican. This was Johnson's introduction to Texas. This incident perhaps inspired Johnson to become adept in the handling of a six-gun. Self-preservation in frontier Texas had little to do with formal law. He later became an expert with a revolver. He also learned the art of roping from some of the best Texans in the trade and was later considered one the best ropers in both Wyoming and Alberta.

Most of Johnson's work consisted of searching for elusive longhorns. The trick was to rope an animal and get it snubbed to a mesquite tree. When the men had enough of them secured, they would bring up a bunch of quieter cattle, work the mavericks in with them, and so take them to the ranch. Sometimes they hazed them in one at a time, and a man who could not handle his rope and his horse could meet with disaster. Their ropes were made of rawhide, as many as eight strands braided, rubbed, and oiled. Once, Johnson saw one of these ropes break, the whiplash end of it striking a Mexican across the stomach, laying it open and killing him. These ropes were sometimes used as weapons of war; many men have been dragged to death at the end of one.

Though Johnson loved Texas, he became increasingly homesick. So, at fourteen, he decided to leave Texas and started for home with only his horse, rope, bedroll, and gun. After several days on the trail, as he was riding through a grove of oaks, he heard shots and the sound of a galloping horse coming toward him. Suddenly a Mexican came into view around a corner, riding hard with a six-gun in his hand. Johnson's horse shied and threw up its head at the sight of him. This perhaps saved Johnson's life; the Mexican fired, hitting the horse in the middle of the forehead. The horse dropped, instantly killed, but Johnson was able to jump free and fire a shot that killed the Mexican.

Even in Texas it was not usual for horsemen to come galloping around corners, guns blazing. But the cause soon became apparent. A group of Texas Rangers were pursuing the Mexican. They were rather impressed by the young boy's shooting and took him back to their camp, where he discovered that their captain was related to his grandmother. This relative was obviously impressed by Johnson's ability with a revolver and suggested that he join the Rangers, which until this time had been a loose militia, usually brought together to rid the frontier of Comanches or Mexicans. The Rangers were probably eager for recruits since they had just been reconstituted that year (1874) after a period of opposition toward them under Reconstruction policy.[4] But Johnson was too intent on returning home. So the Rangers gave him a new horse, and he got a job with an outfit trailing cattle north on the Western Trail to Dodge City. This herd of cattle numbered about two thousand. About a dozen men and sixty or more horses were needed to trail such a herd. The trail boss rode ahead, scouting out the trail and looking for good watering places and fords. He would stop on a rise of land and signal directions with his arm or his hat. He signalled, too, when they were approaching a watering place, so that the herd could be swung downstream if possible and the greatest number could drink at one time. The cook, too, went ahead with the chuckwagon and the horse wrangler with the remuda. On this drive Johnson rode in the swing position. The two best men rode

Frederic Remington, *Stampeded by Lightning* (1908). Remington was undoubtedly influenced by the work of Eadweard Maybridge, who was the first to use a series of trip cameras to capture the movement of a galloping horse. Here Remington has perfectly caught the horse's moment of suspension at the gallop.

point. Then came the men on swing and flanks. Behind, in the dust, came the inexperienced men on drag.

The herd, being creatures of habit, soon became used to the trail. But the wild, high-strung longhorns often stampeded. Lightning or an unusual noise could set them off. Although Johnson spent his life among cattle, he rarely mentioned stampedes. He took them for granted. They were just part of the day's or night's work. "Of co'se we had stampedes," he would say when asked. "We just tried to get the cattle circling." It was typical of his kind that he would downplay the dangers of such a drive, but these were very real. Numerous crude graves along the cattle trails were a mute reminder of the cowboys who had been crushed beyond recognition by a stampeding herd on a stormy night. Yet there is practically no evidence of any of these cowboys shirking their responsibilities during a stampede. And it is doubtful that it was the dollar a day and grub that kept them to the mark. It was an important part of the cowboy code that they respond to stampedes instantly. Any cowboy who shirked his responsibility would be an instant outcast. There was a strong cowboy ethic that most adhered to: it called for being loyal, almost to a fault, and basically honest. "When the chips were down, you could count on them. What more can anyone say of a man."[5]

Wallace Stegner, the Pulitzer-winning author who grew up on the Saskatchewan-Montana border in the early twentieth century, had this to say about the cowboy code:

> They [cowboys] honored courage, competence, self-reliance, and they honored them tacitly. They took them for granted. It was their absence, not their presence, that was cause for remark. Practicing comradeship in a rough and dangerous job, they lived a life calculated to make a man careless of anything except the few things he really valued.[6]

As a small boy, Stegner would conjure visions of his life as a cowboy:

> I would be bowlegged and taciturn, with deep creases in my cheeks and a hide like stained saddle leather. I would be the quietest and most dangerous man around, best rider, best shot, the one who couldn't be buffaloed. Men twice my size, beginning some brag or other, would catch my cold eye and begin to wilt, and when I had stared them into impotence, I would turn my back contemptuous, hook onto my pony in one bowlegged arc, and ride off.[7]

At the same time, however, Stegner acknowledged the other, darker side of the cowboy character: "the prejudice, the callousness, the destructive practical joking, the tendency to judge everyone by the same raw standard."[8]

Other accounts of the period offer graphic evidence of the difficulties encountered in getting cattle from Texas to the Kansas cattle towns: great suffering from lack of water, death or injury from stampeding cattle, and, of course, the Native threat. The Comanches were not militarily defeated until 1875, a year after Johnson rode the Western Trail to Dodge City. James Cook, who was trailing cattle that same year through Dodge to Ogallala to sell to Maj. Frank North and Bill Cody, had many stories of Comanche raids in his classic account *Fifty Years on the Old Frontier*. Cook said that the Comanches were mainly intent on procuring guns and ammunition or running off the stock. Their favourite trick was to gallop through the cattle herd dragging a buffalo hide to make the cattle stampede. Cowboys got into the habit of not sleeping too near the campfire in case of ambush. "Occasionally some unfortunate stockrider would stop a bullet or an arrow. But that was part of the business."[9] One cowboy described a cattle stampede in very realistic terms: "The ones in front go like hell, plumb afraid of the ones behind are goin' to run them over, and the ones behind run like hell to keep up."[10]

Frederic Remington, *The Stampede* (1910). This was Remington's last sculpture. It brilliantly shows the rider's determination and control in the midst of chaos.

Cook, when reminiscing about cowboys up the Texas trails, added, "A large percentage of the boys I have known ... were honest and true as steel to their employers.... The real cowboy would never desert a herd in order to protect himself from heavy weather. Many have gone to their deaths in blizzards, tornadoes and bad thunderstorms by staying with the herd."[11]

In 1874, fortunately for Johnson and his herd, the Comanches were rather preoccupied with what would be their last campaign against the whites. Not far to the west of the cattle trail to Dodge, the Battle of Adobe Walls took place on the Canadian River in June 1874, supposedly pitting twenty-eight buffalo hunters from Dodge against a huge party of Comanches.[12] Actually, as the fame of Adobe Walls spread, so did the disparity in numbers. Initial eyewitness reports calculated one hundred buffalo hunters and teamsters against two hundred Indians. Soon it became twenty-eight against five hundred and within a few years twenty-six against a thousand.[13] Though the hunters had no business being where they were – an area forbidden to white hunters by the Treaty of Medicine Lodge – the battle gave the army the necessary excuse to wage a protracted campaign against the Comanches led by one of the best Indian fighters in the business, Col. Ranald Mackenzie. By the fall of 1874 his bulldog methods had thoroughly demoralized the Comanches; they capitulated the following year. The real cause of Adobe Walls was the railroad, which split the northern and southern buffalo herds and created a booming market in hides that led, by 1875, to the southern herd's extinction.

Johnson, until he reached Dodge, was probably unaware that this drama was taking place so near the trail to Dodge, though he may have learned at Fort Griffin that the Comanches were in open hostility. The trail that he was following was the new Western Trail, which was just starting to replace the famous Chisholm Trail to Wichita, Newton, and Abilene. These towns were in the process of shrivelling up and dying as settlers spread west into the region of the Chisholm Trail, and the cattle trail was forced to shift westward.

The new Western Trail originated west of San Antonio and then went more or less straight north to Dodge before veering somewhat to the west on its way to Ogallala. The first stop was Fort Griffin on the Clear Fork of the Brazos. Here federal troops looked on with seeming unconcern as buffalo hunters set out from the Flat, home to a typically haphazard frontier collection of dance hall girls, gunmen, prostitutes, and professional poker players. The buffalo hunters were not fazed by the fact that they were encroaching on territory guaranteed exclusively for Native hunting by the 1867 Treaty of Medicine Lodge.[14]

After Fort Griffin, the trail crossed the Salt Fork of the Brazos, the Big Wichita, and the Pease, before arriving at Doan's Crossing on Red River. Here Corwin and Jonathan Doan built a store in 1874 to sell supplies to hunters and cowboys. Although they advanced credit to literally hundreds of cowboys over the years, according to J. Frank Dobie, they never lost a dime from their cowboy customers. Some would go several hundred miles out of their way to repay their loans.[15]

From Doan's Crossing, the trail led across two more forks of the Red and then across the Washita, very near the site where, in November 1868, Custer clinched his fame as an Indian fighter by attacking and slaughtering a band of peaceful Cheyennes. It continued across several forks of the Canadian and on to the Arkansas, where the ramshackle beginnings of Dodge City, five miles west of Fort Dodge on the old Santa Fe trail, clung to the north shore, in constant danger of being blown off across the treeless plains.

When Johnson reached Dodge, the cattle boom that would make the town so famous was still a few years away. Dodge would take off as a cattle town in 1876 with the building of cattle pens, replacing Wichita as the centre of the cattle trade and becoming the largest cattle market in the world – and the wildest town in the West – before its demise in 1885. But the extension of the Santa Fe line to Dodge in 1872 had already resulted in the beginnings of a "pitiful masquerade of false front buildings," as Owen Wister would later describe other such western towns. Dodge had begun as a camp

Remington's sketch "A Row in a Cattle Town" perfectly catches the result of mixing guns with alcohol along the cattle trails.

called Buffalo City, whose purpose was to sell liquor to the soldiers at neighbouring Fort Dodge. When the railroad arrived in 1872, it was renamed. By 1874, Dodge was a booming hide depot for the buffalo trade, which shipped several hundred thousand hides annually from 1872 to 1874.[16] In the first three months of its existence alone, Dodge shipped out 43,029 hides and 1.4 million pounds of buffalo meat. That first winter, more than a hundred buffalo hunters froze to death out on the plains. As Johnson approached Dodge, the entire countryside was littered with thousands of buffalo hides staked out to dry and rows of bone ricks randomly constructed along the tracks. Hides sold for two to four dollars, bones for fourteen dollars a ton.

In 1874, Dodge had a somewhat haphazard air, as thousands of buffalo hunters, freighters, and railway navvies erected tents or hastily built quarters and jostled with the soldiers from the nearby fort for elbow room at the mushrooming saloons. There was, of course, no government or law. Dodge had no official marshal until 1876. When Johnson was in Dodge, Billy Brooks was acting in that capacity unofficially, but that year an irate buffalo hunter ran him out of town.[17]

The closest thing to law in Dodge in 1874 was a vigilante committee, which, according to Col. Richard Dodge, the commandant at Fort Dodge, was composed of the worst element in the town. The year before, this group had dragged one of his Black soldiers out in the street and cold-bloodedly

A FIGHT IN THE STREET.

Frederic Remington, "A Fight in the Street" *Century*, October 1888. The saloon was the American West's most popular killing ground; a number of sheriffs met their death in attempting to defuse the effects of liquor and bravado.

murdered him. Col. Dodge could do nothing; Dodge City was out of his jurisdiction and the nearest civilian law was in Hays City.[18] He was not allowed to interfere with civil matters, on pain of losing his commission.

Despite the escalation in the supposed number killed in Dodge as the legend grew, there is no question that Dodge, when Johnson passed through it in 1874, was a wide-open town; the Boot Hill Cemetery was starting to do a creditable business.[19] There is no proper record of clients buried there. Most were unceremoniously deposited in unmarked graves. Yet, despite the large amounts of money floating around Dodge in those early days – there were no banks yet – crimes of property were very rare. There was an odd double standard at work; property was sacred, especially if it was a horse, but life was not. And women, even prostitutes, were much safer than they would have been in many eastern cities. The violence was almost exclusively between men, and it was usually triggered by drink.[20]

There were as yet no Wyatt Earp or Masterson brothers, or "Doc" Holliday and his prostitute inamorata, Big Nose Kate, to oversee Dodge's virtue.

But the town was beginning to stir. By the time the railroad arrived, Dodge boasted a general store, three dance halls, and six saloons,[21] and the usual collection of urban parasites was drifting in to take advantage of the buffalo trade. And, although an ordinance went into effect early in 1874 prohibiting concealed weapons in Dodge City, it was obeyed about as assiduously as the one prohibiting gambling and frequenting prostitutes.[22] Virtually everyone in Dodge, south of the "dead line" that marked the limits of law enforcement, went about armed to the teeth.

A killing in the south end of Dodge was treated in the most casual way; it was not considered murder if both men were armed, due warning was given, and the loser was shot in the front. People usually expressed concern only if property was destroyed. Southern cowboys, for whom the "Lost Cause" was still a living issue, created most of the violence. Their greatest ambition was to "tree" a northerner or to make life miserable for a northern lawman.[23] Add liquor and violence would almost inevitably follow.

But Johnson had no special adventures while in Dodge, or at least none that he wanted recorded for posterity. Undoubtedly, he made a stop at the Long Branch Saloon on Front Street, which was established the year before by Ford County's first sheriff and later became one of the most famous watering holes in the West. After the cattle were delivered, he drew his pay and headed for home.

2: The Black Hills (1875–76)

When Johnson reached home, he found that the family had moved to Rochester, Minnesota, a thriving little town on the Zumbro River. Although his father had been offered the chair of mathematics at Carleton College, Northfield, he had refused it. Instead, he opened a meat market in Rochester, put a friend in charge, and then acquired a stagecoach line running from Rochester to Zumbrota, a distance of about thirty miles. Johnson's father was a good horseman who took great pride in his horses, and the stagecoach line proved to be a profitable undertaking.

Another little sister, named George Lucretia, had been born while Johnson was in Texas. Ebb let her play with his silver-mounted spurs, his prize possession, but he was disgusted with her name. He said, "You might just as well have called her 'Tom.'" And that is what he called her for the rest of his life.

As there were good schools in Rochester, Johnson's father tried to persuade him to pursue an education, but he refused. He was much more interested in the stagecoach line, so his father allowed him to take over some of the driving. He became a good driver and loved working with the horses, but he found the life tame and the routine dull after his experiences in Texas. Johnson was not interested in the staid, respectable life of Rochester; he had been bitten too thoroughly by the West. He itched to leave home and finally persuaded his father to let him go. In the fall of 1875, at the age of fifteen, he headed for the Black Hills as a stagecoach driver.

The Black Hills of Dakota Territory had just exploded onto the American consciousness; gold had been discovered and a full-scale stampede was underway by 1875. There was, however, one annoying complication to overcome before the gold could be properly exploited. The Black Hills belonged to the Lakota Sioux, and they were understandably testy regarding the invasion of their sacred hills by hordes of miners.

Prior to this invasion, there had been persistent rumours of gold in the Black Hills for many decades. But it was not until 1874 that these rumours were given real substance by the report of the military expedition to the Hills under George Armstrong Custer. This expedition had been sent by General Philip Sheridan, commander in chief of western forces, purportedly to scout out the possibility of establishing a military post on the western side of the vast Sioux Reservation, ceded to the Lakotas by the Treaty of Fort Laramie in 1868. It was thought by the army that a post strategically located in the heart of the Sioux hunting territory would dissuade the Sioux from raiding the isolated white settlements that were creeping westward into Lakota country.[1] And they had become increasingly restive as the Northern Pacific Railway approached their hunting grounds.

Custer departed from Fort Lincoln, near Bismarck, Dakota Territory, a town that had taken on an added bustle and importance after the Northern Pacific arrived there three years before. His expedition resembled a cross between an elaborate hunting party and a picnic, complete with a military band mounted on white horses and a train of more than a hundred wagons. Among this party of over one thousand men was a sprinkling of scientists, journalists, and two "practical miners," who were counted on to recognize gold if they saw it. Officially, the purpose of the expedition was to search for a suitable site to build a military post, but, clearly, an important unofficial purpose was to verify the rumours of gold.[2] The expedition became very suspect and promised to arouse Sioux hostility when Custer's official report did indicate, in a guarded way, the presence of gold in the Black Hills. Nowhere in the report did Custer even mention the ostensible purpose of the expedition – finding a suitable location for a fort.[3]

Custer's report triggered the rush to the Black Hills the following year. His official report and his more unguarded interviews with newspaper reporters soon after his return resulted in headlines trumpeting the discovery of a new El Dorado. And his deceit in actively prospecting for gold in country ceded in perpetuity to the Sioux, with all the due solemnity and lack of conviction of the treaty process, was to be repaid in the early summer of 1876 when Custer and his cavalry columns stumbled on a very large and exceedingly unfriendly gathering of Sioux and Cheyennes camped on the Little Big Horn River in southern Montana. It was only fitting that Custer, in the annihilation of his force that followed, should pay the price for the miners' invasion of the sacred territory of the Sioux.

To give the army its due, it did make some attempt to stem the flood of miners to the Black Hills in 1875. The region was closed to whites, and General Sheridan ordered the army to remove all prospectors from the area and burn their wagons. But it was like attempting to stem a migration of locusts. By the fall of 1875 there were fifteen thousand miners in the Hills. Gold became more of an incentive during the economic depression of 1873: hordes of footloose men – and some women – were not about to have their pursuits of happiness checked by the niceties of an Indian treaty. And so, the Black Hills by the fall of 1875 had begun to take on the appearance of a collection of anthills.

If the tone of Annie Tallent, the first white woman to travel to the Black Hills, is any indication, the white migrants considered the Lakotas to be barbarians with no redeeming features who, by God's wish, had to be pushed aside to make way for civilization. In her book, *The Black Hills or Last Hunting Grounds of the Dakotahs*, there is no hint of guilt for invading Lakota land; it was silly to have made a treaty in the first place. Here, in Tallent's little book, is an all-too-typical attitude of white settlers in the American West. Gold was clearly God's bounty, and it was utterly ridiculous not to exploit it just because some former promise had been made to some wandering Indians. Repeatedly, serious friction with Native peoples, which then escalated into open hostilities, began with this dismissive attitude.

In November 1875, President Grant met with his Secretary of the Interior, Zachariah Chandler, and Generals Sherman and Crook. They decided to solve the Sioux refusal to sell the Black Hills by issuing an ultimatum. All Sioux must return to their reservations by January 31, 1876. Any who did not would be considered hostile. This ultimatum was tantamount to an unprovoked declaration of war. These men knew that the Sioux who were off their reservations in the winter could not travel back to them even if they wanted to. The officials' action was completely disingenuous. And the Sioux had not provoked this policy; in fact, they had shown extraordinary restraint toward the illegal miners in their sacred Black Hills.[4]

In the 1868 treaty with the Sioux, negotiated in the aftermath of the Bozeman Trail wars, the Black Hills were "set apart for the absolute and undisturbed use and occupation of the Indians." But in 1877, after the Custer fight, Congress repudiated the 1868 treaty through bullying some Sioux leaders into renouncing it, legally opening the Black Hills to prospectors. Deadwood continued to develop unabated. The situation was so blatantly dishonest that one court remarked, "A more ripe and rank case of dishonourable dealings will never, in all probability, be found in our history." Finally, in 1980 – more than a century later – the Supreme Court of the

Charles M. Russell, *Stagecoach* (1920). Courtesy of the Amon Carter Museum of American Art, Fort Worth.

United States affirmed the decision of lower courts and awarded the Lakotas a total, including interest, of $122.5 million.[5] To date, the Sioux have refused to accept the money.

As Johnson headed for the Black Hills in the fall of 1875, the gold rush to that area was providing a bonanza for the owners of stagecoaches, and they were quick to take advantage of it. Johnson's father was offered a good price for his outfit and sold it to a man who wanted Johnson to stay on as driver. Reluctantly, George Johnson gave his son permission to go. Johnson, now fifteen, accompanied the outfit of horses, Concord stage, men, and supplies as they went by rail and then by riverboat to Fort Pierre, near the junction of the Bad River and the Missouri, in what is now South Dakota. They picked up a load in Fort Pierre and started west, Johnson driving the six-horse team. On the coach with him was a guard, armed with a rifle and a sawed-off shotgun, and two outriders.

The Fort Pierre route was the shortest route to the Black Hills, though not the most travelled. Being the shortest route, and since Fort Pierre was located on the Missouri River, a major artery to the northwest, the Pierre route soon became the primary route for supplying the region. But, in 1875, Johnson and the other Pierre stage drivers were pioneering a route through

rough and potentially dangerous country. It says something about both Johnson and the times he lived in that a boy of fifteen was given this kind of responsibility.

Somewhat later, an alternate route from Cheyenne to Deadwood was opened by Gilmer and Salisbury, but it didn't really start operating until April 1876. This route roughly followed the famous Cheyenne–Black Hills Trail, which was almost identical to present-day Route 87 between Cheyenne and Chugwater and cut east across the Platte at Fort Laramie. From Fort Laramie, the route went north to Lusk and Deadwood, essentially following today's Route 85.

Four routes to Deadwood were developed in the next few years. The shortest, from Pierre on the Missouri River, was roughly 200 miles; from Bismarck, also on the Missouri, it was 225 miles. The longer routes branched off from the Union Pacific Railway at Sidney, Nebraska (285 miles), and the longest of all was from Cheyenne (325 miles).[6]

Later, when the Pierre–Deadwood route was in regular operation, the journey took about forty-eight hours and, even with frequent stations for a change of horses and some refreshment, was considered a tough one. Passengers were reminded not to put grease on their hair because of the persistent dust of the Badlands. The heat in summer and the icy winds in winter were equally trying on these treeless plains. When Johnson drove this route, the conditions were even more primitive.

Johnson's route began at old Fort Pierre, a former fur trade post whose recorded history went back to the mid-eighteenth century when La Verendrye buried a lead plate there and claimed the territory for France before travelling on to the Black Hills. The post had now almost completely disappeared, soon to be replaced by the mushroom-like growth of the new Pierre, which sprouted as a result of the Black Hills stampede. The stage route, for the most part, wound through the desolate, treeless Badlands, periodically crossing such suggestively named streams as Frozeman, Deadman, and Dirty Woman. The only really difficult river crossing was on the Cheyenne River, which was deep and had very steep banks that made it necessary to roughlock the wheels during the descent. After the Cheyenne River, it was a relatively short run to Box Elder Creek, over the divide, and down to Rapid City, one of the earliest communities created by the gold rush. Here the Pierre route was joined by the stage route from Sidney, Nebraska, which, together with Cheyenne, was on the Union Pacific line. The Cheyenne and Sidney routes later became the two most popular ways for passengers to reach the Black Hills.

Neil Broadfoot, *Butterfield Stage*, 1985. There was actually very little Sioux hostility toward the Deadwood stage. Broadfoot is one of the foremost illustrators of historical canoes.

In the spring of 1876, the stage route was extended from Rapid City through to Sturgis – a grubby little town that would be closely associated in the popular imagination with Poker Alice Tubbs and her bevy of somewhat faded "prairie flowers" – and then on to the new town of Deadwood, which was fast becoming the focal point of the gold rush. Johnson spent a lot of time in Deadwood in 1876 and thus witnessed this extraordinary town in its infancy.

Unlike many of the stage drivers who came after him, Johnson never had trouble either from the Sioux or from bandits. The Sioux, in 1875, were unaccountably quiet in light of the illegal invasion of their lands. This was a source of great frustration for military planners who argued that it was time for a showdown with the Sioux. The Sioux had refused all overtures from the Allison Commission of 1875, which had attempted to buy the Black Hills from them. So it was now argued that a campaign against the Sioux would solve the dilemma of the army's helplessness in preventing miners from entering the Hills. But the Sioux were giving them no pretext for a campaign. This did not, however, prevent the army from launching its disastrous campaign of 1876.

There were also few problems from bandits in 1875 and early 1876. Later, after the Sioux raids of 1876 subsided, it would be open season on stagecoaches, but fortunately Johnson had quit driving by that time. Johnson therefore missed the likes of Sam Bass and Persimmon Bill, a member of Dunc Blackburn's Hat Creek gang, whose notoriety rested on stagecoach robberies on three successive nights in June 1877.[7]

The first holdup of a stagecoach did not occur until the end of March 1877. But after that, there were a great many assaults on stagecoaches transporting gold from Deadwood until an effective system of shotgun messengers and bulletproof coaches was devised.

The occupation of stage driver was surrounded by a considerable aura of glamour. It took great skill to handle the ribbons of a six-horse Concord with room for a dozen or more passengers and, on a good stretch, capable of exceeding eight miles an hour. These Concord coaches, made by the Abbot-Downing Company of Concord, New Hampshire, became a trademark of the West. About three thousand of them were produced and sent all over the world. They were painted a distinctive red with yellow running gear and intricate scrollwork and were manufactured mostly from oak and white ash. The interiors were fitted with fine leather, polished metal, and wood panelling. But the main feature – the feature that made them distinct from all other coaches – was their suspension. Instead of metal springs, the Concord had thoroughbraces – multiple strips of leather riveted together and running lengthwise. The body of the coach rested on these leather strips and on nothing else. The lateral sway of the coach was controlled by two simple straps attached from the frame to the body; these could easily be adjusted like a belt. The Concords were unique at the time in producing a swinging motion instead of the harsher up-and-down jolting of conventional springs: another triumph of Yankee ingenuity.[8]

There was a decided art to driving these coaches, especially in keeping the leaders, swing team, and wheelers all pulling evenly. It also took considerable experience to handle the brake properly; a good driver could perform on it "with a rhythm similar to an organist manipulating pipe-organ pedals."[9] And it took steady nerves to live with the constant fear of attack from road agents and the Sioux.

When Johnson began driving the route to Deadwood in the spring of 1876, the town was just coming into existence. In early March, there were fifty prospectors there; by April, a townsite had been laid out, and by fall, it was swarming with people. Most of them were intent on finding gold, but the smart ones were intent on relieving the lucky prospectors of their gold, mostly through whisky, gambling, and prostitution.[10] Deadwood, with dizzying speed, became the typical false-front western mining town, presided over initially by the usual group of urban parasites who astutely sniffed out the great potential for vice in the raw town. Deadwood in these

Deadwood in 1876, a haphazard collection of false-front buildings and tents. Deadwood Public Library.

early days attracted a great many unemployed loafers, and in the absence of any real authority, the atmosphere was one of almost total licence.

Deadwood's era of lawlessness, as was the case with all the famous western towns, was fleeting, but there is no question that Deadwood when Johnson knew it was exceedingly lawless (though the reality was but a pale reflection of the legend that was to follow.) As historian Watson Parker concluded, "It is impossible to avoid the conclusion that Deadwood was a violent town."[11] Between 1876 and 1879, thirty-four people were murdered there, and the Sioux killed another sixty-three.[12] Bill Longly, the Texas outlaw who claimed to have killed thirty-two men, drifted to the Black Hills in the early days and later described its atmosphere. "There was no law at all. It was simply the rule of claw and tooth and fang and the weakest went to the wall. When the majority of people got down on a man, they simply took him out and strung him up on a limb, and they had a big spree on the strength of it."[13]

Herman Glafcke, editor of the *Cheyenne Daily Leader*, blamed the situation squarely on the federal government:

> It is surprising that neither the Government of the United States, through its officials of the U.S. Marshalls [sic] office, nor the County Commissioners, through the officials of the Sheriff's office, have made any effort whatever to pursue and capture the highwaymen who have waylaid and stopped the U.S. mails ... and interrupted travel on the public highway.[14]

And there were many lynchings. The first legal hanging did not occur until 1882.[15] Most violence resulted from the lethal mixture of alcohol and guns, but it would have been unthinkable to actually take seriously the town ordinance meant to discourage the carrying or discharge of weapons in the town. It was an article of faith among Deadwood citizens, all armed to the teeth, that crime could only be prevented by carrying guns. This seems extraordinarily illogical, but, in the absence of effective law, it did make sense. And it is refreshing to note that violence in Deadwood was not entirely sexist. The first ball, the earliest attempt at a "polite social affair," was shot up by a woman with a fine sense of democracy, who had not been invited because of her doubtful virtue.[16] Then there was Calamity Jane Cannary, who entered the Hills as a prostitute with Crook's army in 1876 and became an almost instant legend for her drinking and brawling, as well as for her great warmth and generosity.

There developed, after a time, law of a sort in Deadwood, a mixture of the military; a marshal and sheriff; and an assortment of bounty hunters, hastily deputized posses, and, somewhat later, railway detectives and Pinkerton agents. But, on the other side, the outlaws preying on the gold stagecoaches had a sophisticated system of communications and organization that was almost impossible to break up.[17] Clearly, there was great frustration with this system of law; otherwise there would not have been instances of vigilante mobs liberating suspects from the law and lynching them. This occurred in at least five well-recorded instances involving road agents who had preyed on the Deadwood gold shipments. In 1877, Cornelius "Lame Johnny" Donahue, who allegedly had committed several murders in Texas before coming to the Black Hills, was taken from the stagecoach escorting him to prison by eight masked men and, struggling and kicking, lynched. For a short period, Lame Johnny had been a deputy sheriff in Custer County, but someone from Texas recognized him and exposed his violent past.[18]

The next year, two suspects from the Canyon Springs robbery, who were being escorted to trial by agents of the law, were taken from a stagecoach by five masked men and lynched.[19] Next came Dutch Charley, lynched by a group who first overpowered two deputy sheriffs.[20] Then "Fly Speck" Billy was lynched in similar circumstances in 1881 for killing Abe Barnes, a freighter, at Custer City. He, too, was seized by a mob from the sheriff while being taken to trial.[21] And, finally, there was Big Nose George Parrott, whose end is discussed below. In his case, an armed mob descended on the jail where he was incarcerated and took him by force from the law.

The evolution of Deadwood, in a few short years, from a raw brawling frontier town to a rather sober community of Victorian proprieties makes fascinating reading. The first wave of people, the placer miners and assorted hangers-on (saloon keepers, gamblers, and prostitutes made up a third of Deadwood's initial population), soon gave way to the second, more permanent wave who were intent on establishing law and order, stabilizing economic and political structures, and replicating eastern social standards of polite society. In this evolution, Deadwood was typical of all the frontier towns of the West. In Deadwood, even in 1876, the forces of propriety were already at work, attempting to counteract the saloons and brothels with churches, schools, and other institutions of culture and refinement, such as Jack Langriche's theatre and the Deadwood Opera House. By 1879 most of the sharpers, confidence men, and drifters had departed, leaving Deadwood "as orderly as any eastern city of its size."[22]

Contrary to legend, and similar to almost all western towns, the miners' egalitarian democracy was soon to be replaced by the steady control of a small group of merchants, bankers, and professional men who were intent on establishing stability and a social atmosphere imported directly from the East. Throughout the history of frontier urban development, it was this element of society that quickly assumed control of the economic, social, religious, and cultural life of new communities. Generally, they were recognized as the natural leaders of the town, and most other residents acquiesced in the "better people's" determination to impose "civilized" eastern standards and a stratified social structure on the new community. Understandably, these people have become the villains of western legend because it so goes against the grain of American folklore that this elitist group should have controlled frontier democracy and thwarted the grassroots will of the people.

But when Johnson knew Deadwood, this transformation had hardly begun, and he was probably unaware of anything but the wide-open, bawdy atmosphere of the new town. Everyone knew everyone else in Deadwood.

Johnson said that Calamity Jane was a calamity, alright, and that Wild Bill Hickok wasn't all that wild. He said that Wild Bill was a handsome man and a fine physical specimen, but he considered him a phony. He spent most of his time playing poker and was murdered while doing so – shot in the back of the head by Jack McCall in the summer of 1876 in the Number Ten Saloon. Johnson described McCall as a "nobody who thought he was playin' Hell." McCall was first acquitted by a sympathetic jury in Deadwood and later retried, convicted, and hanged in Cheyenne. It is most interesting that a Deadwood jury would have sympathized with the cold-blooded murderer of a supposedly popular celebrity. Perhaps the purveyors of myth, who generally cast Hickok in a positive light, are not quite on the mark in this case. Maybe the folks in Deadwood didn't consider him a celebrity, just a somewhat faded gambler who had it coming. Or perhaps it just says something disturbing about a casual frontier attitude toward guns and killing.

In his short career, Hickok had been arrested several times for vagrancy and, while a lawman in 1871, had operated out of the Alamo Saloon in Abilene – he was more a gambler, in other words, than a lawman. Eugene Hollon called him a psychopath who played both sides of the law.[23] Franz and Choate comment that, while in Abilene, he spent more time at the Alamo than in doing his duties, which he mostly left to his deputies. Abilene got rid of him at the end of the cattle-trailing season.[24] Yet the mythology surrounding him was so strong that someone like President Dwight Eisenhower, who was raised in the 1890s in Abilene – where Hickok had been marshal in 1871 – was very strongly influenced by him and what he saw as Hickok's code of the West.[25]

Johnson also knew Wyatt Earp in Deadwood. Earp was in-between stints: he had served as a policeman in Wichita from 1875 to 1876 and then as an assistant marshal in Dodge City in 1876, where he moonlighted as a faro dealer at the Long Branch Saloon. He left Dodge at the end of the cattle season in 1876, obviously drawn by the stories of the great riches to be had in Deadwood. Curiously, there is no mention of Earp in most of the standard accounts of Deadwood. This was all before he was launched to fame in 1881 by the fight at the O.K. Corral. That event, of course, brought him national fame, and consequently his earlier life was embroidered in keeping with his role as a national hero. But in 1876 he was only someone who was extra quick and straight with a gun, a semi-drifter who was wanted for horse stealing in Oklahoma.[26] There is no evidence for many of the exaggerated claims that, for instance, are found in Stuart Lake's biography.[27]

In Deadwood, according to Johnson, Earp was in the firewood business. "Why not?" Johnson said. "There was good money in getting it out.

There was a 'right smart' of it around. That's how Deadwood got its name." According to Stuart Lake, who did get this detail right, Earp spent the winter of 1876–77 in the firewood business and made an absolute killing in the process.[28] Lake's notes in the Huntington Library mention that Earp had told him that he outfitted himself in September 1876 for Deadwood and, when he arrived, started hauling firewood, netting $120 to $130 a day.[29] This was very good money, but the work was not steady. So, as Earp told Lake, he also rode shotgun on gold shipments out of the Hills in the winter of 1877, one run carrying the "breathtaking" sum of $200,000. Earp was armed with a brace of single-action Colt .45s, a Winchester repeating rifle, and a Wells Fargo regulation short-barrelled shotgun.[30] Several miles outside Deadwood, the stagecoach was shadowed by two groups of horsemen, but perhaps the reputation of Earp was enough to keep the gold shipment safe. Johnson said that Earp's marksmanship was never in question. There was, in fact, no record of Wells Fargo working out of Deadwood, or any record of Earp working for the company. But Earp's memory was only slightly fuzzy. The Cheyenne and Black Hills Stage and Express did bring out a $200,000 shipment in the winter of 1877, and Earp was listed as a "special shotgun messenger."[31] According to Robert DeArment, Earp acted as shotgun messenger on this single run from Deadwood to Cheyenne in the spring of 1877.[32] When he left Deadwood, he returned to Dodge in July to resume his duties as marshal. Earp later compared the atmosphere of Deadwood to that of Dodge, commenting that, although there were far more gamblers and outlaws in Deadwood, it was far more law-abiding than Dodge. The difference, he thought, was that there were practically no Texans there and thus no mobs of toughs to terrorize the town.[33]

In a number of ways, Hickok and Earp had similar backgrounds. Both had been born in Illinois and made their reputations as marshals of turbulent cowtowns. Both possessed unquestioned bravery and saw the law not so much as a calling as an occupation perfectly compatible with their real love – gambling. And both were to have their reputations inflated beyond recognition, so that it is now very difficult to separate truth from legend. However, it can be said that neither was very effective in his day-to-day duties as a peace officer.[34]

Johnson also knew some of the notorious criminals who drifted into Deadwood. Flyspeck Billy was mostly associated with the town of Custer. Speaking of him, Johnson said, "He was just a damned nuisance. Not even a good badman." Johnson said that Flyspeck Billy was lynched for a foolish murder that he committed and, being written up in the local paper for want of other news, became more infamous in death than he ever was in life. His

Charles M. Russell, *The Hold up (Big Nose George)* 1899. Russell's painting depicts a holdup by George Parrott's gang between Miles City and Bismark. Amon Carter Museum of American Art, Fort Worth.

real name was James Fowler, and he has been described by Mari Sandoz as a slight, almost beardless, youth who got his nickname from the generous "spatter of very dark freckles across his nose."[35] He was taken from the sheriff and lynched for having killed a freighter named Abe Barnes in Custer City.

Johnson also ran into Big Nose George Parrott, who drifted into the Hills in this period. He was the leader of a gang that included Frank Towle, Tom Reed, Charley Ross, and Dutch Charley and haunted the Deadwood–Sidney route. By the spring of 1879, the shotgun messengers guarding the gold shipments were becoming too effective, so Parrott moved on to the more steady and relaxing occupation of stealing horses in Montana. He was later lynched, and part of him was made into a pair of shoes, proudly worn by the later Governor of Wyoming (see chapter 3).

Johnson laughed at the mention of Deadwood Dick; there was no such person. He was the invention of a man named Edward Wheeler, a dime novelist, who brought out his first inane "Deadwood Dick" novel in 1877. There followed a series of Deadwood Dick dime novels in the 1870s and 1880s, depicting the character as a sort of Robin Hood figure who is forced to step outside the law because justice cannot be found in the courts.[36] Simplistic and silly, the books nonetheless reveal some deeply held beliefs among many Americans. Their theme would be echoed in *The Virginian* and also in the real-life actions of the big ranchers in the Johnson County War.[37]

Johnson had some harsh words for some of the supposed lawmen of the time, a few of whom were as bad and trigger-happy as the outlaws. Daniel Boone May, Johnson thought, was one of the bad ones. May arrived in Deadwood in 1876, riding shotgun on a stagecoach. According to Johnson, May wantonly had killed several men whom he accused of resisting arrest.

Daniel Boone May, in September 1878, was guarding a stagecoach with John Zimmerman. The two had caught wind of an intended holdup, so they rode several hundred yards behind the coach, hoping to lure the robbers into an attempt on the stage. Everything went according to plan, and in the ensuing gun battle they killed one of the robbers, whom they buried without ceremony. But they subsequently discovered that the man they had killed was Frank Towle, a veteran of several gangs, including that of Big Nose George. And, best of all, Towle had a price on his head. So May rode out to Towle's grave, dug him up, cut off his head, and brought it back the 180 miles to Cheyenne in a sack as evidence for the reward. Unhappily, the Laramie County Commissioners argued that May had not proven that he had killed Towle. So back in the sack went Towle's decomposing head, and May went on to see if he would have better luck with the Carbon County authorities. Alas, they too argued that May had only proven a certain brashness and lack of squeamishness in carting about a rotting head.[38] However, May did gain a certain notoriety through this episode that stood him well in his duty as a shotgun messenger. If it was known that he was guarding a shipment of gold, that stagecoach was given a miss. He gained the reputation of capturing and killing more outlaws, both stagecoach robbers and horse thieves, than any other shotgun messenger. But, as Johnson mentioned, he also had the reputation for killing captives unnecessarily. For instance, May faced murder charges in the death of "Curly" Grimes, an outlaw generally considered one of the best horse rustlers on the plains. May, together with William Llewellyn, helped capture Grimes in the summer of 1877, and while they were escorting him to Deadwood for trial, Grimes attempted to escape. May and Llewellyn shot him down and killed him. In the inquest that followed, the two were charged with murder. Although the jury found that the killing of Grimes was not justified, the ensuing trial in August 1880 rendered a verdict of not guilty. Understandably, May acquired a mixed reputation. When last heard of, he was in South America, involved in a mining venture.[39]

Johnson was in Deadwood when one old character named Phatty Thompson arrived there with a wagonload of eighty-two cats. As the place was becoming overrun with rats and mice, every woman in the settlement wanted a cat – even though they sold for ten dollars and up, those of finer pedigree going for as high as twenty-five dollars.

Although Johnson was only sixteen, he was tall and strong for his age, and he knew how to take care of himself. One day he got into an argument with a man who was abusing one of the stagecoach horses. When the man came at him with a knife, Johnson picked up a neck yoke and dropped him with a blow to the head. Thinking he had killed the man, he left Deadwood in a hurry. Years later he said that he was surprised and shocked at the thrill he felt as he struck the man down. "This was a wa'nin' to me." And so he took his horse and saddle, bedroll, and gun and joined forces with a scout attached to the Fifth Cavalry named William F. Cody.

3: Bill Cody (1876–78)

When Johnson first rode the Great Plains, large herds of buffalo still roamed the West. From a high hill, he once saw a herd that he estimated to be over a hundred thousand head. On several occasions, he forded a river behind a herd and found the trail deep in mud for a quarter of a mile from the water dripping off many thousands of buffalo. These buffalo still numbered in the millions at mid-century. But the great herds were to become extinct in an alarmingly short time – by 1879 in Canada and shortly after on the American plains.

On the Canadian side, most of the buffalo were killed by Native and Métis hunters, mostly for the fur trade, Canada's premier industry. But, on the American plains, professional buffalo hunters like Bill Cody accounted for much of the slaughter.

Johnson, when reminiscing about Cody and Hickok, considered Cody far more worthy of a place in history than Hickok; however, in later years, he damned Cody with faint praise. He said that Cody was not a frontiersman – not in the same class as Kit Carson or Portuguese Phillips – but he said that Cody had a fine seat in the saddle, was strikingly handsome, a crack shot, an excellent showman, and a virtuoso liar. Johnson, just after the Custer debacle, happened to be in the right place to witness a Cody incident that was to become central to the Cody mystique and to feature prominently in his Wild West show.

Johnson was perhaps not being quite fair to Cody. Certainly, Cody became a master at embellishing his image, but he was no fraud. He did not initiate the embellishments, though he later contributed to the Cody legend with great enthusiasm. Clearly, Johnson shared the same reservations

Frederic Remington, *Coming and Going of the Pony Express* (1900). The company of Russell, Majors and Waddell established the Pony Express Service in 1860. Remington has depicted one of the 190 waystations on the route.

toward him as the other Deadwood freighters and stage drivers, who re-referred to Cody as "See Me Bill" because he was always seeking notoriety.[1] Johnson said that the real frontiersmen that he admired had a strict code of truth. Exhibition and boastfulness, unless tongue-in-cheek, were not part of that code. Cody was clearly suspect, as was Hickok, with his silk shirts and carefully coiffed and perfumed hair.

Stripped of the dime novel absurdities, Cody was still an extraordinary man. Born in Iowa in 1846 to a father who came from Canada, he was a product of "Bleeding Kansas" in the 1850s and of the restless flow of Americans to the plains. He grew up, much as Johnson, drifting from one excitement to another. To a reader a century later, shielded from most dangers and largely looked after by the state, his life seems implausible. But it was actually rather typical of those on the "cutting edge" of the frontier. What made Bill Cody special is that, through a combination of luck, ability, and self-promotion, he became the best at what he did and was not diffident about letting people know. His self-promotion started early and – because many of his supposed exploits were considered quite possible by the standards of the day – he was believed not only by American audiences, but by his first important biographer, Don Russell. Russell claimed that Cody, at

THE COWBOY LEGEND

the age of fourteen, was a Pony Express rider, during the very brief period of that institution's existence in 1860 and 1861, and he was credited with one of the longest rides ever performed by the Pony Express.[2]

He was already, he claimed, an Indian fighter when he was only fifteen. Russell stated that Cody was part of a group led by Bill Hickok that attacked a Sioux village on Clear Creek in northern Wyoming in order to retrieve stolen horses in 1861. Later, the town of Buffalo, which held such a prominent place in Wister's novel, would be built near this spot.

It seems, however, that Cody began to embroider his reputation at an early stage. Both of the above claims are convincingly debunked by Cody's recent biographer, Louis Warren. Warren states that Cody's claim to have ridden for the Pony Express was pure fiction. Cody claimed that he rode for the Express in 1859 – but it did not yet exist then. None of the stations he listed was the right one. Three eyewitnesses, who said that they saw him ride, made their statements long after the event. Moreover, the third one, Alexander Major, one of the three owners of the Pony Express firm, dictated the account long after in a ghost-written biography by the dime novelist Prentiss Ingraham, which was paid for by Cody! Cody's sister Julia remembered that Cody was at home and going to school during this period.[3] The second claim – the raid on the Indian village at Powder River with Bill Hickok – has also been debunked by Warren, who has found that Hickok was some distance away in Nebraska in 1861.[4]

Cody's reputation began to build shortly after the Civil War when he became a scout for the army in its quest to subdue the Plains Indians. By 1868 he was chief of scouts for the Fifth Cavalry and was recognized in army circles for his superior scouting abilities and for his outstanding courage, for which he was awarded the Congressional Medal of Honor.[5] He became generally regarded as the western army's foremost scout.

At the same time, his reputation became established in another line of work – the wanton destruction of the once-vast herds of buffalo. No name is more clearly associated with this extermination – although Cody was far from the only buffalo hunter in the West, he was one of the most successful. Cody fluctuated between scouting and providing buffalo meat for the Kansas Pacific, one of the railways that were sprinting across the continent now that the Civil War and the South's freeze on westward railway building had ended. Cody was a commercial buffalo hunter from the fall of 1867 through 1868. Buffalo hides in this period were turned into robes and coats; then, in the early 1870s, a new method of tanning led to a great demand for buffalo leather for industrial belts, especially in Europe.

Buffalo were pathetically easy to kill. All a buffalo hunter had to do was position himself downwind from the herd and then try to drop the lead cow through the heart, so that she would fall on the spot and not disturb the herd. Then the rest of the herd would usually just mill around her. A good hunter could kill a large number from one spot with a high-powered rifle. Cody calculated that in eighteen months as a market buffalo hunter, he killed 4,280 buffalo. His favourite buffalo gun was a 50-calibre Springfield needle gun, which had great accuracy and impressive killing power.[6]

In the final period of the buffalo extermination in the 1870s, roughly 5,000 white hunters were involved. After the invention, in 1871, of a method of turning buffalo hides into industrial drive belts and military equipment, the buffalo trade became extremely lucrative. Russell Barsh claims that the annual white commercial buffalo harvest was twice that of the Native hunt, which totalled about a million buffalo per year, but this statistic is disputed by Louis Warren.[7]

According to Warren, despite the great publicity surrounding the white buffalo hunters of the period, the majority of buffalo hunters were Native. In 1870, for instance, the vast majority of the 200,000 robes brought to American trading posts on the Missouri River were brought there by Native hunters, intent mainly on trading for guns.[8] Whichever claim is closer to the truth, the sad fact is that the southern herds were gone by 1878 and the northern ones by 1883. On the Canadian prairies, the buffalo were effectively exterminated by 1879.[9]

Russell writes of a much-publicized contest with a well-known buffalo hunter, William Comstock, to see who could slaughter the most beasts in the shortest time. Cody was proclaimed champion buffalo hunter of the plains, due in part to the accuracy and penetrating power of his .50-calibre breech-loading Springfield, affectionately christened "Lucretia Borgia" because of its deadliness.[10] But Warren claims that the contest never took place, at least not as Cody described it. At the time of the alleged match, Comstock, an army scout, was wanted for murder and on the run.[11]

In 1869 the first transcontinental railway, the Union Pacific, was completed. Immediately there was a rush of tourists to the West, and Cody's fame was substantial enough that he was in great demand as a guide for the very rich, often titled, gentlemen who wished to make a hunting excursion to the Great Plains. These shooting parties were executed with great style, and who better to lend drama to the occasion than Bill Cody, with his finely honed ability to spin a yarn and turn the uneventful into an adventure.

These hunting excursions did no harm to Cody's reputation. One of his more famous clients, the Earl of Dunraven, was a correspondent for the

Daily Telegraph, so Cody was already well-known in England when he later appeared there with his Wild West show. A hunting expedition mounted in 1871 by General Sheridan, with Cody as guide, included several prominent eastern journalists, including August Belmont and James Gordon Bennett Jr. of the fashionable *New York Herald*, Leonard Jerome, known as the "King of Wall Street" and a large stockholder in the *New York Times*, Leonard's brother Lawrence Jerome, and Charles L. Wilson of the *Chicago Evening Herald*.[12] Bennett, that same year, had sent Henry Morton Stanley to Africa in search of the presumed Doctor Livingstone. The theme of Bennett's writing, which focused on the actions of both Livingstone and Cody, was the bringing of light to dark, savage places. Later, the unifying central theme of the Wild West show would be the taming of the Indian frontier by the white forces of progress.[13] Sheridan's party included an escort of one hundred cavalry and sixteen wagons of provisions.

Cody's reputation did not suffer from the description of him that found its way to eastern papers: "Tall and somewhat slight in figure, though possessed of great strength and iron endurance; straight and erect as an arrow and with strikingly handsome features." Cody chose his costume carefully, to accent his white horse – a soft-fringed buckskin suit, crimson shirt, and his trademark wide hat. This party left in its wake six hundred buffalo, two hundred elk, and sundry other luckless animals, slaughtered for the pure sport of it.[14] Undoubtedly, weary from the hunt, the evening campfire conversation would turn, with unconscious irony, to the difficulty of convincing the Indians to abandon the chase and embrace the "advanced" civilization of white people.

Cody's most famous client in this period was the Grand Duke Alexis, the son of Tsar Alexander of Russia. Once again, General Sheridan planned this excursion, which was to include a hundred or so somewhat pliant Sioux, hired to stage a buffalo hunt and war dance. It seems that the army had its own modest part in developing the formula that Cody was later to use so effectively in the Wild West show. (Cody carefully avoided the word "show," a word that implies something artificial. To persuade audiences that this was the real thing, Cody used the title "Buffalo Bill's Wild West," later adding "Congress of Rough Riders of the World.")

The Grand Duke's cavalcade, numbering roughly five hundred, set off in January 1872 in search of anything that moved. Pictures of Alexis convey a soft, indulgent impression, and it seems that he was not terribly adept with firearms; Cody had his work cut out in ensuring that the Grand Duke would pot a buffalo before returning home. But, finally, after a very large expenditure of ammunition, Alexis did manage to connect with a luckless beast,

Studio portriat of George Armstrong Custer (left) and Grand Duke Alexis, son of the Czar of Russia. Library of Congress, LC-USZ62-42305.

and Cody, greatly relieved, was able to order the uncorking of quantities of champagne.[15]

However, Cody was not the main attraction for the Grand Duke's hunt. That honour went to George Armstrong Custer and the Sioux chief, Spotted Tail. Throughout the hunt, Cody was clearly in Custer's shadow; he was to find the buffalo and Alexis would give chase. Later, on the train, Alexis continued the hunt, firing away with great jollity through the train windows and watching the wounded animals limp off to die. During the evening entertainment, the Sioux dance, Custer flirted shamelessly with Chief Spotted Tail's sixteen-year-old daughter.

In 1872, Cody was still a bit player; his dime-novel notoriety had not yet fully kicked in. He was not, for instance, in the official photographs. Later, after Custer's death, Cody had to splice his photograph next to those of Custer and the Grand Duke to show the nation what good friends they had been. In fact, Cody and Custer didn't particularly like each other; they were in each other's light.[16]

Alexis was escorted across the plains in as much pomp as the army could muster, in an open four-horse carriage driven by Bill Reid, an overland stagecoach driver and good friend of Cody for whom the Grand Duke expressed much admiration. Previously, Cody, who was more than a little casual about family matters, had left his wife and daughter with the Reids for a year or more when the Fifth Cavalry was stationed at Fort McPherson, where Reid ran the trading post.[17] Bill Reid was a good friend of Johnson's, and it was perhaps through this connection that Johnson met Cody and briefly joined forces with him. As mentioned earlier, Bill Reid's son, Jack, was a close friend of both Johnson and my father. It was Jack who introduced Johnson to my parents.

It was during the year of the Grand Duke's hunt that Cody was invited to New York by some of his hunting clients. There, Cody sought out someone he had met briefly in 1869 in the West, on his return from the battle of Summit Springs in Colorado – a fascinating fraud who went by the name of Ned Buntline.[18] It was Buntline (Edward Zane Carroll Judson) who guaranteed Cody's fame, first through several hurriedly written dime novels and then as the driving force behind a stage production of Cody's exploits, as pictured in the dime novel. In 1869, Buntline produced the first of his four dime novels about Cody, *Buffalo Bill: The King of the Border Men*. This novel began Cody's reputation as a western hero, which, in turn, led to his appeal as a hunting guide. Buntline would be followed by Prentiss Ingraham, who cranked out 88 dime novels about Cody. All told, there were more than 550 dime novels written about Cody![19]

In late 1872, Buntline produced a play in four hours, grabbed some men off the street and retooled them into ferocious Sioux and Pawnee chiefs, and, not least, convinced Cody that he could face an eastern audience. And so was born the first stage "Western."[20] As it turned out, Buntline almost unwittingly brought the dime novel to the stage and thus launched a formula that was to remain remarkably unchanged over more than a century of stage, movie, and television. The stage show was an instant success. As one critic said, "Everything is so bad it is almost good."[21] With the West as the setting, it could not lose. Cody began his climb to international celebrity. At first, the show featured Wild Bill Hickok, but his time with the show was brief because he "had a voice like a girl" and annoyed the other actors by shooting too close to their legs, leaving nasty powder burns.[22] After his stint at acting, Hickok drifted to Cheyenne where he spent most of his time gambling. He married a widow who owned a circus, toured briefly with the circus, and then left his new wife for Deadwood. There, as we have seen, he had the bad luck to join a card game at the Number Ten Saloon in which he was not able to take his usual seat with his back to the wall. He exited this world, August 2, 1876, at the hands of a cowardly murderer.

* * * * *

Meanwhile, Cody was about to become involved in an incident that would become the central attraction of the Wild West show. As it happened, Johnson was there at just the right moment to witness the event. Understandably, the army of the west was horrified by Custer's annihilation by the Sioux and Cheyenne at the Little Big Horn in the summer of 1876. Punitive expeditions were mounted by the army, and Cody was quickly called back to service with the Fifth Cavalry. Initially the Fifth Cavalry, under General Wesley Merritt, was to join forces with General Crook in the area of the Custer fight, but Merritt was informed by the Indian agent at the Red Cloud Agency that several thousand Cheyennes were planning to leave their reservation near Fort Robinson in northwestern Nebraska in an attempt to join forces with Crazy Horse's Sioux. The agent stressed the urgency of the situation, claiming that the Indians had become arrogant and threatening on hearing of Custer's demise. So Merritt quickly changed plans, deciding instead to try to contain these Cheyennes if they attempted to leave their reservation.

After a lightning march of eighty-five miles in thirty-one hours while subsisting on hardtack,[23] seven troops of the Fifth Cavalry – 500 men in all – did manage, early in the morning of July 17, 1876, to intercept part of Little Wolf's band of Northern Cheyenne on Hat Creek (otherwise known as Warbonnet Creek – Johnson called it Indian Creek). The conflict took place where the Indian trail to the west crossed the creek, on the border between Wyoming and Nebraska, 150 miles northwest of the Red Cloud Agency. The army had successfully remained hidden from the Cheyennes, who knew nothing of the army's presence until they saw two army couriers in advance of the supply wagon train galloping toward the hidden soldiers. At once, a group of Cheyennes began to move toward the couriers, and Cody, being in an opportune position, suggested that they be intercepted.[24] Cody was in the vanguard of the troop and ready for action in his scouting costume of black velvet, slashed with scarlet and trimmed with silver buttons. He was accompanied, according to Warren, by a number of scouts serving under him, many of them probably Shawnee.[25]

Cody's stage outfit of black velvet and silver trim, which he wore when he killed and scalped Yellow Hair. Buffalo Bill Center of the West, Cody, Wyoming.

At this point, the accounts of what happened next seem to vary according to the imagination of the teller. An incident such as this is both fascinating and frustrating for the historian, since rarely do eyewitness accounts agree. And it is little short of magic how many extra "eyewitnesses" can materialize as an incident gains momentum and notoriety. First, it is interesting to trace the evolution of Cody's own account of what became known as the Yellow Hand incident. (The Cheyenne man's real name was Yellow Hair, or Hay-o-wei, because of the blond scalp that he carried about with him.) This Yellow Hair is not to be confused with the illegitimate son that General Custer supposedly had with Monahsetah, his Cheyenne captive from the Battle of the Washita in 1868.[26] Cody's first description is contained in a letter to his wife, written the day following the fight:

> We have had a fight. I killed Yellow Hand a Cheyenne Chief in a single-handed fight. ... Sent the war bonnet, shield, bridal [sic], whip, arms and his scalp to Kerngold [who had a clothing store in Rochester] to put up in his window. I will write Kerngold to bring it [the scalp] up to the house so you can show it to the neighbors.[27]

Cody's killing of Yellow Hair was a very minor incident in the history of frontier warfare, but it took on an elevated status because it was the first retaliation for Custer's death. As well, Cody's showmanship certainly caught the public's imagination.

Three years later, in 1879, and obviously warming to the subject, Cody gave the following description of the fight in his autobiography:

> I finally suggested that the best plan was to wait until the couriers came closer to the command, and then, just as the Indians were about to charge, to let me take the scouts and cut them off from the main body of the Cheyennes. ... I rushed back to my command, jumped on my horse, picked out fifteen men, and returned with them to the point of observation. ... We instantly dashed over the bluffs, and advanced on a gallop towards the Indians. A running fight lasted several minutes, during which we drove the enemy some little distance and killed three of their number. The rest of them rode off toward the main body. ... We were about half a mile from General Merritt, and the Indians whom we were chasing suddenly turned upon us, and another lively skirmish took place. One of the Indians, who was handsomely decorated with all the ornaments usually worn by a war chief when engaged in a fight, sang out to me in his own tongue: "I know you, Pa-he-haska; if you want to fight, come ahead and fight me."
>
> The chief was riding his horse back and forth in front of his men, as if to banter me, and I concluded to accept the challenge. I galloped toward him for fifty yards and he advanced toward me about the same distance, both of us riding at full speed, and then, when we were only about thirty yards apart, I raised my rifle and fired; his horse fell to the ground, having been killed by my bullet.
>
> Almost at the same instant my own horse went down, he having stepped in a hole. The fall did not hurt me much, and I instantly sprang to my feet ... we were now both on foot, and not more

Charles M. Russell, *First Scalp for Custer*. The fanciful depictions of Cody's killing and scalping of Yellow Hair added greatly to Cody's fame.

than twenty paces apart. We fired at each other simultaneously. My usual luck did not desert me on this occasion, for his bullet missed me, while mine struck him in the breast. He reeled and fell, but before he had fairly touched the ground I was upon him, knife in hand, and had driven the keen-edged weapon to its hilt in his heart. Jerking his war-bonnet off, I scientifically scalped him in about five seconds. … As the soldiers came up I swung the Indian chieftain's top-knot and bonnet in the air, and shouted: "The first scalp for Custer."[28]

Just for a start, there are two problems with this account. The first, and most glaring, is that Cody spoke no Native language. Therefore, he would have had no idea what Yellow Hair said, if, indeed, he did say anything. Also, not being an avid reader of dime novels, Yellow Hair would have no idea who Cody was. It is clear that Cody's account in his autobiography was written to square with the play that Cody had commissioned in the fall of 1876, *The Red Hand*, or *First Scalp for Custer*.[29]

1876 was not a good year for the western army: first Crook's humiliation at the Rosebud and then the Little Big Horn. Americans badly needed a boost, especially as they were enduring a period of economic depression and political scandal. Cody gave them what they badly needed. The skirmish on the Warbonnet was pretty small stuff, with only one killed and possibly two others. But Cody's "first scalp" caught the popular imagination, and Cody was shrewd enough to capitalize on the incident. Soon, the duel with Yellow Hair became a central feature of the Wild West show, re-enacted with a high degree of dramatic licence. The short-range gun duel of Cody's first account now became a hand-to-hand struggle to the death with Cody finally holding aloft the reeking scalp and uttering the now immortal words. Poor Yellow Hair had the ignominy of being dispatched nightly by a white guy in a stage outfit. And to give authenticity to the scalping finale, Yellow Hair's actual scalp was on display for paying customers. Audiences loved it and, though undoubtedly aware that the facts were embellished somewhat, probably believed in the essential truth of the drama.

The message that audiences were to take away from this climax of Cody's Wild West extravaganza was the conquest of savage America. In Cody's version, however, the Indians were the aggressors; the whites were only reacting to violent Indian savagery. Many of the Native actors, who nightly worked themselves into a state of frenzy, had been, like Sitting Bull, the real thing. They must have had some very mixed feelings when they were instructed to imitate false depictions of themselves.[30]

It will come as no surprise that Johnson's account differs somewhat from Cody's. It is not clear in what capacity he happened to be at Warbonnet Creek, but he was probably a minor scout under Cody. When the Cheyennes appeared on that early morning, Johnson must have been one of the fifteen men mentioned in Cody's autobiography who accompanied him in charging the Cheyennes as they tried to intercept the couriers. Johnson said that when the Indians saw Cody and his men, Yellow Hair, son of old Chief Cut Nose, ran out in front of the other Cheyennes and executed a sort of war dance, thumping his chest and making signs that he wanted to fight. The distance between Cody and Yellow Hair was about three hundred yards. Cody dismounted and, with his horse standing broadside to the Indian, laid his rifle across the saddle and fired a high drop shot. Yellow Hair fell dead – shot through the chest. Johnson said it was a fluke shot; Cody's marksmanship was fantastic, but with the rifle and the ammunition available then, and at that distance, no man could shoot that accurately. It had to be a fluke. The Indians fled back to their main party, which made no further attempt to join Sitting Bull. Cody disgusted Johnson when he so falsified facts in his autobiography and in the Wild West show; he forever lost Johnson's respect. Johnson never could decide whether Cody really did believe that he had uttered the words, "The first scalp for Custer."

In all this, one thing is clear. Cody was an inveterate liar. He had fabricated his Pony Express career, his buffalo-killing contest with Comstock, his expedition with General Sherman to negotiate a treaty with the Comanche and Kiowa, and now the essential details of the Yellow Hair incident.[31]

However, can we believe Johnson's account? It varies in several important details from several accounts of other eyewitnesses. First, we can safely conclude, as Johnson said, that Cody was a virtuoso liar. The various accounts of the incident make it clear that there was no duel at close quarters. But, after that, no two accounts agree completely, so we will probably never be satisfied that we know exactly what happened that morning.

The two accounts thought to be most reliable are those of Charles King, then a lieutenant, and trooper Chris Madsen, a signalman stationed on a butte some distance away, who both witnessed the event from a distance and sharply disagreed on some points. Madsen later prepared a commentary listing twenty-eight points of disagreement with King's account.[32] So what are we to believe? None of the accounts so far, except Cody's, came from someone at close quarters. What credence can we give to Johnson's account, since he claims to have been with Cody at the time?

First, the recorded testimony is very vague concerning who was with Cody during the encounter. Cody said there were fifteen individuals, but named none of them. Other reliable accounts have said there were only seven or eight, but only one scout, Jonathan White, has been clearly identified.[33] So it is entirely possible that Johnson, though not named in any of the existing accounts, was with Cody at the time. It is unlikely that Cody was lying when he claimed that fifteen others accompanied him; a smaller number would have made his feat seem all the braver. The two witnesses, King and Madsen, probably could not see all that was happening in hilly terrain and from some distance, one with field glasses and the other with a telescope, both of which limited the field of vision.

Does Johnson's account come close enough to those of King and Madsen to be believed? Unfortunately, all three accounts are annoyingly vague, but in broad outline they are not that far apart. All three speak of a short preliminary skirmish. At this point, Madsen remembered Cody and Yellow Hair firing simultaneously, Yellow Hair's horse going down, and, almost at the same moment, Cody's horse stumbling in a hole and unseating him. Native testimony backs up this point.[34] Johnson did not mention this part of the action, but it would fit with his memory of events that there was a preliminary skirmish, after which Cody found himself on foot and in a position, as Johnson claimed, to make a deliberate long-range drop shot across his saddle at his now-stationary foe. King said only that at this moment

Cody "connected with a well placed shot."[35] But Madsen claimed that Cody knelt, took deliberate aim, and killed Yellow Hair with a shot through the head, at the same moment that Yellow Hair fired at him.[36] Do these details discredit Johnson's version? Perhaps not. Madsen gave his testimony more than sixty years after the incident.[37] Memories do become a bit selective and vague over half a century. Johnson, too, when recounting this incident to his daughter-in-law, was remembering an event long past. But a detail such as shooting over a horse's saddle is one that is likely to stick in one's mind. And it is entirely logical that this is how it happened; Cody's horse undoubtedly was accustomed to Cody making similar shots during a buffalo hunt and so would have stood still. Also, since Yellow Hair, though apparently wounded, was still in a position to fire at Cody, it made sense for Cody to use a horse as a shield so that he could make a deliberate shot. It would be interesting to know whether the weapon in question was, in fact, the famous Lucretia Borgia.

Johnson's version should be given at least as much credence as those of Madsen and King, the only two that are generally given much weight. As already mentioned, Madsen gave his account over sixty years after the event. King, on the other hand, recorded his account soon after, in his book *Campaigning with Crook*. But King's reputation for truth is in serious question. At the time of the Yellow Hair incident, King was moonlighting as a special correspondent for the *New York Herald*. Later he became a novelist, writing sixty-nine novels between 1885 and 1909. He has been accused of not letting the truth spoil a good story.[38] In this case, King was clearly trying to create a heroic battle for the Fifth Cavalry out of a no-account little skirmish.

This incident has been dissected, partly to satisfy the reader concerning Johnson's credibility, but, more importantly, to make a general point. Very rarely does the historian of the West have the confidence that he or she has struck pure truth. Of course, this is true for all historical fields, but the American West is particularly tricky. Usually the more diligent the research is, the more uncertain the historian becomes, faced with ever-mounting conflicting evidence. It is almost as if many westerners, even at an early stage, were determined to make their country live up to the myth that was already being manufactured in the East. In the case of the Yellow Hair scrap, an ordinary account would not do. Cody concocted a hand-to-hand duel to spice up the episode and, with retelling, casualties began to mount. In fact, Yellow Hair may have been the sole casualty, as the *Cheyenne Daily Leader* had remarked, "It is a pity that only one 'good Indian' is the result of this campaign." But as the incident took on national appeal, new "eyewitnesses" emerged to give their versions, some claiming as many as eleven extra "good

Indians"; several others claimed to have killed Yellow Hair and depicted Cody as jumping in only to liberate his scalp.[39] As Don Russell, an authority on this incident, has observed, no two versions agree. There are significant disagreements between the official army version and those of King and Madsen. Then there are the claims of five people who said that they killed Yellow Hair, and the eyewitness who swore that Cody killed Yellow Hair in an hour-long duel with knives within sight of Fort Robinson.[40]

The most bizarre account of the fight came in 1936 when an old-timer claimed that the enmity between Cody and Yellow Hair began on the stage in 1874 when Yellow Hair, a member of the cast, insulted some female members of the show, and Cody flattened him. At that moment, Yellow Hair swore vengeance![41]

It also appears that numbers have been inflated shamelessly. Instead of the 800 Cheyennes attempting to escape their reservation that is recorded in some accounts, there may have been as few as 30. General Carr reported:

> There were not over 30 Indians in sight at any time and we had over 400 men. There were a few sacks of flour destroyed, three Indians killed, 12 ponies captured and a few went back to the agency.[42]

There were only about 200 Cheyennes on that particular reservation, and General Merritt reported seeing only seven with Yellow Hair.[43]

And then there is the Native side. In 1930, Beaver Heart, a Northern Cheyenne man who had been at the event stated:

> I have heard the story as related by him [Cody] regarding the fight, and the fact that Yellow Hair challenged him, this is not true. Buffalo Bill, whoever he was, could not talk Cheyenne, and Yellow Hair could not talk English or Sioux, and I do not know how these people could talk to each other. ... Furthermore, Yellow Hair was not killed by any one man as far as I could see, as the whole two troops of soldiers were firing at him. If Buffalo Bill was one of these soldiers he stayed with them until Yellow Hair was killed, and he didn't come out and engage Yellow Hair single-handed.[44]

The army was also most happy to inflate events. When Cody's 1879 autobiography appeared, General Carr wrote the preface and General Sheridan wrote an endorsement – on army letterhead – calling the book "scrupulously correct." In return, Cody dedicated the book to Sheridan. Clearly, senior army officers endorsed Cody's inflated depictions of frontier army life to make themselves and the army appear in a very favourable light.[45]

In 1906, Cody wrote General Carr of his plan to re-enact the battle of Summit Springs and asked for a testimonial of his actions at the battle. Cody added that he hoped that the general would be a guest of honour at the opening performance at Madison Square Garden in New York. As expected, Gen. Carr wrote the testimonial, putting Cody at the centre of the action and essentially following Cody's version of events.[46]

The arch-inflator of them all, George Armstrong Custer, made no mention of Cody in his own self-aggrandizing writing, and went out of his way to praise other scouts, especially William Comstock. Cody got around the fact that there was no mention of him – but a very effusive mention of Comstock – in Custer's *My Life on the Plains* by concocting the fictitious contest with Comstock for the boast of champion buffalo murderer.[47] Custer and Cody were clearly rivals for popular adulation and disliked each other. But, after Custer's dramatic death, Cody realized that Custer was now a national martyr of dramatic proportion. So he quickly manufactured a friendship and, for most of his life, traded on this supposed friendship as, night after night, he raised the reeking scalp of Yellow Hair and told the audiences that he was the first to avenge the killing of his great friend. It worked beyond his most calculated imaginings.

The verdict on Cody is inescapable; his version of events became increasingly fraudulent. And there is something a little sickening in his calculated preparation for the encounter with Yellow Hair. Sensing that there was good publicity in the offing, he had donned for the conflict his Wild West show's Mexican vaquero outfit of black and scarlet velvet, trimmed with silver buttons and lace.[48]

The verdict on Custer, too, is a little sickening. At the battle of Gettysburg, Custer, like Cody, wore a uniform of his own design – black velvet, with gaudy coils of gold lace. But there was no question of his courage. He rallied his Michigan troops against Jeb Stuart's attack and played a significant role in the Union victory and, thus, in the outcome of the war. Custer always believed that he possessed an inflated destiny and did all he could to help it along. When he attacked Sitting Bull at the Little Big Horn on June 25, he was all-too-conscious that the Democratic National Convention opened in Saint Louis on June 27. Although Samuel Tilden was the clearly favoured candidate, there was still time, after a brilliant defeat of the Sioux, for a last-minute "draft Custer" movement.[49]

But the blame for distorting events cannot rest merely with Cody. Though certainly an opportunist who was happy to falsify the facts, he was reacting to an American propensity to create a western folk mythology that so distorted truth that it is sometimes very difficult for the historian to separate fact from legend. If Cody wanted to remain at the forefront of the popular imagination, which he clearly did, no ordinary stirring deeds would do. His embellishments to the Yellow Hair story, which so disgusted Johnson, were necessary to keep the attention of his audience, which demanded of its heroes absurd feats and, of its villains, impossible depths of depravity, in keeping with the popular belief that America was the "Biggest and the Bestest." The seeming limitless gullibility of audiences and the reading public continually astounds historians looking at this period. It was as if they really did believe in the inflated history that Cody and others like him were manufacturing. And it was not just American audiences that could so easily suspend their disbelief. Later, when Cody took Europe by storm with his Wild West show, Europeans, too, proved to be remarkably gullible. If Cody was not to be relegated to obscurity, it was necessary to "improve" the facts.

In 1883, Cody's stage show, which had achieved success through the seventies, was about to go to a much higher level. That year, Cody's truly dreadful melodrama was happily terminated, and there emerged, instead, "Buffalo Bill's Wild West," which Cody refused to call a show, arguing that it was the recreation of the real thing. Buffalo Bill's Wild West was to be a huge outdoor extravaganza, replete with cowboys, Indians, Mexican vaqueros, bucking horses, wild buffalo, the real Deadwood stagecoach, and much more. The beginning of the rodeo can be seen in "Cow-Boys' Fun" – bucking horses, roping, steer riding and races. Cody's exhibition was to become phenomenally successful in both America and Europe and would last until 1916 – a total of thirty-three years! The only setback that first year came with the wild buffalo riding. Cody insisted on riding Monarch, a buffalo bull that most of the cowboys refused to ride. Cody landed in hospital for two weeks, a period that some alleged was the only time that summer that he was sober.[50] Buffalo Bill's Wild West first opened in Nebraska at the Omaha fairgrounds; it never looked back.

An instant star of the Wild West was Phoebe Ann Moses – Annie Oakley – who joined Cody's troupe in 1885, the same year that Sitting Bull joined and Cody added a new finale – the scalping of Yellow Hand. Perhaps no other American woman in outdoor show business became more famous, even long before Rodgers and Hammerstein's musical hit *Annie Get Your Gun*. She dazzled crowds with her combination of modesty and the unladylike ability to do such things as shooting a cigarette from her husband's mouth or a dime held between his fingers.[51] This was certainly an excellent

Poster for Cody's Wild West. Cody played shamelessly on his supposed friendship with Custer. The "Last Stand" was often the finale of the show.

formula for maintaining a very respectful husband! Her nickname "Little Sure Shot" came from one of her chief admirers, Sitting Bull, who was with Buffalo Bill's Wild West for only one season in 1885. Some have seen Sitting Bull as mercenary, interested more in money than in dignity, but Sitting Bull sent almost all the money he made that summer back to his people or gave it to bootblacks and street urchins who hovered around the show. He could not understand how such a rich country could let its children exist in such poverty.[52]

One of Cody's greatest inspirations in the creation of the Wild West was the hiring of a large number of recently defeated Sioux. He was among the very first to have "real Indians" playing themselves. Why the Sioux, in effect, joined the enemy to re-enact their own demise still remains, to some degree, a puzzlement. But there were good reasons. For a start, they could make good money and see the wider world. Perhaps the real answer is in the numbing hopelessness of the reservation. Many of them would do just about anything to escape that purgatory. Also, Cody was very careful to have them play the "good Indians." The bad ones were played by non-Indian extras, and the really evil element was always the Mormon polygamist with his retinue of abused wives.[53] Black Elk, a Sioux who had fought at the Little

Big Horn, aptly summed up possible reasons why some Sioux joined Buffalo Bill's Wild West: "I wanted to see the great water, the great world and the ways of the white man."[54]

In 1887, Buffalo Bill's Wild West achieved international stature when it was included as part of the American Exhibition at Queen Victoria's Golden Jubilee at Earl's Court, celebrating the Queen's fiftieth year on the throne. Cody arrived in London with a cast of 209, which included almost 100 Sioux, 200 horses, and eighteen buffalo.[55] The high point of that season for the Wild West was clearly the command performance for the Queen. It was so successful that a second command performance had to be arranged for all the crowned heads of Europe who gathered in London to honour Queen Victoria. By the time Cody and his troupe left England, it is perhaps fair to say that Cody had so thoroughly indoctrinated the British that their view of the American West, probably for generations, was essentially that of Buffalo Bill's Wild West. In an era when empire was celebrated and Darwin's ideas concerning the survival of the fittest were popular, the British certainly agreed with the Wild West's central theme: the virility of the Anglo-Saxon and the triumph of that breed over all others.[56]

According to one of the performers, the Queen was so carried away by the performance that she rose and saluted the American flag, the first time a British monarch had done such a thing since the American Revolution. This made terrific press back home in America, but the truth was somewhat different. Cody had the flag dipped in deference to her, and she acknowledged the gesture with a royal nod.[57]

A very significant element in the success of Buffalo Bill's Wild West in London was the same theme that so resonated with American audiences – the issue of racial decay. One of the central themes of the show was the revitalization of the Anglo-Saxon on the frontier. The English had the same fear in the late nineteenth century that their ruling class was becoming soft and effete.[58] These themes – the fear of racial decay and eastern effeminacy, and a belief that the West was the seat of Anglo-Saxon revitalization – would be at the centre of Wister's later writing. The Queen's jubilee came at the height of empire, and Cody's message certainly resonated among British people who had a passionate belief that it was their country's mission to send their best to the far-flung frontiers of the world.

After captivating London and clearly amusing Queen Victoria, Cody next descended on Paris, his arrival coinciding with the celebration of the completion of the thousand-foot Eiffel Tower, the centrepiece of the 1889 Exposition Universelle. Curious Parisians watched the entourage disembark a hundred Sioux Indians in brilliant war paint, Mexican vaqueros,

Poster from Rosa Bonheur's famous painting of Cody and his white horse (1889). Cody was a superb horseman, an attribute which was at the forefront of his Wild West.

Eskimo sled dogs and the erection of corrals for the many horses and buffalo At the centre of all this was Buffalo Bill's luxurious tent with its special display – once again, Yellow Hand's actual scalp![59]

As in London, the main theme of the Wild West extravaganza was the triumph of white civilization and the taming of the West. This theme fit very nicely with the American inventions brought by Thomas Edison, demonstrating the miracle of electricity and the telephone and telegraph. American progress was clearly on display.

At first, the French were a bit aloof, as if Euro Disney had just invaded, but they quickly began to soften when the wife of a French nobleman eloped with a Sioux warrior.[60] Then Annie Oakley utterly charmed them too with her combination of dazzling shooting and folksy ways. Soon, Buffalo Bill became the most celebrated American in Paris since Benjamin Franklin. The themes of Cody's Wild West enthralled Parisians: the Pony Express, an

Yellow Hair's belongings including his scalp, which Cody took on tour with The Wild West. Audiences in London and Paris lined up patiently to see the famous "first scalp for Custer". Buffalo Bill Center of the West, Cody, Wyoming.

Indian ambush of the Deadwood Stage, bronco busting and sharpshooting, an Indian attack thwarted by the cavalry – and Cody!

Rosa Bonheur, the most celebrated animal painter of the era, happened to be in Paris, and she, too, became enthralled with the Wild West. She produced altogether seventeen paintings of the Wild West; her painting of Cody on his white horse became one of her most famous.[61]

Finally, Cody introduced Parisians to his new finale – his hand-to-hand duel with Yellow Hand and the dramatic scalping. The Parisians loved it and lined up to file past Cody's tent, which held Yellow Hand's war bonnet, shield, gun and scabbard – and scalp.[62] The young Norwegian painter Edvard Munch wrote home to his father, "Bilboa Bill is the most renowned trapper in America. ... Bilboa Bill took part in several Indian wars ... among other things in a big fight with a well-known Indian Chief and took his scalp with a knife. The knife and scalp are displayed in his tent."[63]

Paris was followed by a tour of Rome, Venice, Austria-Hungary, and Germany. While on this tour, Cody decided to return to the United States to dispel charges that he was mistreating "his" Indians. He happened to return at a very touchy moment for relations between the US government and the

Sioux – and Sitting Bull. Government officials believed that Sitting Bull was one of the main forces behind the Ghost Dance movement of 1890, which was unsettling the Sioux. A Paiute mystic named Wovoka was preaching a doctrine of non-violent resistance to white colonialism. The Sioux developed their own version of Wovoka's religion, including the belief that if they wore special ghost shirts and danced the Ghost Dance, they would bring back the pre-contact "old" world and their ancestors would rise again. The evil whites would disappear and the buffalo would return, in preparation for the appearance of a Native messiah. It seems to have been only in the Sioux version, as taught by Kicking Bear, that the ghost shirts must be worn to repel bullets. The army's slaughter of the Sioux at Wounded Knee, using the newly invented Gatling gun, ended that particular belief.

This "Ghost Dance craze" was part of a larger phenomenon seen worldwide among colonized peoples. These messianic religions were a backlash against colonial domination and, in one form or another, preached that if indigenous populations returned to their true beliefs, the bad things would disappear and the good times would return. Pontiac's Rebellion was one example; Tecumseh's brother, the Prophet, preached a similar doctrine. There were clear overtones of a messianic religion in Louis Riel's message in 1884–85.

James McLaughlin, the Indian agent at the Standing Rock Agency, was convinced that Sitting Bull was at the centre of the Ghost Dance religion and recommended that the army arrest him. On Cody's arrival in New York, he was given a telegram from General Nelson Miles requesting that he come to Chicago. There General Miles convinced him that the country was facing a serious Indian war. It seems clear that Cody only intended to speak to Sitting Bull and try to persuade him not to go to war, but then came another telegram from Miles: "Confidential: you are hereby authorized to secure the person of Sitting Bull and deliver him to the nearest com'g officer of U.S. troops."[64] Meanwhile, Agent McLaughlin telegraphed the Commissioner of Indian Affairs to say that a military arrest of Sitting Bull would provoke a war; it would be far better to have his Indian police do the job. McLaughlin's plea went all the way to President Harrison, who had Cody's order rescinded.

Two weeks later, in December 1890, the Indian police on the Pine Ridge Agency launched a pre-dawn raid to capture Sitting Bull and remove him from the agency, but about 150 of his followers were alerted and resisted the police. In the melee that ensued, Sitting Bull was killed by one of the Indian police. Eleven days later, the US cavalry surrounded a large group of Sioux who had fled their reservation after Sitting Bull's death. When the army's

Gatling guns fell silent at Wounded Knee, almost two hundred Sioux lay dead – mostly women and children.

It so happens that when I was researching my doctoral thesis on the Mounted Police and Canadian Native policy, I came upon an account in the Mounted Police files of an incident of Sioux horse stealing by one of Sitting Bull's followers. Sitting Bull and over 5,000 Sioux were in Canada after the Battle of the Little Big Horn until the spring of 1881. The Mounted Police confronted Sitting Bull and asked that the culprit be turned over. Sitting Bull persuaded them, instead, to leave the horse thief to Sioux justice. Sitting Bull had the accused man stripped naked and staked out in a mosquito swamp for a goodly time, a far worse punishment than the Mounted Police had in mind. I happened to remember the name. It was the same name as the Indian policeman, Bull Head, commander of the Indian Police, accused of killing Sitting Bull on that cold December morning in 1890!

The Wild West reached its pinnacle in 1893 at Chicago's slightly belated celebration of the four hundredth anniversary of Columbus reaching the Americas at the World's Columbian Exposition, with the newly christened subtitle *Buffalo Bill's Wild West and Congress of Rough Riders of the World*. Two new additions that year were the actual log cabins of Theodore Roosevelt and that of the recently murdered Sitting Bull, the latter complete with a Sioux guide to gleefully show visitors the bullet holes from that December morning in 1890.[65] There is perhaps more than a small irony that Buffalo Bill's popularity reached its zenith precisely at the moment that the American frontier was officially pronounced dead. As Cody was immortalizing the violent conquest of the American West, almost across the street, Frederick Jackson Turner was giving his address to the American Historical Association on "The Significance of the Frontier in American History," remarking on the American census department's 1890 announcement that there was no longer a frontier in America. (This theme will be pursued again in chapter 7 in the context of Turner's frontier thesis and the influence of Roosevelt, Cody, Wister, and Remington on popular beliefs about the frontier.)

Cody had leased fifteen acres at Chicago for Buffalo Bill's Wild West because the organizers of the world's fair wouldn't allow it to be an official act. Over the six months of the fair, the Wild West averaged 12,000 people a day, a total of almost four million. Cody made about a million dollars from the Chicago tour (thirty million dollars today), part of which he used to establish the town of Cody, Wyoming.[66]

After the Chicago exposition of 1893, the Wild West persisted for many years, well into the twentieth century. There is no question that Cody and his Wild West had an enormous influence on the popular perception of the western American frontier both in the United States and in Europe. And what of Cody the man? It is too easy to belittle him as a charlatan. He was certainly happy to play into the dime-novel image of the West, but he was larger than life and it says much that he gained, and kept, the loyalty of so many. Perhaps Annie Oakley said it as well as any:

> I travelled with him for seventeen years – there were thousands of men in the outfit during that time, Comanches, cowboys, Cossacks, Arabs, and every kind of person. And the whole time we were one great family loyal to a man. His words were more than most contracts. Personally I never had a contract with the show after I started. It would have been superfluous.[67]

* * * * *

Soon after the Yellow Hair incident of 1876 and after Cody had returned to the stage, Johnson left his employment with Cody and drifted around the West. It is unlikely that Johnson was bothered by the demise of Yellow Hair. He was a man of his time and shared the current attitudes toward Native people. As a child in Minnesota, he was weaned on the lurid details of the Santee Sioux uprising in 1862. In Texas, he encountered the Comanches first-hand and undoubtedly shared some of the Texan antipathy for those people. Later he became involved in several skirmishes with the Apaches and learned to hate them. The Osages he dismissed as a "no account outfit." In Wyoming, he grew to respect the Cheyennes, but he continued to hate and distrust the Sioux. Like most of his contemporaries who grew up on the frontier, his attitudes toward Native people were shaped by overblown stories of ambushed wagon trains, kidnapped women and children, and unspeakable torture. Of course, the whites were blameless!

Johnson would say very little about the period between being a scout for Cody at the death of Yellow Hair and becoming a cowboy in Wyoming, but he did acknowledge that he had spent most of that time in Arizona, Colorado, Indian Territory, and the Staked Plains of Texas. And it was at some time during that period that he and a few companions got into a scrape with some Apaches that almost ended his life. While travelling through Apache country, he and his friends were ambushed by Apaches who fired at them from behind an outcropping of rock high on a hillside. They retreated to the shelter of the timber and, while one watched for any move the Apaches might make, the other two cut a pile of brush, which they tied in a large bundle with their saddle ropes. Then, rolling the bundle in front of them, they started up the hill toward the Apaches. Johnson was on the end where the brush was thinnest. The Apaches kept shooting and finally hit Johnson. He dropped as if dead. The other two, riled by the loss of their friend, redoubled their efforts, got into a strategic position, and managed to kill all three Natives. When they got back to Johnson, they found him just regaining consciousness, the bullet having spent its force on the brush. The bullet lodged in his chin and left a scar for life. After patching him up, his companions happened to catch a glimpse of two Apache women making off with the horses of the dead Apaches. They took off after them and killed them both.

On another occasion, Johnson was part of a group that came upon a man who had either been tortured and killed by Apaches or dismembered after death. They had cut off his genitals and stuffed them in his mouth. It is perhaps this story that Wister hinted at in *The Virginian*.

And while Johnson was in the Black Hills, he, of course, encountered the Sioux. Actually, the Sioux were surprisingly peaceful while Johnson was in the Hills, but there were incidents and the whites in the area were understandably jumpy. Any Sioux was automatically considered a hostile. On one occasion, Johnson and a man named Kneebone rode up to a house and found two terrified women, a mother and daughter, who told them that two Sioux had been watching them all day from a hill behind the house. Kneebone took his rifle and stole quietly out the front door. There were two quick shots and then he was back. He said, "They won't trouble you any more." He had not even bothered to walk up the hill to see if they were dead; Johnson added that Kneebone could not have been less concerned had they been coyotes. Kneebone later came to Alberta with Johnson. In hindsight, this casual brutality toward the Sioux is shocking, considering the fact that Johnson and his fellow frontiersmen were the trespassers on Sioux land and, in most cases, the Sioux were merely retaliating against white incursions. But this logic was lost on the great majority of frontiersmen.

* * * * *

For a time after the Yellow Hair incident, Johnson went back to driving stage and then drifted for a while. He happened to be in Laramie, Wyoming, in 1876 when he found himself in the middle of a gunfight between Laramie's marshal and two men who were making their escape on horseback. Johnson fired at one of the men and to his surprise, the man dropped from his horse, dead.

The marshal, Nat Boswell, was obviously grateful and persuaded Johnson to stay on for a while as one of his deputies.[68] This Johnson did, but he had to lie about his age, being only sixteen at the time. He had great respect for Boswell, saying that he was one of the real lawmen, quiet and determined – nothing like "Hickok and that set." Boswell was one of the famous lawmen of the West. In the late 1860s, he had been elected the first sheriff of Albany County (which included Laramie), and in 1876, when Johnson knew him, he had recently been appointed marshal of Laramie. He later became the chief detective for the Wyoming Stock Growers Association. His quiet style and iron determination did much to reverse the earlier reputation of Laramie as one of the wickedest towns in the West, where lynchings, including that of the former marshal of Laramie, Sam Duggan, were common.[69] Johnson would never say much about those days, but he did admit years later, when excavators found two bodies under an old building in Laramie with bullet holes in their heads, that he knew who they were.

On one occasion, he and Boswell went in search of an outlaw, known to be a dangerous character, who was thought to be in a small abandoned log cabin. Boswell and Johnson found the cabin and approached it at night, leaving their horses some distance away. Then they took up their positions, one hidden in the woods in front of the cabin and one behind it. Just at daybreak, the outlaw stepped out of the cabin door, looked around, and then, as they had expected, began to urinate. While thus preoccupied, he heard the order to put his hands above his head. Resistance was rather pointless; he was soon handcuffed and on his way back to Laramie.

They started back single file, Boswell ahead and Johnson behind the outlaw. Shortly, they came to a difficult muskeg where they had to walk and lead their horses for some distance. Boswell, being a humane man, took the handcuffs off the outlaw and allowed him to lead his horse. Several times Johnson noticed the outlaw's hand steal forward to take Boswell's rifle from the scabbard, but he always just missed getting it. Finally, Boswell caught him at it and shouted, "Shoot the son-of-a-bitch!" But that was not necessary. Johnson had had a bead on him all the time; if his hand had touched the gun, he would have been shot.

Johnson was probably lucky that his short stint as lawman was not more eventful. Two years later, two of Boswell's deputies were murdered by Dutch Charley's and Big Nose George's gang. The next year, 1879, Dutch Charley was captured, admitted his guilt – in fact, bragged about it – and, soon after, was liberated from the law by a group of masked citizens in Carbon, the hometown of the two deputy sheriffs he had murdered. They promptly lynched him. The headline in the *Cheyenne Daily Sun* was joyfully upbeat:

DUTCH CHARLEY TAKES HIS LAST DANCE in a HEMP NECKTIE, WITH TELEGRAPH POLE FOR a PARTNER. The coroner ruled him dead from exposure.

In 1881, a similar fate befell Big Nose George Parrott. He was arrested by two deputies, and, while being transported by train, he, too, was liberated from the law in Carbon. He was first subjected to a "faux" hanging, with the same objective as present-day waterboarding, and when he had confessed to the murders of the two lawmen, Widdowfield and Vincent, he was returned to the two deputies. He was subsequently tried for murder and convicted. According to one witness, when a sentence of death was pronounced, he "wept like a child and broke down completely." In the spring of 1881, shortly before his execution date, he attempted to escape but was foiled by his jailer's wife, who alerted the town with several shots. He was subdued, and, later that night, an armed mob descended on the jail, took him to a telegraph pole, and attempted to hang him. The mob made several very bumbling attempts to hang him and then Big Nose George pleaded with them to let him do it right. He then climbed the ladder to the top of the telegraph pole and managed to strangle himself properly.[70] He had achieved, by now, a celebrity status, so his remains were in some demand. An enterprising young medical student, John Osborne, later to become governor of Wyoming, was given the body "for medical study." He partially skinned George and made him into various mementoes, including a pair of shoes and a medicine bag.[71] He also sawed off the top of his head, which was later found doing effective duty as a doorstop.[72]

Life in Laramie did not appeal to Johnson for long. He took every opportunity to work among cattle and to mingle with the Texans who were driving herds into southern Wyoming. After a year or so of drifting, he decided that working cattle was really the thing for him. While in Cheyenne in 1878, he decided to sign on with a cow outfit that had located in the new cattle country of northern Wyoming.

4: Wyoming (1878–88)

While in Cheyenne, in 1878, Johnson met a man who would greatly influence his life. Johnson, now eighteen, had experienced more than most men twice his age. For the moment, he seemed content to drift from one experience to the next. Fred Hesse changed all that. Hesse was an Englishman who had come to the American West in 1873. He first went to Texas, where he worked as a cowboy. Four years later, he came north as the trail boss of a herd belonging to John Slaughter, one of Texas' most famous cattle barons. When Johnson met him, he was working for John Sparks, a stockman who ranched in the Cheyenne district and later became Governor of Nevada. Hesse was to become, the following year, foreman of the Frewen brothers' newly formed 76 Ranch on the Powder River. Johnson's friendship with Hesse would result in Johnson, too, signing on with the 76, a decision that would shape the next, and most significant, decade of his life.

In 1878 there was, as yet, no settlement in northern Wyoming. Among the first to venture into the country as prospective ranchers, and the first to stake a claim in the Powder River country, were the two eccentric English brothers, Richard (Dick) and Moreton Frewen. The Frewen brothers came west to hunt in the Yellowstone and Jackson Hole country of northern Wyoming in the fall of 1878. Although they had been warned to leave before the heavy snowfall came, they did not start east until December. Typical of a certain type of Englishman, they ignored the warnings, but somehow managed to bumble through, taking their pack train up Ten Sleep Canyon and crossing the Big Horn Mountains through a barely navigable pass. When they reached the lower slopes of the Big Horns and the upper branches of the Powder River, they were so taken with the country that they decided to

Fred Hesse, the foreman of the Powder River Cattle Company, who hired Johnson in 1878. He became Johnson's mentor and lifelong friend. In 1892, Hesse was one of the leaders of the Johnson County war. American Heritage Center, University of Wyoming.

locate a ranch there, which they called the Big Horn. When they returned the next year to establish the ranch, one of the first things they did was to hire Fred Hesse as foreman, and Hesse, in turn, hired Johnson as a ranch hand, partly because Johnson was one of the few non-Natives at the time who was familiar with the Powder River country. Hesse continued as foreman until 1890, when he started his own ranch, the 28, south of Buffalo on Crazy Woman Creek.

    The Frewen brothers were among the very first to take advantage of the fact that two major impediments to ranching had recently been removed from northern Wyoming – the buffalo and the Native population – thus leaving the region free for cattlemen to grab one of the finest cattle ranges in America. Before 1878, cattle had already populated southern Wyoming, but farther north the hostile Native frontier had prevented settlement. The census of 1880 listed only 637 people in Johnson County, where the Frewen brothers located in northern Wyoming.

1882 Studio portrait of Everett Johnson, Kirkland Studio, Cheyenne, Wyoming. Glenbow Archives, NA 2924-12.

The census of 1880 gives a rather surprising picture of how the Wyoming cattle frontier was evolving from virgin range to serious overcrowding. Although northern Wyoming was very sparsely settled in 1880, the census gave a very good indication of how Wyoming's cattle frontier was developing. Of 311 men listed as "stock growers," only two were from Texas, far outnumbered by the 29 from New York, the 26 from Pennsylvania, the 29 from England and the 19 from Canada. Ownership of the big Wyoming ranches was largely in the hands of those from the Northeast, the Midwest, and England, Scotland, and Ireland. And the picture is consistent when it comes to cowboys. Of the 669 listed in 1880, only 25 came from Texas, far outnumbered by the 58 from New York, and roughly the same as the 23 from Massachusetts and the 22 from England. At least in Wyoming in 1880, the vast majority of cowboys came from the North, and about two from the Midwest for every one from the Northeast. Besides Texas, the only other southern state with a significant representation was Missouri (53). Given the recent claim that up to one-third of cowboys on the western range were

Black, it is surprising that only two Blacks were listed as cowboys on the Wyoming range (and nine Indians.)[1]

Everett Johnson is listed in the 1880 census as a former Virginian, twenty years old, living with Effingham and William D. Warner in Crook County. He is termed a "cattle herder." Also listed for Crook County is Michael Henry, thirty-eight years old, his wife, Catharine, thirty-five years old, and their daughter Elizabeth, eighteen years old. More of her later! Mike Henry is listed as the owner of a "road ranch."

If even the Frewen brothers could recognize superb cattle range in the dead of winter, then it takes little imagination to understand the Native population's determination to defend one of the finest buffalo ranges on the Plains from white encroachment. The dry, elevated climate of Wyoming produced native grass that cured on the stalk and did not lose its value when frost came. This simple fact explains much of the blood that flowed in the Native peoples' attempt to block white migration into northern Wyoming.

Before the Frewen brothers first glimpsed the Powder River country from the top of Ten Sleep, this future cattle empire had been, for over a decade, a battle zone between Native people and whites. Several important incidents occurred in the struggle for the Powder River country, which involved close friends of Johnson's. These incidents formed a vital prelude to the Wyoming cattle empire; Johnson's recounting of them to his daughter-in-law Jean, especially the information he passed on to Jean regarding the Wagon Box Fight of 1867, sheds some important new light on early Wyoming history. This information came from his good friend Bill Reid, who was involved in the battle. Reid's account of the Wagon Box Fight has not appeared before in print, except for a brief version in Andy Russell's *The Canadian Cowboy*, which Russell got from Reid's son Jack.[2]

NORTHERN WYOMING AND THE WAGON BOX FIGHT

White pressure on this area of northern Wyoming began the moment the Civil War no longer distracted Americans. Once again, the nation's focus was on the West and many thousands poured westward, many of them rootless victims of the dislocation of war. The vast majority of them were seeking economic opportunity, which is no surprise. But this wave had been hardened by war, so their inevitable clash with those who considered the Great Plains their home was to be even more ruthless than usual. And the Native people of the Plains, for their part, had a clear sense that their backs were to the wall, so they fought this white advance with ruthless determination.

Before the Civil War, the line of white advance had already crossed the Mississippi, once thought to be the dividing line between America and the "permanent Indian frontier." The Native peoples of the Plains in the 1830s and 1840s had watched the seemingly endless migration of wagon trains cross the so-called Great American Desert on the way to Oregon and California. So now, after 1865, California and Oregon were relatively settled and whites were closing in on the Great Plains, America's last frontier. It is easy to understand both the Native peoples' anxiety and their intransigence. The earlier facile rationalization of Indian removal was no longer possible. There was no more unwanted land to dump them on. So the people of the Plains faced the stark prospect of dispossession and forced confinement on reservations. Small wonder they fought with such determined ferocity.

There was no solution to this clash of cultures. Neither side would bend sufficiently to find a middle ground. Plains culture simply could not find a meeting ground with the most powerful force in American culture – the idea of progress. At the raw, grassroots level, this idea was largely an aggressive economic imperative, and woe to anyone who got in the way of the plainsmen's pursuit of happiness.

Americans headed west into this last Native bastion with few restrictions. The Northwest Ordinance of 1787 was the blueprint of western development; it spelled out a policy of local self-determination for most aspects of the American advancement across the continent. The army, of course, was on the frontier to uphold federal policy, but the army had practically no control over that element at the edge of white advancement that caused most of the trouble with Native people. As has already been seen in the Black Hills gold rush, the army was reluctant, and largely powerless, to curb the aggressive push of Americans westward, whether guaranteed by treaty or not. By and large, the army in the West, from top to bottom, shared the frontiersman's antipathy toward Native peoples and believed equally in the American dream of replacing them since Native peoples were perceived as just drifting over vast tracts of virgin land that could be put to better use. In a somewhat fuzzy way, a great many Americans held the belief, some honestly and many fraudulently, that it was ordained by God that the land be tilled and made productive. Clearly, the Native peoples were not living up to God's definition of effective land use. Thus, there was no moral dilemma in dispossessing them and shunting them on to reservations, where agents of civilization could offer them the blessings of Christian salvation and instruction in proper land owning. Then there were those who did not go in for fancy philosophizing and just believed that Natives should just be got rid of at any opportunity.

Before the Civil War, many thousands of Americans followed the Oregon Trail along the North Platte and into the area that would become, in 1868, Wyoming Territory as they made their way to California and Oregon. The vast majority had stopped in Wyoming Territory only long enough to scratch their names on Independence Rock.

But this was to change dramatically in the 1860s, due largely to the coming of the Union Pacific, which reached Wyoming in 1867, and the emergence of a mining frontier in Montana and Idaho. Even before the railway came, large numbers of emigrants were drawn to the newly developed Bozeman Trail, which branched off the Oregon Trail at Bridger's Crossing in southeastern Wyoming and headed north through the Powder River country to the new diggings in Montana.

John Bozeman, a Georgian, had pioneered the shortcut from the Oregon Trail to Montana Territory in 1863 and by the next year, despite intense hostility, the trail was in heavy use, since it was faster and less expensive than the river route by way of the Missouri River to the Montana diggings. The next decade of northern Wyoming's history was to consist primarily of Native hostility along the Bozeman Trail. Strangely, the fighting was with the Sioux and Cheyenne, who did not even belong there. The entire length of the trail was in Crow country, recognized as their land under the Horse Creek Treaty (or Fort Laramie Treaty) of 1851. But, beginning in the 1850s, the Sioux and Cheyenne began to invade Crow territory and drove the less numerous Crow westward beyond the Big Horn Mountains in north-central Wyoming.

The Bozeman Trail ran through the last good hunting grounds east of the Big Horn Mountains, in the valleys of the Big Horn, Rosebud, Tongue, and Powder rivers, as these rivers made their way to the Yellowstone. By midcentury, the powerful Lakota Sioux, who could mount over 3,000 warriors, and their allies, the northern Cheyennes and Arapahos, were pushing the far less numerous Crow and Shoshoni west into the mountains. Despite the Treaty of Laramie, the Sioux, Cheyennes, and Arapahos in 1857 waged war against the Crow and appropriated important parts of their buffalo hunting territory.[3]

Contrary to the general belief, the wars of the Bozeman Trail had nothing to do with the violation of treaty rights. All the skirmishes and battles between the army and the Sioux and Cheyenne in the decade following the Civil War – the Fetterman Massacre, the Wagon Box and Hayfield fights, the

Battle of Rosebud Creek, the Custer battle, the Dull Knife battle – were all fought in Crow territory. And it is no surprise that the Crow sided with the American army in all these engagements against their traditional enemies.[4]

From the inception of the Bozeman Trail in the 1860s until the subjugation of the Sioux and Cheyenne in the wake of the Custer fight in 1876, there was an almost constant state of turmoil along the trail, as the Sioux, Cheyenne, and Arapaho attempted to stem the white migration into their newly acquired hunting grounds. And, after the massacre of peaceful Cheyennes under Chief Black Kettle at Sand Creek in late November 1864 by Colonel Chivington's Colorado militia, the Native peoples of the northern plains took on a new ferocity. Sand Creek was the turning point and it became the symbol of a war to avenge that cowardly and duplicitous action.[5] Native attempts in 1864 to close the route to whites travelling from the Oregon Trail to Montana prompted, first, the Connor expedition of 1865 and, subsequently, the policy of establishing military posts along the trail to facilitate the white migration into land guaranteed by treaty to Native peoples. General Patrick Connor, in 1865, led a column of roughly a thousand men up the trail to subdue the Native population. Connor was accompanied by 179 Pawnee and Winnebago scouts. There was no love lost between these Native groups. He surprised a group of Arapaho and extracted a promise of peace. But this left the Sioux and Cheyenne still intractably unreformed. Their uncharitable attitude toward sharing their territory with the military column invading their country might just possibly have had something to do with one of General Connor's orders to his men:

> … you will not receive overtures of peace or submission from Indians, but will attack and kill every male Indian over 12 years of age.[6]

General Connor's orders were "bluntly genocidal."[7]

Several years earlier, Connor – then a colonel – on January 29, 1863, with his California volunteers, had attacked a Shoshone camp in the southwest corner of present day Idaho. In "one of the deadliest massacres in American Indian history," now known as the Bear River Massacre, Connor and his men killed at least 250 men, women, and children. One man said he counted 493 dead Shoshone

In 1866, Colonel Henry B. Carrington was ordered to consolidate the work of the Connor expedition by establishing a chain of forts along the Bozeman, including Fort Reno at the Powder River crossing, Fort Phil Kearny near present-day Sheridan, and Fort C. F. Smith in southern

Montana. Carrington's army, starting with Carrington himself, was not very prepossessing. Carrington was a political appointee, generally resented by officers who had survived the Civil War, and few of his men were veterans. Under Carrington, they would receive little training. The post commander at Fort Laramie remarked, as they departed for the Powder River country, that they were "the worst cavalry I have ever seen."[8] These were the poor devils that the government was sending to subdue the Sioux and Cheyenne nations!

The US Army after the post-Civil War demobilization was a rather pathetic affair, badly paid and little respected. By 1874, Congress would budget for only 27,000 soldiers to patrol both the West and the South at the height of Reconstruction. But recruitment was so dismal that the army could muster only about 19,000 poorly armed and provisioned soldiers.[9] The army in the West suffered from low morale and serious levels of desertion. In the 1870s, the army lost one-quarter of its strength from desertion; over a longer period, from 1867 to the 1890s, one-third of the western army deserted, perhaps partly due to the regular soldier's pay – a measly fifty cents a day![10] And this western army was a very mixed lot. Half were immigrants, desperate to have any sort of job; one-third of Custer's army were Irish.

It is worth pointing out, considering the importance of Frederic Remington to this story, that it was Remington who created a very different image of the western army in the public eye. His drawings and paintings – more than 700 of them on the themes of western war and violence – changed the public's perception of that army. Remington was intent on depicting reality and generally he did so, but his army was relentlessly Anglo-Saxon, and his record of the passing of the frontier, with all its dust, sweat and violence, pictured the western army in a very heroic light. Americans couldn't get enough of it.[11]

The army in northern Wyoming spent most of its time constructing forts and providing protection for wagon trains headed for Montana. Large parties were generally safe from raids, but many stragglers were picked off. Then, on December 21, 1866, a small contingent of soldiers was sent out from Fort Phil Kearny under Captain W. J. Fetterman to protect a party of civilian woodcutters.

Captain Fetterman, a Civil War veteran, held a pronounced contempt for both his commanding officer's caution and for the fighting ability of the Sioux and Cheyenne. Clearly disobeying Carrington's orders to refrain from pursuing hostiles beyond a certain point, he allowed himself, in a very Custeresque fashion, to be drawn into a carefully prepared ambush led by Crazy Horse. Fetterman was completely taken in by the old decoy trick, a favourite in Plains Indian warfare. His small force suddenly faced several thousand Sioux, Cheyennes, and Arapahos, who swarmed up out of nowhere to overwhelm these green recruits who fumbled frantically with their muzzle-loading Springfield rifles or the cavalry's unfamiliar new Spencer carbines.[12] The two civilians accompanying the soldiers, who were armed with Henry repeating rifles, could make little difference to the outcome, although, from the very large number of Henry casings surrounding them, it appears that these two civilians fought to the bitter end.[13] His entire force of eighty-one was destroyed. No one was left alive and only one was spared the indignity of scalping and mutilation. Those who came to their relief found what appeared from a distance to be a scattered collection of pincushions; the Sioux, Cheyenne, and Arapaho released roughly 40,000 arrows that day. The Native force was armed mostly with bows and a smattering of smoothbore trade guns, acquired from Métis traders.[14] Inept troops with muzzle-loading rifles were no match for Native warriors who could put half a dozen arrows into the air at the same time. Almost before it started, the worst defeat inflicted on the army in the West thus far was over. Fetterman, the architect of this total slaughter, perhaps had a last-minute change of mind concerning the effectiveness of Native warfare as he was run over by American Horse's mount and clubbed to death.[15]

The estimate of the number of Native warriors killed or wounded ranges from a mere handful to Utley's estimate of as many as one hundred. Bray argues that as few as eleven were killed and roughly sixty wounded.[16]

Understandably, the troops at Fort Phil Kearny were in a profound state of shock when they saw the dismembered bodies of their comrades.[17] The wide reporting of this scene would later reinforce the view on the frontier and in American society generally that the only proper fate for Native people was to be swept from the face of the earth. Even if the beleaguered garrison understood Native motivation, which is unlikely, they undoubtedly would not have sympathized with the Native religious belief that the body entered the spirit world in the condition in which it left its other world. By depriving them of their limbs and other parts, they were consigning these soldiers to hell.[18]

Those left at Phil Kearny expected an attack at any moment. The weather was bitterly cold, and help was depressingly far away. Only 119 men, including civilians, survived to fend off the expected attack. The nearest relief was Fort Laramie, more than two hundred miles away. And those who were left to defend the fort had no illusions concerning their fate should the enemy overwhelm them. No one slept that night, least of all Colonel Carrington, who wrote to his superiors, "No such mutilation as that today on record."[19]

Obviously, word of the disaster must be got out. John Phillips, later to be a close friend of Johnson's, volunteered to run the gauntlet through the surrounding enemy; there ensued one of the most famous rides of the West, a ride that was far more spectacular than Paul Revere's modest little ride, and one that was far more dangerous. Revere, when captured, merely had his horse confiscated. Phillips, if captured, faced death and dismemberment.

John "Portuguese" Phillips, born Manuel Filipe Cartoso in the Portuguese Azores, was a well-known figure on the frontier. He happened to be at Phil Kearny waiting for the mining season to open. On the night following the massacre, he volunteered, at a price, to attempt to slip past the enemy and take dispatches to the nearest telegraph, 190 miles away at Horseshoe Station (south of present-day Douglas, Wyoming). He set off in a raging blizzard on Carrington's favourite Thoroughbred, with his saddle bags stuffed with hardtack and oats.[20] Phillips made the ride in three and a half days, arriving on Christmas Eve at the telegraph station to alert the outside world of the Fetterman disaster. He then continued on to Fort Laramie, arriving the next night in dramatic fashion at the garrison's Christmas ball, staggering from fatigue and barely able to speak. Phillips' horse, which had so gallantly made the 236 miles in four days, through intense cold and huge drifts, died soon after. Phillips collapsed and took weeks to recover.

Portuguese Phillips' ride has become a part of American folklore and, over time, has become almost as distorted as Cody's later affray with Yellow Hair. Popular accounts have him galloping non-stop to Fort Laramie through hordes of bloodthirsty savages. But even the respectable accounts do not agree. Two of the leading experts, Dee Brown and Robert Murray, disagree on key points. This underscores the difficulty of verifying the actions of minor players like Johnson who, at this stage in his life, was primarily a witness, either first or second hand, to the opening of the West.

The nation was in a state of shock at the news of the Fetterman massacre, and a majority of Americans probably agreed with the sentiments of General Sherman's telegram to President Grant:

> We must act with the utmost vindictive earnestness against the Sioux even to their extermination, men, women and children.[21]

Red Cloud, the leader of the force that annihilated Fetterman's troops, also called for the extermination of the American troops invading his country. And it should be remembered that, after the wanton butchery of Black Kettle's band of peaceful Cheyennes at Sand Creek in 1864, Colonel Chivington's Colorado militia had mutilated many of the dead and skinned a number of women to make purses.[22] It was a period of savage war on both sides, with plenty of incidents of barbarity to harden frontier attitudes into intransigence.

Johnson was a good friend of Phillips in later years and considered him to be one of the most remarkable men he ever met. He first met Phillips through Bill Reid, who was also at Phil Kearny at the time of the Fetterman disaster. Phillips had been a frontiersman and civilian scout and had developed the typical hatred of Indians associated with that type. He would not hesitate to shoot an Indian on sight and counselled Johnson to do the same as a matter of self-preservation.

On one occasion, Phillips and Johnson were riding down toward a ford on Crazy Woman Creek when they saw a Native man ahead of them driving a few cattle. Phillips simply shot him, took his knife and scooped out his insides, filled his stomach with rocks, and sank him in the river. He then took the cattle and, with Johnson, trailed them south until they reached a place where they could be left. It clearly never occurred to Phillips to stop the man and question him about the ownership of the cattle. The frontier bred hard attitudes, with little room for seeking a middle ground of understanding. And it does not seem that Johnson protested Phillip's actions; he probably fully agreed with them.

Natives believed that Phillips was a devil; according to Johnson, he looked the part – high cheekbones, a black pointed beard, and narrow black eyes "sometimes terrible, sometimes gleaming with malicious amusement." Even in later years, he was incredibly wiry and active. Johnson had a huge admiration for his courage and daring and considered him invincible. He regarded him as one of his very special friends.

There were many Native attempts on his life, but Phillips always escaped. Johnson recounted one story about four Natives who ambushed him and dragged him from his horse. But he managed to draw his knife, cut the rope, and stab two of his attackers. The others tried to escape, but Phillips got to his horse and rifle and shot them both. He became the constant target of ambushes; on one occasion, his ranch buildings on the Chugwater were burned down and all his cattle killed. Yet, despite his enemy's best efforts, he died in his bed in Cheyenne in 1883 at the age of fifty-one.

* * * * *

Johnson's other great friend in early Wyoming days was Bill Reid, previously mentioned as a good friend of Bill Cody. Reid was one of that breed of plainsmen who made the West – tough, fearless, and without guile. In 1866, he was part of the group of civilian contractors, hired to build the forts on the Bozeman Trail, who had accompanied Colonel Carrington. He too was a close friend of Portuguese Phillips. It was Jack Reid, Bill Reid's youngest son and one of my father's greatest friends, who gave his account of his father's time at Fort Phil Kearny to Jean Johnson.

Bill Reid had earlier been a Pony Express agent and stagecoach driver; he must have been an expert driver to have been chosen for the job of driving Grand Duke Alexis on his tour of the West in 1872. And by the time he signed on to accompany the army on the Bozeman Trail, he was a seasoned Indian fighter, a skill that was to prove very useful the next year when he was at the centre of the Wagon Box Fight of August 1867. His account of the Wagon Box Fight is included here because it was part of Johnson's story and, more importantly, because it provides important new information about that rather neglected moment in western history.

Reid's skill as an Indian fighter was much in evidence, for instance, in the fall of 1861 while stationed at Rocky Ridge, Wyoming, on the Rocky Ridge–Salt Lake City run. A group of Arapahos stole a large number of Shoshoni horses and then drove off all the stock at the stage station. Reid and a number of Shoshonis under Chief Washakee set off on foot in pursuit and came on the Arapaho camp in the Wind River Mountains. Reid and the Shoshonis hid for the night and then attacked at dawn, first setting fire to the long grass and brush. The Arapahos tried to fight their way out, but were all killed. Not only were all the horses recovered, but about two hundred Arapaho horses were also taken. A grand celebration and war dance followed, and then the victors returned home, Reid with a trophy for his wife, which he casually dropped in her lap – the ear of an enemy who had wounded him with an arrow. Her reaction to the gift is not recorded. She had an especially warm welcome for Chief Washakee, whose very ill son she had once nursed back to health.

On another occasion, about 150 warriors attacked Reid and some others while he was driving stage near the Sweetwater. He and the others cut the horses loose and, in a sort of rehearsal for the Wagon Box Fight, turned the coaches on their sides to form breastworks. The fight lasted for two days. Reid was shot through the back and had to be brought out on the running gear of one of the coaches. Several of the defenders were wounded by arrows, but Reid said that when they discovered that the arrows were not poisoned, no one worried much about the wounds.

In 1876, Reid was to become chief of scouts under General Crook at the Battle of Rosebud Creek, just nine days before Custer's fateful decision to split his command and attack the largest known camp of Sioux ever assembled, presided over by the cream of Sioux leadership – Crazy Horse, Gall, Little Wolf, and, of course, Sitting Bull.[23]

By the time that Reid hired on in 1866 to provide timber for Fort Phil Kearny, he was clearly a very seasoned Indian fighter, far more experienced than the green troops who were there to protect him and his companions. In fairness, after the Fetterman debacle, the army did send out more competent troops and officers and armed them with the new retooled breech-loading Springfield rifles. By the summer of 1867, the troops at Phil Kearny were no longer the disgrace they had been the previous winter. But they were now fighting enemies emboldened by the ease with which they had snuffed out inept troops armed with old, muzzle-loading rifles. In the spring of 1867, the Sioux and Cheyenne began to lay elaborate plans for a campaign to drive the intruders from their hunting grounds for good. The plan, as it unfolded under the direction of Red Cloud, was to mount simultaneous attacks at both Fort Phil Kearny and C. F. Smith. These two battles would be the climax of Sioux and Cheyenne hostility along the Bozeman Trail until the Custer disaster almost a decade later.

Throughout June and July, they intensified the level of harassment at both forts and then, on August 1, they launched a major attack against the soldiers and civilians at work in a hayfield near Fort C. F. Smith. The next day, they unleashed a similar attack against the woodcutters and their military escort on a high meadow, six miles west of Fort Phil Kearny. In the open high meadow, Company C of the Twenty-Seventh Infantry had constructed a defensive enclosure using fourteen overturned wagon boxes, stripped of their running gear. They then drilled firing ports through the floors of the wagon boxes.

By July of 1867, the army along the Bozeman Trail now numbered about 900 officers and men at the three forts, Reno, Phil Kearny, and C. F. Smith, and another 500 building Fort Fetterman as the southern anchor of the system. Meanwhile, during July, after the annual Sun Dance, a large group of Sioux and Cheyenne gathered on the Little Bighorn River to plot strategy for further attacks on the forts. Unfortunately for their cause, they couldn't decide which fort to attack first, so, after much bitter argument, they finally decided to split the force, 500 to 800 mostly Cheyenne opting to attack Fort C. F. Smith, and about one thousand Sioux and Cheyenne making Fort Phil Kearny their target, under the leadership of Red Cloud.[24] The force that attacked Fort Phil Kearny was comprised mainly of Oglalas, Sans Arcs, some Miniconjous, and a number of Cheyennes. Crazy Horse and Man Afraid of His Horse were the principal leaders.[25] It is interesting to speculate what

Site of the Wagon Box Fight, 1867, in nothern Wyoming. Author's photo.

might have been the outcome if these two forces had remained united against one objective.

The Wagon Box Fight of August 2, 1867, has become an important part of western American folklore. Here the army took its revenge for the humiliation of the Fetterman disaster. The clear message of the Wagon Box Fight has come down to us that a small number of troops, entrenched behind overturned wagons and using improved firearms, were able to hold off huge numbers of Native attackers. Later Red Cloud was to say that he lost the flower of his fighting force at the Wagon Box Fight.[26] For the Sioux and Cheyenne, the Wagon Box Fight was a major humiliation; they were not to attempt another major offensive until forced into one a decade later by another Fetterman – the supremely overconfident George Armstrong Custer – who became the victim of his overweening ambition and disastrous judgment.

The attack on the wagon box camp began at six o'clock in the morning with the attackers driving off the mule herd. Crazy Horse led the initial attack on the woodcutters' camp in the woods, where they were felling trees. Four woodcutters and two soldiers were killed at this point. The rest raced to the wagon box defences. Red Cloud orchestrated the overall attacks, but he was unable to copy the tight unity of purpose of the Fetterman fight. The bank of Piny Creek gave the warriors protection until the last hundred yards, and then the attack required a charge over completely open ground, except for a dry gully, which gave further protection. Those with guns were concentrated here. Also, from the protection of this gully, the attackers lobbed fire arrows into the enclosure to ignite the hay and manure.

Certainly, the defenders behind the fourteen overturned wagons thought that their time had come as they watched what seemed like thousands of Sioux and Cheyenne swarm toward them on that clear summer morning. Acting Corporal Samuel Gibson, one of the defenders, said he would never forget the looks of grim determination on the faces of his comrades. They knew they had little chance; the fate of those with Fetterman crowded out all other thoughts. As they waited, Gibson watched Sgt. Frank Robertson, a veteran of Indian wars, calmly and deliberately unlace his shoes and tie the laces together with a loop at one end for his foot and another at the other end to fit over the trigger of his rifle. Other veterans followed suit. No one spoke.[27] It was better to end your own life than to die by torture.

The initial tactic of the enemy was the one that had always proved successful in fighting the army. They rode to within 150 yards and waited for the discharge of the defenders' rifles and the glint of the ramrods as they reloaded. This was the signal to ride the defenders down. But there were no ramrods; instead, for the first time in their wars with the army, they met a steady field of fire. Repeated charges on horseback throughout the morning and early afternoon took a terrible toll, with virtually no effect on the defenders.

The battle lasted until mid-afternoon, when the attackers made their last desperate attempt to overrun the defences. Suddenly, the tense silence was broken by an eerie humming and a low chant, and then the chilling sight of many hundreds of the attackers, naked except for a breechcloth, advancing in a wedge, slowly and deliberately, led by Red Cloud's nephew, Lone Man. They continued to advance through murderous fire until they were almost touching the defences. But they could not withstand the intensity of the fire and finally broke and fled. Their extraordinary courage accomplished nothing. Further charges were equally futile. Finally, a general mounted charge was driven off.[28]

Soon after, the booming of a howitzer was the first indication that a relief column was approaching. As the tension broke, the grim silence changed to whooping and sobbing.[29] Their last sight of the attackers, as the defenders returned to the fort, was a long train of horses three or four abreast and a quarter-mile long, carrying away the dead and wounded. Only six soldiers were killed and two wounded that day, while estimates of Native losses range from thousands (more than were actually there!) to the estimate of Captain James Powell, who thought about sixty Natives were killed and twice that many wounded. Robert Utley put the number of Sioux and Cheyenne at the Wagon Box Fight at between 1,500 and 4,000, with casualties at between 400 and 1,000.[30]

The outcome of the Wagon Box Fight, needless to say, was an enormous relief to both the defenders and the army, which could not afford the indignity of another Fetterman fiasco. The army had acquitted itself well. But there is a degree of unfairness in the established verdict on this incident. On the monument at the site of the fight, which describes the engagement as "one of the famous battles of history," are listed by name the soldiers of Company C, Twenty-Seventh US Infantry, who took part in the fight – two officers and twenty-six soldiers. The plaque also states that "four unknown civilians" helped to repel the three thousand warriors under Red Cloud whom the army claimed took part in the Wagon Box Fight. Most of the literature on this fight echoes this plaque, leaving the impression that the civilians were, at best, incidental to the fight.

Bill Reid was one of those "unnamed" civilians and, if his account is to be believed, he and the other woodcutters were anything but incidental. Reid, at the time, was wagon boss for the group of woodcutters that the firm of Proctor and Gilmore had contracted out to build forts for the army and to provide the forts with firewood. As Robert Murray has noted, these civilian employees at western military posts have not received the recognition they deserve. Many of them, like Bill Reid, were seasoned frontiersmen. Often their steady, cool behaviour was vital to the success of a military defence against hostiles.[31]

The established wisdom seems to be that in the interval between the Fetterman disaster and the Wagon Box Fight, the quality of troops, leadership, and arms at Fort Phil Kearny improved markedly. Thus, when seasoned troops with improved weapons faced even overwhelming numbers at the Wagon Box Fight, the new discipline, coupled with the improved firepower of the new breech-loading "trap door" Springfields, were more than a match for the enemy. The real significance of the Wagon Box Fight, it is said, is that it was the first time that the army in the West had used breech-loading rifles against Native enemies; their devastating effect left the Sioux and Cheyenne chastened for a decade.

The biggest advances in weaponry from the Civil War to the western frontier period were in the development of breech-loading rifles and metallic cartridges, replacing muzzle-loading rifles and paper cartridges. But the new metal cartridges could pose one very serious problem. In some rifles, and especially the retooled Springfield, the hot metal of the cartridges in extended firing expanded and tended to jam in the chamber.[32]

There is clearly some truth in the army's argument that the breech-loading Springfields were a significant improvement, but their argument was too pat. First, it is not quite realistic to argue that this metamorphosis in the quality of the troops took place between December 1866 and August 1867. And were these new breech-loading Springfields really such a vast improvement over the old muzzle-loading variety? The accepted accounts of the engagement, for the most part, are based on the official army reports of Captain James Powell, who commanded the troops, and of Major B. F. Smith, who led the relief column. Understandably, they would portray the role of the army in the best possible light, especially with regard to the increased firepower of the new rifles. But these same rifles a decade later were involved in the other total massacre of troops in the West. Custer's men, too, were armed with breech-loading Springfields, while many of the Sioux and Cheyenne now carried "Spirit Guns," the much superior Henry and Spencer repeating rifles. About a quarter of them had the new Winchester repeating rifle, which the army refused to buy because of its expense.[33] According to Douglas D. Scott and Richard A. Fox Jr. in *Archeological Insights into the Custer Battle*, their conservative estimate of Native firearms at the Custer fight put them at 370, of which at least 192 were repeating rifles.[34] In fact, the army continued to fight in the West with the decidedly inferior Springfield until the 1890s, when it adopted the Krag repeating rifle. The Springfields had a superior stopping power, range, and accuracy to the Henry and Spencer repeating rifles, but at close range there was no contest; the speed of the repeating rifle, as an 1879 Army Ordinance Report made clear, made them far superior in close combat.[35]

In July 1867, the troops at Phil Kearny were issued with .50-calibre Springfield-Allin breech-loading rifles, to replace the old .58-calibre Civil War Springfield muzzle-loaders that the infantry had previously used. But these rifles were by no means the best ones available. They were a quick and easy adaptation of the old Springfields. The National Armory in Springfield, Massachusetts, developed a method of converting the muzzle-loaders to single shot breech-loaders and, at the same time, reducing the rifles from .58- to .50-calibre by reaming the bores to accept .50-calibre liners, which were then brazed into place.[36] These rifles were a distinct improvement over the old ones, but the army was clearly more concerned with economy than with efficiency in its decision to remodel the old rifles. The remodelled Springfields were still distinctly inferior to other newly developed rifles. And to make matters worse, in an engagement like the Wagon Box Fight, where rifle barrels became too hot to touch, the Springfield became "slower than Hell" because, when the breech became hot, the spent casings were often hard to extract. This, too, was to become an important issue in the Custer disaster.

William Murphy, a soldier who witnessed the Wagon Box Fight from a distance, remarked that the Springfields were only good for eight or ten shots and then it became necessary to eject the cartridge with a ramrod, since the ejector cut a groove in the rim of the cartridge.[37] To make matters worse, as the post records of Phil Kearny show, the soldiers had only used the rifles for about two weeks before the Wagon Box Fight and had not had any target practice with them.[38]

The same problem with the overheated Springfields was recorded a decade later at the Custer battle. By then, it had become a Native tactic when facing Springfields to wait until Army rifles became heated and started to jam. Unlike the brass shell casings of today, the copper casings of the .45-calibre ammunition were far more malleable. After rapid fire, "the extractor mechanism had a tendency to rip through the flange at the bottom of the heat-softened shell, leaving the barrel clogged with remnants of the exploded casing." The soldiers' only recourse was to try to dislodge the mangled shell with a knife – a laborious and increasingly nerve-racking procedure, especially when the enemy was massing for a charge.[39]

Bill Reid said that most of the woodcutters were armed with .44-rimfire Henry repeating rifles and Colt revolvers that used the same ammunition; each wagon had a case of 500 rounds of ammunition. One, at least, of the civilians was armed with a Spencer repeating rifle. A civilian teamster named Smyth stated that he had two Spencer carbines and two colt revolvers, which he fired through auger holes in the wagon boxes.[40]

The Henrys were vastly superior to the Springfields, taking sixteen shells at a time, loaded through the butt. The Henry was unquestionably the finest American rifle of the period. It had been developed by B. Tyler Henry, who worked for Oliver Winchester; it was the first really successful rifle to be manufactured by Winchester's company, the New Haven Arms Company.[41] It became the most feared gun of the Civil War and soon became the favourite gun of western Indian fighters. Its only drawback was that it was too heavy and the barrel too long to be an effective cavalry weapon. Military reports during the Civil War stressed that it was almost impossible to overrun a position defended by Henrys. As Confederate general John Singleton Mosby stated, "It was useless to fight against them." Confederate troops echoed his sentiments. When Sherman's troops used the Henry on their march through Georgia, Confederates described it as "that damned Yankee rifle that you loaded on Sunday and fired all week." The promotional literature boasted that it was capable of firing sixty shots a minute, putting it in a class all of its own. Despite this marked superiority, the Union army during the Civil War did not purchase many and continued, to the end of the Indian wars in the West, to supply its troops with the decidedly inferior Springfields.[42]

There is certainly more than a little irony in the fact that Custer himself attributed the great success of his Fifth Michigan troops at the decisive battle of Gettysburg to the firepower of the Spencer repeating rifle, a rifle not even as good as the Henry.[43] And again, in 1868, Custer's cavalry was armed with the Spencer carbines when they attacked a peaceful Native camp on the Washita River.[44] As one authority on Civil War guns has said, "The army [in the post–Civil War period] repeatedly found itself outclassed by Indian warriors bearing superior rifles and revolvers."[45]

Various accounts state that there were either four, five, or six civilians in the Wagon Box Fight.[46] Reid said there were five.[47] It is plausible to argue that the firepower of five men with Henrys equalled or exceeded that of four or five times that number of soldiers with Springfields. No attempt is being made here to belittle the soldiers, but it is realistic to argue that the woodcutters had a crucial role in the fight. Indeed, several soldiers in the fight stated later that they thought they were all going to be killed and that their time had come. It could be that their time would, indeed, have come except for the devastating power at critical moments of the Henrys. Many of the Native corpses were piled within yards of the barricades. Is it possible that the Native peoples' new respect for the army, which was the chief legacy of the Wagon Box Fight, was based on misconception, on the belief that it was the soldiers, not the civilians, who could unleash such devastating firepower? It is quite likely that it was the coolness of experienced civilian frontiersmen, armed with the latest weapons, which saved the day at the Wagon Box Fight. These woodcutters were all seasoned marksmen; the soldiers were anything but!

Reid held the Springfields in contempt but not the soldiers who had to use them. He had only praise for them. The soldiers were rather less charitable toward the woodcutters. They are scarcely mentioned in the official reports; there is certainly no indication that they made a significant contribution to the battle. Soldiers who were there have left several reminiscences of the fight, and they, too, hardly mention the civilians. Two such accounts, by Private Samuel Gibson and by Corporal Max Littman, make it appear that the woodcutters took little or no part in the battle. Another, by Private Frederic Claus, leaves the impression that the woodcutters were all hiding in the woods during the battle and only joined the soldiers after the fight was over.[48] These self-serving versions can perhaps be explained in several ways.

First, witnesses admitted that they were so concentrating on their own survival that they did not have a clear picture of the overall battle. In addition, flaming arrows caused the hay and dry manure to ignite, producing a terrible stench and heavy smoke throughout the fight. It was very difficult to see all that was going on in the compound, and panicked, milling horses within the circle of wagons made the situation worse. Moreover, it is only natural that the army, which had come under intense criticism after the Fetterman fight, should try to capitalize as much as possible on their victory.

One final point about the effectiveness of the Henry rifle in the hands of a cool and experienced plainsman like Bill Reid: F. G. Burnett, one of the participants in the Hayfield Fight that erupted at almost the same moment, commented that most of the troops were armed with breech-loading Springfields, while the civilians were armed with Henrys and Spencers. The exception among the troops was Captain D. A. Colvin, who was armed with a Henry and a thousand rounds of ammunition. Colvin was a crack shot; by the end of the day, the dead were heaped in front of him. Burnett stated that he doubted if there was any man living who had killed more Native warriors in one day than Colvin. Burnett claimed that Colvin alone probably killed about 150 of them.[49] Even allowing for exaggeration, it appears that one gun at the Hayfield Fight accounted for the equivalent of between one-third and one-half of the total number of Native deaths that were officially recorded by Captain Powell at the Wagon Box Fight.[50] It is interesting to note that the next year, in the standoff at Beecher's Island in 1868, a company of fifty frontiersmen, armed with Spencer repeating carbines, held out for seven days against overwhelming odds: 6,000 to 7,000 Sioux and Cheyennes.[51]

At the risk of belabouring the issue, three points can be made. First, it seems clear that the American government, through misplaced economy, was allowing its troops in the West to be needlessly slaughtered for want of proper arms. Second, the apparent success of the breech-loading Springfields at the Wagon Box Fight probably lulled the government into an unwarranted sense of satisfaction in its policy, thus contributing to the later Custer disaster.

Third, and most significant, the Wagon Box Fight and the Hayfield Fight give us a glimpse of the future, a nightmare future of the transformation of warfare from individual bravery and initiative to that of the methodical slaughter of the industrial age. At the Wagon Box Fight (and the Hayfield Fight), traditional Native tactics of warfare suddenly became obsolete, just as traditional European tactics did in the First World War. At the Battle of the Somme in 1916, which became the symbol of the senseless slaughter of that war, waves of brave men were scythed down by the impersonal "two inch tap" of the German machine guns mounted on tripods. Many years after the Wagon Box Fight, Red Cloud admitted that in that battle he had lost half his warriors. Their extraordinary bravery had meant nothing against the new weapons of the industrial age. The drama of a handful of soldiers and civilians fending off the full power of the Sioux and Cheyenne nations had obscured the real significance of the battle. Just as the increased firepower of Mr. Colt's revolving pistol in the hands of the Texas Rangers transformed Indian warfare in Texas, so too did the dramatic improvements in rifles, the direct legacy of the Civil War. Though this message was obscured by the ineptitude of the army at the Rosebud and Custer battles a decade later, the improvements in weapons, symbolized by the Henry, doomed Native resistance to white advancement. Though it was not recognized at the time, August 1867 marked the end of the ability of the Native nations of the West to stem the white flood.

The lesson to the Native side was that they must arm themselves with better weapons. At the Fetterman battle, fewer than 10 percent of the warriors had guns, and most of these were smoothbore flintlocks from the fur trade era. The lesson of the Wagon Box Fight was that they must upgrade their weaponry. In the following decade, much of this was accomplished. At the Custer fight, many of the Sioux were armed with the new repeating rifles, mostly acquired from Métis traders of the Canadian plains – at the price of a good horse. In 1876, Custer faced a newly armed foe, 50 percent with firearms and 10 percent with the latest repeating rifles.[52]

* * * * *

After the Wagon Box Fight, Bill Reid continued for a while as a wagon boss for the army. Then, in 1869, he was sent to Fort McPherson, where his first son George was born in 1872. He was later stationed for a while at Fort Laramie, and he then established the BP Ranch on the Laramie River. His youngest son, John, was born there in 1882.[53] In June 1876, Reid was a wagon master and chief of scouts under General George Crook at the Battle of Rosebud Creek, nine days before Custer met his end at the Little Big Horn.[54]

In 1881, Bill Reid guided Theodore Roosevelt on a hunting trip in Dakota Territory. Roosevelt was greatly taken with Mrs. Reid, especially her stories of the incredible hardships of her early life. He persuaded her to write her reminiscences, which fortunately she did. These reminiscences, passed on by her son Jack to Jean Johnson, provided the information about her husband's role in the Wagon Box Fight.

Johnson became a regular visitor at the Reid ranch, and it was probably here that he met Portuguese Phillips, who had a ranch not far away on the Chugwater, High Kelley, an Indian trader who had a stage station at Chugwater, and the famous Liver Eating Johnson, whose nom de plume came from his rumoured habit, considered an eccentricity even on the frontier, of eating his Native foes' livers. He was a scout and bullwhacker in early Wyoming and later ranched for a while on the Laramie River but couldn't settle down. He decided, instead, to become a lawman. Quite late in life, he became a US marshal at Red Lodge.

MORETON FREWEN AND THE 76

Shortly after the Wagon Box Fight, northern Wyoming was to have a decade of relative peace. Though their losses at this battle, and the subsequent Dull Knife battle five months later, gave the Sioux and Cheyenne a tremendous jolt, the government had already decided, because of the Fetterman massacre, to close the Bozeman Trail. This it did in 1868. Fort Laramie and the newly built Fort Fetterman (on the Platte River near present-day Douglas) could protect southern Wyoming. For a decade, northern Wyoming was not inundated with settlers. It was only when the Black Hills were invaded by white miners in 1875 that the Sioux and Cheyenne again initiated hostilities. Then, even though spectacularly successful at the Battle of the Rosebud and the Custer fight, which inflicted on the western army their worst defeat to date, the Native victory was short-lived. It was no longer possible to stall industrial America's push west. The buffalo, the Natives' major source of food, fled the country as soon as large numbers of Sioux and Cheyenne gathered, making long major campaigns against encroaching whites an impossibility. So the victors of the Little Big Horn capitulated or fled to Canada or Mexico. About 5,500 chose Canada, and some remained there until the spring of 1881, when Sitting Bull finally surrendered to American authorities.

Five months after the Custer fight, the Cheyenne were hunted down in a secluded spot on Powder River and, in what has become known as the Dull Knife Battle, were soundly defeated, thus ending Cheyenne hostility and clearing the way for white settlement. This fight took place on the Red Fork of the Powder, in what would become known as the Hole-in-the-Wall country, later made famous by Butch Cassidy, Sundance Kid, and their cohorts, who were collectively known as the Wild Bunch. This spectacular country, once the Native people were defeated, was to become part of the cattle range of the Frewens' 76 Ranch, so named for the ranch's brand, which reflected

Frewen's arrival in America in 1876. The 76 Ranch would establish a line camp at the Hole-in-the-Wall, twenty miles west of where the main house, the Castle, would be built.[55]

In 1878, with the buffalo and Native people removed, the Powder River country was ready for grabbing. As has been seen, Moreton and Richard Frewen, the two slightly dotty Englishmen, were among the very first to take advantage of these changed circumstances. Native people were now mostly on reservations or had fled to Canada or Mexico. The buffalo had been effectively exterminated; by 1877, only small straggling herds were left. So, after 1877, northern Wyoming lay there for the taking, as did vast tracts of Montana. Collectively, these areas were the last virgin tracts left in that immense cattle frontier that spread from Texas to the Canadian border in the astonishingly short period of two decades. By 1885, ranchers in Wyoming and Montana were already looking north to Canada for grazing land because they had, in a decade, overstocked the northern American ranges. The golden era of ranching in northern Wyoming lasted only from 1879 to the mid-1880s.

The vast majority of the ranching and cowboy history and literature strongly emphasizes the role of Texas and Texan cowboys in the diffusion of cattle throughout the West. But recent scholarship is showing that the story is more complex – and interesting. Richard Slatta's superb *Cowboys of the Americas* leads the way. Slatta's fascinating book shows how richly textured the ranching and cowboy story really is, without taking anything away from Texas. His work demonstrates how shallow Wister's beliefs, discussed in the next chapter, were about the Anglo-Saxon makeup of the cowboy.

Terry Jordan's *North American Cattle Ranching Frontiers* is also a seminal work in comparative cowboy and ranching history. Jordan, too, takes the emphasis off Texas and rightly expands it to discuss the traditions of the Scottish Highlands, Northern Ireland, Wales and the hill shires of England, as well as different Spanish traditions and the transplanted English traditions of the Carolinas, which found their way to east Texas, there to mingle with those of Mexico. As the cattle frontier moved north from Texas, it also mixed with those of California and the American Midwest.

Throughout the Americas, the horse and the country suited to ranching gave these diverse traditions a unity. As Jordan points out, much of the allure of cowboying was the "imagined" freedom it gave.[56] There was a vast difference between a cowboy on a horse on the open ranges of the Americas and a cattle drover plodding behind a cow with a stick! Foremost in a cowboy's mind was pride in horsemanship, and a contempt for those who walked.[57]

The real life of the cowboy was monotonous and full of drudgery, and it is true that he was just a hired hand without capital. There is nothing particularly romantic, for instance, about Andy Adams' depiction of the early cowboy.[58] But add a horse and a gun at his belt and the image of the cowboy is transformed. In an era of open ranges and endless vistas, with the ability to ask for his time (money owed to him) and move on if an employer displeased him, the cowboy really was a free spirit, far removed from the wage slavery of industrial America. He could easily move from job to job, with all his earthly possessions tied behind the saddle.

The horse, of course, was the key to cowboy life. Until the horse was reintroduced to the Western Hemisphere by the Spanish (after becoming extinct there in prehistoric times), the Great Plains were seen as a hostile wasteland. The horse unlocked the potential of that region for both Native buffalo hunters and white cattlemen, and gave the region its romantic aura.

The grasslands of the Western Hemisphere produced a unique specimen in the mounted cattleman and, though the cowboys of Texas, Argentina, and Alberta were different in both important and superficial ways, they shared a unique culture and prestige with their cousins, the Australian drovers, the Russian Cossacks, the South African Boers, and many others around the world. They embodied a mystique special to the man on the horse.

* * * * *

The two Frewen brothers were able to stake their claim to a huge area of prime grazing land before other ranchers began to invade the country. They established their headquarters slightly east of the junction of the north and middle forks of the Powder River. Here they built a large log house in the style of an English hunting lodge, later to become known as "Frewen's Castle." The "Castle" had a stairway imported from England and a forty-foot square living room with a gallery for musicians on special occasions.[59] Altogether, according to Lawrence Woods, they laid claim to 4,000 square miles of grazing land, eighty-miles long north to south and fifty miles from east to west.[60] The 76 claimed two million acres in 1882, with only 160 acres actually owned. At this point, their range ran 34,000 cattle, 450 horses, and somewhat over 8,000 sheep.[61] According to another range authority, Maurice Frink, the ranch, in 1885, had no deed or lease land and a total herd of 48,625 head. Dividends to investors were 6 percent in 1883 and 4 percent in 1884.[62] Agnes Wright Spring calculated that, at the height of its opulence, the 76 ran 60,000 head on the Powder, Tongue, and Rawhide Creek, with

Frewen's Castle, with its imported stairway and style of an English hunting lodge. American Heritage Center, University of Wyoming.

line camps along the middle and south forks of Powder River.[63] Johnson, too, said that the 76 at maximum ran 60,000 head and had fifteen brands other than the 76 brand. Fred Hesse was the foreman on the home ranch and E. W. Murphy on the Rawhide ranch. Johnson worked under Hesse as one of his four assistant foremen. Hesse had about thirty cowboys working under him.[64] Agnes Spring also estimated that, in the early years of the open range up to 1882, British returns on ranching investment were often over 50 percent, a figure that is hard to believe, even in good years.[65]

Moreton Frewen was the real force in this ranching enterprise; Richard did little more than provide capital. And in short order Moreton became a definite presence on the Wyoming ranching frontier, though perhaps he was not fully appreciated by the more democratic elements on the Wyoming frontier. He had been born into the near-aristocracy of England to a landed family with extensive holdings in Lincolnshire, Sussex, Leicestershire, and Ireland. He embodied just about every quality that made Americans bristle. His life in England, by his own admission, appears to have been a constant round of weekend country parties, gambling, horseracing, and womanizing. At the latter, he was particularly accomplished, having included in his list of conquests one Lillie Langtry, later the King's mistress. During his time at Cambridge University, he had spent most of his time racing horses and carousing at his many social clubs, before being finally "sent down" because of his almost complete disregard for the educational possibilities at Cambridge.

But Frewen had another side. While dissipating his inheritance in a mere three years, he had the honesty to observe in his autobiography that his class no longer had a purpose in England, being largely caught up in an "infectious orgy of idleness and frivolity, largely devoid of social conscience."[66] While casting about for some new diversion at the end of the 1877 fox-hunting season, he was invited by John Adair to visit his Texas ranches. En route, he met General Sheridan, "a little red-faced explosive cavalry officer" who filled him with tales of the Upper Yellowstone. And in Dodge City, he met Bat Masterson, who gave him a long discourse on bad men. It was all in the eyes, Masterson said. The ones with brown eyes were not to be feared; their badness was of the "stage property" order of things. It was the grey or blue-gray eyes that held real menace.[67]

And so it was that, Frewen – after spending a month as a guest of Charles Goodnight, Adair's ranching partner – found himself, along with his brother, at Fort Washakie (later to be Owen Wister's starting point for several hunting trips) in early December. Any normal person, at this point, would have called it a season. But the Frewens were that combination of the effete and the bloody-minded that scorns common sense. They decided that they wanted to see the much-talked-of Powder River country, and no rational arguments about the impossibility of crossing the Big Horn Mountains in winter were about to deter them. They probably would have joined the statistics of silly Englishmen being killed doing ridiculous things if it had not been for the luck of running into a large herd of buffalo which happened to be going their way, providing a "snow plow" through the passes.

On reaching the eastern side of the Big Horns, one of the glorious views in the American West opened to them. Moreton said of his first glimpse of the Powder River country:

> Near two hundred miles south we could see Laramie Peak. To the east was the limitless prairie, the course of Powder River showing its broad belt of cotton woods fading out in the far distance. To the northward we could see clear up to the Montana frontier, a full two hundred miles. Not a human habitation was in sight. …

The northern Wyoming range before the great Die-up of 1886–87. Wyoming was the ultimate "cattle country," too arid for agriculture, but ideal for cattle grazing. American Heritage Center, University of Wyoming.

> Montana, Alberta, what is now Saskatchewan, up to Peace River … it was a virgin prairie, just waiting for man. How amazing the idea that for five hundred miles at least this immense area was destined to fill with settlers and their cattle during the next five years.[68]

A "virgin prairie" just waiting for "man"! The original people, like the buffalo, were to make way so that "man" could make God's garden bloom.

The Frewens instantly fell in love with the Powder River country and decided to locate a ranch there the next spring. At first they called it the Big Horn Ranche. By April 1879, they were back in Wyoming, wasting no time in building the "Castle" and buying their first herd of 4,500 head from Tim Foley for $70,000. The ranch soon became the Powder River Ranche, with 76 as the brand. (The ranch was generally known as the 76). Other herds followed, so that by 1882, when Moreton bought out his brother's interest in the ranch, he claimed that the 76 range covered 20,000 square miles and had 40,000 head of cattle.[69]

The house, "Frewen's Castle," was to become the social centre of northern Wyoming's cattle industry, particularly after Moreton married Clara Jerome, the eldest daughter of Leonard Jerome, one of the principal owners of the *New York Times*. She was considered one of the reigning beauties of Paris at the end of the Second Empire. Her sister married Lord Randolph Churchill and was thus the mother of Sir Winston Churchill.

In his autobiography, Frewen made no mention whatever of even his foreman, Fred Hesse, let alone a mere cowboy like Johnson. Similar to Owen Wister later, he was interested only in those who counted; the ranch almost seemed to be an excuse for a prolonged summer house party and a lodge for hunting in the Big Horn Mountains. The Castle's guest book bulged with the signatures of titled English, mostly there for the superb hunting in the Big Horn Mountains. They would set off for a day's hunt in their White Melton riding breeches, leaving behind the bemused cowboys who had saddled their mounts. One can imagine the conversation in the bunkhouse after one of these intrepid hunters bagged the ranch's milk cow in the bushes, mistaking it for a vanished buffalo. Another absent-mindedly walked off a cliff to his death. Others were somewhat more competent. Topping that list was Lord Caledon (father of Field Marshal Earl Alexander of Tunis, one of Canada's most popular governor generals), an Irish peer who had come west to live with the Blackfeet. When he returned to Ireland, he took several Wyoming elk for his deer park and two bears that lived in his stables. In preparing for his western adventure, he had slept in the garden and instructed his footmen to see that his blankets were kept damp.[70]

For a brief moment, the ranch was graced by the presence of Frewen's new wife, Clara, but one visit to the primitive atmosphere of the Castle was more than enough for her. She had been trained for a different life. Clara's mother seems not to have understood the classless nature of America; she has been described as one of those desperate American mothers who set her sights on marrying her three daughters to European royalty.[71] She and her daughters were, for some time, fixtures at the French court, but Madame Jerome's hopes were dashed by the fall of the Second Empire in 1870. So, on to England, where daughter Jennie was soon greatly fancied by Lord Randolph Churchill. At first, Mrs. Jerome thought she could do better than a Churchill, but finally, after some hard bargaining on both sides, the match was made final.

Leonie married an Irish cavalry officer, but soon broke into the rarified circle of British nobility. For many years she was the mistress of Prince Arthur, Duke of Connaught, the youngest son of Queen Victoria, who later became the governor general of Canada during the First World War.

It was now Clara's turn and, for a while, it went well. But Clara's chances of marrying a title were dashed when Lord Randolph, her entree into London society, was almost involved in a duel with the Prince of Wales and was consequently ostracized from London society. Thus, she had to settle for the next rung down.

Meanwhile, Leonard Jerome was usually left in New York by his wife and daughters to oversee the Madison Square mansion, with its ballroom and opera house. But he was forced to inform his wife that he could no longer keep his women at the centre of English society. And so it happened that Clara was in New York when Moreton made his first American journey, stayed with the family, and saved her from the ugly fate of marrying someone who was merely rich. Despite her mother's displeasure, and her sister Jennie imploring her not to marry into the rough West, she and Moreton were married in 1881 and shortly thereafter headed for Wyoming to spend the honeymoon at the ranch. Clara, with her riding habit from the Bois de Boulogne and her maid to ensure that her shoelaces were tied, since she had never in her life tied her own laces, lasted only a short time in Wyoming. She never returned.[72]

A year after their marriage, partly no doubt as a result of Clara's extravagance, and more so because Richard withdrew his money from the venture, Moreton was forced to sell shares in his ranch, now called the Powder River Land and Cattle Company. He was able to raise 300,000 pounds ($1.5 million) by appealing to a number of his rich friends and acquaintances. He then formed a board of directors, at first headed by the Duke of Manchester, lord of the bedchamber to the Prince Consort, and later replaced by Edward Montagu Stuart Granville Montagu-Stuart-Wortley-Mackenzie (otherwise known as Lord Wharncliffe and later Viscount Carlton of Carlton). The board also included such names as the Earl of Rosslyn; Baron St. Oswald; the Earl of Dalhousie; Lord Henry Nevill, son of the Marquis of Abergavenny; Baron Grinthorpe; Sir Frederick Milner, the son of the Earl of Lonsdale; Baron Dunsany; Baron Belper; Viscount Anson, son of the Earl of Lichfield; and Alfred Sartoris, whose brother had married Adelaide Kemble, opera singer and sister of actress Fanny Kemble, Owen Wister's grandmother. The interest in western ranching among those on this list may have had something to do with Frewen's claim that they could make 60 percent on their investment on the Wyoming cattle frontier.[73]

Frewen was unrealistic in thinking that he could finance a large ranch alone, or with only his brother. Almost all the early big ranches on the open range were joint stock ventures, with boards of directors and annual dividends. And, as will be seen later, Frewen's estimate of an annual return of

60 percent on investments was wildly unrealistic, although Maurice Frink estimated that some Scottish ranching companies were making 30 percent on their investment on the open range. Many Scots borrowed in Scotland at very low rates and then got higher rates in the United States.[74]

Frewen was now able to return to Wyoming with $1.5 million to invest in the new company. By 1884, the Powder River Cattle Company covered 4,000 square miles, and spilled over into southeastern Montana. The ranch claimed two million acres of public land, but actually owned only 160 acres – the land where the Castle was situated![75] It ran 50,000 head of cattle, had a hundred cowboys on the payroll, and claimed a dividend of 24 percent. The actual figure may have been closer to 3 percent.[76]

The investors were in for a shock. Very quickly the bubble burst; by 1885 the Wyoming range was overstocked as hundreds of others took advantage of free land and, sooner than most could have imagined, the warnings of sober Scottish economic journals came to pass. The ranching craze could only last as long as those who had an equal right to "free" land did not contest it. Overstocking and plummeting cattle prices, as well as the disastrous winter of 1886, effectively destroyed the Powder River Cattle Company, in company with hundreds of other ranches on the northern plains. And, in 1885, there was an ominous note in the report of Fred Hesse, the foreman of the 76. Rustling was becoming a major problem.[77] John Clay, the manager of the huge Swan ranch, was to write of this period, "From the inception of the open range business in the West and Northwest, from say 1870 to 1888, it is doubtful if a single cent was made, if you average the business as a whole."[78]

But, in the meantime, Wyoming became the centre of an international investment frenzy. Perhaps because Wyoming represented the end of the romantic free grass era in the US, it took on a special aura. As Mari Sandoz has said:

> The rest of the cow country would have other important pursuits and industries: Texas her vast plantations and farm areas; Colorado, Montana, and the Dakota Territory their mines and wheat; Nebraska and Kansas as well as some others their corn and wheat. All these would be cattle states, but Wyoming would be the truest, the purest cow country.[79]

Perhaps it was this special aura that attracted such an inordinate amount of eastern and foreign investment in the cattle business. The combination of adventure, romance, and money was irresistible.[80] The Frewens represented only the beginning of an invasion of British capital into northern Wyoming.

There is a glaring irony in the fact that Wyoming, which more than any other region of the Plains became associated in the American mind with the ranching frontier, was in reality an enclave of British capital. There is the further irony that the compelling character which Owen Wister created in *The Virginian*, a character that was so appealing to an American readership because he embodied so many of the ideal American virtues, was based, at least in part, on Johnson, a wage hireling of British investors.

Certainly many of the early ranchers in Wyoming were tough and individualistic men who carved their cattle empires from the wilderness through perseverance and energy: pioneers of the sort that spawned the legend. But, in reality, they were overshadowed in Wyoming by those who saw this last frontier in terms of a compatible mix of adventure and investment. With astonishing speed, eastern American money poured into Wyoming ranching. Yet this money was soon eclipsed by even more substantial English and Scottish investment.[81]

British investment in American ranching coincided with the height of the British Empire. Britain was becoming vastly rich through foreign investment. Already, by the 1870s, huge amounts of British money had gone into American canal and railway building. Now cattle ranching seemed to offer one of the greatest returns of all since the land was free and only a few cowboys were required to look after huge numbers of cattle. It seemed too good to be true – which, of course, it was. As well, British interest in ranching was prompted by the very large export trade in beef to Britain, and by the invention of refrigeration.[82] By the late 1870s, fifty million pounds of refrigerated beef and 80,000 head of live beef were exported annually to Britain. And by 1880, there were reports of 30 percent profits – or more – in American ranching.[83]

By the time the Wyoming cattle range opened, rich Scots and Englishmen were already in the habit of organizing "exploring parties" to the American West. Most of these "top shelfers" shared an enthusiasm for shooting anything that moved. This was the heyday of the weekend shooting parties at English country estates. It was also the period of the English mania for travel and adventure literature. The result was that the English began to focus on the American plains frontier, especially after Bill Cody brought his Wild West show to England. So off they went to rough it in the West, loaded down with custom-made firearms, folding rubber baths, and, on occasion, silver tea services; one wanted to experience the frontier, but one did not want to be mistaken for an American.

A number of them hired specially fitted railway cars, which came into fashion in the late 1870s to take hunting parties west. These cars provided every comfort, including a porter, waiter, and cook. The supplies, including dog boxes and "hunting costumes," were kept in the accompanying baggage car. And, undoubtedly, on the trip across the plains, many read one of the most talked about books of the time – J. S. Brisbin's *Beef Bonanza: or How to Get Rich on the Plains*, published in 1881.

The western shooting party over, many Englishmen returned home, both enchanted with the Great Plains and also buzzing with excitement over the financial prospects of making huge dividends by investing in a ranch on "free land" in this vast inland sea of grass that had so recently been cleared of the "Red Indian" menace.

Even the Scots got excited. John Clay, the best known of them on the Wyoming ranching frontier, wrote in breathless terms of his first sight of the Wyoming grasslands, "There is a freedom, a romance, a sort of mystic halo hanging over those green, grassy, swelling divides that was impregnated, grafted into your system."[84] Sober Scottish trade journals began to feature technical articles on the spectacular returns on investment that western ranching could expect. Only in the small print was it mentioned that these vast ranches were being established on the public domain; the land that was owned by the companies was usually a very small proportion of what was "claimed" by right of occupancy. In some cases, these ranchers owned no land at all, and title rested only on prior occupancy. Thus the investment was very risky in the long run.

This was the era of British world dominance, both economic and military. The British, at the height of empire, exuded all the insufferability that accompanied that position. British ways were clearly superior; they appeared not to remember that they had been humbled by upstart American colonists only a century before.

During this period, there was a very large export of capital throughout the world, and western American ranching seemed to be one of the most lucrative ventures going. Very considerable amounts of English and even larger amounts of Scottish capital poured into western ranching, following in the tradition of huge British investment earlier in the century in American development. By the mid-1880s, twenty-nine foreign companies, almost all of them English or Scottish, controlled over twenty million acres of ranching land in the United States – much of it public domain.[85] This situation so upset many Americans that it resulted in a Senate investigation in 1884.[86] Several years later, just before the terrible winter of 1886, petitions flooded Congress. In 1887, Congress enacted a law stating that no foreign individual or corporation holding 10 percent or more of stock in a ranch could own public land in the territories.[87] In the early eighties, a committee of Congress estimated that foreign interests controlled 100 million acres of US soil, in defiance of "the rights of honest and humble settlers."[88]

From a purely economic point of view, this British investment was generally a good thing, providing the US with much-needed capital, particularly in the costly expansion of transportation. It was also very important in developing the ranching frontier and helping make possible the flow of western livestock to the markets of the East and Europe. Scottish corporations like the Texas Land and Cattle Company of Dundee, or the even more famous Scottish Matador, which ran sixty thousand head on two million acres, or the Wyoming Cattle Ranch Company, managed by John Clay, which claimed four thousand square miles of Wyoming grazing land, injected many millions of dollars into the American economy. Together with their counterparts in New York, Boston, Chicago, and Philadelphia, these mostly absentee investors established a ranching frontier in the 1880s that was an extension of eastern American and British business at the height of its exploitative mentality. When the axe fell on this ranching empire in the killing winter of 1886 and most British investors decamped, they left behind a great deal of investment money that was very important in developing America's Great Plains.

But the ambition of these investors was to clash head on with an even more powerful belief. The western frontier was America's destiny, a belief that set Americans apart. It was an article of faith for millions that the frontier was there for ordinary Americans to better their lives and to extend the limits of democracy. Free land was fundamental to the American drive for economic advancement among a type of people who, in Britain and Europe, were alleged to be prisoners of a class-ridden system. It was extremely galling for Americans of this sort to find, when they arrived to take up their free homesteads, that supercilious foreigners or rich absentee investors from the East were claiming much of the good grazing land in Wyoming. It was an article of faith with Americans that there would be no established church and certainly no aristocracy. Understandably, serious nativist attitudes came to the surface. As well, there was to be a period of rather intense class tensions between the moneyed ranchers and the "little people," which found an outlet in rustling and squatting on the big claims. These tensions culminated in the Johnson County War of 1892 in northern Wyoming between the big ranchers and those who wished to have a modest part of the Wyoming range.

The tensions which caused the cattle war of 1892 came primarily from American land law. By the 1880s in Wyoming, there was very serious tension between large landowners and both the cowboys who wanted to start their own spreads and those who entered the country as homesteaders. The Homestead Act of 1862 gave 160 acres of free land to anyone who "proved up" in the required fashion. It became an important symbol of American democracy, and it was a policy that worked very well in large areas of both the American and Canadian West, but in the semi-arid grasslands of Wyoming, it was a disaster. Homesteaders only wanted the well-watered river bottoms. The big ranches could not possibly buy all the land required to run big herds; their land became useless if it did not include access to water. Anyone who has travelled through Wyoming knows that water is the issue, not land. Whoever controlled the water effectively controlled the land to the next watershed. The bitter fights in the Wyoming ranching country were all about water.

In 1879, in his Report on the Lands of the Arid Region of the United States, John Wesley Powell, fresh from descending the Grand Canyon of the Colorado River and about to become, in 1881, the Director of the US Geological Survey, was the first to argue that the Great Plains could not support a conventional system of agriculture and that its lands could not sustain unlimited development. The trans-Mississippi West wasn't called the Great American Desert for nothing! Powell argued that grazing was the only safe and logical use of shortgrass country. He urged the government to divide the arid West into four-section parcels (2,560 acres). But, in a triumph of ideology over pragmatic good sense, the federal government decided that it could not possibly tolerate such a "feudal" and "undemocratic" policy.[89] The government had certain expectations for the region, and common sense wasn't going to change the situation. So Powell's report was ignored, as was a similar report several years later.[90] In 1912, the Kincaid Act would be the first federal act – and it only applied to northwestern Nebraska – to dispose of federal land for grazing purposes. But the government would still not contemplate leasing western land.

Over the decades, the federal government experimented with other laws for shortgrass country. But as Deborah Donahue argues in *The Western Range Revisited*, all these policies were largely failures, leaving a situation of "chaos and anarchy" and serious overgrazing, in "an atmosphere of the absence of the most elementary institutions of property law."[91] Each time a policy of leasing shortgrass country was proposed, the "antiquated Jeffersonian ideal of the yeoman farmer" killed it.[92]

The 1862 Homestead Act was seen as the "safety valve" of American democracy. All Americans, not just those with money, were entitled to the free land of the West. The US government did make a minor concession to the arid climate of the West by passing the 1873 Timber Culture Act, which added another 160 acres to the original free quarter section in shortgrass country, if the applicant planted trees on forty acres within four years. And American officials did flirt with a policy of selling large tracts in shortgrass country at attractive prices, or of leasing large tracts of land as was already done in Australia and would soon be done in western Canada. But Congress finally argued that it was more important to fill the West with settlers, so it passed the 1877 Desert Land Act, giving an added section of land to settlers for $1.25 an acre, if they irrigated a portion of it. Not until the 1930s did the Taylor Grazing Act finally introduce a leasing system to shortgrass country.[93]

But the Taylor Act, which established a Bureau of Land Management (BLM), did not settle much. Even today across the arid West, but especially in Nevada, the issue of the use of public land is still very tense. Recently, there have been examples of armed resistance by western ranchers to the BLM's attempts to protect the public lands from overgrazing. Large groups of protesters, armed with semi-automatic rifles and handguns, argue that the land is free and the federal government has no right to it. Emotions have reached a point where a few police officers and BLM rangers have been killed or wounded. Environmental activists charge that western overgrazing of public lands has resulted in large parts of the western ranching country being on the brink of ecological collapse. On the other side, a large number of conservative western ranchers have formed powerful lobby groups to promote state ownership of land and, also, state stand-your-ground laws such as that in Florida. Once again, it is easy to see how federal land law has been crippled by states' rights.[94]

Through a combination of filings under homestead, pre-emption, timber-culture, and desert-land entries, an individual could obtain ownership to 1,120 acres of free land. But this was not anywhere near enough even for subsistence ranching in shortgrass country. Calculating that it required forty acres to run each head of cattle, 1,120 acres would only sustain twenty-eight animals.[95] Many concluded that fraud was the only answer. It became common for cattlemen to get their cowboys or friends and relations to make added claims to an area. For instance, Thomas Sturgis, the secretary of the Wyoming Stock Growers' Association, was charged with filing fifty-five desert claims in the names of people from New York, New Jersey, and Massachusetts.[96] Often cattlemen got their cowboys to file claims for them on choice meadowlands with good water, which they filed as desert land.[97] In this way, they tried to control bottomland and keep newcomers from filing on the all-important watered sections of their accustomed range.

In theory, ranching in Wyoming could be enormously profitable. All that was required was to buy a small amount of land on water and then turn cattle out on the public domain. Because of the altitude and dryness of Wyoming, the native grass cured on the stalk and provided good feed all winter. Branded cattle could be turned out on the open range to be rounded up periodically for the branding of offspring. Overhead, wages, buildings, and equipment were minimal. A cowboy cost $30 a month, $40 for a top hand and $125 for a foreman.[98]

But the system only worked on a range that was not overstocked with cattle or disputed by newcomers. In the early days, convention created established ranges. On the early open range, custom dictated that the first one in a valley claimed it as far as the next watershed.[99] Early outfits like the 76 could lay claim to areas somewhat larger than modest countries, if they had the capital to stock the range. But as the Wyoming range became crowded in the 1880s and as the newly created railways brought waves of settlers, the old conventions could not persist. By 1885, there were 1.5 million cattle in Wyoming Territory, far more than the range could sustain in bad years.[100] Insatiable greed, by 1885, had nearly destroyed the range. The robber baron mentality had gone mad with visions of great wealth built on little outlay and minimal effort. Vast areas of the Great Plains had been, with the greatest deliberation, divested of buffalo and Native people and then, in a blindingly short time, had been virtually destroyed through unthinking greed. The only solution these western robber barons could see was to bully the newcomers, erect illegal fences, and resort to violence.

The new cattlemen had every legal right to share the public domain, as did the new settlers to a quarter section on land that, by convention, not title, was considered to belong to the early ranchers. This doomed the early cattle empires. Previously the cattle barons had been against a system of individual leases, of the kind that were being established north of the border in Canada; now they were all for it, but it was too late to have their view prevail.

By the mid-1880s, as the northern Wyoming range became congested and many newcomers and cowboys from the big spreads began to establish their more modest ranches and homesteads, the large owners began to lobby strenuously for a lease system. But their efforts were not successful; the opposition was too strong. Their opponents could muster compelling arguments that reserving the public domain for privileged monopolists was antithetical to democracy and a perversion of the American belief that free land was for the benefit of all and the crucial underpinning of a free society. These were noble sentiments, certainly, but unrealistic in Wyoming. The result was that tensions between big and small ranchers escalated during the 1880s, finally culminating in the "Invasion" of 1892, that extraordinary episode in Wyoming history that stands as a major indictment of both land law and criminal law in the American West.

Add to the above the issue of the weather. In good years, cattle could winter on the open range, as had the buffalo for thousands of years. Early cattlemen assumed that cattle could just replace the buffalo. But even before the disastrous winter of 1886–87, hard winters had taken an unacceptable toll. The lesson of the winters of 1886–87 and 1906–7 was that winter grazing had to be supplemented on the northern plains with hay put up for use in severe weather. Unlike buffalo and horses, cattle cannot effectively paw through crusted snow and are more selective grazers than both buffalo and horses. Unlike buffalo, cattle won't roam over large areas, so they tend to overgraze an area.[101] In bad winters, cattle on the open range died in the thousands.

After the winter of 1886–87, the mystique of making a fortune by simply turning vast herds of cattle out on the open range vanished and, by 1895, the number of cattle on the western American range declined by two-thirds. The vacuum thus created by this decline was quickly filled by sheep, which are able to graze where cattle will die. Sheep poured into Wyoming to outnumber the cattle ten to one.[102]

The lessons of that terrible winter of 1886–87 were intensely painful but ultimately positive. The cattle barons whose habit it was to just turn up for roundups and then flee back to the Cheyenne Club left the country to the stayers. The essential lesson was that the size of the herds must be reduced and the cattle must be helped through rough winters with stored hay. And some land must be owned and fenced so that winter feeding could be controlled. Astute cattlemen came out of the die-up winter better off because they learned the lessons and were able to buy stock at very depressed prices.[103]

But the winter of 1886 had one other effect. Previously, cowboys had counted on drifting from one job to the next and, if unemployed over the winter – which many of them were – taking advantage of the grub line (the tradition of out-of-work cowboys over the slack winter months finding food and a warm bunkhouse wherever they went) until spring. But everything changed with that terrible winter. The grub line was ended and immediately rustling became a serious problem for the big ranches.[104] At the same time, with the arrival of the railway in northern Wyoming in 1887, and with the lure of new dry farming techniques, the pressure on the big ranches multiplied.

Charles M. Russell, "Waiting for a Chinook." The catastrophic winter of 1886–87 effectively ended the open range and the era of big ranches. The terrible lesson of that winter was that smaller numbers of cattle that were fed hay over the winter survived very well. Montana Historical Society, Helena, Montana.

Actually, for all his financial ineptitude, Frewen had seen the situation in Wyoming coming and had pleaded with his board as early as 1884 to diversify by sending cattle north to the Alberta ranges. That year Frewen had sent his foreman of the southern herds, E. W. Murphy, to investigate the Alberta range.[105] And in 1885 Dick Frewen went north to Montana and Alberta to see whether conditions there would be better than in Wyoming.[106]

Just before the apocalyptic winter of 1886, which in some areas of the northern plains killed most of the cattle, Frewen had written to Clara, "I dread the coming of winter; if it is a severe one, half the cattle in Wyoming will die for sure."[107] Unfortunately, his board did not sufficiently heed his predictions and agreed to send only a small number of cattle to Alberta. Those that were sent came through the winter in good shape. By 1887, the Powder River Cattle Company was in the process of liquidation. After losing this battle with the board, Frewen was forced to resign as manager of the 76, just before the roof fell in.[108]

Frewen left Wyoming with much bitterness, convinced that his ranch would have survived had the board taken his advice to move more cattle to the superior range in Alberta. However, a look at his subsequent career gives one doubt in his overall ability. In a way he was a British robber baron, but without the killer instinct. He was later involved in a bewildering array of schemes, but none of them prospered and he was left deep in debt. His nephew, Winston Churchill, certainly considered him an embarrassing failure. His daughter's wedding was attended by four cabinet ministers and a number of gatecrashers – creditors who presented him with writs "of varying antiquity."[109]

Frewen's relationship with his daughter Clare was anything but benign. She became a well-known sculptor, and her arch-conservative father almost disowned her when she travelled to the Soviet Union on commission to do the busts of Lenin and Trotsky.[110]

Frewen can be seen as an arrogant fool – and many did view him in that light. Yet some of his schemes were visionary, if impractical – a British colony in Kenya, railways in Canada to Hudson Bay and to Prince Rupert in British Columbia to be the gateway to the Orient. His friend Rudyard Kipling remarked, "He lived in every sense, except what is called common sense, very richly and widely. ... If he had ever reached the golden crock of his dreams, he would have perished."[111]

* * * * *

What Johnson thought of Frewen we will never know. He hardly mentioned him. Perhaps Frewen never even met Johnson. The real work of the ranch did not involve the Castle, and nothing in Frewen's autobiography would lead us to believe that he ever became familiar with the cowboys. Johnson had much to say about his foreman, Fred Hesse, but Frewen and his guests appear not to have been part of the real ranch life of the 76. The tone of Frewen's writing suggests that the cowboys were there to look after his investment and provide local colour for the guests.

Eighteen miles downriver from the home place was the cow camp with its log house and stables, corrals, and hen house. It was here that the ranch crew carried out the main work of the ranch. Johnson and the other hands would have seen little of life at the "Castle." They lived in a very different world. The social world of the Castle had very little to do with the real world of ranching. Most of Johnson's memories were of the people he worked with. And they were a very mixed lot. Not surprisingly, he remembered best those who had some notoriety.

Johnson said that he knew some of the Daltons and Youngers and on one occasion rode some distance with Jesse James in Texas. The West was

Members of the Wild Bunch, otherwise known as the Hole-in-the-Wall Gang. From left: Harry Lougabaugh (Sundance Kid), Will Carver, Ben Kilpatrick, Harvey Logan, and Butch Cassidy. Photo taken in 1900. American Heritage Center, University of Wyoming, H 714 wg.

full of those with reputations who made ends meet with a little cowboy work. In Wyoming, he had many friends of somewhat shady reputation and he claimed that, without exception, they were capable cowhands while working for the big outfits. He added that by nature most of them were reckless and most were also crack shots. Most had a sublime disregard for danger and an intense loyalty to their friends.

Two, in particular, became good friends of Johnson's. One of them turned up at the 76 and asked for work, giving his name as Cassidy. Johnson later learned that his real name was George Leroy Parker. Johnson took an immediate liking to Cassidy and kept him under his wing. Cassidy had the makings of a good cowboy and was also witty and good-natured. Johnson, no slouch himself, was astonished at how fast he was with a gun, even though he was hardly more than a boy. The other one that he especially remembered, Harry Longabaugh, worked for the 76 at the same time. The three became very close friends. (Later, when Johnson was married in Alberta, Harry Longabaugh – a.k.a. the Sundance Kid – would be his best man.) All his life, even after they "went bad," Johnson retained a great affection for both of them.

Johnson said that he, and everyone else who knew them, both admired and trusted Cassidy and Longabaugh. They never forgot anyone who befriended them and were never known to kill, except in self-defence. Johnson added one other detail about Longabaugh; he claimed that Pat Garrett, the killer of Billy the Kid, had shot Longabaugh's brother Edward. Johnson referred to the Kid as "that dirty little killer." Johnson had ridden with cowboys who knew the Kid well. It took a particular genius to turn him into the stuff of legends – including a ballet![112]

One day at the 76, a stranger rode up to some of the cowboys and, pointing to Johnson, asked who he was. Cassidy answered, "Why that's my pa." The 76 hands were delighted by this and the name stuck, even though Johnson was only about five years older than Cassidy. From then on Johnson was "Pa"; the name even followed him to Canada, where it became "Dad."

Johnson liked to tell another story about Butch Cassidy. Eggs were scarce in Wyoming, and hens were highly valued. (Wister would give the hen Em'ly central billing, and say more about hens than cattle in *The Virginian*.) Cassidy stopped at a ranch house one particular day and asked if he could have something to eat. While the rancher's wife was preparing the meal, he drew his revolver and shot the heads off several of her hens. The woman was furious, but Cassidy tried to make amends by presenting her with a gold coin for each of the hens he had killed. She was not greatly mollified.

Johnson also knew some of the others who would become the Hole-in-the-Wall gang: Ben Kilpatrick, known as the tall Texan; Bill Carver; and the Logan brothers, Lonnie, John, and Harvey. Johnson thought the Logans were a bad lot, and after Lonnie and John were shot for rustling in Montana, he thought that Harvey became a cold-blooded killer. Johnson hated him and called him a rattlesnake. He said that Harvey Logan had the worst eyes he had ever seen. He accused Logan of leading Cassidy astray. All of the gang met a violent end except, perhaps, Butch Cassidy, either shot or, in the case of Kilpatrick, with an ice pick in the head.

Johnson did not make it clear whether these men constituted a gang when he knew them, but it is obvious that they became familiar with the Hole-in-the-Wall country during this time and would later use it for holding stolen stock and for hiding after holdups. For both purposes the country was ideal. A huge area of good grassland was accessible only through a few narrow gaps in the spectacular red cliffs that border the country on the east and run almost unbroken for fifty miles. A very few men could hold a large herd. And if trouble came, it was easy to retreat into a narrow and very steep canyon to the west. A few men could have held a modest army at bay.

The Hole-in-the-Wall is actually a narrow gap in the wall of red cliffs that run for many miles. A road now runs throught the "hole". A few gunmen strategically positioned at this point could hold off a small army. Author's photo.

The red cliffs of the Hole-in-the-Wall country. These cliffs made a perfect barrier for containing stolen cattle in this ideal grazing land. Author's photo.

This steep cayon at the back of the Hole-in-the-Wall country was an ideal place for a hide-out after the Wild Bunch's many train robberies. Author's photo.

The country is still isolated, thrilling, and, so far, unmolested by the tourist industry.

Cassidy's and Longabaugh's joint criminal escapades were not launched until after Johnson had left for Alberta, but Johnson still kept in touch with their careers through the cowboy network and continued to have a soft spot for them, arguing that the atmosphere in Wyoming which spawned the Johnson County War had much to do with turning them bad. And he believed, as was almost certainly the case, that they had both met their ends in a shootout in Bolivia in 1908.

Harry Longabaugh was born near Philadelphia in 1867 and first came west in 1882, at the age of fifteen, to work for his uncle in Colorado. He headed north four years later in 1886, first to work for the Suffolk Cattle Company near Newcastle in Crook County, Wyoming (now Weston County).[113] There he was hired on as a horse wrangler. (It is also believed that in 1886 he worked for the Lacy Cattle Company in Utah.) After a few weeks at the Suffolk ranch he moved on, according to Donna Ernst, to the N Bar N ranch, the Home Land and Cattle Company, which, in 1886, had over 60,000 head of cattle on the northern range. He was listed as one of those who drove cattle north for the ranch from New Mexico to Montana in 1886.[114]

Longabaugh was apparently heading back to the N Bar N to look for work when he spent some time on the Three V Ranch in the northeastern corner of Wyoming, owned by an English syndicate and managed by John Clay, a future president of the Wyoming Stock Growers' Association. In February 1887, Longabaugh stole a horse, saddle, and revolver from Alonzo Craven, a cowhand on the Three V.[115] He was soon arrested, escaped, was again arrested, and almost escaped again. After that, he spent the next eighteen months in the new jailhouse at Sundance, Wyoming – thus the name that followed him for the rest of his life. It is believed that when he was released, he was part of the gang that robbed the San Miguel Valley Bank in Telluride, Colorado.[116]

Although not stated by any of the principal authors writing about Butch Cassidy and the Sundance Kid – Anne Meadows, Larry Pointer, Richard Patterson, and Donna Ernst – it must have been some time in 1886 that both of them worked for the 76 and, thus, became Johnson's friends. Richard Patterson writes that it is a possibility that Longabaugh might have worked temporarily for the 76 and, perhaps, might have moved cattle north to Alberta with Johnson in the summer of 1886.[117] If this was the case, it is odd that Johnson didn't mention this to Jean. However, it remains a possibility and would help to explain why Longabaugh came to Alberta a few years later.[118]

Shortly after leaving Alberta in 1892, Longabaugh and two colleagues, Bill Madden and Harry Bass, robbed a train in Montana. The other two were caught and put in the Montana State Prison. Longabaugh escaped. Not much is known about him from then until the late 1890s when he joined the famous Wild Bunch. This group, whose regular members included Harvey Logan, Will Carver, Ben Kilpatrick, and sometimes Lonnie Logan and Flatnose George Currie, made the headlines with regularity but, like Billy the Kid, their fame caused them to be blamed for far more than they possibly could have accomplished. It is established that in 1899 they robbed the Union Pacific near Medicine Bow, Wyoming, the squalid little town where Wister starts his novel. They blew up the safe and escaped to Hole-in-the-Wall with around $30,000.[119]

However, this line of work was becoming somewhat unrewarding. The railroad companies were fighting back, using such unsportsmanlike tactics as boiling oil, Gatling guns, hand grenades, hoses to spray steam, and special "posse cars" especially fitted out for instant pursuit.[120] So the Wild Bunch sought happier fields for professional development. They ruled out the Canadian West because of the Mounted Police. South America appeared to be a good choice since it was not in the immediate orbit of the Pinkerton detective agency.

It seems that the Wild Bunch's last fling in the US was robbing the Great Northern in Montana in 1901. Then the gang split up, and Cassidy and Longabaugh, after a high-rolling stint in New York City, headed for Argentina. In Argentina, Cassidy, Longabaugh, and Longabaugh's companion, or wife, Etta Place, together purchased four leagues of public land (25,000 acres) and established a cattle ranch.[121] That might have been the end of it if the Pinkerton Agency had not caught wind of them and proved them wrong about the reach of their influence. So on to Chile, with perhaps a last parting bank robbery in southern Argentina in 1905. The relentless Pinkerton agency gave the following description of Longabaugh: five foot ten, 165–175 pounds, blue eyes, bowlegged, brown hair, and going by the following names: Harry Alonzo, Frank Jones, and Frank Boyd.[122]

Then, at least for Longabaugh, came the last robbery, in November 1908, in southwestern Bolivia. According to the established version, dramatically portrayed in the film *Butch Cassidy and the Sundance Kid*, they robbed the Aramayo payroll and, soon after, an armed patrol confronted them in San Vicente. According to the Bolivian army version, the army cornered the two bandits in a rented room in the village and quickly dispatched them both after a short gun battle.[123]

Immediately, awkward questions emerged. Nothing conclusive was found to identify the robbers. If the two were Butch and Sundance, their actions were totally out of character. They were known for their meticulous planning, careful and fast exit plans, and the lengthy endurance training of getaway horses. For instance, horses were carefully chosen; the first getaway horse was a sprinter, the second a stayer, with lots of "bottom." No posse could catch them. After the Aramayo robbery, the bandits stayed around with a stolen mule and allowed themselves to be caught in a room with no possibility of escape.

Whoever they were, the two gringos were quickly buried and meagre records filed. Over the years, a large question mark hung over the proceedings and theories abounded. In late 1991, Anne Meadows and her husband, Dan Buck, went so far as to have the bodies of the San Vicente bandits exhumed, with the help of a team of US and Bolivian forensic scientists led by internationally acclaimed forensic anthropologist Clyde Snow. The result:

Professor Snow was "reasonably certain" that one of the bodies was that of Harry Longabaugh; there was no certainty about the other.[124]

This uncertainty has led to the theory that Butch Cassidy either escaped or was not there at all. Larry Pointer's book *In Search of Butch Cassidy* argues that Cassidy did not die in Bolivia and, after 1908, was seen by a number of people who knew him, including his youngest sister, Lula. Perhaps this is just like Elvis sightings, but doubt persists. Pointer argued that Cassidy became William T. Phillips, who lived in Spokane and died during the Great Depression. However, handwriting analysis was inconclusive, and computer analysis matching photos of Phillips and Cassidy, according to Richard Patterson, "all but rules out the likelihood that Phillips was Cassidy."[125] But the uncertainty still persists. For instance, Phillips went to Alaska in 1912 to prospect for gold and ran into Wyatt Earp, who was running a gambling joint in Anchorage. Earp later said he had run into Cassidy in Alaska and commented about him, "Outlaws are made, not born."[126] Earp was not alone; a significant number of people who knew Cassidy well swore that they had seen him – and talked to him – in the 1920s and 1930s.[127] The mystery will probably continue.

If Larry Pointer is right, Cassidy ended his days in Spokane in 1937 as a rather pathetic figure who had been destroyed by the Depression. He spent part of his last few years on trips to Wyoming, digging about in a futile attempt to find some of his buried loot. He even made a rather pathetic attempt to kidnap a rich man in Spokane, before being carted off to die in a nursing home.[128]

THE JOHNSON COUNTY WAR

Butch Cassidy, the Sundance Kid, Nate Champion, the Hole-in-the-Wall gang, and many other "rustlers" came of age in the Wyoming atmosphere of the 1880s. If Johnson had not gone to Alberta in the late 1880s, it is not altogether clear where his loyalties would have lain when the turbulence of the period came to a head in 1892 in what has become known as the Invasion or the Johnson County War. He perhaps had little loyalty for Frewen and his English stockholders, but his loyalty to Fred Hesse and the ranch itself was very strong. Hesse was one of the principal leaders of the Invasion, and Johnson remained intensely loyal to him. Yet he could understand the animosity of many of the so-called rustlers who seethed at the arrogance of those who considered it their right to appropriate public land and police it through their stock association. Though he could not condone rustling and was a member of more than one vigilante group in the 1880s, Johnson did not want to get involved in the showdown that he could see coming. He was square in the middle – with a strong loyalty to Hesse, but closely linked to one of the rustlers who would be his best man when he married in Alberta: the Sundance Kid.

Johnson said that by the late 1880s the atmosphere was too much for him to take. After the disastrous winter of 1886–87, many of the big outfits were laying off cowboys, many of whom now turned to cattle killing and rustling to keep from starving. The ranges of the 76 were particularly vulnerable, and Johnson found his vigilante duties increasingly distasteful. As will be seen in the next chapter in the discussion of vigilante law, he had already lost his girl over the supposed lynching of his friend Steve; the chances were good that he would have to lynch others that he knew.

When he was recounting this period to Jean Johnson, one incident stuck in his mind that summed up the atmosphere of the time. As Johnson and another 76 cowboy were returning to the ranch from Buffalo, they spotted a settler who had been digging a well. The man was asleep on a side hill. Johnson's companion, who was a crack shot, fired a shot at his hat to give him a scare. The man did not move and when Johnson went over to him, he found him dead, shot through the forehead. Unfortunately, he had pulled his hat down too far. Though Johnson was furious, he never betrayed his ranch mate. This killing was undoubtedly blamed on the big ranchers.

Johnson said that, by 1887, cattle rustling had become an epidemic and the big ranchers could do little about it because the sheriff at Buffalo, Red Angus, sided with the rustlers and did next to nothing to stop them. At the time of the Invasion, Angus was in his early forties. He was well-known in the saloons and brothels of Buffalo – he had once been on the other side of the law, and his first wife had been a prostitute.[129] Stolen cattle could easily be disposed of, especially to construction crews in Montana. There was also a thriving business in selling stolen beef to local butchers.[130] Johnson thought that the cattlemen were goaded into taking the law into their own hands.

From this atmosphere emerged the Johnson County War. It was certainly one of the most bizarre events in the history of the American West. Johnson had already left for Canada before the violence erupted, but the event is essential to the telling of his story since he claimed that he saw it coming and that he left Wyoming to avoid the inevitable showdown between the big cattlemen and those they claimed were stealing them blind.

The primary cause of the war was western land law. Much has been written about this famous incident in western history, with the usual villains being the arrogant cattlemen who wanted everything for themselves and would not share their land with the new settlers who were flooding into Wyoming after the coming of the railway. Certainly the big ranchers had made a terrible mistake in believing that they could hold on to vast tracts of public land by prior right of occupancy, instead of arguing, when they had the chance, for a lease system similar to the one that developed on the western Canadian range. Extraordinarily, there was no land office in Johnson County until 1888.

At a meeting of the Wyoming Stock Growers' Association in Cheyenne in 1879, the big ranchers voted unanimously against a proposal for a lease policy. But, by 1884, they had vehemently changed their minds. At the meeting of the Cattle Growers' Association of America, Thomas Sturgis, representing the Wyoming cattlemen, spoke eloquently for establishing a lease system on the public domain similar to that in Australia, New Zealand, and Canada. But, by now, it was too late. Congress would not budge.[131] In 1885, when the Wyoming range was bulging with cattle, the Wyoming cattlemen voted unanimously through the WSGA for a lease system and tenure to their land. But Wyoming and the West in general were filling up with those who saw public land as a sacred democratic trust; the new settlers saw the stockmen's proposal as an abuse of that trust.[132]

It is popular to view the Johnson County War as a fight between the cattlemen and the homesteaders. This is a false picture. Certainly, homesteaders were arriving in Wyoming in the late 1880s by way of the new railway during a period of more than average rainfall to take up homesteads on the usually sparse cattle range. But northern Wyoming land, for the most part, was not suited to agriculture. The fight was really between the big ranchers and the small ranchers, who were increasingly taking up land in the 1880s and who were only trying to stake a claim to their fair share of Wyoming grasslands. Unquestionably, among these small ranchers were some who were outright rustlers and a number who were not overly scrupulous about adding to their herds at the expense of the big ranches. There were also a number of cowboys in this latter group who had worked for one or more of the big outfits and didn't like either their sense of entitlement or the new rules they had put in place, lowering wages and ending the established custom of riding the grub line.

The arrogance of the big ranchers is seen in the fact that, by the mid-1880s, 125 cattle companies were putting up illegal fences on public land in the West.[133] So many ranchers in Wyoming, and elsewhere, were illegally fencing the open range and filing fraudulent claims to land that, in 1887, President Cleveland had federal troops stationed in Cheyenne with the express purpose of pulling down illegal fences.[134] Joe DeBarthe, the editor of the Buffalo *Bulletin*, wrote in 1891: "The big cattlemen ... have grabbed up all the rich creek bottoms they could ... and the rest of the state was their range ... when a man who had been working for one of their outfits had the audacity to take up 160 acres of land for himself the big fellows blackballed him."[135]

But, all this aside, especially if one views the war from the vantage point of the Alberta range at the same point of development and under similar circumstances, one can see very forcefully that the basic issue was land legislation. In this shortgrass country, where forty acres or more were required to feed a single head, ranching or sheep raising were the obvious choices. Large tracts of land were necessary for ranching beyond a mere subsistence level. But how was this to be accomplished, given both the letter and the philosophy of the Homestead Act? Free land was a sacred trust, meant to be shared democratically, for the people of the West. There was nothing democratic about your average cattle baron! But it could be argued that Wyoming was not set up for democracy. Large holdings were required for a cattle industry, which was clearly how Wyoming could add to the wealth of the nation. John Clay added an argument seldom considered. By taking the stand it did on democratic principles, Congress crippled the western beef industry. Because of this, millions of Americans suffered from a higher price for beef and less beef in their diets.

To add to the complications for the ranchers, in a country where water was at a premium, prospective homesteaders or small ranchers would obviously try to stake their claims in watered valleys, which were few but critical to the success of the big ranches. Cattle range was of no use whatever unless it had easy access to water. A homesteader's or small cattleman's fence was a very serious threat.

In the absence of effective law in Wyoming, both sides now behaved badly. In their staggering arrogance, the big ranchers bent the law shamelessly and argued that they had the right to hold their accustomed range, even if at the point of a gun, and by putting up illegal fences on public land. They also formed an increasing number of lynching parties to rid the country both of outright cattle thieves and of the more casual rustlers. Many of the early cattlemen got their start by sweeping the range for stray cattle – mavericks – but now that practice was becoming a hanging offence. One of the early newspapers of the area, the *Big Horn Sentinel*, which began in 1884, recorded "an endless litany of lynchings, seemingly a new one or two every week."[136] Even with an allowance for shameless overstatement, lynching seemed to be a common practice. *The Sentinel* claimed that, in

1884, there had been "considerable lynching in the last six months, at least fifty lynchings in this period."[137] The paper commented that most killings in Johnson County were settled by a coroner's jury with the usual verdict of "justifiable homicide."

Lynching blossomed because the ranching industry of Wyoming was completely stymied by the unwillingness of the law to apprehend cattle rustlers; local juries in Buffalo, the only centre of population in Johnson County, simply would not convict cattle rustlers, no matter how compelling the evidence. The hostility toward the cattle barons was so great that it was almost impossible to get people to testify or a jury to convict. Emerson Hough commented that the cattle barons and their high-handed association were so detested in Johnson County that it became almost a moral code to brand a few of their cattle. Rustlers were seen as democratic heroes.[138] He claimed that the big ranches had brought suit against 180 rustlers and got one conviction for petty larceny – a penalty of eighteen dollars![139]

At the same time that the big ranchers complained bitterly of ineffectual law in Johnson County, Buffalo brought in a new city ordinance that levied a fine of up to $25 for a woman wearing a Mother Hubbard on the streets of the town. (A Mother Hubbard was a loose-fitting dress that was clearly too risqué for the refined sensibilities of Buffalo.[140])

Helena Huntington Smith, who made a careful study of cattle stealing in northern Wyoming in her book on the Johnson County War, stated that in 1887 there was one case of rustling in Johnson County, which was dismissed; in 1888 there were five cases, four of which were dismissed and one given a small fine; in 1889 there were thirteen cases – all dismissed![141] After that, the cattlemen gave up on the law. A presiding judge in Buffalo in 1889, Judge Micah C. Saufley, commented that four men arraigned before him for rustling were "as guilty as any men I have ever tried" and added that he did not know how the stock interests were to protect themselves.[142] John Clay said much the same. He mentioned one rustler who was caught red-handed, but the jury wouldn't convict. Soon after, the man was drygulched.[143]

After the winter of 1886, the opposition to the WSGA grew more powerful and vocal, with the new governor of Wyoming, a granger named Thomas Moonlight, adding his weight to the forces opposed to the big ranchers. By the end of the decade, juries routinely refused to convict rustlers on the grounds that the WSGA had used high-handed methods in arresting them. The situation was somewhat ironic since the citizens of Buffalo on these juries were now lashing out at an association that was a shadow of its arrogant former self after the Great Die-Up.[144]

So what was the cattle industry to do? By the mid-1880s in Wyoming there had been only two legal executions, both of them of mixed-blood Natives, while there were a large, but uncounted, number of vigilante executions.[145] The industry tried to act through the Wyoming Stock Growers' Association by hiring a number of stock detectives and by ramming odious legislation through the Wyoming legislature. The Maverick Law of 1884 stated that any unbranded strays were the property of the WSGA, and the sale of these animals would be used to hire stock detectives – and to buy rope for lynching! This was breathtakingly high-handed law. The WSGA took the unbranded stock of small ranchers – who were not allowed to be members of the stock association – for the benefit of the large ranching members of the WSGA.[146] Mari Sandoz claimed that this maverick law lit the powder under the Johnson County War.[147]

Before Red Angus became Buffalo's sheriff, Frank Canton had held that post from 1882 to 1886. He was also appointed deputy marshal for Wyoming Territory in this period. During his stint as sheriff, Canton had broken up a notorious horse-stealing ring and was responsible for sending nineteen cattle and horse rustlers to jail. But, in the 1886 elections, Canton, a firm Republican, didn't even run against the Democratic candidates, first E. U. Snider and then William G. "Red" Angus. He knew he didn't stand a chance in Democratic Buffalo. Under Snider and Angus, the number of arrests dropped "precipitously." This reflected the Democratic anti-cattle baron sentiments of Buffalo. Only five rustlers were sent to prison under their watch.[148] After the Maverick Law of 1884, Buffalo simply voted down the Republican ranchers and began refusing to convict men for rustling. The term "rustler" now became a badge of honour! Angus added to the cattlemen's rage by appointing Thad Cole, a known rustler, as his deputy. And in 1889, Frank Canton, as a deputy marshal, worked up an unsuccessful case against six men he considered the worst rustlers in Johnson County. The cattlemen concluded that the Wyoming legal system was just a waste of time.[149]

Frank Canton's career says much about American frontier justice in the nineteenth century. He was born Joe Horner and, by his mid-twenties, he was in jail in Texas for both bank and highway robbery. After several jail breaks, he fled Texas and changed his name. In the 1880s he became, in quick succession, a stock detective, sheriff, and deputy marshal in Wyoming. He took a prominent part in the Johnson County War. In 1896, when he was a deputy marshal, he shot and killed another deputy marshal in one of the very few real walk-downs in the West. He had accused the man and his two deputy marshal brothers of being rustlers and in league with the Dalton gang. In 1898 he became the only lawman in the interior of Alaska during the gold strike. From 1900 to 1906, he was a bounty hunter in Oklahoma. He ended his life as an honorary major general of the Oklahoma militia. There were a surprising number of lawmen like him who flirted with both sides of the law. He was also touted as a serious candidate for Wister's Virginian, even though he had only met Wister once.[150]

It was in the atmosphere of the impending Johnson County War that Owen Wister visited Buffalo in 1891 and came away as a fierce apologist for the vigilante arguments of the cattlemen. His attitude, no doubt, was coloured by his impression of Buffalo, which he shared with his mother:

> Something terrible beyond words. If you want some impression of Buffalo's appearance, and all the other towns too, think of the most sordid part of Atlantic City you can remember. A general litter of paltry wood houses back to back and side to back at all angles that seem to have been brought and dumped out from a wheelbarrow.[151]

The frustration of the cattle barons led to the utterly bizarre plan that Major Wolcott and some of his cronies hatched in early 1892, a plan to hire twenty-five Texas gunmen, fill a wagon with dynamite, and descend on Buffalo with the intention of blowing up the courthouse and killing those on a blacklist of about seventy people, starting with Sheriff Angus. Then, in the delusional minds of the ringleaders, life would go on as before, with control of northern Wyoming snugly in the hands of the WCGA and state politicians sympathetic to the large cattle interests.

Before writing Wolcott and his co-conspirators off as a coterie of delusional crackpots, it is important to realize that according to WSGA president John Clay, the Invasion was supported by every large cattleman in Wyoming and had the strong moral backing of both Wyoming senators.[152] The real answer to the question of the cattlemen's state of mind can be found in Montana. It seems clear that the success of both waves of Montana vigilantism deluded the Wyoming cattlemen into believing that they could copy the Montana vigilantes, and even take things to another level. Before discussing the Johnson County War in detail, it is necessary to give a short synopsis of Montana's two vigilante eruptions, which undoubtedly had an important influence on Wyoming's vigilantes.

In the early 1860s, at the end of the Bozeman Trail, the mining frontier of Montana erupted in violence, first at Bannack and then Virginia City. In the absence of law, the first Montana vigilantes were born. Between 1863 and 1870, they lynched at least fifty men. The standard argument is that they were just filling a legal void. But this argument, even if conceded in the early stages of their work, masks a very troubling legacy. In the gold diggings of Bannack and Virginia City, after the vigilantes had cleared the area of the hard core criminals who were terrorizing the diggings, they had the bit in their teeth and continued, with alarming enthusiasm, to lynch men for increasingly flimsy reasons.

The first wave of vigilantes did not disband when law finally came to Montana. They went on to lynch vagrants, along with some who were just suspected of a crime, without any thought of due process. As Frederick Allen in *A Decent, Orderly Lynching* commented, "Over a six year period they killed a total of fifty men, many of whom were not guilty of capital crimes, some of whom were not guilty of any crime at all."[153]

In 1863, Idaho Territory, which included large parts of the present-day states of Idaho, Wyoming, and Montana, was formed without appropriating any money for government or civil and criminal law. The locals were just to muddle through – the ultimate in local self-determination. The general rule was that, when a town in the West became incorporated, by law it had to elect a marshal, but until then, it could go without formal law. Town marshals were usually just uneducated men who had a facility with guns.[154] As the miners of Montana were to find out soon enough, they didn't make a terrifically wise choice in electing Henry Plummer to see to their legal needs.

In 1863, the miners of Bannack elected Plummer as their sheriff. They soon discovered that he was the ringleader of the most effective gang in the area. Before they realized their mistake and lynched him, events were already unfolding that should have given advocates of vigilantism some pause. In late 1863, a mass meeting of miners was called to pass judgment on a man who was accused of murdering a boy carrying a considerable amount of gold. The man was convicted on very flimsy evidence after three full days of deliberation. For most miners, there was a serious flaw in this legal structure. There was gold to be dug, and they were just not willing to make this sort of trial a habit. From this frustration was born the first Montana vigilance committee of over one thousand citizens, led by a man with the wonderful name of Paris Pfouts.

Almost immediately, this committee showed an alarming tendency: when members had second thoughts about the guilt of a suspect, they were threatened at gunpoint by the zealots.[155] At an early stage, two men were lynched for merely warning a suspect that the vigilantes were looking for him. There were serious flaws in the functioning of the group, but they got the main job done. Sheriff Plummer was apprehended and duly hanged.

However, shortly after Plummer's hanging, the next target was Jose Pizantia, "The Greaser," a Mexican considered a general nuisance. He was dragged from his shack by a howling, racist mob and strung up. More than two hundred bullets were fired into his swinging corpse. And the leaders of the vigilante committee stood passively by and just watched. Perhaps most disturbing of all, the newly appointed chief justice of the territory also stood passively, powerless to intervene.[156]

The next five who were lynched had done nothing to warrant capital punishment, but no one seemed to question the vigilantes. And the vigilantes didn't take kindly to criticism. Two men with legal training who questioned their methods were just run out of town.[157] If things had stopped there, a plausible argument could be made that their actions were necessary, but after lynching thirteen men, some of whom were unquestionably rotten, the vigilantes were just getting into stride.

Next came J. A. Slade, an annoying drunk, who had a habit of shooting up the town. They hanged him just for being obnoxious. The most shocking aspect of the murder of someone like Slade is that there was not the slightest ripple of protest in the East about his killing. His killing and many more like it were entered into the Congressional Record without comment. This was just the West, after all! It was really eastern attitudes being played out on a western stage. Worst of all, the casual attitudes seen here toward the law were to become ingrained in Western culture.

Then, in 1864, the Bannack vigilantes lynched a man merely for criticizing them. The victim was just a harmless drunk who had the temerity to speak out against their increasingly despotic methods. He was number twenty-seven.[158]

In the fall of 1864, the new Chief Justice of Montana Territory, Hezekiah Hosmer, found himself in a major confrontation with the vigilantes. They were simply not prepared to disband as law came to Montana and their lynchings became increasingly dubious. Number thirty-seven was just a pickpocket. And by 1870, well after the establishment of the machinery of law in Montana, they were still hard at work. They took two men who had robbed a drunken man from the sheriff and lynched them in front of a large crowd. These two were numbers forty-nine and fifty. Dimsdale, in his first-hand account of this period, wrote that this sort of hanging sometimes attracted crowds of five to six thousand spectators.[159] After number fifty, vigilantism needed a rest until, of course, it started all over again with Stuart's Stranglers in the mid-1880s in eastern Montana. Montana did not have a legal hanging until 1875. And in 1883, the editor of the *Helena Daily Herald* was still urging the revival of "decent orderly lynchings."

He was shortly to get his wish. On the eastern Montana range in 1884, in an atmosphere very similar to that of the Wyoming range, with the absence of any effective law, Granville Stuart, a rancher and, at the time, president of the Montana Stockgrowers Association, assembled a group of vigilantes to rid the range of rustlers. At the time, he was the manager of the largest open-range ranch in Montana. The group soon became dubbed "Stuart's Stranglers." They became the most notorious vigilantes in Montana, but they were not the only ones at the time. It is claimed that his squad killed between eighteen and twenty-four rustlers in one summer alone.[160] Their actions precisely mirrored those of the Wyoming vigilantes.

In a clear reference to Stuart's vigilantes, in 1884 Inspector A. R. Macdonell of the Canadian Mounted Police reported to the commissioner that a US official had told him that, in the last year alone, twenty horse thieves had been lynched in Montana Territory.[161] Macdonell added, perhaps with a slight tone of wistfulness, that the Americans were able to deal with horse stealing more effectively than the Mounties because they didn't have to worry about the niceties of the law. They just took law into their own hands.[162] The comment, of course, was tongue-in-cheek. The Mounties believed fiercely that vigilantism was one of the greatest curses of the United States.

Certainly, some of the Stranglers' victims were guilty. Others were just in the wrong place at the wrong time. But they were just as dead. In one case, Stuart and his posse took four men from a US deputy marshal who was escorting them to Fort Benton. They were taken to a cabin, lynched, and then had the cabin burned down around them.[163]

Exactly as in Wyoming, their actions were condoned by the governor of Montana, who argued that vigilantism was necessary until the area became more settled. But, as in Wyoming, the issue was not a lack of law and order on a raw frontier. It was the doubtful quality of the law under the elective principle. As in Wyoming, the big cattlemen could expect no sympathy from the courts. Some members of the association urged the members to raise a small army of cowboys, as they were about to do in Wyoming. Among the most enthusiastic for this solution was Theodore Roosevelt![164]

In both Wyoming and Montana, the cattle barons just assumed that they could use deadly force to protect their interests. And Stuart claimed that the actions of his group stopped rustling in eastern Montana for many years.[165] One historian of the Canadian–American ranching frontier has gone so far as to argue that western American vigilantism "might well have been more effective" than the efforts of the Mounted Police in the Canadian West in dealing with rustling.[166] In effect, the ends justify the means. It is perfectly fine to subvert the law if it gets the job done. This is an alarming argument if taken to the logical conclusion – that any group can take the law into its own hands if it feels justified. Just as troubling was the real situation in the American West, where many vigilante mobs "liberated" suspects from the protection of properly constituted lawmen and "jerked them to Jesus." And, in the long run, western vigilantism, because of the false mythology that has grown up around it, has bred a contempt for the law that has persisted into the twentieth and twenty-first centuries in mainstream America.

This argument for the effectiveness of vigilantism is based primarily on the vigilantes of Montana, both the early ones on the mining frontier of the early 1860s and "Stuart's Stranglers," who in 1884 purged the eastern Montana range of many of its horse-stealing rustlers. Warren Elofson argues that the early vigilantes on the Montana mining frontier were so successful that "peace and security came to the people ... for robbery became almost unknown."[167] Maybe, but at what price? Frederick Allen's *A Decent, Orderly Lynching* makes it all too clear that early Montana vigilantes went well beyond lynching guilty men. Without any form of trial, they began lynching mere suspects, and then men who were just a nuisance. There is a price to pay for subverting the law, especially the long-range price of entrenching a cavalier attitude toward the law.

As for the later group, Stuart claimed in his autobiography, *Forty Years on the Frontier*, that his vigilantes effectively ended rustling in eastern Montana, where law was ineffective in the early days of the ranching frontier. "This clean-up of horse thieves put a stop to horse stealing and cattle stealing in Montana for many years."[168] But Stuart even contradicted himself, stating a year later, in 1885:

> The stealing is as bad as ever this summer, but a great deal of it is by those lovely Government pets the Crow and Piegans. The white thieves don't seem to have any regular headquarters as last year which makes it difficult to get on to them but I think we will fetch 'em yet.[169]

And in 1891, Stuart admitted, "We have helped to convict about a dozen of them [horse thieves] but the supply seems perennial."[170]

The seeming success of Stuart's Stranglers in the mid-1880s was instrumental in the thinking of the Wyoming cattlemen when faced with the same problem. The Stranglers were essentially a small private army of cowboys, formed by the big cattlemen of Montana to rid the territory of rustlers. The big ranchers of Wyoming in 1892 just took the principle to a higher level in hiring a small army of Texas gunmen. Stuart's vigilantes cannot be seen in isolation. Their actions led directly to those of the Wyoming vigilantes and then to an idolizing of the idea of vigilantism in Montana history.

Lynchings in Montana continued after statehood and the organization of state law. In fact, lynchings continued into the twentieth century and became surrounded by mythology. In 1920, government officials, cashing in on the romance of the early lynchings, named the highways from Butte and Helena to Yellowstone National Park the Vigilante Trail. Also in the 1920s, a Vigilante Day Parade was launched in downtown Helena. And to crown it all, in 1956, the Montana state patrol added the numbers 3-7-77 to their shoulder patches and shields on their car doors. The numbers, now famous in Montana folklore, signified a three-dollar ticket out of town on the 7:00 a.m. stage, by order of the secret committee of seventy-seven. Throughout Montana history, the early vigilantes have continued to be honoured as heroes.[171]

How could anyone defend vigilantism who has read the powerful indictment of vigilantism and lynching in Walter Van Tilburg Clark's *The Ox-Bow Incident*? It is a chilling account of mob psychology and the fate of an innocent man who happened to be in the wrong place at the wrong time. The evidence of wrongful lynchings in the American West is easy to find. Vigilantism in the American West can only be considered a major indictment of American law.

There is certainly no validity to the contention of Warren Elofson, the leading academic apologist for western vigilantism, that the Montana vigilantes were essentially "an effective extra-legal citizen action committee ... a demonstration of self-government." And he is clearly wrong in stating that "In most cases they [vigilante groups] seem to have worked directly with regular lawmen. They rounded up suspected criminals and turned them over ... to be tried in the courts."[172] Frederick Allen's impressive and detailed work on the Montana vigilantes demonstrates definitively just how wrong Elofson is in his contention that Montana vigilantes worked with the law. They came close to being at war with the law!

The real problem with vigilantism is that it simply cannot merely be seen as a temporary expedient until real law arrives in a region. Over and over, vigilantism continued after law arrived, often in opposition to that law. Apologists for vigilante law usually argue that vigilante "justice" was a temporary expedient which filled a vacuum in the absence of legally constituted law. But in an overwhelming number of cases, this argument rings false. In a great many cases, the victims were liberated from good, honest, competent lawmen. The vigilantes were motivated by a disdain for the law, an impatience for the slow wheels of justice or, in the case of the Wyoming vigilantes, a firm belief that they could find no justice in the "people's law" of Buffalo.

In the larger canvas of the West, vigilantes in more settled areas were all too often motivated by the belief that, if someone was clearly guilty, or looked guilty, why waste time and money on lawyers and pettifogging procedures? Clearly, here was the slippery slope of justifying a contempt for the first principle of law – the presumption of innocence until guilt was proven. And vigilantism bred a long-term attitude of contempt toward the law, an attitude that still thrives. Certainly, when Stuart became the US Minister to Uruguay and Paraguay in the 1890s, his vigilante background was not considered a political liability, even at the highest levels of American government.

There are clear parallels between the situations in Montana and Wyoming in the eighties and that in Cochise County, Arizona, where the turbulent town of Tombstone was situated. There, in the fall of 1881, the famous shootout between the Earps and Doc Holliday and the Clantons and McLaurys at the O.K. Corral became a national sensation, soon dramatized beyond recognition. The shootout was actually a rather squalid little affair, brought on by a number of incidents and by liquor (in the case of Ike Clanton, who precipitated the incident through drunken bravado and then left the scene at high speed). But, in the background, is yet another example of the clear failure of American law. John C. Fremont, the pathfinder, conqueror of California in the Mexican War, Civil War general, and first presidential candidate for the new Republican Party, was now, in 1881, the governor of Arizona. He was greatly distressed by the situation in Cochise County, but lacked the power to do anything much about it. Law was totally in the hands of local law officers, in this case the largely inept Sheriff Johnny Behan and Deputy Marshal Virgil Earp, who saw Behan as a political hack far more interested in collecting taxes than in trying to catch rustlers. Fremont tried to get the Democratic legislators of Cochise County to form a local militia to deal with the threat of Apache raids, stagecoach holdups, and rustling, but the legislators were far more interested in economy, so nothing happened. In this atmosphere, the citizens did the logical thing – they formed a Citizens Safety Committee to counter the ineptitude of the law. In this stalemate between sheriff and deputy marshal, vigilantism seemed the only answer.[173]

The Johnson County War was clearly not a unique event. Its background had much in common with many other incidents in the West, but it was clearly the most extreme example of vigilantism on record. Looking back, it is hard to imagine how the plan for the invasion of Johnson County could be anything more than the embarrassing plot for a B-grade movie, but it all happened. The Texas gunmen materialized, followed by the wagon of dynamite and an assortment of ranch owners, managers, and foremen, the ranch owners mostly sophisticated eastern men of business with Harvard and Yale pedigrees. Many have blamed the "lordly English" for the situation in Johnson County but, by 1892, practically all the English were gone, contrary to local popular prejudice.[174] By 1889, three years before the war, almost all of the English investors in Wyoming ranching had left, eighteen in the last fifteen months, because of the winter of '86.

John W. Davis has argued in his recent book, *Wyoming Range War*, that the cattle barons precipitated the war for staggeringly selfish reasons: to keep control of the range, to get rid of competition, and to kill those who had witnessed their illegal lynchings.[175] He claims that the criminal case records for 1891, for instance, do not support the ranchers' allegations that rustling was endemic. But John Clay, for one, argued that by 1891 the ranchers had given up on the law and had decided to follow the path of Granville Stuart and his Stranglers in Montana, so they were no longer trying to get rustlers arrested. "The miscarriage of justice became so notorious that ... if a prisoner pleaded guilty he was not punished."[176] One historian has argued that even many lawmen began to condone lynching after they watched men get off who they had arrested red-handed. Lynching had the obvious attraction of "no appeals, no writs of error, no attorney's fees."[177]

Davis's book is important reading on the Johnson County War; he includes much careful research and gives a vivid picture of the war from the vantage point of hundreds of Buffalo citizens who rallied to defend their town from the Invaders. But his conclusion of unalloyed perfidy on the part of the cattlemen leaves a niggling doubt about their motives. Certainly the leader, Frank Wolcott, was capable of inflamed and stupid acts. But what about someone like Hubert Teschemacher, a man of high moral principles, who claimed that the ranchers had no choice given the utter failure of the law to protect ranching interests?[178] What about Willis Van Devanter, the Invaders' legal counsel, who was appointed in 1911 to the Supreme Court of the United States? Or Acting Governor Barber and Senators Carey and Warren? It is hard to imagine all of them acting for the reasons given by Davis. The real culprit in all of this was ineffectual law.

By 1892, Wyoming was a state with a supposedly functioning political and legal system. The ranchers behaved as if northern Wyoming was still raw frontier requiring – and justifying – vigilante law. On the face of it, the Regulators, as they became called, did not have a leg to stand on; their arguments and actions were utterly absurd. Yet, it could be argued, they were driven to some kind of action by their lack of legal protection. First the Great Die-Up, and now they watched their herds dwindling from theft, with no legal recourse.

The last straw for the big ranchers was the formation in 1892, in defiance of the WSGA, of the small ranchers' unofficial Wyoming Farmers and Stock Growers Association. It gave notice that it would hold its round-ups one month before the official WSGA roundup, from which they were excluded. This set in motion the plan of the big ranchers to punish these upstarts who were defying the WSGA and, it was assumed, robbing the big ranchers blind.[179]

The events of the war have been told too often to rehash here in detail.[180] A special six-car train was assembled in April 1892, three cars for horses and three for men, equipment, and dynamite. It is quite clear that the Union Pacific, which provided the special train, knew its purpose, as did both state senators, Carey and Warren, and Acting-Governor Amos Barber.[181] Documents showed that both senators were completely committed to the cause of the Invaders; they were even involved in posting a list of rustlers who were to be given twenty-four hours to leave the country before they would be hunted down and killed.[182] The records of two of the leaders of the Invasion, Dr. Charles Penrose and W. C. Irvine, clearly indicate that the Invaders planned to kill nineteen or twenty of those they thought were rustlers and then drive many more out of the region.[183] It defies logic how sophisticated and worldly men imagined that they could get away with such a hare-brained scheme in a region that was now a state, not a raw frontier.

At Casper, this entourage disembarked and proceeded north for Buffalo with dynamite now packed in buckboards, stopping at the Tisdale TTT Ranch, where Wister in 1891 had witnessed Bob Tisdale, in a fury, gouge out a horse's eye (see chapter 5).[184] Their plan to take over Buffalo, blow up the courthouse and kill those on the blacklist came unstuck when they encountered two of the prime suspects, Nate Champion and Nick Ray, at the KC Ranch, an old 76 line camp on the middle fork of Powder River. A shootout ensued in which precious time was lost. It took too long to kill Champion and Ray; they finally had to burn Champion out before they could gun him down. Meanwhile, Buffalo was alerted, and a large citizen posse was quickly assembled. Now it was the cattlemen and their hired Texas thugs who were the hunted. They barricaded themselves at Dr. William Harris's TA Ranch, thirteen miles south of Buffalo, about halfway from the KC Ranch to Buffalo, to await the posse. When they arrived, another shootout ensued, resulting in a stalemate until federal cavalry from Fort McKinney near Buffalo rescued the cattlemen from their very embarrassing situation. The

Buffalo, Wyoming in the 1880s. American Heritage Center, University of Wyoming.

cavalry rounded up the "Invaders," mostly for their protection, and lodged them first at Fort McKinney and then at Fort Russell to await trial.

The trial took place at Cheyenne and resulted in an acquittal, surely a gross mockery of the law. The WSGA had lots of money for the cattlemen's legal defence; Johnson County simply could not afford a long and complicated trial. By the time of the trial, the full machinery of the national Republican Party was in action, and it was even alleged that President Benjamin Harrison's influence came to bear. By the end of this legal charade, it was clear that the cattlemen were backed by the entire Republican machine, from the president and Wyoming governor and senators to the legislature, courts, and army.[185] Altogether, a low moment for American law.

And what to make of the thoughts of John Clay after the Insurrection? Clay, a prominent Scottish cattleman and president of the WSGA at the time of the War, was first told of the plans for the War when he was visiting Major Frank Wolcott at the VR on July 4, 1891. He thought the plan was impossible, but later he clearly changed his mind and wrote in his book *My Life on the Plains* that the War was for a just cause:

> Great reforms are brought about by revolutionary methods. The Boston Tea parties, the victories of Washington, were protests flung world-wide against a Teutonic dictator.

The Invaders of Johnson County after they were taken into protective custody by the army at Fort Russell. American Heritage Center, University of Wyoming, 15768.

This invocation of revolutionary tradition to justify the squalid actions of the cattle barons is truly extraordinary, coming from a transplanted Scot and a sophisticated businessman. The quote does demonstrate the power of revolutionary ideology in the oddest circumstance, and it is also fascinating in its reversal of villains; the humble settlers and small-time rustlers are now transformed into overbearing Teutonic dictators! The cattle barons were just doing their patriotic duty.

It is also interesting to realize that the place where Wister first discovered his western theme was the same place where one of the West's most extraordinary plots was hatched. One of the main fascinations of this remarkable incident for those who study comparative frontiers is to see how differently the same kind of people can act under different circumstances and under different legislation. The leaders of the Invasion were essentially the same sort of people who were to become the acknowledged leaders of the early Alberta ranching frontier. In a different setting and with different laws, they set the tone for early Alberta ranching, with little opposition. Of course, they were backed by strong federal land legislation which favoured them at the expense of prospective settlers.

This should have been the end of the story, but there was more to come. After their thorough humiliation, the cattle barons turned on the sheep ranchers, who were coming into northern Wyoming after the depletion of the cattle on the northern range after the winter of 86. The Johnson County range war settled very little. The most vicious phase of the range violence was yet to come. In the years 1903 to 1909, long after law should have been entrenched, nine sheep wars erupted in Wyoming, culminating in the Ten Sleep raid of 1909. A number of Johnson County ranchers argued that, if this infestation of sheep was not discouraged, the range would soon be destroyed for cattle. They argued, with some truth, that sheep, with their sharp teeth and close cropping, made the range untenable for cattle. The big ranchers' solution was to establish arbitrary "dead lines," beyond which sheepmen went at their peril. At the same time, the WSGA hired a contract killer, Tom Horn, at $70 a head to terrorize the sheepmen and to kill rustlers. Horn was good at his job. Single-handed, he caught all the members of the Langhoff gang, a group of horse rustlers who had a small ranch next to the vast Swan ranch. After long, drawn-out court proceedings, the rustlers' penalties were very slight. After that, the WCGA decided there would be no more courts! Horn was instructed to kill known and suspected rustlers.[186] But the times had changed. Horn was arrested for his vigilante work and hanged in 1903 for his crimes.

In 1909, for the first time in these sheep wars, a number of cattlemen's hired guns were arrested and five of them were sent to prison. The fact that the law finally acted seems to have dissuaded the cattlemen from further terrorizing the sheep men. This ended a very ugly period in the American West, from 1870 to 1920, in which there were about 120 incidents in eight western states of cattlemen terrorizing sheepmen – all prompted by a fight over public land. At least 54 men were killed, and 50,000 to 100,000 sheep slaughtered. Half the men killed met their end in the ironically named Pleasant Valley War in Arizona. After 1920 the sheep wars just petered out.

* * * * *

It was just as well that Johnson left for Alberta before the Johnson County War erupted. His mentor, Fred Hesse, was one of the main leaders in the war, and Johnson was certainly a member of a number of vigilante groups. Yet he had a close friendship with Butch Cassidy and the Sundance Kid, and probably many others who were not overly scrupulous about other men's cattle. He would have been in an impossible position.

5: Owen Wister and Wyoming (1885)

Before the Great Die-Up and the Johnson County War, Wyoming was, indeed, the ideal cattle country, a land of breathtaking vistas and seemingly endless cattle range. To this cattle Mecca Owen Wister was sent in the summer of 1885 to restore his fragile health. That summer Johnson took a leave of absence from the 76 and eventually drifted down to visit Mike Henry's 88 Ranch near Fort Fetterman. Johnson had at one time been engaged to Lizzie Henry and still remained a good friend of the family. It was while he was staying at the 88 that the manager of a nearby ranch, Frank Wolcott, heard that he was in the area and, being short-handed, asked him to help out with a dude who was about to arrive from the East.[1] This eastern greenhorn, as it happened, was Owen Wister, who was making his first visit to the West. Two spinster friends of his mother – Maisie Irwin, who operated a private girls' school in Philadelphia, and her assistant Sophy – accompanied him. They came west, it seems, to keep an eye on Wister's delicate health.[2]

This was the first of many trips to the West for Wister. He came in 1885 as a young man in his mid-twenties, sent by his family doctor in the hope that the West would help cure him of one of the most fashionable complaints of the period – frayed nerves, or "neurasthenia" in the popular jargon of the time. Wister had recently graduated from Harvard and was about to enrol in law school. He was in a most uncertain frame of mind about his future. His first love was music, and for a while he hoped that he might make a career as a pianist. But this was not to be. Though very accomplished, he was probably not quite good enough to pursue a career as a professional pianist and, besides, his father, who controlled his finances, discouraged his ambitions. These years of training, though, would certainly not be wasted. At this stage in his life, he had no serious pretensions about becoming a writer; these thoughts would not enter his head until the early 1890s. But when at last he found his calling and produced the first great western novel, an important part of its appeal rested on Wister's acute ear and his masterful ability to pick up the cadences of western speech and expressions peculiar to the West.

All of this was far in the future. Wister came west in 1885 as an effete tourist whose real love was for the old cultures of Europe. He was not drawn, it seems, to the rawness of Wyoming, only to the possible restorative power of its air. It was not until he reached Wyoming that something, quite unexpectedly, stirred within him and set in motion thoughts that would germinate for the best part of a decade before taking precise shape.

Two things are clear from Wister's first western diary of 1885. He certainly did not come to Wyoming with thoughts of writing. The sparse entries are those of a tourist more interested in hunting and in his close circle of contacts than with any notion of seeing Wyoming and its people through literary eyes. Yet it is equally clear that he fell hopelessly in love with Wyoming. After a stop in Cheyenne to sample the famous Cheyenne Club, Wister and his chaperones left the train west of Cheyenne and set off for the Wolcotts' VR Ranch by stage. It was at the Cheyenne Club that Johnson first met Wister and his two companions. He picked them up at the club and accompanied them by train to Rock Creek and then fifty miles by stagecoach to the VR Ranch.

The Cheyenne Club was unique in the West and just the sort of place to make Wister feel at home; it was the foremost anomaly on the frontier. It became the focal point for the big ranchers of Wyoming, which is why, shortly before Wister's visit, Cheyenne was reputed to be the richest city per capita in the world.[3] The Cheyenne Club rivalled the best clubs of New York and London with its superb French chef and impeccably trained servants from Ottawa. It is not hard to see why it attracted the cream of British and eastern American ranching investors, most of whom spent more time in Cheyenne than at their ranches. Dinner jackets, not chaps, served as the dress code, and many members seemed less interested in cattle than in supporting the new Cheyenne Opera House, whose formal opening included satin programs scented with just a hint of perfume. One legendary dinner in 1883 for forty-two members, at which the English members entertained the Americans, demolished sixty-six bottles of champagne – more than a bottle and a half per member.[4] There was much to celebrate. In those heady days, profits from cattle in Wyoming fluctuated, according to Agnes Spring, from 50 percent to 100 percent.[5]

Perhaps, while at the club, Wister might have run into Van Rensselaer Schuyler Van Tassel, who was one of the first major investors in northern Wyoming and whose family was featured in Washington Irving's *The Legend of Sleepy Hollow.* Or perhaps Wister encountered G. A. Searight of Austin, Texas, whose Goose Egg Ranch south of Casper on Poison Spider Creek would allegedly be the setting for the baby swapping incident in *The Virginian.*

On July 4, on the way north from Cheyenne, Wister recorded in his diary:

> I can't possibly say how extraordinary and beautiful the valleys we've been going through are. They're different from all things I've seen.... You never see a human being, only now and then some disappearing wild animal. It's what scenery on the moon must be like. Then suddenly you come around a turn and down into a green cut where there are horsemen and wagons and hundreds of cattle, and then it's like Genesis.[6]

In one of his first letters from Wyoming to his mother, he told her that "the air is better than all other air. Each breath you take tells you that no one else has ever used it before you."[7]

Wister arrived on July 6 at the VR Ranch near present-day Douglas, whose cattle range extended along both sides of the North Platte River, and met his "delightful" hosts, Major and Mrs. Wolcott. He was soon ensconced in a tent on the lawn and began a routine of daily rides on his "broncho," a wise little animal, it seems, who registered its disgust at having an eastern dude aboard by almost immediately lying down with him.

There is a most interesting passage in the diary for July 10, only four days after arriving at the VR. Something in the Wyoming atmosphere had already triggered the germ of what was to become, a decade later, Wister's great mission to place Wyoming and the cowboy at the forefront of the American consciousness. Appended to a lament on the lack of a true American type is this observation:

> Every man, woman and cowboy I see comes from the East – and generally from New England, thank goodness – If that's the stock that is going to fill these big fields with people our first hundred years will grow to be only the mythological beginnings in the time to come. I feel more certainly than ever, that no matter how completely the East may be the headwaters from which the West has flown and is flowing, it won't be a century before the West is simply

Major Wilcott's VR Ranch near Glenrock, Wyoming, where Owen Wister and Everett Johnson spent the summer of 1885 together. American Heritage Center, University of Wyoming, R151-VR.

the true America with thought, type, and life of its own kind. We Atlantic Coast people, all varnished with Europe, and some of us having a good lot of Europe in our marrow besides, will vanish from the face of the earth. We're no type – no race – we're transient. The young New Yorker of today is far different from the man his grandfather was – even when the grandfather was a gentleman. The young Englishman of today is not so different from his grandfather – for the Englishman is a congealed specimen – a permanent pattern – while each generation of us is a new experiment. All the patriotism of the War doesn't make us an institution yet. But this West is going to do it. I wish I could come back in two hundred years and see a townful of real Americans – and not a collection of revolutionary scions of English families and emigrants arrived yesterday from Cork and Breman, for that is what our Eastern Cities are today.

At the same time, he expressed his ideas more succinctly to his good friend John Jay Chapman:

> [Easterners] are too clogged with Europe to have any real national marrow. No matter how completely the East may be the headwaters from which the West has flown and is flowing, it won't be a century before the West is simply the true America.[8]

On the face of it, these passages seem rather strange. It would have been difficult at the time to find an American more "varnished with Europe" than Wister. And it would have been difficult to find a worse snob – except for his mother, who, as Wister commented in a letter to her, would have hated Wyoming. Yet, in these simple, uncultured westerners, Wister thought he had discovered the future of America. The logic seems deficient, but what is fascinating is that Wister's mind – in a sudden, almost unconscious revelation – was beginning to shape his great theme. Although this revelation would take some time to be represented in his writing, Wister learned more about ranching that summer of 1885 than at any time later. Most of his subsequent trips would be for the purpose of hunting or searching for other western themes. So, almost a decade before Frederick Jackson Turner's famous essay on the significance of the frontier, Wister's own frontier thesis was beginning to stir in his brain. Perhaps this should not be too surprising because the frontier was a subject of interest for most Americans of the time. The beliefs that Turner distilled in his 1893 thesis were certainly not novel. But in 1885, everything in Wister's upbringing and intellectual training should have prepared him for a role as a prime skeptic of Turner's argument.

Turner's thesis is perhaps best expressed by Gertrude Stein, who observed that "in the United States there is more space where nobody is than where anybody is. That is what makes America what it is." Turner was a bit more expansive. His great contribution to American thought was to distill in one short essay what had been in the air in one form or another for the best part of a century. In language that caught the imagination, he made it clear that what was important in American civilization was not the product of European culture; instead, it was the result of the frontier. The distinctive American character had been shaped through American history by the freedom and equal opportunity that the frontier imparted. (See chapter 7 for a further discussion of Turner.)

It is rather a puzzlement why this line of thought should have appealed to Wister. Perhaps opposites attract. He was most unhappy with his country as he saw it in the 1880s and was drawn – as were a number of educated, cultured Americans of the time – to the culture of Europe. The intense ugliness of the Gilded Age in America was overwhelming; a great many of his "set" escaped either literally or spiritually to Europe or retreated into their exclusive enclaves. If Wister's music career had flowered, he might have become, like his mother's good friend Henry James, an expatriate.

Instead, he discovered the West and gradually began to believe that here lay the solution to America's moral and physical ugliness. This was not to be an easy discovery, for the strengths he found in the West were his own weaknesses. Almost all that he stood for – culture, education, pedigree, wealth – meant nothing under the harsh scrutiny of the western gaze. It would not have been an enjoyable discovery that the ingredients of his considerable self-importance were considered liabilities in Wyoming. Later, in *The Virginian*, he was able to produce a very successful self-parody, juxtaposing his ineptitudes in the areas that really counted with the Virginian's strengths. But in 1885, it is doubtful that he was able to do this easily.

It is clear, too, from the first diary that his view of the cowboy was still in its infancy. After a month in Wyoming, he observed:

> They're a queer episode in the history of this country. Purely nomadic, and leaving no trace of posterity, for they don't marry. I'm told they are without any moral sense whatever. Perhaps they are – but I wonder how much less they have than the poor classes of New York.

There is no hint in this passage that a decade later Wister would have self-consciously decided to become the Kipling of the American West and the literary champion of the cowboy. In 1885, he seemed to view the cowboy with a combination of fascination and condescension. It is perhaps not reading too much into this first diary to argue that Wister in 1885 was mainly preoccupied with the arresting scenery of Wyoming and with his small circle of friends, which now included the Wolcotts. He had practically nothing to say about the cowboys he met whom, it seems, he regarded as picturesque employees, there to make his time more interesting. This attitude perhaps explains why there is no mention of Johnson in this diary, even though Johnson spent a lot of time with him that summer; he was not someone that counted.

There is very little mention, either, of the 76 Ranch, yet some of the cowboys in *The Virginian* were recognizable to Johnson as 76 hands, so it is probable that in the summer of 1885 Wister and Johnson rode from Wolcott's ranch to the 76. And, in *The Virginian*, the distance from Medicine

Bow to Judge Henry's ranch is 263 miles. That is roughly the distance from Medicine Bow to the 76 Ranch.

There is also no mention of Mike Henry in the diary, yet it is known that Wister was a guest at the Henry ranch that summer for a week, escorted there by Johnson. Proof of that is to be found on a barn door at the Henry ranch, where Wister carved his initials beside those of numerous cowboys. (I saw the initials "OW" carved on the door when I visited the Henry Ranch, together with Buckeye, Slim, and Eb – the name that Johnson went by in Wyoming). So the initial inspiration for Judge Henry in *The Virginian* is nowhere mentioned by Wister in his correspondence, then or later. This could be merely an oversight, but perhaps not. The fact that neither Mike Henry nor Johnson was mentioned in Wister's diary is consistent with Wister's focus in the diary on his tight little social set. But what is intriguing here is that Wister could lament in his diary that easterners were "all varnished with Europe," and yet in 1885, he seems to have behaved exactly as he had Molly Wood's family behave toward the Virginian in the novel; he, like her family, could not see beneath the rough exterior and treat westerners as more than intriguing frontier types. Perhaps someone like Wister was so accustomed in Philadelphia and Boston to keeping the common people at bay that it was hard to break the habit. It is ironic that over the next half decade Wister would not only come to value men like Henry and Johnson, but also find his mission in portraying them to the American public as the natural aristocracy of America.

Mike Henry, known in the area as "Judge" Henry, was in many ways an ideal model for Wister's host in *The Virginian* – a much better model than his real host, Frank Wolcott, who had all the snob appeal that Wister initially found attractive. Wolcott was a distinctly unpleasant man when he became tired of being a charming host; Mike Henry, on the other hand, came close in real life to Wister's Judge Henry.

Born in Athlone, Ireland, in 1840, Henry come to New York as a child and there attended military school. He then enlisted at the age of thirteen as a bugler in the regular army. In 1855 he came west with the command of General William S. Harney and first saw the Oregon Trail. After serving in the Civil War, he again enlisted in the army and was involved in considerable Indian fighting, including the Battle of the Rosebud under General George Crook in 1876. The next year, he took his discharge after serving for thirty years and filed on land, first at the mouth of House Creek and then along the Bozeman Trail near Brown's Springs, in the northern part of Converse County, named for a soldier who had his scalp lifted at that spot. He was one of the very first ranchers in the northern part of Converse County.

The Henry ranch was initiated in 1878 and became one of the more enduring success stories in Wyoming history. It weathered the disastrous winter of 1886 and by the turn of the century was running 3,000 head of cattle.[9]

By the time Wister visited the Henrys for a week in 1885, their 88 Ranch, on La Prele Creek, south of Douglas and only a short ride from Wolcott's VR Ranch, was well-known in the area for its cattle and horses and was also a stage relay station for the Patrick Brothers' stage line. The Henrys ran a roadhouse there, and Mrs. Henry cooked for the guests. Perhaps it was this involvement in trade that excluded the Henrys from Wister's diary. But it appears that, in retrospect, the visit was very important to Wister. Not only does it appear that Judge Henry in *The Virginian* was based partly on Mike Henry, but, also, two of the bronco busters working on the 88, "Chalkeye" and "Red-Wing," were included in the novel. Family tradition also has it that two of the babies who were switched at the Bear Creek barbecue were Henry boys, a story that Wister heard while staying with the Henrys and used to good effect in *The Virginian*.[10] According to the Henrys, this baby switching occurred at the Searights' Goose Egg Ranch, which was started in 1879 at the confluence of Poison Spider Creek and the Platte River (nine miles northwest of present-day Casper).[11] Johnson also claimed that the baby swapping really did happen, and his account supports the Henry family's claim that the swapping took place at the Searight Ranch and that the two Henry boys were among the victims. The Goose Egg is near the real Bear Creek.[12] Johnson said that he and Jim Drummond did the switching and that there were three babies switched. Wister wrote in his 1893 journal that he heard the baby-swapping story from Jim Neil in Texas, but that didn't mean that the story couldn't have originated in Wyoming. Stories like that would pass quickly up and down the cattle trails.

According to Johnson, part of the character of Molly Wood, the heroine of *The Virginian*, was based on Mike Henry's daughter Lizzie. She ran the post office, which was located on the 88, and later married Frank Merrill, a rancher and member of the Wyoming legislature. They lived at the Double Box Ranch, eighteen miles north of the 88.

It is not known whether Wister met Henry again after his 1885 trip. It is interesting to speculate whether Wister, in retrospect, saw in Henry during that short visit the basis for Judge Henry in *The Virginian*, the figure that Wister meant to represent what was best in the western character, and one of the true builders of the West. Certainly Henry, in later years, lived up to the role. He became one of Wyoming's most respected citizens and a major force in ranching, oil, mining, banking, and real estate. And today the ranching tradition he began is still strong. His great-grandson, Mike, still

Mike Henry's 88 Ranch at the time that Wister visited the ranch in 1885. Courtesy of Bill Henry, Mike Henry's grandson.

runs the 88, which now covers some 30,000 acres.[13] When asked about the character of Judge Henry in Wister's novel, Johnson said that there was no question in his mind that it was based on Mike Henry. "It was Mike Henry, no question. It sure warn't Wolcott."

Wolcott's VR Ranch (for Victoria Regina – Queen of England) was, and still is, located on Deer Creek (pronounced "krik" in Wyoming) where it flows out of the Laramie Mountains, about ten miles south of Glenrock. Here, in 1878, Major Frank Wolcott, a Kentuckian of Scottish descent who had served on the Union side in the Civil War, staked his claim. The Mormons had used the land in the 1850s as a supply station for the trek to Utah. Then, when Fort Fetterman was built in 1867, the government had established a hay reserve on the site. Here, in a beautiful lush valley with the Medicine Bow Mountains in the background, Wolcott built his stone ranch house. When Wister visited, the major had established a style that Wister clearly enjoyed – Persian rugs, immaculate table linen, a piano in better condition than the one in the Wister house, and a Chinese waiter, "properly instructed."

Wister visited the VR at its most prosperous moment, though the ranch faced financial problems of which Wister was probably unaware. Typical of so many of the big ranchers, Wolcott, in order to expand, had added partners to the company. The Scottish American Investment Company, headed by Thomas Nelson of the famous publishing firm, invested substantial capital in the ranch in 1885. The VR, when Wister visited, was vilified by the locals as one of those foreign outfits that were robbing the people of their right to the land. Also, typical of so many of the big spreads, the devastating winter of 1886–87 was to cause economic havoc at the VR, which lost a third of its stock that winter. By 1892, when Wolcott led the Invaders in the Johnson County War, he had been forced to turn the ranch over to his creditors, the Tolland Company, though he stayed on as manager. He owed the Nelson family so much money that he was forced to sell them all his stock in the VR. After that, he seems to have drifted out of the picture.[14]

But in 1885, Wolcott was full of optimism and assurance. He had established an impressive cattle empire and was able to entertain his guests in considerable style. Yet there were cracks in his geniality, even toward guests. On one occasion he refused to speak to anyone because camping arrangements had gone awry. Wister also found Mrs. Wolcott most daunting; he recorded in his diary for August 1:

> Mrs. Wolcott has the Puritan virtues and she congealed early. The result is she doesn't understand and gets no pleasure out of new people – and gives them none. She is high minded, narrow, intelligent, clean and capable – but I don't think she has derived a moment's satisfaction from our visit – or a moment's dissatisfaction either.… Its a bad thing to have no humour – and she hasn't a grain.

Wister was far more charitable toward Major Wolcott, but in this he was in the minority. Even Wolcott's friends and associates found him difficult. Malcolm Campbell, who knew him well, described him as a bantam rooster with very positive convictions and violent relations with his neighbours. John Clay, who also knew him well, described him as "a fire-eater, honest, clean, a rabid Republican with a complete absence of tact, very well educated and when you knew him a most delightful companion. Most people hated him, many feared him, a few loved him."[15] Wolcott had been, at one time, a receiver of the United States Land Office and also, for a short time, a US marshal for Wyoming Territory, until a flood of letters and petitions began to flow into Washington, claiming that he was "overbearing and abusive, insolent and dishonest, obnoxious and hateful."[16]

Wister mentions in his diary for July 16 someone who certainly did not fit into the category of the few who loved Wolcott. He mentions the episode casually, but the issue is important both to *The Virginian* and to the atmosphere of law and order in Wyoming. Wister mentions that Wolcott was in a state of rage because one of his former employees was now squatting on prime land that Wolcott claimed. Wolcott had ridden off to have a talk with the man, Brannan, who, Wolcott said, had been goaded into squatting on his land by "a damn scoundrel" by the name of Beach. According to Wister, Brannan, when confronted, asked the Major to step down to his tent where they could talk business. This meant, "How much will you give me to clear out?" "Not a nickel," said Wolcott, who returned home for his rifle before he continued business. Nothing untoward happened, but Wolcott returned home seething, threatening that he would make it hot for them. Wister mentioned nothing more, but the story continues in an article written the next year, which was clearly libellous if not true.[17]

Six months after Wister's visit, Sumner Beach killed Bill Locker, who appears to have been a hired gun sent by Wolcott to clear Beach and Brannan off the disputed land. A random killing here or there in the West at that time is hardly worth mentioning. But the episode is important because, in a minor way, all the ingredients were there that culminated in the violence that erupted in Wyoming in 1892 between the big ranchers and those who also wanted to stake their claim to Wyoming grasslands. Obviously, one of the people who felt victimized by the large landowners wrote the article, which accused Wolcott of being an Anglomaniac – "a lick-spittle to the lordly English; a man who wears knee-britches, parts his hair in the middle and uses a cane." What's more, backed by British gold, he and people like him were defrauding America. What right had "aliens" and their toadies to the heritage of free Americans?

By the mid-80s, as newcomers began to pour into the area and, more important, as ex-cowboys like Beach and Brannan tried to stake their modest claims to land already occupied by the big outfits, hostility flared. The "aliens" became the scapegoats, regarded with a venom instilled in Americans as a legacy of the American Revolution. What right did these foreigners have to swindle honest Americans of their patrimony? The Wyoming Stock Growers' Association was accused of trying to steal the entire territory of Wyoming through a gigantic conspiracy. And Wolcott was using "English gold" and fraudulent claims under the Desert Land Act to defraud "free America."[18] By the mid-80s, a strident Anglophobia had developed in Wyoming because of the scale of British investment, an attitude that is clearly reflected even in scholarly writing and in many present-day attitudes in Wyoming. In retrospect, the British economic presence in Wyoming was very modest compared to the far larger and far more assertive American economic presence in Canada in the twentieth century. But in Wyoming in the 1880s, it must have seemed both odious and overwhelming. Looking back, it is clear that the British left little mark on Wyoming and, in fact, at a critical time in its development, they provided Wyoming with much-needed development capital.

According to the article on Wolcott, British villainy prospered through the Desert Land Act, "one of the most gigantic swindles that has ever been perpetrated on a free nation." There is no question that this act was often used fraudulently in order to acquire large tracts; many of the big outfits added crucial land with water on it in the names of employees or friends and relations who had never set foot in Wyoming. And, of course, once the water was controlled, all the land stretching back to the height of land was automatically included. It is understandable that this situation caused considerable enmity, but the fault was not with the individuals who took advantage of this law; the fault lay with the system. Since the big outfits could not lease the land, they resorted to questionable practices to safeguard their accustomed ranges from usurpers.

Considerable sympathy should be extended to the usurpers. In most cases they were not new settlers; the aridity of Wyoming discouraged farming. Rather, the struggle was mostly between the early ranchers who claimed huge areas because they were there first and ex-cowboys like Beach and Brannan who, in the best American tradition, were trying to make the transition from employee to small rancher. Friction was inevitable because of the scarcity of water in Wyoming, so anyone filing on water automatically took control of all the range near that water. It is not surprising that, in the absence of effective land legislation and criminal law, violence flared.

Wolcott's problem with squatters was not unusual in the mid-1880s. Many people were filing on free land, hoping to build up large herds as had the first comers. And they knew that many of the early cattlemen, while establishing empires, had acquired strays – mavericks – and put their brand on them before someone else did. The temptation was strong to continue this tradition since the herds of the big outfits often mingled indiscriminately on the open range, and a few calves here or there would not be missed. So many ordinarily honest men, who found it easy to bend their consciences because they were taking cattle from those who were unfairly monopolizing the land, condoned cattle stealing. And it was somehow easier to steal from eastern and foreign nobs, often absentee owners who occasionally turned up at the ranch at branding time but otherwise spent most of their time while in the West at the Cheyenne Club.

When Wister first visited Wyoming, the epidemic of rustling was just beginning. On subsequent trips, his rancher friends would undoubtedly have told him that the rustlers were destroying their profits and, even if caught, were rarely prosecuted. In the absence of firm direction from the government, the ranchers had tried to control the ranching industry through the WSGA. However, this body became increasingly unpopular with those who were not members but were still bound by its rules. The result was legal chaos on the range, and it is in this atmosphere that the big ranchers decided to take the law into their own hands.

Vigilante law was as old as the nation. By the time it reached Wyoming, it was enshrined in respectability, largely from its roots in the Revolutionary War, when the theory emerged that the people were justified in taking the law into their own hands to counter the iniquity of British control. There emerged the tradition, now given the sanction of legend, that the people have the right, indeed the duty, to uphold the law in the absence of properly constituted law. If the cause was just, then vigilante law was really just a democratic expression of the people.

One of the most compelling and masterful parts of *The Virginian* deals with this aspect of Wyoming life through depicting the lynching of the Virginian's good friend Steve, the persuasive arguments of Judge Henry for vigilante law, and the final showdown with Trampas, the leader of a rustler gang. All this was based on fact. Wister witnessed the beginnings of the trouble in 1885 in the incident over disputed land. When he next came to Wyoming two years later, he undoubtedly heard more on the issue. In 1889, at the height of the rustler problem, he again visited Wyoming and recorded in his diary:

> Sat yesterday in smoking car with one of the gentlemen indicted for lynching the man and the woman. He seemed a good solid citizen, and I hope he'll get off. Sheriff Donell [Hadsell] said "All the good folks say it was a good job; its only the wayward classes that complain."[19]

Wister made it very clear here and in *The Virginian* whose side he was on. Implicit in his view is a belief in the sanctity of property; it is justified to resort to vigilante law when the law is ineffective, or actually opposed to protecting that property. Wister also alluded to another aspect of the problem. The basis for the legal chaos in Wyoming was class warfare, not the absence of properly constituted authority as the apologists of vigilante law would have you believe.

The incident that Wister referred to in his journal was one of the most famous in Wyoming history. On July 20, 1889, "parties unknown" lynched James Averell and Ella Watson on the Sweetwater near Independence Rock. Their crime – it was alleged – was rustling. It is very hard for the historian to get at the truth in this affair, but it does seem possible that Ella Watson was a prostitute who accepted stolen cattle in trade. Also, she and her friend and oft-time lover, Averell, were squatting and filing on choice land that one of the large ranchers claimed. This, in the eyes of the cattle barons, was the more serious crime. Their deaths were to be a warning to that class of squatters that if the courts did not uphold their position, the big ranchers would do it themselves.

The lynching of Watson and Averell was the most famous incident of vigilante law in Wyoming largely because it is the only case in Wyoming's history of lynching a woman. But there seems to have been many more lynchings, most of them unrecorded, so it is impossible to attempt statistics. The big ranchers thought they had no other choice since the law seemed actively hostile to their interests.[20]

What seems extraordinary, in retrospect, is the justification of lynching and vigilante law by men of education and culture. Anyone reading the Englishman Thomas J. Dimsdale's classic account, *The Vigilantes of Montana*, comes away with an impression of stern, moral, upright citizens reluctantly performing a dirty, but necessary, duty. Much the same impression is left in innumerable other western histories. Clearly Wister in his treatment of vigilante law was merely reflecting the viewpoint of the "respectable" set in Wyoming. He left us a classic defence of the institution, one based very much on reality.

There was nothing fanciful in Wister's account of the lynching of Steve, or in the atmosphere on the Wyoming range that prompted that lynching. According to Johnson, Steve was a real cowboy who worked at one time for the 76 and then drifted off to consort with doubtful company. True to the story, Steve had been a good friend of Johnson's. It was only late in life that Johnson told Jean in confidence any details of his lynching. He made it clear that Wister got it more or less right, except for the fate of Steve.

At one time Johnson had been very close to Steve. Together they had worked on roundups, camped on many lonely trails, hit town to celebrate, and shared hardships. Once, in the desert, they had come close to dying together. They had run out of water and had only the dew from their blankets to sustain them until they were lucky enough to stumble on a spring.

Charles M. Russell, "The Necktie Party," 1918. Russell has caught perfectly the atmosphere of grim determination and necessity as a group of vigilantes does its distasteful duty.

Steve was the only one to call Johnson "Jeff." It was an affectionate name he used to rib Johnson. He kidded Johnson about his loyalty to the South and to Jefferson Davis; in private he used the name Jeff because Johnson was very bristly about the South. It is not clear how Wister learned of this private nickname.

Unfortunately, Steve left the 76 and fell in with some bad company who began stealing 76 cattle, a relatively easy pastime given the extent of the 76 range. But they ran out of luck and were followed as they were driving some stolen stock to Idaho. Finding themselves closely pursued, they scattered. Steve was captured, and it fell to Johnson as leader of the posse to hang him.

Johnson told Jean near the end of his life what really happened then. He said that he led Steve some distance from the rest of the posse, ostensibly to find a suitable lynching tree. He tied the noose around Steve's neck as he sat on his horse under the hanging tree and then gave the horse a slap. Steve stayed with his horse and rode for his life. Johnson had tied the knot so it would give. As Steve took off, Johnson galloped after him and after some distance fired a few shots. When he returned and said that Steve was dead, no one doubted his word. It was difficult for Johnson to make this decision; in common with most cowboys, he was loyal to his outfit. But he knew that he had removed Steve from the scene as effectively as if he had killed him. Steve understood that Johnson was risking his life to save him. He made his way to Idaho, changed his name, and never returned to Wyoming. All the people involved in this story were dead before Johnson divulged the real story.

A puzzlement remains. Wister in the novel has the Virginian, while in the throes of delirium after being wounded by Indians, say, "Steve, I have lied for you." This comment means nothing in the context of the story. Why then did Wister put it in? Could Wister perhaps have overheard Johnson talking in his sleep? Johnson recognized the country that was the setting for Wister's lynching of Steve and for the chapter "Superstition Trail," which Wister thought was the best part of the book, as did Roosevelt. Johnson and Wister had ridden the country together, and according to Johnson, Wister described it accurately.

Backing for Johnson's account comes from a somewhat unexpected source. Moreton Frewen in his autobiography had the following to say:

> Readers of that delightful book of Owen Wister, The Virginian, will recall references here and there to the "76 Outfit" and its shadowy "boss," this writer. The hanging of the outlaw by a protectionist posse was a real episode and I was both coroner and chairman of the jury of four who, high up there in the mountains above the south fork of Powder River "viewed the remains" and at a discreet distance returned an open verdict.[21]

Several interesting arguments can be drawn from Frewen's memory of events. First, it can be argued that the lynching that Frewen spoke of formed the basis for Wister's description. His account and Johnson's agree, and both recognized Wister's setting for the lynching in *The Virginian* as the actual location. Second, the lynching had to happen before Frewen left Wyoming in 1885. This is surprisingly early for a Wyoming lynching, but it gives credibility to Johnson's claim that he told Wister about the lynching in 1885 and either described the country where it took place or showed it to Wister. Third, and most intriguing, Johnson's claim that Steve escaped in the manner described is a little hard to swallow. Yet Johnson told Wister that two men were lynched, and Wister faithfully recorded that fact in a most effective way, contrasting the behaviour of the two men on the point of death. But Frewen mentioned seeing only one body; it is most unlikely that he would forget the presence of another. A lynching would tend to stick in the memory in a vivid and accurate manner. Thus Frewen inadvertently gave credence to Johnson's admittedly doubtful story about Steve's escape.

One of the more intriguing and effective aspects of *The Virginian* deals with Molly's abhorrence of vigilante law and Judge Henry's justification of the institution, an argument that at last convinces Molly so that there can be a final reconciliation with the Virginian, which Wister means to represent the acceptance by New England of western standards. Well, in real life, this was apparently not the case. Johnson said that Molly rejected him for good because she thought he had murdered a good friend. Apparently the western arguments for lynching left her eastern scruples quite unmoved.

Judge Henry's rationalization for lynching in the novel is masterly and, on the surface, reasonable. First, it is ingenious that Wister should have the argument presented by a former federal judge and an easterner. To some degree, certainly, Wister was presenting the defence of many of his friends who were involved in the Johnson County War. Wister, too, was masterful in invoking the classic argument for vigilante law, an argument firmly grounded in democracy and Revolutionary tradition.

First Wister established the gulf between eastern and western law. Molly's aunt, on being presented with the Virginian's picture in western garb, with a gun at his waist, exclaims, "I suppose there are days when he does not kill people." Wister is then able to contrast the law suitable to an ordered, settled society to that in the raw West where institutions have yet to be forged. This sets the scene for Judge Henry's defence of western lynch law. Wister ignored the reality, of course, that it was safer to be in Wyoming in 1885 than in New York City!

Judge Henry begins Molly's education by pointing out that right and wrong are not absolutes; they vary with circumstances. Lynching southern Blacks is vastly different from lynching Wyoming cattle thieves. The former demonstrates the barbarity of the South; the latter indicates that Wyoming is becoming civilized. When Molly suggests that lynching Wyoming cattle thieves defies law and order, the Judge invokes an argument with all the sanctity of the Revolution behind it. In answer to Molly's accusation that vigilantes take the law out of the hands of the courts, the Judge agrees but asks, "What made the courts?" "The Constitution." "How did there come to be any Constitution?" "The delegates." "Who elected them?" "The people." "So you see," said the Judge, "at best, when they lynch they only take back what they once gave." And besides, the Judge argues, the courts in Wyoming had not been convicting rustlers, so it was necessary, in order to bring civilization to Wyoming, to circumvent the courts. "And when the ordinary citizen ... sees that he has placed justice in a dead hand, he must take justice back into his own hands where it was once in the beginning of all things ... so far from being a defiance of the law, it is an assertion of it – the fundamental assertion of self-governing men, upon whom our whole social fabric is based."

Here is Thomas Paine with a vengeance. Wister's arguments come, virtually unaltered, from Paine's *Common Sense*, that brilliant revolutionary tract that shaped the course of American history, giving credence to the notion of some distant golden age before monarchy and aristocracy perverted the just will of the people. Of course, Paine's arguments were based on utter nonsense, but that did not prevent them from having enormous influence on people who wished to believe.

And Judge Henry's arguments, though based on pure sophistry, invoked that same powerful belief in the sovereignty of the people and thus appeared plausible to the credulous. But Judge Henry has turned Paine upside down. The Judge is defending the vigilante practices in Wyoming of a group who represented an American moneyed aristocracy, a small minority who were not prepared to abide by the duly constituted will of the majority of settlers in Wyoming. How was this to further civilization? Clearly the result was not the furthering of civilization but, rather, the anarchy that culminated in the Johnson County War.

Judge Henry's argument does not bear analysis. In effect, he is saying that the people can circumvent the institutions they have created if they don't like the way they are functioning. In theory Judge Henry was arguing the "higher law," the belief that moral values transcend legal statutes. This is a most compelling argument when directed toward British misrule in the 1760s, which brought on the American Revolution, or the slavery issue, but what about Wyoming law in the 1880s? In effect, Wister was saying, through Judge Henry, that a small group of the "right people" could flout the law if that law didn't quite suit them.

Wister was arguing for the only possible justification for vigilante law – the obligation of the good people to establish law and order on a raw frontier. But Wister was being dishonest. Wyoming in the late 1880s was not a raw frontier; by 1890, it was a state whose law was not functioning because the elective principle in American law guaranteed that the rich, privileged ranchers would not be protected. It is somewhat ironic that they were in the same boat as the Native peoples of the West, both victims of popular prejudice.

Many Americans would like to believe in the mythology of western vigilante law – that good citizens were doing their duty as the advance agents of civilization. There is clearly some truth to this view, but, in reality, this aspect of vigilante law was completely overshadowed by an uglier sort of truth. For every rustler "jerked to Jesus" by upright citizens, there were many who were taken from jails by mobs who were not especially interested in proof of guilt or due process of law. These mobs, of course, felt little awe for the lawman, who often looked on helplessly as his charge was liberated from his care and "stretched" on the nearest lamppost or suitable tree.

Anyone who has read Walter Van Tilburg Clark's *The Ox-Bow Incident* will be disabused of romantic or honourable notions of lynching. This shocking little book lays bare the base motives and frightening mass psychology that so often lay behind many lynchings. Clearly, vigilante law was resorted to in most cases not because of an absence of law, but because the law was either not working or was not respected.

Also, try as he might, Wister could not separate western lynching from that in the South. The two were linked, both products of a violent society. Wister's picture of eastern decorum and western violence rings false. Many scholars, such as Paul Gilje in his *Road to Mobocracy*, argue convincingly that eastern America became increasingly violent in the nineteenth century as large numbers of Americans embraced the belief, sanctified by revolution, that law was the servant of the people.

Southern lynching, too, cannot be divorced from the western brand, despite Wister's attempts to separate them. They both sprang from the same disrespect for the law. What made southern lynching so much worse were the added ingredients of racism and sexual paranoia, which gave southern mobs a unique level of depravity. But there are also descriptions, from Montana for instance, of crowds of 5,000 or 6,000 coming long distances to view a "good lynching."

It is perhaps not a coincidence that lynching began as a southern custom, though the terrorizing of Tories in Virginia during the Revolutionary era is really not all that different from the hangings in Salem of those who were thought to stray from community standards and were accused of being witches. But it was in the South that lynching was to endure, not as a substitute for law in new country, but as a pre-emption of law in supposedly settled and civilized communities. And the excesses of southern lynch mobs became condoned by community leaders, including state governors.[22]

American statistics on lynching are staggering. From 1889, when the *Chicago Tribune* began to keep count, until 1927, when the practice began to go out of fashion, there were 3,224 recorded lynchings, the vast majority in the South. Only about 4 percent of these lynchings were performed in the West (and about 7 percent in the North.)[23] Not surprisingly, most of the lynchings were in the Black Belt, where, by the late 1880s, lynching had become the standard method of social control. For extremes of depravity, Texas led the field. As in so many other things, Texans did nothing by halves. Texas, of course, was born in lawlessness and turmoil. But instead of lawlessness being confined to a formative period, it grew as the state matured, fed, it seems, by the proud vision of Texans taking charge of their destiny with both fists and not waiting on legal niceties.

It is perhaps unfair to single out Texas, except that the worst extremes took place there in the wave of southern lynchings that suddenly erupted in 1889. These Texas lynchings so disgusted Wister that they may have been very important in convincing him that his cowboy hero should not be a Texan. The South in that year seemed to be taken over by a sudden paranoia regarding Black sexuality.

Perhaps the ultimate depths were reached in Paris, Texas, in 1893 with the hideous torture and burning of Henry Smith for the alleged rape of a little girl. A crowd of ten thousand, many of them brought to the scene by special trains, gathered around the specially built platform to watch the spectacle and savour the animal screams as Smith's eyes and tongue were burned out with hot irons, prior to him being doused in oil and set alight.[24] And this was by no means an isolated incident.

WYOMING AND THE GENESIS OF THE VIRGINIAN

Vigilantism and western law in general have been considered here in some detail for two reasons. First, they were a central issue in the American West, an issue that gave the West its fundamental character and mystique. Second, this issue assumed a large importance in *The Virginian*. The hanging of Steve, the final showdown with Trampas, and the agonizing of Molly over the laxity of western law form critical parts of the novel.

Johnson told his daughter-in-law that Wister stayed close to the truth in this part of the book. Steve did exist, and so did Molly. Johnson maintained that there was a Molly Stark, who really did come from New Hampshire. He was very reticent when speaking about her, but did comment, "there was none of that drop the handkerchief sort of nonsense." He said that he did get into a scrape with Indians, as described in the book, but it was Lizzie Henry, not Molly, who found him and lifted him into the buckboard. When he said that Molly could not possibly have lifted his weight onto the buckboard, a gentleness in his voice seemed to imply that this was to her credit. Johnson also said that it was Lizzie, not Molly, that he rescued from the stagecoach, which was stuck in the Medicine Bow River. This was an act, Johnson remarked, which required a certain amount of co-operation from the lady.

In the novel, Molly, after much soul-searching, is reconciled to western law – the lynching of rustlers and the code of honour that required a man to stand up to a challenge. Johnson would not say much about this, but he made it clear that the real Molly Stark did not become reconciled; this was the reason for their parting.

I discovered the link between Wister and the fictional Molly Stark quite by accident. While in Concord, New Hampshire, researching both Wister's old school, St. Paul's, and the Concord stagecoach, which Johnson drove into Deadwood, I discovered by chance that Wister, while at St. Paul's, was a frequent visitor at the Stark house in Dunbarton, seven miles southwest of the school. The elderly Stark sisters, Charlotte and Harriet, were in the habit of entertaining boys from the school, including Wister. Harriet died in 1872, a year before Wister arrived at St. Paul's, so he would only have met Charlotte, who was a regular visitor to the school. Undoubtedly, this is where Wister learned of the Stark sisters' connection to General John Stark of the Revolutionary War and his wife Molly. It was General Stark, the commander of the New Hampshire militia in the pivotal Saratoga campaign and in the defeat of the British at the Battle of Bennington in 1777, who uttered the famous words, "Tonight our flag floats over yonder hill or Molly Stark sleeps a widow."[25] Here again is an example of Wister using real people in his writing.

However, when it came to the villain of the book, Wister did not use his real name. As he made clear, he was inspired by a man named Henry Smith in his portrayal of Trampas, but he wanted his villain, like his hero, to have a mystique. In real life, according to Johnson, Trampas was a man named White Clay George or Frank Bull – if those were his real names – a cattle rustler and killer who had been run out of several states and territories.[26] So Wister's Trampas was an amalgam of Henry Smith's character and looks and White Clay George's (or Frank Bull's) actions.

Early in *The Virginian*, there is an episode that is now firmly entrenched in American folklore. During a poker game, Trampas calls the Virginian a "son-of-a-bitch." The Virginian draws his gun, places it on the table, and utters the now immortal words, "When you call me that, *smile!*" Johnson could recall no such incident, but he did say that Wister probably got his

The Stark house in Dunbarton, New Hampshire, that Wister visited while at St. Paul's school. Wister probably based Molly Stark and her connection to General John Stark of Revolutionary fame on the Stark family of Dunbarton. Author's photo.

inspiration for the scene from the regular gambling at Glenrock, where Johnson's friend Monte Cunningham was a dealer. Later, Cunningham followed Johnson to Canada and the two remained close friends. In referring to those famous words, Johnson commented that Wister was puzzled when Johnson called someone "that old son-of-a-bitch." Wister said, "But I thought you liked him." Johnson explained that it was all in the way you said it – "a term of endearment or something that could get you killed."

There is a further explanation for this event in Wister's notes. In his Frontier Notes, 1894, is the following passage: "Fetterman Events, 1885–1886. Card game going on. Big money. Several desperadoes playing. One John Lawrence among others. A player calls him a son-of-a-b–. John Lawrence does not look as if he had heard it. Merely passes his fingers strokingly up and down his pile of chips. When hand is done, he looks across at the man and says, 'You smile when you call me that.' The man smiled and all was well."

And the shootout did not happen as the book depicted, in a classic "walk-down" on the main street of Buffalo. Wister was central to the creation of the ritual shootout on the street, the two steely-eyed antagonists walking slowly toward their destinies. In fact, this scenario virtually never happened. The vast majority of western shootings happened in saloons, the result of liquor, or from ambush. In Johnson's case, White Clay George (or Frank Bull) rode into Buffalo determined to settle with Johnson and, in anticipation of the meeting, got increasingly liquored up. He told Jim Drummond that he would shoot Johnson if he saw him. Drummond warned his friend and Johnson decided that things had been said that could not be ignored. So he armed himself with two revolvers, one in a holster and the other tucked into the front of his pants – not a usual practice amongst shootists. Johnson walked to the Occidental Hotel, entered the bar, and placed himself facing the door. When George came in the door and saw Johnson, he started to draw. Johnson killed him with two shots. The coroner decided that it was a clear case of self-defence; there was no inquest.

A happy ending, except for Molly's reaction. In the real world, she did not fall into Johnson's arms after the killing. She was repelled by the atmosphere of violence in Wyoming, by the lynchings and killings. That Johnson was at the centre of these things caused a permanent rift.

Unfortunately, I cannot prove that White Clay George (or Frank Bull) even existed. Attempts to trace him through court records came to nothing. But it would have been unusual if they had. Though Johnson did not give the date of his killing of George, it had to be before he left for Alberta in 1886. The newspapers in northern Wyoming at this stage were in their infancy, so the absence of any account of the shooting in the press means nothing. Also, as Johnson stated, the killing was considered self-defence, so there was no inquest, and no mention of the incident in the fledgling court records in Buffalo. Because the court records in Buffalo revealed nothing, I was sent to a nearby funeral home where the coroner's records of that period were kept. When I explained my mission, the owner as much as told me that I was wasting my time. He said he could show me a number of unmarked graves from that period. "If it was considered a fair fight, they just planted the loser, no questions asked." So, no records of Mr. George, if that was his real name, seem to exist.

Wister provides no help. A very careful scrutiny of his writing provides no clue about whether he based the killing of Trampas on an actual incident. He does, however, go into some detail concerning his picture of Trampas. The character of Trampas was clearly based on the personality of a gentleman named Henry Smith whom Wister appears to have first met in 1891 while staying on the ITT Ranch of Bob Tisdale. Tisdale was a thoroughly nasty man with a savage temper. His brutal treatment of horses was to be immortalized by Wister first in his short story "Baalam and Pedro" and then in *The Virginian* in the chapter "Balaam and Pedro." Both accounts were based on an incident that Wister witnessed, in which Tisdale, as Wister watched helplessly, flew into such an uncontrollable fury that he gouged out one of his horse's eyes. Wister agonized over the fact that he did nothing to stop him. The episode obviously preyed on his mind until he was able to absolve himself, at least partially, by having the Virginian beat Balaam senseless for this disgusting act.

"Black Henry" Smith, the model for Trampas, was the genuine thing – a thoroughly bad man, with the magnetism and fascination that often accompanies that type. In fact, he sounds far more interesting than the character that Wister was to construct in the novel. Trampas, put beside Smith, seems to shrink and become a rather lacklustre and one-dimensional villain, without the perverse attraction and evil energy that Smith exuded. Wister described Smith thus:

> He was the real thing, and the only unabridged "bad man" I have ever had the chance to know. He is originally from Texas. ... He has been "run out" of every county he has resided in. ... Smith is at present stealing cattle or, more likely, Mavericking.
>
> Before I forget him, I must describe Smith's appearance. A tall – long-nosed, dark fellow, with a shock of straight black hair on end, all over his head. ... He is so tall he bends down over almost everyone as he talks, and he has a catching but sardonic smile. His voice is unpleasant, very rasping, though not over loud. The great thing is his eyes. They are of a mottled yellow, like agate or half-clear amber, large and piercing, at times burning with light. They are the very worst eyes I have ever looked at. Perfectly fearless and shrewd, and treacherous. I don't see how an eye can express all that but it does. I have sat and talked to Smith, or rather listened to him, he's a brilliant talker ... and he has found me what I set out to be in this world – a good listener.[27]

Wister's preoccupation with Smith's eyes is particularly interesting. Just as a good horseman first looks at a horse's eye in judging its worth, so, too, was it important on the frontier to take account of a man's eyes. They gave you a good estimate of whether you would still be alive at the end of a serious altercation. It was not always how fast you were on the draw; it was more important how cool and steady your nerves were.

Black Henry appears to have been one of the really bad men who gave substance to the legend. When Wister knew him, Smith already brought with him a mystique of violence and killing. Later – and it is not clear whether Wister was aware of this – Smith became a leading member of the Red Sash gang that terrorized Johnson County in the aftermath of the Johnson County War. He had been one of the leading candidates on the Invaders' blacklist of rustlers. Johnson knew him well, since he had worked both for the Powder River outfit and for the EK. Shortly before the Invasion, in the atmosphere of retribution toward the big ranchers, he became a leading member of the group that looted and indiscriminately terrorized the settlers of Johnson County. Meanwhile, Sheriff Angus and his deputies, the alleged champions of the little people, demonstrated their utter ineptitude in protecting people against the gangs of thugs that preyed on the community. Smith was finally indicted both for trying to burn down Fort McKinney and for the murder of George Wellman, a special US marshal. He was freed on both accounts for lack of evidence, largely the result of Sheriff Angus's ineptitude in investigating the case.[28]

There is an interesting footnote to Wister's acquaintance with Smith. It seems clear that Smith gave Wister the inspiration for his first published story on the West, "Hank's Woman." In his journal for June 17, 1891, Wister records:

> Some of Smith's conversation: "That's a terrible plain woman Hank's got. All driven and dried up. Looks like a picture on one of those shoo-fly boxes. But she's jest as joyous as one of these leave-me-alones. Old Westfall hates her. He calls her that buckskin son of a bitch. ... Got that boy Mose down at the EK yet? ... Got the oldest-looking head in the world on him. Looks as if it'd wore out four bodies. ... Old Gregg's a cunnin' man. Wanted a woman. Couldn't get none in this country as was willin.' Went out to England and fetched one along aback. Told her he had a large interest in the Powder River Cattle Company. Well, she comed and learned he had an interest. Had a cookin' interest in the roundups sometimes. But she couldn't find her way out of the country. Had to stay with Gregg. She'd been raised under a wharf there in Liverpool and like as not she'd have struck west if she started out for England. She's here yet."
> In all this I omit many pungent expletives.

When "Hank's Woman" appeared, Wister's first western story, its theme was somewhat altered, but there is no question that it was based on Smith's story. It is worth noting that this story introduced Lin McLean, but not the Virginian. The story is somewhat contrived and gives no hint of the huge talent still seeking an outlet. And it is perhaps interesting that Wister began his western writing with a small and rather squalid story. There is no hint of the great theme that is germinating. As will be seen later in chapter 8, Johnson knew Henry Smith in Alberta – he referred to him as Hank and considered him a friend.

"Hank's Woman" was not Wister's first attempt at western writing. Before that, he had written "The Story of Chalkeye: A Wind River Romance" in 1891, but had never finished the story. It is worth noting again that Chalkeye was the name of a real cowboy who worked for the 88. It seems clear that, from the start, Wister was basing his western stories on real people and real incidents. Yet these people and incidents are hardly mentioned in Wister's journals. Thus it is not puzzling that Johnson is nowhere mentioned in any of Wister's journals. Neither was Chalkeye. Neither was Mike Henry. Wister obviously had a good memory and included many people and episodes in his writing that were not in his notes. It is important to add that Wister's journals before 1891 are very sketchy; it was only in 1891, when he self-consciously proclaimed himself to be the bard of the American West, that he began to record many western details in his notes. But even then one searches in vain for most of the stories that were used in *The Virginian*. Most of these he kept in his head.

One last point about Wister's first western manuscript, "The Story of Chalkeye." A somewhat shadowy figure by the name of Link Trampas is introduced and features in Wister's first attempt to deal with western justice. Wister has Trampas ruminating on western justice:

> No sir. Why, when any unmerited shooting takes place in this country, we don't think well of it. A man is apt to be shunned after doing such a thing. And if its very bad, he's a sight likelier to get his medicine here than where yu' have attorneys and juries and female witnesses for the accused moppin' and slobberin' with their nose-rags. Why sir, men have to get out of this country on account of public opinion more'n they do in the States. There's a man down the river right now will have to look to himself or – "There yu' go James," said the cook nudging the packer. "Why can't yu' leave poor Link Trampas alone?" "I'm naming nobody," said Chalkeye severely. But when a man's word and deed comes to be mistrusted, Wind River ain't a good place for him.

Trampas was created early in 1891, before Wister met "Black Henry" Smith. Probably "Black Henry" was in the back of Wister's mind as he honed the character of Trampas, but the idea of Trampas was there earlier, and it is reasonable to argue that the original inspiration for Trampas came from Johnson's description of his troubles with White Clay George, culminating in the shootout in the bar at the Occidental Hotel. Certainly, there was no doubt in Johnson's mind on this score. He said that the character of Trampas and the events surrounding him in *The Virginian* were about an even mix of truth and imagination.

Finally, what credibility can be given to the claim that Johnson was the original inspiration for the Virginian? To begin with, it becomes clear that, in the strict sense, there was no "Virginian," a figure closely based on a real figure like Daniel Boone. Part of the enormous success of the book was certainly Wister's genius in creating a figure who embodied what Americans wanted to believe about themselves, a figure who was mysterious enough to ride down through the ages as the ideal American type. If Wister had linked his Virginian with any one person, the mystique would have vanished. Wister was always very cagey when asked who the real Virginian was. He was coy on this score and must have had much fun deflecting the persistent questions about the identity of his hero. But the figure of the Virginian did not come entirely from his imagination. When one looks at the short stories that became the basis for the novel, it is obvious that Wister initially was intent on accuracy in his western stories. It was only later, when he incorporated these episodes in the novel, that he attempted to create a folk hero. At first, he saw himself more as an accurate recorder of western life and people. His early western stories were based on real people – Chalkeye, Lin McLean, Mike Henry, and Molly Wood – and those familiar with Wyoming often recognized the settings. Only later did he see himself as a writer of the literary imagination, rather than as a recorder of the frontier West. His early stories, though interesting, are earthbound. None of them attempted to soar.

The hints that Wister does give us regarding the Virginian are deliberately frustrating. In the preface of the first edition of *The Virginian*, he had this to say: "Sometimes readers enquire, Did I know the Virginian? As well, I hope, as a father should know his son." This statement is not terribly helpful. Perhaps Wister was saying only that he knew cowboys well enough to draw an accurate image. Later he was to make other statements that have led others to jump to conclusions that were perhaps unwarranted.

Undoubtedly, readers with a thorough knowledge of the subject might be skeptical concerning the latest pretender. Who has ever heard of Everett Johnson? Where is the slightest mention of him in all Wister's detailed notes? Is his name merely the latest to be added to the very large file in the

Wister Collection at the University of Wyoming – or the equally large one at the Library of Congress – of Virginian claimants who, like Gilbert and Sullivan's cousins and aunts, can be reckoned up by dozens? The file is bulging with letters and newspaper clippings concerning this or that cowboy who happened to meet Wister and supposedly unloaded his life story on the author. The files testify to Wister's great success in catching something real in the western atmosphere more than they bolster any claims that can be taken seriously.

But there are two claims, besides Johnson's, that bear serious scrutiny. First, Wister's daughter, Fanny Kemble Wister, who took a deep interest in her father's work and finally edited his western journals and letters, has argued vigorously that the character of the Virginian was based on Charles D. Skirdin.[29] But, as Darwin Payne, Wister's foremost biographer, has stated, this is clearly wrong.[30] Wister did not meet Skirdin, at Fort Bowie, Arizona, until October 1893 – after the Virginian already had appeared in several stories.

In 1894, Wister got to know Skirdin at Fort Bowie and recorded his impression of him in his journal:

> His story, literally and faithfully recorded, would make a book as absorbing as Robinson Crusoe, and he's only twenty seven now, but his life has made him look thirty five! His search and discovery of his family, a taking of many years for which he saved all his money, is deeply touching. Skirdin is uncouth, ugly, and knows only what he has taught himself. But his talk is as simple and strong as nature, and he has a most beautiful eye. The officers place a high value on him.
>
> We grew very intimate, riding about the hot hills, and our views of life were precisely similar. His native wisdom is remarkable, and now and then he says something that many a celebrity would be glad to phrase himself.[31]

At the end of the 1894 journal are twenty-five pages of "frontier notes," which Wister's daughter did not include in the published version of his western writing. Among these notes are a number of Skirdin's anecdotes, but none of them is even remotely similar to the stories that appear in *The Virginian*. It is most difficult to understand how Wister's daughter arrived at the conclusion that Skirdin was the Virginian. She must have seen these notes and realized how little of Skirdin's life was similar to that of the Virginian. Skirdin, for a start, was not a cowboy. He was the wrong age (the

Virginian in the novel was the same age as Wister), and he was not physically similar. The Virginian was certainly not "uncouth and ugly." Then, of course, there remains the slight problem that the character of the Virginian had started to take shape before Wister ever laid eyes on Skirdin.

Undoubtedly, there was some of Skirdin in the final character of the Virginian. Wister was very fond of Skirdin and thought he embodied western virtues more than any westerner he had met. But Skirdin's life, though fascinating, did not even remotely fit the pattern of the Virginian's life. Clearly, the episodes of *The Virginian* were not based on Skirdin's experiences. What probably led Wister's daughter to advance this claim was a statement that Wister made in 1908 concerning Skirdin. He had become a Philadelphia policeman and had been sent to trial for killing a man while in the line of duty. Wister testified on his behalf, stating in court: "That man embodies all the characteristics of the hero of my novel 'The Virginian.' While no person was the actual prototype of the character, Skirdin, more than any man, embodies the type. ... I have often hunted with him and he was absolutely fearless, but exceptionally quiet and peace-loving."[32] It is important to note that Wister was making this statement in the context of saving Skirdin from jail and was careful to say only that he represented a *type* of man reflected in *The Virginian*. Wister was careful to keep the Virginian anonymous, thus preserving his mystique. Wister's testimony on behalf of Skirdin was the only time he identified someone closely with the Virginian, and he was careful to qualify his remarks. Later, in 1916, Wister would write in *Roosevelt: The Story of a Friendship* that he had met Skirdin in 1893 and that "much of him went into the Virginian, about whom I had written 'Em'ly' and 'Balaam and Pedro' before I met Skirdin, who *reminded* [author's emphasis] me of my own creation."[33]

The only other serious contender was George West, Wister's guide on numerous hunting trips. Darwin Payne has persuasively advanced the claim, but there are a few problems with the argument. First, Payne argues that before the Virginian appeared in "Baalam and Pedro," the character of Lin McLean, who appeared in Wister's first two western pieces, "Hank's Woman" and "How Lin McLean Went East," was based on George West. Payne then argues later that the Virginian was also George West. Payne is probably partly right, but the argument is unconvincing since Lin McLean and the Virginian were very different characters. Obviously both could not have been closely modelled on the same man. It seems that Payne associates West with Lin McLean largely because part of the story in "How Lin McLean Went East" was based on an event in West's life. And West, to a degree, fits the picture of Lin McLean – a footloose, carefree, irresponsible, woman-chasing cowboy.[34] But why is it that Wister called him Lin McLean, which was Jim Drummond's real name? According to Johnson, the character of Lin McLean did come close to Drummond's. So it would seem that the character of Lin McLean was perhaps a composite of Drummond, West, and probably others. What is important to note here is that Wister based his first cowboy, Lin McLean, on someone he met in the first summer of 1885, and someone who was never mentioned in his journal or letters.

How likely is it that George West was a model for Lin McLean and also for the Virginian? The answer depends on how far you take the argument. It is plausible to argue that there was some of West in both characters. Wister was initially very fond of West, and on his first meeting described him as "much better looking than any of us."[35] West, though a recent transplant from New England, had acquired many of the characteristics that Wister so admired in western cowboys. It is clear from his journal that Wister was at first in awe of George West. But it is equally clear that it would have been extraordinarily difficult for Wister to transform a New Englander into the soft-spoken, courteous Southerner, an aspect that was a central part of the Virginian's character.

But, by the time he came to write *The Virginian*, much of that awe had soured. By 1892, a decade before the publication of *The Virginian*, Wister was becoming distinctly annoyed by West's frequent requests for money and by his obsequious gratitude. "You are good, Wister, and a Christian if there are any on earth. ... Yes, you are a friend to me & the best I have ever had or will ever have I know. I never thought one man could love another as I have grown to love you."[36] A short time later, West asked for another loan and Wister refused. The somewhat grovelling tone of West's letter is so at odds with the remote, proud character of the Virginian that it is impossible to see the connection.

In 1900, just as Wister was immersed in the final development of the Virginian's character, George West wrote to Wister to inform him that he had just been arrested for stealing cattle. His candidacy becomes less and less convincing.[37]

Perhaps the journal entry of June 9, 1891, is the most telling evidence that George West was decidedly not the Virginian. His daughter's editing of his diaries and journals omitted this passage, so Wister's true feelings toward West have not been generally known. Wister wrote:

> Olmstead tells me that West broke out drinking last winter. I am deeply sorry. I hope it was only an "after-glow." Olmstead certainly thinks he is making more attempt at steady occupation than

ever before. West, himself, wrote me he had not been altogether an angel. But I drew from that that it wasn't serious or he would not have spoken of it. He has every gift for success, but that moral volatility (I'm beginning to think) will never let him get anywhere. I am not quite sure I ever thought anything else.

These words were written *before* the Virginian appeared in "Baalam and Pedro." Wister and West remained friends for many years, but Wister was obviously no longer in awe of West when he began to create the character of the Virginian. The moral laxity that Wister soon recognized in West makes it very difficult to believe that West, in more than a marginal way, could have been the model for the Virginian. West comes much closer to Lin McLean, Wister's first cowboy, who made his way through life on good looks and charm but lacked the iron core and unflinching standards that set the Virginian apart.

Again, in a journal entry not included in his daughter's published diaries and journals, Wister recorded an observation on George West on July 17, 1893, at a time when the character of the Virginian was taking definite form:

> But next year West will be just as far behind [despite Wister's frequent loans]. ... What can one do with such a man? ... He thinks he will give up his ranch because the winters are too long. If he does seek towns and gets work on some railroad, I think he will go to pieces with dissipation as he did once before – only then he was 20 and now he is 34. ... When I first began to know him well, six years ago, I was always wondering at his moral volatility – he has seen rough days and little else since then, but the volatility remains unprecipitated. With this, he has almost the most loveable nature I have ever known.

George West the Virginian? Hardly. And there is not a shred of specific evidence from his life that events in his life formed a basis for the novel.

There are really no other serious contenders for the title. Many names have been put forward as influencing Wister in developing aspects of the character, but only one other name seems to have much credibility. In 1895, while in New Mexico, Wister met Dean Duke, a colourful ranch foreman. Wister's 1895 diary is full of Dean Duke and his terrific stories, one of which was probably the inspiration for the four chapters in *The Virginian* dealing with Dr. McBride, the pompous preacher who finally leaves the Sunk Creek

Ranch in a state of high dudgeon after the Virginian has kept him up all night ministering to his loss of desire "aftah the sincere milk of the Word." Wister recorded in his journal that the preacher had just been giving a sermon under a tree to the cowboys on Duke's ranch and had informed them that "The Lord will come here – I tell you he will take possession of this valley." At this point, a cowboy whose attention had drifted and had only half caught the last sentence piped up, "The Hell he will. If he does that, Duke will law him out of it."[38]

Wister, too, was obviously taken with the type of cowboys on Duke's ranch. He commented in his journal, "They are the manly, simple, humorous, American type which I hold to be the best and the bravest we possess and our hope for the future – they work hard, they play hard, and they don't go on strikes."[39] Wister's view of the cowboy had certainly matured in a decade! In 1885, he would never have called cowboys America's "hope for the future." A decade had wrought a dramatic change in his thinking.

Duke, like Skirdin, undoubtedly influenced Wister's later thinking on the character of the Virginian as it appeared in the novel, but obviously neither could have been *the* Virginian since he met both of them after the Virginian had already appeared in several short stories. Yet these two were the only ones that Wister ever identified as being linked with his character, Skirdin as "embracing the type" and Duke as the ex post facto model for the Virginian.[40]

Perhaps one more small group of contenders should be mentioned. Wister had a good friend from Harvard days, George Waring, who had settled in the small village of Winthrop in the Methow Valley of Washington. Wister visited Waring in 1892, partly to hunt in the spectacular Cascade Mountains. He came again in 1898 with his new wife Molly to spend part of their honeymoon. Waring was a lifelong friend, the product of a prominent New York family who went west in disgrace because of an inappropriate marriage. Over the strenuous opposition of his parents, he had married his stepmother's sister, Helen Clark Green, who was more than a decade older. Waring in 1892 ran a small general store in Winthrop (now a western theme town!). Wister was appalled by the degraded life his friend was leading but understood the attraction of the country. Several ideas for stories resulted from his first stay; one about cockroaches found its way to "The Right Honorable the Strawberries."[41]

Anna Green Stevens, Waring's stepdaughter, claimed, "when I asked Owen Wister who was the Virginian, he said it was a composite picture of three men, Milton S. Storey being the principle [sic], my daddy, and Pete

Bryan." Methow Valley residents also claimed that Wister wrote *The Virginian* in Winthrop in 1901.[42] As Darwin Payne has observed:

> Claimants for the honor of having served as the original model of the Virginian continued to surface. Wister, quietly amused, never publicly disputed any of them. ... The same year another newspaper article from Methow Valley in Washington declared Milton Storey to be the Virginian, and his wife the model for Molly Stark. Wister's private comment was "nonsense." Another account, with an even more unlikely claimant for the honor, emerged in 1924 when the former governor of Puerto Rico, E. Montgomery Reily, wrote to ask if the assertion by his former chief of police that he was the model for the Virginian were true. The man since had been discharged for bootlegging. Other claims were equally farfetched.[43]

Certainly Wister did not make George Waring his model! The rather ridiculous claims of Winthrop are all too typical of the dozens that sprouted seemingly everywhere Wister had trod once his fame began to spread.

So what are we left with? How do we reconcile Wister's statement at Charles Skirdin's murder trial in 1908 that "no person was the actual prototype of the character" with his statement in the preface of the first edition of *The Virginian*, "Did I know the Virginian? As well, I hope, as a father should know his son." It would seem that as the fame of the novel increased, Wister became increasingly coy about the character he had conceived. To link the Virginian with someone specific would utterly destroy the mystique. Besides, Skirdin and West did not go on to distinguished futures. Skirdin ended as a watchman, sweeping floors, and West was arrested for stealing cattle.[44] So Wister was very careful about linking real people to his hero.

What is very clear, however, from a careful reading of all Wister's western letters and journals and his early articles, is that Wister, certainly at first, saw himself as a chronicler of western stories and people, not as an artist of the imagination. He prided himself on the authenticity of his stories and tried to capture real people in his stories. So it is likely, at least at first, that the emerging character of the Virginian in the early 1890s was based on someone real, or a combination of real people. If this was the case, Wister gives us practically no help, except for the above quoted statement in the preface of *The Virginian*.

In retrospect, however, Wister did mention one other who influenced his character. On his first western trip, in 1885, he met a man named Morgan, a Virginian, who was the proprietor of a stage stop. Morgan's wife was ill and Wister recorded in his diary how taken he was with the man's extreme gentleness in caring for his wife. Almost fifty years later, in the preface of *The Writings of Owen Wister: The Virginian*, Wister was to say that this man was the original inspiration for his Virginian. What can be made of this? In one sense, not very much. This was a fleeting meeting with someone who certainly did not inspire a picture of a cowboy. But, in another sense, this chance meeting probably did trigger something important in Wister's mind. One of the most striking characteristics of the Virginian was his quiet gentleness toward both women and horses, so at odds with the general stereotype of the cowboy at the time. Wister was obviously greatly drawn to southern manners at their best. This later became abundantly clear when he wrote *Lady Baltimore*, a sympathetic study of upper-class Charleston. What so caught the public's imagination when the Virginian appeared fully developed in 1902 was his combination of the western democratic spirit and the manners of the Old South. Wister had created a hero who was unlike any of the dime-novel cowboys who went before him.

It was not a coincidence that Wister chose a Virginian for his hero. He was consciously distancing his hero from both the literary stereotype of the time and from the average American cowboy, both of whom had Texas origins. Wister was not at all fond of Texas, and he was not greatly drawn to the typical Texas cowboy. His fastidious upbringing caused him to draw back from the bumptious, swaggering, coarse, and violent cowboy that he, fairly or unfairly, associated with Texas. And there were a great number of this sort of cowboy who had drifted up from Texas to make the cattle towns of Kansas legendary for roughness and violence.

Wister made it very clear in his 1893 journal why his cowboy hero would not be a Texan. In a passage omitted by his daughter in the published version, he had this to say:

> It is unlucky for Texas that so large a part of her people come from the Southern poor white trash. It is said of them that they have all the vices of the peasant and none of his virtues. They live in the dregs of dirt and poverty. ... The men seldom have the courage to work steadily at any honest calling; but they are bold enough to shoot their enemy in the back any time they can catch him not looking. I have heard more stories of cowardly murders here than I have ever heard before. And it is a serious thing to be a witness against any man, for he, or his brother or cousin, will shoot you sooner or later. In fact a man who is likely to be

a witness at a trial not yet come off is likely to be killed by some unknown person as he sits by his lighted window in the evening.

The journal goes on to remark on the epidemic of cattle rustling and the shocking number of murders in the area – thirty-four in the previous year and a half. And Wister was no kinder to Texas women, whom he thought put on the most ludicrous airs even though they were of a low class. Wister mentioned a man named Philpot who was known as Price "because Texas ladies could not possibly say Philpot and feel pure."[45]

Wister, of course, was being terribly unfair to the average Texan. Yet it is important to reveal his attitude toward Texans because it caused him to reject the Texas cowboy as his model and to look for someone very different. He sought a striking contrast to the sort of cowboy – a product of dime novels and the Wild West show – then in the popular imagination.

Instead, Wister chose a Virginian as his ideal cowboy. In doing so, he was probably consciously distancing himself from what he so disliked about the South – the ignorance, intolerance, and closed-mindedness of the common people, the marked propensity for violence and lawlessness, the lack of ambition. His cowboy hero, instead, reflected the standards of the older, more cultured Tidewater South, to which he was greatly attracted. Though Wister's cowboy was supposedly of humble origin, thus giving him the popular appeal of a Horatio Alger figure, he reflected the standards of the old planter aristocracy, standards which, of course, were not confined to the aristocracy itself. The Virginian embodied the code of the Old South – the intense pride of region, an understated courage and code of manliness, an elaborate deference to the right sort of woman, an iron moral code, a gentleness unless aroused, and, above all, a prickly sense of honour. No wonder the most popular author in the South in the nineteenth century was Sir Walter Scott. The cavalier tradition of the South was lifted almost literally from the pages of Scott. What Wister obviously did was to transplant this cavalier tradition to the western plains.

The hero's southern background was central to Wister's thinking. His next book after *The Virginian* was very different, based as it was on the elite society of Charleston, South Carolina. But *Lady Baltimore* actually has a close tie with *The Virginian*. Both novels are a close study of cultured southern beliefs and manners, though in very different settings. Wister, of course, had a strong southern background through his mother's side of the family, one that he clearly valued highly.

When *The Virginian* was eventually published, Wister must have been surprised by the instantaneous and overwhelming enthusiasm for the book.

The cover of the first edition of *The Virginian*, 1902. Author's copy.

Wister was not a particularly modest man, but he could not have anticipated how completely his Virginia cowboy would catch the imagination of Americans of all regions and levels of sophistication. The extraordinary outpouring of letters to him showed equal enthusiasm from New England literati and from western cowboys.[46]

Wister had tapped into something vital in the American psyche, and the situation was not without irony. The horrors of the Civil War were still of recent memory. Many thousands of northerners died to eradicate the blight of slavery but, more importantly for most of them, they fought to keep the Union intact. To accomplish this, in the broadest sense, the southern mentality had to be brought to heel. Prior to the Civil War, national politics had become impossible due both to the intransigence of the southern mind on the issue of slavery and the South's determination to preserve a distinct society. So there is a striking irony in the fact that a mere forty years after a war that northerners blamed on an impossible southern outlook, the figure of the Virginian emerged, the embodiment of that intransigent southern outlook.

It took the country by storm. Wister's hero became by far the most popular American folk hero for generations, in all parts of the country. Wister was consciously attempting in his novel to bring about a reconciliation between North and South, but in his wildest imagining he could not have dreamed how successful he would be. Behind the willingness of the North to become reconciled with the South was a general abandonment of the cause of Blacks after Reconstruction. But there was something more. There was something immensely attractive in the southern code of honour and in the southern refusal to be caught up in the frantic northern pursuit of crass material progress. The Virginian, the embodiment of the southern ethic, stood in stark contrast to the vulgar excesses of the Gilded Age, which deeply embarrassed thinking Americans. For millions of Americans, increasingly anxious over the future of an urban, industrial society at a very unattractive stage, the Virginian reassured them that the simple, honest virtues of Jeffersonian America were not lost.

Finally, even if it is plausible to the reader why Wister decided to make his hero a Virginian, there undoubtedly remains a degree of skepticism that Wister chose as his cowboy the particular Virginian who is the preoccupation of this story. Why, after so long, does he suddenly emerge from nowhere? Why is there not the slightest shred of evidence in Wister's voluminous writings that the two ever laid eyes on each other? Considering the number of pretenders to the title, it would be daft to accept uncritically that Everett Johnson was the real Virginian. The West was, and still is, full of old-timers with active imaginations, who embroidered the facts and included themselves in as many stirring events as they could get away with. Was Johnson just one more?

There appears to be almost no proof that Johnson was the Virginian. (See chapter 8.) His case rests mostly on circumstantial evidence and on the credibility of his story. First, the known facts. There is no doubt that he was in Wyoming in 1885, that he worked for the 76, and that he was at Major Wolcott's VR Ranch when Wister visited and saw him roping during a roundup – an important episode in the book. Fred Hesse described him as his trusted man, a kind of assistant foreman. Hesse put Johnson in charge of annual roundups for the 76, and it was Johnson whom Hesse sent to scout Alberta for good range for 76 cattle. But there is no evidence that Johnson and Wister were friends.

Physically, Johnson fit the picture. He was the same age as Wister, just as Wister described the Virginian. Wister had his twenty-fifth birthday at the VR Ranch, and Johnson turned twenty-five in the fall; Wister had described the Virginian as being twenty-four. Johnson was the right build, tall and lean; he had black hair and the rather "swarthy" complexion of the Virginian. He had, by all accounts, a striking appearance, especially while on horseback. And according to Johnson's daughter-in-law, Wister described his eyes exactly – a dark blue, and able to change colour like the moods of the sea.

Wister stressed the Virginian's horsemanship and skill with a rope. Later, in Alberta, Johnson was considered one of the foremost ropers in the Canadian West and was chosen to do a roping exhibition when the future King George V and Queen Mary visited Canada in 1901 and were given a taste of what would eventually become the Calgary Stampede. He was also renowned for his horsemanship in Alberta. He was continually asked to compete against Alberta's top bucking rider, John Ware, to determine who was number one, but he would not compete against Ware because Ware was Black. Johnson's southern roots never left him!

Perhaps the most intriguing aspect of the identity of the Virginian concerns the character that Wister developed. The Virginian was not Wister's first cowboy. In creating Lin McLean, Wister demonstrated his early fidelity to the realistic, typical cowboy – charming, rough, picturesque, somewhat lacking in ambition, and morally ambiguous. Darwin Payne is probably right in arguing that George West served as the primary model. Yet there is the fact that Jim Drummond's real name, according to Johnson, was Lin McLean. So, it would seem that Jim Drummond was also a model for Wister's first important cowboy. If Lin McLean had remained Wister's only cowboy, Wister would never have emerged from the ranks of second-rate writers. Lin McLean's character is interesting and believable, but does little to stir the imagination. His character differs little from what had gone before in cowboy literature.

But somewhere before the emergence of the Virginian in 1892, Wister's mind began to turn to quite a different sort of cowboy. His moment of genius – and it was the only one in his career as a writer – was to create a cowboy who was not at all typical. Yet the enormous success of his character resulted in generations of real and want-to-be cowboys modelling themselves on the Virginian, who was a throwback to the old Virginia planter aristocracy. Wister gave his Virginian a humble background, thus surrounding him with an aura of upward mobility based on character and a desire for improvement through education, one of the most powerful of American beliefs. Otherwise, the character that Wister fashioned, consciously or otherwise, was based not on that of the typical cowboy, but on the characteristics of the old planter aristocracy of the upper South. The Virginian was neither bumptious, crude, boastful or, as was so often the case, bashful to the point of painful silence. The character that Wister created was that of the southern gentleman – with an unshakable code of ethics, an extreme deference to women, a quiet understated assurance, a love of horses and a great gentleness with them (which was not typical at that time on the open range), and an almost exaggerated quiet, unless aroused. Perhaps most characteristic of all, the Virginian embodied the pronounced code of honour by which all southern gentlemen lived – and often, because of the code of the duel – died. The violence latent in the southern gentleman was close to the surface but was of a type very different from the spontaneous and volatile violence of the typical Texas cowboy. At one point in the novel, Wister described his Virginian as having an "aristocratic introspection" that set him apart.

What Wister did was to create a character that transcended his particular surroundings and caught the national imagination in a most extraordinary way. His character had enough of the western patina to appeal to his western readers and strike them as authentic. But the Virginian also possessed the dignity and sophistication to free him of purely local appeal. And, of course, he possessed the mystery that readers found irresistible. How did Wister, who prided himself on the authenticity of his writing, concoct such a character? Well, it is humbly submitted that Wister, beneath the artistic licence of the novelist, was describing the only cowboy he seems to have encountered who represented the aristocratic roots of the Old South that Wister so admired, and later described so fondly in *Lady Baltimore*.

So Johnson was the proper "type" to be considered as Wister's model. But that obviously is not enough to convince the reader. What can be made of Johnson's reminiscences? These are only believable if there is other strong evidence. I could find no proof to back his assertions that there was a teacher named Molly Wood; that he had a friend named Steve, who was supposedly lynched; that there was a baby swapping at the Goose Egg Ranch; that he killed a man named White Clay George in a fashion similar to the killing of Trampas. Certainly local Wyoming lore reinforces his contention that the baby swapping did, in fact, take place at the Goose Egg and that a shootout did take place at the Occidental Hotel in Buffalo, which formed the basis of Wister's story. But no proof exists that Johnson was involved in either incident.

During the years that I tried to find hard evidence for Johnson's version of events, first in Wyoming and then among the Wister papers in Washington, Philadelphia, and Boston, I had some low moments. I could find nothing. In each case, there was an explanation, but still, it was depressing.

There were no letters from Johnson in the Wister papers. Johnson claimed that Wister wrote to him a few times, but he did not answer the letters because he was too self-conscious about his lack of education. And there was another reason. Johnson was not that close to Wister. In 1885, Wister was not particularly likeable, and Johnson had the somewhat humiliating job of looking after him. This situation is certainly hinted at in the novel. The Virginian, for the most part, remained aloof from his eastern charge and rarely allowed an intimacy to develop. Johnson said that it was considered degrading to have to look after an eastern dude and that he took a lot of ribbing from the boys. But, more important, Johnson had a considerable pride of ancestry and a fierce loyalty to Old Virginia, yet he found himself in the humiliating position of being considered an interesting but ignorant cowhand by a snobbish northerner. It is clear from Wister's early journals that he had not yet developed the appreciation of the cowboy "type" which, a decade later, would cause him to write his "Evolution of the Cow-Puncher," his eulogy to the cowboy as the finest type that America had produced. In 1885, it is clear that Wister was careful to associate only with the "right" people and, understandably, he would have exuded an air of condescension toward rough and uneducated cowboys. Johnson, in turn, undoubtedly had his own air of condescension toward this effete easterner who had to be looked after like a child and had not yet learned how to associate easily with cowboys. Exactly this situation is alluded to in the novel.

In each case, the lack of any supporting evidence can be explained. It quickly becomes evident to the researcher of Wyoming history that very little "proof" exists for many events in the 1870s and 1880s. The newspapers and legal records for northern Wyoming are very haphazard indeed. It is virtually impossible to verify anything concerning the life of someone like Johnson who was not an important force in the community. Ordinary cowboys just do not emerge from the newspapers, diaries, or biographies of the period. Even a decade later, the situation was dramatically different, but in the earlier period, people were too busy doing things to bother about recording them.

There is one more argument to add, one that on the surface might appear rather weak but does have some force. Johnson recorded his memories to Jean before a rather substantial body of material involving both Wyoming and Wister emerged. Yet nowhere in his manuscript is there any statement that is clearly false. If Johnson had been spinning a story out of whole cloth, it is almost inevitable that he would have tripped himself up somewhere.

But it was still deeply depressing that I could find so little "proof" of his story in general, and none when it came to the Wister connection. Yet I did not lose faith in his credibility for two simple reasons. My father knew Johnson well. My father was one of the most astute judges of both horseflesh and human character I have known. He could not abide the slightest kind of embroidery in someone's stories. I can remember a number of embarrassing moments in our house when a guest's picturesque story shrivelled under my father's "look." So when he said that Johnson was the real thing, I knew he had to be.

But more importantly, my father and others testified to the existence of practically the only proof linking Johnson to Wister. Shortly after the publication of *The Virginian*, Wister sent a copy to Johnson. Unfortunately, this book and a few letters from Wister were lost in a house fire. But there is no question in my mind that the book existed. Both my father and mother told me that they had seen the book with its inscription: "To the hero from the author. Owen Wister."

6: Alberta (1888–1904)

In the fall of 1885, shortly after spending the summer escorting Wister, Johnson left Wyoming for Alberta, riding his big black horse, Monte (renamed Sailor in Canada). When he reached Alberta, by way of the old Indian trail that ran practically unbroken from Mexico to Canada, he stopped at the ranch of Joe Trollinger on Mosquito Creek, midway between Fort Macleod and Calgary. He looked over the range and was pleased with what he saw. The grass could support far more cattle than could the Powder River country, the land was well sheltered, and he was told that stock wintered easily in the area, famous for its chinook winds. Besides, a cow worth twenty-five dollars in Wyoming went for forty in Alberta.

Fred Hesse had asked him to scout the Alberta range for good grazing land. By 1885, Moreton Frewen was acutely conscious that northern Wyoming was overstocked and was desperately trying to persuade his board in London that as many cattle as possible should be moved to Alberta. As early as 1883, Frewen, who has come down to us in Wyoming history as the quintessential English twit, was ahead of most in predicting the end of the free range in northern Wyoming.[1]

Fred Hesse's reports to Frewen in 1885 undoubtedly reinforced Frewen's belief that the company was facing a crisis. Hesse estimated the loss of cattle over the previous winter at 15 percent, significantly greater than in previous years.[2] The number of calves in 1885 was way down from the previous year, and the 76 herd was down to 48,550 from 55,000. The range in Johnson County was in bad shape from overgrazing. (The earlier refusal of the large ranchers to countenance a lease arrangement was now coming home to roost!) The dividend of the Powder River Cattle Company had been a

Typical ranching country of southern Alberta. The chinook winds in winter dropped their moisture in the mountains and often blew enough snow off the range to allow grazing all winter. Glenbow Archives, NA 67-6.

mere 3 percent in 1884; clearly, some new solution was necessary. So, at roughly the same time that Johnson was looking over the range in Alberta, the shareholders of the 76 sent Dick Frewen in 1885 to look at grazing land in Montana and Alberta. He sent back a glowing report from Fort Macleod, in southern Alberta, and, acting on that report, Moreton Frewen went to Ottawa to pay a visit to his friend Sir John A. Macdonald, prime minister of Canada, to see if the 20 percent import duty on cattle could be waived.[3]

The situation in 1885 was somewhat complicated because, under pressure, Moreton Frewen had resigned as manager of the Powder River company and had been replaced by someone who opposed moving any cattle to Alberta. But by 1886, after some threatened resignations on the Board by those opposed to moving herds to Alberta, the opponents were finally persuaded that the herds should be moved – largely because of the very serious overgrazing of the northern Wyoming range. Horace Plunkett became manager and ordered Hesse to make the necessary arrangements to move cattle north. There was now some urgency in the situation because the cattle had to cross the Canadian border before September 1, 1886, in order to avoid the import duty. To complicate matters, the man who was to supervise the drive, E. W. Murphy, was caught in the middle of the feud between Plunkett and the Frewen brothers. He had been fired in 1885 for being short on the count of some cattle being moved to the Powder River range.[4] The Frewens thought the charge was absurd. But Plunkett refused to rehire him, undoubtedly because Murphy was too loyal to the Frewens, who were making Plunkett's life miserable with their attempts in London to control the board.

Eventually, in May 1886, the responsibility for the drive to Alberta was taken out of Plunkett's hands, and Murphy was rehired to supervise the drive. Johnson was sent north that same month to scout the trail, and on June 25, 7,500 head were started north with Johnson as trail boss. He had carefully studied the route that the cattle should take, stopping briefly in the Judith Basin in Montana to visit a budding artist friend named Charlie Russell, whom he knew from several roundups. The cattle were divided into three herds, which Johnson trailed slowly over the five hundred miles to Mosquito Creek, after first killing all the late calves, which would not have survived the winter. The cattle arrived in Alberta in August in good shape, ready to face the winter, and just beating the import duty deadline. They were then driven to the land that Johnson had scouted in 1885, which the company had now leased in E. W. Murphy's name – grazing land on Mosquito Creek and the Little Bow River, midway between Fort Macleod and Calgary.[5] (The land was leased for twenty-one years at one cent an acre per year.) Murphy was pleased, reporting that the cattle had come through well and that Alberta had ten times the grass that Wyoming had.[6]

Frewen decided to lease land in Alberta because Canadian law gave him security of tenure on his leased land. There would be no overstocking, as was the case in Wyoming by 1885. He intended to keep the stock in Alberta for two years because Canadian law stipulated that American lessees could circumvent the 20 percent import duty if they kept the cattle in Alberta for at least that long.[7]

Moreton Frewen came to Alberta in early October to inspect the herd, and he, too, was well pleased, until he happened to drop a cartridge into a campfire, which exploded and embedded some rather painful shrapnel in his leg.[8] When he saw the Alberta range, Frewen felt vindicated in his view that as many cattle as possible should be moved north, and he wrote Clara the same month that he hoped all the Powder River cattle could be moved to Alberta – that it was the only salvation for the company.[9] Seeing the relatively virgin Alberta range only confirmed his view of several months earlier when he had visited Wyoming and reported to Clara: "I don't see how we can avoid heavy loss this winter again. It is impossible to disguise it, the business has quite broke down on these ranges. There never can be any recovery. ... I dread the coming winter; if it is a severe one, half the cattle in Wyoming will die for sure."[10] What needs stressing here is that it was not just the freak winter of 1886 to 1887 that destroyed the old era of the open range in Wyoming. The writing had already been on the wall for several years.

The winter of 1886–87 was also severe in Alberta, but the 76 herd survived reasonably well, with few losses.[11] Other ranchers didn't fare so well. A. E. Cross on the a7 lost 60 percent of his stock, Walter Skrine, 70 percent. The average loss in the Calgary area was 25 percent and in the Medicine Hat and Highwood country, 50 percent.[12] But the situation was far worse in Wyoming. Fred Hesse reported in the spring of 1887 that the Powder River herds just melted away; that winter killed 75 percent of the herd.[13] The 76's Alberta herds thrived on their new range, but the company could send no more cattle north to Canada from the ravaged grasslands of Wyoming because the Canadian import duty was now in place. By 1888 the Powder River company was facing bankruptcy; by 1889, the Wyoming herd was down to 13,000 head.[14] The ordinary shareholders had lost their entire investment – so the company was forced to sell the Alberta herd.[15] They sold it in 1889 to Sir John Lister-Kaye of the Canadian Agricultural Coal and Colonization Company, to become part of the enormous Stair 76 Ranch. In 1890, Pierre Wibaux, a Frenchman ranching in Montana, bought what was left of the Powder River herd.[16]

Lister-Kaye, in many ways, was the Moreton Frewen of the Canadian range, a flamboyant English aristocrat with grand ideas. His dream was to form English colonies in the Canadian West and to this end, he imported Englishmen, horses, sheep, and pigs, which he established on ten different farms and ranches. But by 1895, his ventures had soured and, like Frewen, he was replaced as manager by his board and eventually frozen out. The company continued until the disastrous winter of 1906–7 in Alberta, which killed about two-thirds of the livestock. In 1909, the directors disposed of all their land to the meatpacking firm of Gordon, Ironside and Fares (for whom Johnson later worked). That firm operated the 76 until the 1920s when it sold the ranch to Canada Packers, thus ending the 76.[17]

Meanwhile, Johnson had returned to Wyoming in the fall of 1886, leaving behind four of his crew who decided to stay in Alberta – Roy Cowan, Tom Lusk, Blue Osborne, and a cowboy Johnson referred to as Nigger Tom. But he was not to remain there for very long. He could see that the great days of Wyoming ranching were gone. The Powder River Cattle Company was going under, and if that great company could not make it, there was little hope for the other big ranches. He was also greatly disturbed by the atmosphere of hostility between the old-timers and both the new settlers and the cowboys who were trying to establish ranches on land claimed by the big ranches.

Hunting party in the Wind River country, 1887. Wister is standing, pouring a drink for their Native guide. Laurie and Jean Johnson believe that the man second from the right, with his hand on the tent flap, is Everett Johnson. Photo by Copley Amary. American Heritage Center, University of Wyoming.

But before he left permanently for Alberta, he was to have two brief encounters with Owen Wister, who had come back to Wyoming in the summer of 1887, this time to hunt in the Wind River country. Wister had written to Johnson of his plans and had suggested that they somehow meet. Johnson said that he caught up with Wister's party several days out of Fort Washakie and had a short visit. Although there is no mention of Johnson in Wister's journal for 1887, Wister does mention in his journal entry for August 9 that a cowboy had come into camp when they were about ninety miles from Fort Washakie. Several days earlier, Wister had recorded that he had shot a magpie and stewed it for dinner. Johnson, without knowing what Wister had written, remembered that Wister had shot a hawk and stewed it. So it seems possible that this cowboy was indeed Johnson.

And there is, perhaps, a small mystery involved in this meeting. In Wister's published journals and letters, his daughter has included a picture of this hunting party that Copley Amory, one of Wister's two Boston friends on the trip, provided. The caption identifies George West as the person seated third from the left. But all the members of the hunting party are identified in the caption. So who took the picture? Johnson's son, Laurie, and his daughter-in-law, Jean, have said that there is no question in their minds that the man identified as George West was actually Johnson. The cowboy in the photograph bears his unmistakable attitude, and the scar on his chin from an Indian scrape in Arizona is evident in an enlargement.

Wister came back again to the Wind River country in 1888, and Johnson saw him again briefly, but he gave no details of the meeting. The fact is, Johnson liked Wister but didn't attach much importance to the friendship. All his life he was very reticent about his friendship with Wister. It was his friends who had worked on the VR with him in 1885, Roy Cowan, Monte Cunningham, and Lorenzo Smith, who noised it about, after the novel came out, that Johnson was clearly the Virginian. Johnson put far more stock in his friendships with his Wyoming cowboy friends.

Before leaving Wyoming forever, Johnson paid a short visit in 1888 to his mother, who lived near Rochester, and then returned to Wyoming to say his goodbyes. Although he would remain fiercely loyal to the country of his birth, Alberta was to be his home for the rest of his life. As he rode north driving a team and buckboard and trailing his favourite cut horse, Johnson noticed that much of Montana looked overstocked and overgrazed. And he could see the changes that were taking place in the range industry. Barbed wire was intruding itself everywhere he looked, and cowboys were losing the aura of the free range, spending less time in the saddle than in the somewhat demeaning tasks of fencing, haying, and tending crops.

On reaching Alberta, Johnson stopped for a time at the Quorn Ranch, on the south side of Sheep Creek, or Stony Crossing as it was then called, just west of Okotoks. An English syndicate that ran about 5,000 head of cattle owned the Quorn, one of the big ranches of southern Alberta. But the owners were mainly interested in horses. The ranch was named for the famous Quorn hunt, one of the foremost in England, and the real aim was to produce horses for the British Army and for the English hunting field. To this end, one hundred Irish mares and a half dozen top Thoroughbred stallions had been imported. At this time, the Quorn was raising the finest horses in Alberta.[18]

Johnson recalled that the first night there, he went in to dinner and the first man to sit down was a tall Black cowboy. Johnson stood back, expecting the man to be ordered out, but all the other men sat down, and Johnson reluctantly did the same. He had never before sat at dinner with a Black man, and he could not understand how the other cowboys seemed to be on

John Ware and his family, 1896. Ware came to Alberta up the cattle trail from Texas and was considered by many to be Alberta's finest bronco rider. Glenbow Archives NA 263-1.

equal terms with him. He happened to be in presence of John Ware, one of the most respected cowboys on the Alberta range. Johnson later grew to have great regard for Ware but could never bring himself to be familiar with him.[19] The talk at dinner was mostly of horses. The Quorn's horses were clearly very fine, but no match in toughness to the cow ponies that had evolved from the Arab and Barb stock of Spain and North Africa. In the Quorn breeding program can be seen the beginnings of a major Alberta industry that owed much to the influence of the early English ranchers.

From the Quorn, Johnson moved on to Calgary, where he helped a friend, Charlie Perry, move some horses to the Ghost River country west of the city. This spectacular foothills country, with the backdrop of the Rocky Mountains, would be the future home of Johnson's son Laurie and his daughter-in-law Jean. The family is still ranching there. On the way back to Calgary, he stopped to visit his two old friends from the VR, Roy Cowan and Blue Osborne. Then south to the Bar U Ranch, where he had agreed

Fred Stimson, shareholder and a manager of the North West Cattle Company, which owned the Bar U Ranch. His roots in the eastern townships of Quebec are very clear in this portrait. Glenbow Archives, NA 117-1.

to be foreman, replacing George Lane in 1889.[20] Lane had been the ranch's original foreman, but he left the ranch to go into the business of buying cattle. Johnson agreed to go to the Bar U when the 76 folded. The ranch was owned largely by the Allan family of Montreal, owners of the Allan Steamship Lines and Canada's richest family. Fred Stimson, one of the shareholders of the North-West Cattle Company, as the Bar U syndicate was called, managed the ranch. When Johnson was hired by Stimson, he came with an impressive reputation. An early rancher, Lachlin McKinnon, described Johnson as "one of the top cow-hands who came up from Wyoming."[21] This was a view seconded by D. H. Andrews of the 76, who now ran several ranches for the Canadian Land and Ranch Company. His recommendation for Johnson stated: "A first rate cowman, in fact, I think about the best all around cowman in this country, and he is very good with young horses."[22]

The Bar U buildings looking west. The last building on the left was Fred Stimson's house. Glenbow Archives, NA 466-12.

The Bar U Ranch buildings with Pekisko Creek in the foreground. The ranch is now a National Historic Site. Author's photo.

The Prince of Wales and George Lane, owner of Bar U, in 1919 during the Royal visit of that year. As a result of this visit, the Prince of Wales fell in love with the ranching country of southern Alberta and decided to buy an adjoining ranch, the Bedingfeld Ranch, which he renamed the EP Ranch (for Edward Prince). Glenbow Archives, NB 16-149.

The Bar U was situated in the heart of Alberta's ranching country, in rolling foothills country southwest of Calgary, with the Rocky Mountains close at hand. The ranch possessed some of the best cattle grazing land in the West. Sheltered timbered valleys protected the stock in the winter, and frequent chinook winds cleared the land enough for grazing. As late as the 1950s, these winds allowed the ranch to feed very little hay through the winter.[23]

Stimson established the Bar U in 1882 and was the driving force in the formation of the syndicate. The ranch started with a capitalization of $150,000. Sir Hugh Allan and his brother Andrew each had 250 shares, which together represented a third of the total shares.[24] The foundation herd of 3,000 head had been brought from Idaho by Tom Lynch and a group of cowboys that included John Ware. By 1890, when Johnson was foreman, the Bar U had over 10,000 cattle and 800 horses, including several superior imported stallions. Among them was the imported Thoroughbred stud Terror, one of the finest horses Johnson ever saw. At this point, the ranch had 158,000 acres under lease.[25] Stimson, like his neighbour C. M. Martin on the Quorn Ranch, was attempting to breed hunting horses for the British market.[26]

Fred Stimson had married Mary Greeley Smith in 1886. When she came down with scarlet fever in 1889, a nurse was sought. Fortunately, one was found who had just arrived from England and was staying with her uncle, Joe Laycock, at a ranch just north of Calgary called the Grange. Mary Bigland came to the Bar U as Mrs. Stimson's constant companion. She and Johnson soon saw much of each other, since he was the only one that Mrs. Stimson trusted to carry her. They soon decided to marry.

Ebb and Mary were married at the Grange on November 18, 1891, by the minister of Knox United Church in Calgary, Reverend Herdman, who may have been a bit startled by Johnson's choice of best man – Harry Longabaugh, also known as the Sundance Kid. He was in Alberta at the time working for the Bar U. Johnson was thirty-one at the time and Mary twenty-four. He was listed as Presbyterian, and she as "English Church" – Anglican. It is not known where they spent their honeymoon – perhaps at some special spot in the Rockies.

It seems that the Sundance Kid came to Alberta in about 1891, perhaps at Johnson's urging, and worked for both the McHugh brothers on the H2 Ranch and for the Bar U, breaking horses. He also worked at some point for the OH Ranch, north of the Bar U. Longabaugh was twenty-five in 1891 and was wanted at the time by the law in Wyoming for threatening a deputy sheriff. Two years earlier, he had been sentenced to eighteen months in jail at Sundance, Wyoming, for horse stealing – hence the adopted name. In August 1891, he was charged with cruelty to a horse while at the Bar U, but the charge was dropped. Perhaps this is why he was laid off as a "horse-breaker" for the Bar U. He spent the winter of 1892–93 in Calgary as a partner in the Grand Central Hotel, but the partnership with Frank Hamilton went sour for some reason and Longabaugh returned to the US to begin his fabled career as an outlaw.[27]

Soon after they married, Mary, for some reason, convinced Johnson that they should leave the Bar U. He did so reluctantly and took up the job of foreman for the Military Colonization Company Ranch east of Calgary. It is hard to imagine Johnson being happy on the ranch, which had been started by the very eccentric General Thomas Bland Strange to raise horses for the British Army and to train young Englishmen in the arts of ranching. Strange had left by the time Johnson became foreman. It became Johnson's job to deal with a succession of English visitors who came to learn the art of

Form DVS 2

PROVINCE OF ALBERTA
DEPARTMENT OF PUBLIC HEALTH
DIVISION OF VITAL STATISTICS

FOR USE OF THE DEPARTMENT ONLY
08- 1471-1891

REGISTRATION OF MARRIAGE

BRIDEGROOM

1. PRINT name in full: JOHNSON (Surname) — Cyril Everett (Christian names)
2. Trade, profession or kind of work: Foreman
3. Kind of industry or business: North West Cattle Ranchers
4. Bachelor / Widower / Divorced: Bachelor (State which)
5. Age: 31 (In years)
6. Religious denomination: Presbyterian
7. Citizenship (see marginal definition):
8. Racial Origin (see marginal definition):
9. Residence: High River, Alberta
10. Place of birth: Virginia, U.S.A.
11. Name of father: JOHNSON (Surname) — George (Christian names)
12. Maiden name of mother: Lucretea (Surname)
13. Birthplace: Father — Mother

BRIDE

14. PRINT name in full: Bigland (Surname) — Mary Eleanor (Christian names)
15. Trade, profession or kind of work: (If at home, state household duties)
16. Kind of industry or business:
17. Spinster / Widow / Divorced: Spinster (State which)
18. Age: 24 (In years)
19. Religious denomination: English Church
20. Citizenship (see marginal definition):
21. Racial Origin (see marginal definition):
22. Residence before Marriage: Calgary, Alberta
23. Place of birth: England
24. Name of father: BIGLAND (Surname) — John (Christian names)
25. Maiden name of mother: Eleanor (Surname)
26. Birthplace: Father — Mother
27. Date of Marriage: 18 day of November 1891 19...
28. Place of Marriage: Grange Farm, Calgary, Alberta
29. Licence Number: ? Name of Issuer ?
30. Marginal notations (Departmental use only)

31. Signature of Groom / Bride
32. Signatures of Witnesses:
    Name: Harry Longabough — Address: Calgary, Alberta
    Name: Maggie Laycock — Address: Calgary, Alberta

I certify the above stated particulars are true to the best of my knowledge and belief.

Officiating Clergyman or Marriage Commissioner:
Signature: J.C. Herdman
Address: Calgary, Alberta
Religious Denomination: ————
Certificate of Registration Number:

Filed at Calgary, Alberta on the 21 day of November 1891
District Registration No. ? — M.L. Bernard, Signature of District Registrar
(SEE OTHER SIDE)

THE COWBOY LEGEND

General Thomas Bland Strange, an autocratic military figure, was the driving force in the forming of the Military Colonization Company Ranch, whose central purpose was raising horses for the British army and training young Englishmen in the arts of ranching. Glenbow Archives, NA 1847-2.

Previous page: Although John's given names are transposed, and his mother's name is misspelled, as are those of his best man, Harry Longabaugh, and the minister, Rev. J. C. Herdman, this is the genuine wedding certificate of Everett and Mary Johnson, November 1891.

ranching in the wilds of Alberta. It was probably all too reminiscent of his days on the 76, babysitting effete easterners and English aristocracy.

The ranch adjoined the Blackfoot Reserve, and Johnson hired a number of Blackfoot cowboys and learned enough of their language to communicate with them. Chief Old Brass was a frequent visitor. It is important to pause here to point out that Johnson, the Indian fighter, under quite different circumstances became a friend of his Native neighbours, enough so to call Old Brass a good friend. The Blackfoot had not taken part in the 1885 Rebellion, and Johnson could recall no tensions with his Blackfoot neighbours, who were trying very hard to settle in as farmers.

After leaving the Bar U, Johnson stayed only a short time as foreman at the MCC Ranch. In 1893, Gordon and Ironside persuaded him to locate a ranch for them, which they named the Two Bar, in the Wintering Hills south of the Red Deer River. Johnson laid out the buildings in a manner similar to the Bar U. Here, he and Mary had their two sons, Robert Everett and Laurence Branch. In later years, Mary spoke of the Two Bar in a way that made it clear that these were very happy days. Johnson later became a cattle buyer for the company of Gordon, Ironside and Fares who, by 1906, were the largest cattle exporters in the world.[28]

Jean Johnson recalled several of Mary's stories from this time, especially one incident when Johnson was having trouble bringing in a bunch of skittish horses and was trying to corral them. Thinking she could help, she rushed out of the house, which had the effect of scattering the horses "from Hell to breakfast." When she yelled to Johnson, "What should I do now?," he answered, "Go in the house and hide under the bed."

She also recalled, with obvious pride, an incident on Calgary's main street, Stephen Avenue, which at the time was a mixture of mud and construction material. Johnson was riding along the street just as a runaway team and democrat went tearing past. He took off in pursuit, freeing his rope as he caught up. Just as he came even, a large pile of lumber loomed in his path. Mary said it was quite a sight watching him leap the pile and on the landing stride throw a loop over the heads of both horses. The street was busy; his quick action and skill with a rope probably prevented a nasty accident.

****

Most of the big ranches in early Alberta, like their counterparts in Wyoming, owned very little land. The Bar U, for instance, one of the biggest ranches in the Canadian West, at first did not own a single acre of deeded land, although its original two leases in 1881 totalled 114,000 acres. It was not until 1891, almost a decade after its formation, that Stimson applied for a homestead entry. The census that year showed seventeen people living on the ranch. The census also gave an interesting "snapshot" of the Alberta ranching frontier a decade after its inception. It listed those in the ranching community by background: 80 percent came from eastern Canada or Britain (42 percent from eastern Canada and 37 percent from Britain); 17 percent were American.[29] By the next census of 1901, these percentages would change significantly. By 1901, there were fewer American foremen like Johnson on the big ranches and also fewer American cowboys. But the census showed an increase in Americans who crossed the border to take up farms and small ranches.[30] The great American influx into Alberta in

The Bar U general roundup of 1901. The technology of ranching in Alberta was exactly the same as in the American West, but one striking difference is seen in the middle of this photograph. The presence of the Mountie spoke of a very differenct tradition of law on the Canadian ranching frontier. Glenbow Archives, NA 1035-5.

the 1890s went mostly to the farm sector.[31] The statistics point to an important fact. The Canadian ranching frontier in its formative period was overwhelmingly Anglo-Canadian or British. It was only later, when social, legal, and political institutions had already jelled, that Americans began to arrive in numbers, many of them to become small-scale ranchers.

The Alberta ranching frontier that Johnson came to in the 1880s was in many ways similar to that he had left in Wyoming, but there were a few not-so-subtle differences. Certainly, the geography was similar, not so much to Wyoming as to Montana. The Powder River country was far more arid and treeless than the Alberta ranching country in the foothills of the Canadian Rockies. And the practice of ranching was much the same. In terms of technology, the Alberta ranching frontier was an extension of the American frontier. And the Native peoples, who by now had been shunted onto reserves to make way for white settlement, were separated artificially by the Medicine Line. But there the similarities ended. The cultural atmosphere of the Alberta ranching community shared some similarities with its

6: Alberta

Bar U cowboys during the roundup of 1901. A NWMP stock inspector on far left. Charlie McKinnon, foreman of the Bar U, is on the left, boots in the foreground and face hidden. Glenbow Archives, NA 1035-6.

American counterpart, but it was far more English than American and the political and legal set-up was very different. This ranching community was also deeply influenced by a very different frontier past.

From the landing of English colonists at Jamestown in 1607 and at Plymouth Rock in 1620, the American frontier witnessed three centuries of almost constant warfare with Native peoples as Americans moved west, intent on dispossessing these peoples of their lands. As Robert Utley, the distinguished historian of the American frontier concluded, the American frontier saw three centuries of "mutual incomprehension"; neither side was willing to compromise or find some middle ground.[32]

The Canadian frontier developed very differently, largely because of geography – and botany! Canada is uniquely blessed with an arterial network of lakes and rivers, which became the country's early means of transportation and communication. Only 5 percent of Canada is arable. Because of eastern Canada's dense forests, most early travel, of necessity, was by water, using Native bark canoes. And these bark canoes were unique to

Branding a steer, 1893. The practice of "heeling" a steer (throwing a loop under a hind leg) and dragging it to the branding fire has not changed on many ranches since Texas herds started heading north on the cattle trails. Glenbow Archives, NA 5182-1.

Canada. The map of the growth of the birch tree is essentially a map of Canada. As it happens, the bark of the birch tree is the only bark in the world capable of being formed into a good canoe, because the lines of growth of birch bark are transverse, unlike all other barks, whose lines of growth are longitudinal. Unlike longitudinal bark, birch bark can be cut and shaped into the elegant and functional shapes of the surprisingly tough Native birch bark canoe. And this birch bark canoe was found only in Canada and small areas of the northern United States.[33]

Most of Canada lies north of what geographers call the Canadian necklace – the axis of water that begins with the St. Lawrence River on the east and extends west through the Great Lakes, Lakes Winnipeg and Manitoba, the Saskatchewan River system, and, finally, the Athabasca River, Great Slave and Great Bear Lakes and the Mackenzie River to the Arctic Ocean. Above that line lies the Canadian Shield and below, the relatively thin line of agricultural Canada. Because of the unique geography of the Canadian frontier, Canada's borders were defined by canoe exploration and, even though Alberta's ranching frontier was greatly influenced, as was the American frontier, by the horse, this ranching frontier's institutions and customs were mostly determined by the frontier of the canoe, by the autocratic control of the Hudson's Bay Company and, later, by the equally autocratic control of the federal government. The local self-determination of the American frontier was conspicuously absent from the later Canadian frontier that included the ranch country of Alberta.

The result of this geography is the fact that when the French settled along the St. Lawrence River in the early seventeenth century, they quickly realized that it was far more profitable to enter into mutually beneficial trade alliances with Native groups than to dispossess them of land largely unsuited to agriculture. Canada's future lay with water and the bark canoe of Native peoples, in a land with more navigable water systems than any other place on earth. Later on, Native groups in southern Canada were forced from arable land, but only after peaceful relations had been firmly established with French fur traders from the St. Lawrence and English traders from Hudson Bay. When the North West Mounted Police came west in 1874, they were not met with hostility; instead, they were able to take advantage of a legacy of almost three centuries of mutually profitable trade relations on the Canadian frontier. Although the Mounted Police, on their march west in 1874, feared Blackfoot hostility because of the Blackfoot's history of aggression toward American fur traders on the Missouri River, they met with none. The Blackfoot had been trading pemmican for many decades at Fort Edmonton and had formed peaceful relations with these traders. The Mounted Police could thank the HBC for the Blackfoot's friendly reception.

On the political side, when the Dominion of Canada inherited the fur trade's vast domain at the time of Confederation, it had to quickly develop policies and laws for this territory. Canada's Fathers of Confederation consciously forged institutions that were the opposite of those in the United States. As much power as possible should be given to the central government, and there would be no loose talk about the "pursuit of happiness." As Donald Creighton, one of Canada's pre-eminent historians, has said, Canada was brought into Confederation by a generation of mid-Victorian colonials who valued the political system they had inherited and "would have been sceptical about both the utility and the validity of abstract notions such as the social contract and the natural and inalienable rights of man."[34] Canada's fathers were less taken with noble sentiments than with making things work in a practical way. To them, the doctrine that mankind on the loose was innately perfectible smacked of pure humbug.

These same men determined policy for the development of the Canadian West. In sharp contrast to the philosophy of the Northwest Ordinance, the blueprint of the American westward movement, which gave enormous scope to local self-determination, Ottawa's territorial policy kept tight control of all aspects of development in the formative period of the North-West Territories, now southern Saskatchewan and Alberta. A small council, appointed by Ottawa, governed the area. And the federal government completely controlled territorial law and Native relations, in a conscious attempt to reverse what most Canadians saw as a glaring failure in American territorial policy.

In crafting its western policy, Ottawa was continuing an established practice in the West. As part of Confederation, the British government ceded to Canada the vast domain of the Hudson's Bay Company (HBC), at that time the largest private fiefdom in the world – one-twelfth of the entire world! The Company had held autocratic sway over Canada's West in a fashion that left little room for democratic self-expression. All policy was in the hands of its governor, Sir George Simpson, who imposed rules of conduct and policies of trade with the Native peoples that dictated peace. The original charter of the Company had imposed on it the obligation of preserving law and order in its territory, and it was an obligation that the Company took seriously after it acquired a total monopoly of the Canadian fur trade in 1821, the year of its amalgamation with its rival, the North West Company.

The year 1821 was a watershed in the history of the Canadian fur trade and Native-white relations on the Canadian frontier. The moment allows the historian to make several important arguments regarding the nature of the North American frontier. Canadians, in a somewhat insufferable way, love to tell their American neighbours how much more peaceful the Canadian frontier has always been. Not so! In the era of intense fur trade rivalry before 1821, the fur trade frontier in Canada was extremely violent, largely because of the staggering quantities of alcohol used to induce trade. In the maddened pursuit of profit, a number of fur traders were murdered, and Natives were debauched with liquor by unscrupulous traders. In other words, the western Canadian frontier was much like the American frontier; unscrupulous whites had virtually no restraints placed upon them. As a result, Native relations were extremely volatile.

But all this changed dramatically after the Seven Oaks Massacre of 1816, in which the Métis of the North West Company killed Robert Semple, the governor of the HBC's Red River colony, and twenty of his men. As a result of this incident and because of the general tone of lawlessness in fur country, the British government forced the two rival companies to amalgamate in 1821; they came together under the Hudson's Bay Company's name. The atmosphere of liquor and violence between companies changed overnight to one of autocratic, centralized authority. The new governor, Sir George Simpson, issued a series of edicts outlawing liquor in most of Indian Country and establishing a stern code of behaviour toward Native peoples. Literally overnight, he changed the course of Canadian history, imposing on the Canadian West a relative harmony that was in striking contrast both to former days on the Canadian frontier and to the atmosphere south of the border. The critical issue, of course, is that Simpson had no qualms about stifling the self-expression of that small element of riff-raff that, on the American western frontier, knew few restraints and was responsible for most of the violence and disastrous Native relations.[35]

After 1821, the policy of strict social control on the frontier became the Canadian trademark. And when the Canadian government took over the HBC domain after Confederation, it merely continued the company's almost feudal policy of centralized autocracy. All important aspects of western development were tightly held by the federal government – the territorial council, land policy, Native relations and, most critically, the law.

One of the first acts of the government in Ottawa, on acquiring the new domain from the HBC at the time of Confederation, was to establish a police force to assert sovereignty and bring order to the area. The North-West Mounted Police were crucial to the process of continuing the HBC legacy of relative harmony between races. But they were mainly there to oversee the process of making treaties with the plains tribes and shunting them to one side so that white settlement could proceed without fuss. The Mounted Police were the main instruments in this process. Sir John A. Macdonald's National Policy aimed to fill the West by building a transcontinental railway and then enticing settlers with the promise of free homesteads on the American model, with the ultimate goal of replacing the Native hunters with a West full of white farmers.

If one is looking for the principal difference between the Canadian and American plains frontiers, the Mounted Police are the key, both in the atmosphere they created on the Canadian Plains and in the attitudes and policies that led to their formation. Essentially the Mounted Police were the product of a nineteenth-century Canadian belief in strong central government and law, and an equally strong anti-Americanism. The governing generation after Confederation was very consciously attempting to create a counterbalance on this continent to the American "experiment." They believed without question that extreme democracy, strong state rights, and especially a relaxed attitude toward the law had done terrible harm to American development. The American Civil War, Canadians argued, was the logical outcome of a bad system. So Canadians, with an air of smug superiority tinged with grudging envy for the vitality and economic dynamism of America, consciously set about to create something quite different.

The starting point was a more sober view of mankind. Canadian leaders were convinced that American notions of liberty and egalitarianism had led to a minority of undisciplined Americans perverting their society.

Remington sketch of the North-West Mounted Police, *Harper's Weekly*, October 1888. The stern military bearing is a striking contast to western American sheriffs and the Texas Rangers, a loose militia with a great facility with guns.

Canadians constantly commented on the staggering levels of violence and dismal Native relations in the US and concluded that a lack of both social deference and stern law were the principal causes. The Canadian governing class believed very firmly that the lower orders in society must not be allowed the self-expression that was accepted in the US. Clearly, Americans had lost John Stuart Mills' definition of liberty – that it must not infringe on the liberty of others. Canadian political rulers believed that American democracy had all too often become clear licence, the negation of true liberty. Canadian leaders emphatically placed order and stability before personal liberty.

When the North-West Mounted Police was created in 1873 to bring order to and assert sovereignty over Canada's new western empire, it was established as a federal force with almost absolute power over the early destiny of the Canadian plains frontier. At first, they were the sole federal presence in the North-West Territories, other than a few surveyors. They were responsible for all aspects of government policy and quickly became the symbol of both the official Canadian presence on the plains and of the Canadian style.

6: Alberta

In theory, the NWMP established a police state in the Canadian West. The officers were either stipendiary magistrates or justices of the peace. Thus the British system of law, so cherished by Canadians, was theoretically subverted. At first, the Mounted Police held all aspects of the law in their own hands and blandly ignored the independence of the judiciary, so central to the British system. Yet, it can be argued, it was precisely this subversion of the law that resulted in the success of the Mounted Police – and their popularity. They were able to control, with relative ease, the small disreputable white element on the frontier which, under the American system of divided legal jurisdictions and ultra-democratic law, was allowed to run amok, terrifying both Native people and frontier towns.[36] Because the Mounted Police, at first, had complete control over all aspects of the law, their justice was swift. This is a critical consideration when comparing Mountie law to that on the western American frontier. One of the central justifications on the American frontier for vigilantism was that constituted law was too slow and cumbersome – and costly! Too many slick lawyers got criminals off on technicalities. One of the major reasons for the complete absence of vigilantism on the Canadian frontier was that Mountie law was clear and direct – and timely.

The Mounted Police, being removed from the pressure of local influence and, at first, in absolute control of the entire legal system, soon established an atmosphere of order that was in dramatic contrast to that below the border. The stock explanation is that the western movement in the US was spontaneous, while on the western Canadian frontier the law, in the form of the Mounted Police, preceded settlement, rather than following it. This simplistic line of reasoning explains practically nothing. What is important is what the law did when it got there. Law is not a uniform commodity that just happened to find its way to the Canadian West at an earlier stage of frontier development. Law is a fundamental expression of a nation's character, and the legal system that the government imposed on the Canadian plains was very different from the code that shaped the American West.

It is fascinating to see these early Mounties through the eyes of one particular American immigrant from Iowa and the Dakotas. Wallace Stegner recounted his instant impression of the Queen's law hanging in the waiting room of the courthouse at Weyburn, Saskatchewan – the framed portraits of Mounties, representing Canadian law in the West. It was an impression that remained unchanged after half a century.

> The resolute, disciplined faces and the red coats glimmering in the shabby room filled me with awe. I can see the portraits yet;

they were burned into me as if I had been photographic film.... They hang in my head, unaltered and undimmed after nearly half a century, static, austere, symbolic. And if I had known all the history of Canada and the United States I could not have picked out a more fitting symbol of what made the Canadian West a different West from the American....

The important thing is the instant, compelling impressiveness of this man in the scarlet tunic. I think I know, having felt it, the truest reason why the slim force of the Mounted Police was so spectacularly successful, why its esprit de corps was so high and its prestige so great. I think I know how law must have looked to Sioux and Blackfoot when the column of redcoats rode westward in the summer of 1874.

Never was the dignity of the uniform more carefully cultivated, and rarely has the ceremonial quality of imperial law and order been more dramatically exploited. ... But given the historical context, red meant to an Indian of the 1870s friendship and protection, and it is to the honor of an almost overpublicized force that having dramatized in scarlet the righteousness of the law it represented, it lived up to the dramatization.[37]

Even before the Mounted Police arrived in the West, the legal set-up for the western frontier was being established in Ottawa. The 1873 act which created the North-West Mounted Police established a legal framework for the area. Lesser cases were to be tried without jury by two stipendiary magistrates sitting together or by a judge of the Manitoba Court of Queen's Bench. Charges punishable by death were to be sent to the Manitoba court. There was to be a further refining of this act in 1875 and, by 1877, all criminal cases could be tried in the NWT. The first stipendiary magistrates, the senior judicial officers, were appointed in 1876, two years after the arrival of the Mounted Police.[38]

The role of the stipendiary magistrate was terminated with the creation of the Supreme Court of the North-West Territories in 1886, but it should be stressed that, from the moment of the arrival of the NWMP in 1874, effective law was established in the West and only refined by later federal enactments. A rowdy West was never allowed to germinate. Since one of the Supreme Court judges appointed in 1886 was the former Commissioner of the Mounted Police, James F. Macleod, the continuity with early Mountie law was also maintained. These judges were given all the powers of the judges of the Manitoba Court of Queen's Bench.[39]

WHEN LAW DULLS THE EDGE OF CHANCE

Charles M. Russell, "When Law Dulls the Edge of Chance." The North-West Mounted Police ensured that there wold be no vigilantism or lynch law on the Canadian ranching frontier.

It is important to dwell briefly on the Mounted Police because they established policies and attitudes on the Canadian plains that had a profound influence on the emerging character of that frontier, including both the Alberta and the Saskatchewan ranching frontiers. The first thing to understand about the NWMP is that the officers, the ones who dictated policy and set the tone on the frontier, came almost exclusively from the upper levels of Canadian and British society. They brought with them a strong sense of social hierarchy, a devotion to the idea of British law, and a firm belief in Victorian propriety, which translated into a determination that the frontier environment would not get the better of them. They attempted to impose on the Canadian plains, with some success, a rather prim Victorian morality that was in striking contrast to the atmosphere in the American West – no drinking, no gambling, no swearing on Sunday.

The NWMP also brought prohibition with them to the West; it was their only real source of unpopularity with the general population, until its repeal in 1892. The North-West Territories Act of 1875 prohibited the import, sale, exchange, barter, and manufacture of liquor in the Territories.[40] The federal government was determined to end the illicit liquor trade with Native peoples, so western whites were cut off too, unless they could obtain a "medicinal permit" from the lieutenant-governor of the North-West Territories. As time would show, these permits were all too easy to obtain or circumvent. The enforcement of this prohibition was somewhat half-hearted. Its main purpose was to prevent the selling of liquor to Native people; to that end the NWMP were successful. In addition, the NWMP used the all-embracing vagrancy law to clear western towns of transients intent on stirring things up. The prime concern of the Mounted Police was to contain that small element that was responsible for most of the trouble with the Native peoples on the American frontier, and, to this end, they were very successful. The whisky traders from Fort Benton literally evaporated when they discovered that the Mounted Police could, and would, convict them on Native testimony. They decamped very abruptly.

It is not surprising that much ingenuity went into circumventing a very unpopular liquor policy. The stories are legion regarding the smuggling of liquor under the Mounties' noses – hollow bibles being one of the favourite smuggling devices. There is the supposedly true story of a Mountie waiting patiently behind a pillar on a train platform for someone to collect a barrel making a very suspicious sloshing sound. He waited all day near the barrel, while the man who came to collect it, seeing the Mountie on guard behind his slim cover, crawled under the station platform with an auger and some containers, drilled through both the platform and the bottom of the barrel and liberated the nectar. And the Mounties had their own methods of liberating illicit whisky in winter, their favourite procedure being to dump the confiscated whisky in a snow bank and later sneak back for it; they had no fear of eating yellow snow!

Whisky and guns! The two most powerful architects of crime on the American frontier. The post–Civil War American West was perhaps the leading gun culture in the world, a dubious honour that did not diminish in the slightest, nationwide, as the frontier period receded. Federal policy in the Canadian West in the last quarter of the nineteenth century was very consciously established as the antithesis of American practice. The Mounted Police brought not only prohibition to the western frontier but also strict handgun laws (as outlined in the introduction). It was all too clear that most western American crime was urban, triggered by liquor and made lethal by the presence of handguns. So the Mounties brought with them in 1874 a prohibition against carrying handguns in towns.

The Canadian West was as much a hunting culture as its American counterpart; carrying a rifle was normal practice. Handguns were a different matter. There was no practical need for them. On the American range, cowboys got into the habit of carrying them, especially when they were trailing through Indian country. After a time, the revolver became a symbol of the trade. Some American states and territories had laws against carrying handguns but, as Philip Jordan remarked, these laws were universally unobserved, though an exception was usually made for church.[41] Jordan adds that all sorts of Americans carried handguns – judges and lawyers, travelling salesmen. Yet it is the cowboy who is associated more than any other figure with the handgun. Jordan makes an important distinction. Cowboys usually carried their revolvers high on their waist; gunmen slung them low.[42] Although most American cowboys were not expert with guns, the popular image of the cowboy has become firmly associated with the handgun.

In the Canadian West, a number of cowboys carried guns, in spite of the NWMP edict against them. Many cowboy memoirs indicate that most did not carry guns. For instance, Floyd Bard, an early Alberta rancher, stated bluntly that no one carried a gun.[43] Fred Ings said, "I can't recall that there was the rowdy, lawless behaviour of the story books when cowboys went to town. In fact, on trips to town, their guns were generally left at home."[44] Henry Caven remembered much the same: "There was none of the Wild West gunman stuff that the movies portray about early American west days." Wallace Stegner, growing up on the Saskatchewan–Montana border at the edges of the Canadian ranching frontier east of the Cypress Hills, recalled a Montana cowboy by the name of Murphy "who may have been in Canada for reasons that would have interested Montana sheriffs." On the Canadian side, he carried his six-gun on the inside of his coat because "Canadian law forbade the carrying of sidearms." Murphy was finally killed by a Mountie in Shaunavon who was overly jittery: there was bad blood between them, and the Mountie knew that Murphy was carrying his six-gun, although probably only "for reasons of brag" and not with evil intent. "When Montana cattle outfits worked across the line they learned to leave their guns in their bedrolls."[45] By the late 1880s, it was not uncommon for cowboys to carry pistols in the Canadian West, but it was very uncommon for them to use them.

In discussing the American cattle outfits that crossed the border to the area east of the Cypress Hills, Stegner commented on the American cowboy's gun culture:

> But it is likewise true that American cow outfits left their gun-law cheerfully behind them when they found the country north of the Line well policed, that they cheerfully cooperated with the

Mounted Police, took out Canadian brands, paid for Canadian grazing leases, and generally conformed to the customs of the country. They were indistinguishable from Canadian ranchers, to whom they taught the whole business. Many Canadian ranches, among them the 76, the Matador, the Turkey Track, and the T-Down-Bar, were simply extensions of cattle empires below the border.[46]

Stegner could have been describing Everett Johnson. He, too, cheerfully left his six-guns at home and cheerfully adapted completely to his new surroundings in Alberta, though he never lost a deep nostalgia for Wyoming and its culture of excitement and danger – and freedom.

The Mounted Police arrested any cowboy caught firing a pistol in the streets.[47] And, certainly, taking the law into one's own hands was not tolerated. There was no need to carry handguns for personal safety; the commission of an armed crime was treated with the utmost strictness. The upshot of this federal handgun policy was that the Canadian West was almost as peaceful as the East. There was much petty crime and many minor assaults, but very little armed crime.

As different groups migrated to the Canadian West, tensions between groups were bound to surface, as happened when a large group of Mormons came to southern Alberta and settled in the Cardston area, hoping to avoid the worsening atmosphere in Utah over the issue of polygamy. At first, an atmosphere of hostility existed that could easily have flared into open violence. In fact, tensions were so extreme that a number of settlers in the Cardston area requested that the Mounted Police grant them special permission to carry firearms for their protection. The NWMP quickly answered this request, warning the settlers that carrying firearms (presumably handguns) was illegal; such actions would be punished with the "utmost severity."[48] Undoubtedly, if the Mormons had not been protected by the Mounted Police and if the local settlers had been allowed to carry handguns, some incident could easily have turned ugly and escalated into serious violence.

Martin Friedland, former dean of law at the University of Toronto and a leading expert in the area of comparative Canadian–American law, has set forth in lucid and compelling terms the differences between Canada and the United States in the area of criminal law. In his *Century of Criminal Law*, he argues that a critical issue was handgun legislation. This came into effect across Canada in 1892, but earlier in the Canadian West. In 1885, the federal government enacted legislation for the North-West Territories requiring a permit for carrying a handgun. The legislation imposed a jail term of six months for carrying a handgun without a permit. Prior to this, the federal government, in 1877, had put forward Canada's first handgun legislation, stating that, unless a person had reasonable cause to fear an assault, the carrying of a handgun was forbidden. R. Blake Brown adds that "fear of allowing Canada to adopt a gun culture similar to that in the United States thus helped motivate Canadian legislators to adopt new gun measures." This federal legislation applied equally to the West.[49] Because of this handgun legislation but, more so, because of the general legal thinking that lay behind that prohibition, "Canada did not have a wild west. ... The role of the Mounties in the west is one of those myths that turns out to be true."[50] Friedland quotes David Breen in making the point that the control of liquor and handguns in the Canadian West resulted in a relative calm:

> Between 1878 and 1883, only five murder cases were brought before the courts. An incident in December 1895 in which a Texas foreman of [a] ranch beat an adversary to the draw and shot him in the stomach caused the editor of the Macleod Gazette to call attention to the rarity of such incidents with the observation that this was only the second time since the paper was established in 1882 that he had been able to report a gun fight. The police vigorously discouraged the carrying of side arms and the mere pointing of a revolver was sufficient to bring imprisonment.[51]

Hugh Dempsey, in his book *The Golden Age of the Canadian Cowboy*, could find only three accounts of gunfights in Canadian cattle country in the early days, and American cowboys figured prominently in those. Two occurred in 1885, and one early in the twentieth century. Only one man, Robert Casey, was killed during this era.[52] One other incident though is worth recounting, a near killing in Pincher Creek by Jesse Hindman, a man wanted by US authorities. When a man tripped over a bench in a poolroom and knocked him down, Hindman pulled out a handgun and shot at him. For this, he was given five years in jail.[53] Dempsey made a special point of recounting this case, and the severity with which it was treated because it was so unusual. One statistic says it all: there was virtually no vigilante action and not a single authenticated lynching in the Canadian West throughout its history, except for one incident when American vigilantes entered British Columbia to lynch a Native boy (discussed in more detail below).

The overwhelming mission of the Mounted Police, forcefully expressed in so many early reports and diaries, was to establish law and order and to pursue Native relations in ways that were a clear contrast to American policy. The views of the early Mounted Police with regard to the American

West were based to a great extent on their contacts with American wolfers, whisky traders, deserters from the army, and other flotsam of the frontier. It was hard for them to see beyond this perspective, one constantly reinforced by accounts of lynchings, mob violence, and general lawlessness that filled early western American newspapers. The early Mounted Police records are full of lurid accounts of American lawlessness.[54]

The determination of the NWMP to create a frontier very different than the freewheeling frontier of the Americans resulted in an ordered Canadian West in which relations between incoming whites and the Native peoples were rigidly controlled. A complex spiderweb system of patrols was initiated which kept the NWMP in constant contact with the Native peoples and with white settlers. It was at the heart of the Mountie philosophy of preventive law. The cattlemen were particularly well served. There were four division headquarters in cattle country, at Calgary, Fort Macleod, Lethbridge, and Maple Creek. As well, there were numerous detachments in each division, from which daily flying patrols were sent out on a regular basis to protect ranching country. Each of the four largest ranches had a NWMP detachment stationed nearby.[55]

The patrol system, as Carl Betke has pointed out, also gave early settlers a sense of confidence that they were being looked after. Not only were the Mounties on patrol on the lookout for possible sources of crime, they were also to report crop failures and cases of destitution. The federal government, through the Mounties, was committed to providing seed grain in times of crop failure and relief from destitution in the form of food and clothing. It was in the federal interest to populate the West with settlers of good quality. It was up to the NWMP to assess that quality and to decide whether the aid was deserved. The NWMP held very strong opinions on the "deserving and undeserving" poor![56]

This patrol system, perhaps more than any other Mounted Police policy, accounted for their success. Maps of the patrol routes and tallies of the miles ridden on patrol are astonishing. And the voluminous weekly reports of the Mountie patrols make it clear that the force had an extensive and detailed knowledge of the territory under its jurisdiction. These weekly reports also give a far more detailed picture of crime on the Canadian frontier than do the reports in the annual sessional papers. And, in a very pointed reference to American frontier practice, the NWMP put order and the rights of the Native peoples decidedly ahead of the personal liberties of the early whites. (This equation would all too soon be compromised after the Native peoples were put aside on reserves!) One can see in the early Mounted Police actions an uncompromising determination to demonstrate to Americans how to run a frontier.

So the early ranching community was quite effectively protected from Native cattle killing. There would be occasional moments of hysteria, but, for the most part, the ranching community had a very sensible and understanding attitude toward its Native neighbours. There would be, for instance, some anxiety in 1890 when the Ghost Dance religion, which culminated in the Wounded Knee fight, reached its peak among the Sioux. But Mounted Police reports reassured the ranchers in Alberta that the local Native groups were not performing the Ghost Dance but, instead, were "going for the cotillion, eight-hand reels and quadrilles."[57] Somewhat later, the theft of a cake, followed almost immediately by allegations concerning missing gingerbread, fuelled fears of a Native uprising. But, as usual, the NWMP were able to reassure the skittish.

With few exceptions, the early ranching community held sensible attitudes toward its Native neighbours. There certainly was a constant appeal for more NWMP protection, but there was also a general sympathy and understanding on the part of ranchers. A thorough survey of the diaries and letters of this early ranching community clearly demonstrates this. One rancher, H. M. Hatfield, said that the real problems were gophers and cutworms, not Indians.[58] Generally, relations with the Native peoples were friendly, though usually distant and condescending. Government policy, especially in the form of the pass system, resulted in a lack of contact, which in turn guaranteed a lack of friction. The sad truth is that, except on a few ranches situated near reserves, Native people and ranchers had very little to do with each other. Government policy produced two solitudes that rarely interacted, except on festive occasions. Most of the ranching community could carry on as if the Native peoples did not exist.

Some ranchers did hire Native or Métis help, especially at haying time or as cowboys, but the practice was not general. A survey of the photograph collection at the Glenbow Archives in Calgary shows that in the early days of contact, Mounties and ranchers liked to have their pictures taken with Native groups. But later, when the novelty wore off and the Plains tribes were consigned to reserves, these photos became almost non-existent.

By the mid-1880s, the NWMP reported that, due to their patrol system, horse stealing by both Natives and whites had virtually ended, except near the American border, where some American horse thieves were even prepared to stand the Mounted Police off at gunpoint.[59] In the 1880s and 1890s, horse stealing replaced inter-tribal warfare as a major preoccupation for Native peoples, who were forced by circumstances to accept reserve life. Raids across the American border were deemed the most profitable since pursuit by law enforcement had to cease at the border. But after the improved patrol system instigated by Commissioner Herchmer after 1885, which concentrated on the border areas, Native horse stealing declined very significantly. This decline could also be attributed to the new telegraph and the good relations between the Mounties and the US Army and between Indian agents on both sides of the border. By 1890, the agent on the Blood reserve near Fort Macleod, the largest Indian reserve in Canada, could report that horse stealing across the American border had entirely stopped. By 1895, the NWMP could report that Native cross-border horse-stealing raids were "a thing of the past."[60]

However, Native cattle killing was another matter altogether. Even if caught in the act, Native poachers were able to escape through country they knew intimately. The NWMP did fear that ranchers would seek reprisals, but there is very little evidence that they did. The newspapers, of course, gave the impression that there was a Native epidemic of cattle killing. The violence of their language, in most cases, was inversely proportional to their knowledge of the situation. Mounted Police investigations, which had to scrupulously follow even vaguely plausible complaints, almost always found that the newspapers of cattle country grossly exaggerated the situation or had no convincing evidence for their allegations.[61]

Those who question the effectiveness of this patrol system clearly have not read the weekly NWMP reports or seen the map of patrol routes, which resembled a great spiderweb of crossing lines. Through a system of posts and flying patrols, the Mounted Police were able to cover vast areas effectively. These routes criss-crossed their jurisdiction and covered all areas where settlers and ranchers had established themselves or where Indian reserves were situated. It becomes clear from reading weekly Mountie reports that they had a fairly accurate sense of their territory mainly gained from word of mouth as they visited all the settlers in the area. It was only in the Cypress Hills that this system was not effective. The argument that there were too few Mounties to patrol a vast area misses the point. A single Mountie, or Mounties in pairs, could travel a very large area on horseback because there was no threat of attack. The greatest value of the patrol system was that trouble could be anticipated and defused. By keeping in touch with Native groups and white settlers on regular patrol routes, the NWMP were able to anticipate trouble and often resolve it before it became an issue. It is silly to argue, as some have, that it took too long to ride around the circumference of a large area and, therefore, the NWMP did not have an accurate knowledge of the country. The US Army could not initiate a similar system

Charles M. Russell, "Single-Handed," 1912. The NWMP prided themselves on being able to make single-handed arrests in Native camps. In reality, this only worked if Native chiefs cooperated. The practice broke down in the numbing atmosphere of the Native reserve.

because lone soldiers or small groups would have been patrolling hostile country, so the army was forced to follow a policy of retaliation and punishment of the innocent after the guilty were long gone.

The contrast between frontiers would be even more dramatic when Canada's northern gold frontier opened. The difference between the lawless atmosphere of the California gold fields in 1849 and the Klondike in 1898 could not be more striking. The California gold rush saw very little government presence. Lawlessness and racial violence toward Natives, Mexicans, and the Chinese went unchecked. The only effective restraints came from vigilante groups.

In the Canadian North, the first rumours of gold prompted the federal government to send an initial group of Mounties to the Yukon in 1894, four years before the stampede to that region. In the summer of 1898, the government also sent the Yukon Field Force, a militia unit of 203 officers and men, to back up the Mounted Police presence. At the height of the Klondike rush, there were 350 Mounted Police and 200 men of the Canadian Army in the Yukon to maintain order. And, as in the Canadian West, Yukon Territory was governed by a council appointed by the federal government.[62] When the rush of 1898 began, gold seekers were met at the top of Chilkoot and White passes by Mounties who welcomed some of the most hard-bitten miners in existence to Canadian territory and informed them that they required a year's supply of food (2,000 pounds) before they could proceed. Dawson City, the focal point of the gold strike, saw practically no serious crime.[63] The Mounties allowed free-flowing gambling and prostitution in Dawson City, but no guns! Firearms were not allowed in Dawson. Fist fights were endemic in Dawson, but not murders and, as in the Canadian West, there was no vigilantism. There were no lynchings, not even a threat of one. At its height, Dawson City had a population of 40,000, but there was never a murder in any of Dawson's saloons. In fact, during the intense period of the gold rush, from 1897 to 1901, there were only three murders attributed to the gold rush.[64]

Meanwhile, almost within sight of the Mounties at the top of White Pass, lay Skagway in the American panhandle, the entrance to the Klondike at the end of Lynn Canal. Here the legendary Jefferson "Soapy" Smith and his gang terrorized Skagway without opposition from American law. (Smith earned the name "Soapy" from one of his scams – he auctioned off non-existent prizes in soap packages to gullible audiences.) Smith and his large gang of followers from Denver landed in Skagway in 1898. Soon they had taken complete control of the town through threats and well-placed bribes. The Vigilance Committee of 101 was formed to counteract his reign of violence, but Smith just formed his larger Law and Order Society and blatantly continued his robbing and killing spree, usually concentrating on those who had just struck it rich.

The end came for Soapy and his gang when they attempted to rob George Carmack, the man who had first found gold on Bonanza Creek. Carmack's shipment of gold was guarded on its way out of the Klondike by Charlie Siringo, an ex-Texas cowboy and Pinkerton agent, and by Zachary Taylor Wood, the senior Mountie in the Klondike and descendant of President Zachary Taylor. Carmack had caught wind of an attempt on his money, and unbeknownst to Soapy and his thugs, Carmack's Native relations and friends were alerted and suddenly materialized out of the fog, armed to the teeth, in bark canoes. Soapy's gang was forced to back down very publicly; after that, they never really regained the initiative. Shortly, Soapy was confronted by a member of the Vigilance Committee and killed in a shootout. What was left of his gang, after the ringleaders were dealt with by the committee, quickly dispersed. Thus ended Soapy's reign of terror in Skagway, a dramatic contrast to the Mounties' reign of order in Dawson.[65] In the Klondike under Mounted Police control, as Ken Coates and William Morrison state, for the entire period of the gold rush, there was only one instance of a Native killing a white.[66] It is hard to imagine any more striking contrast in institutional differences between nations than this joint gold rush frontier, under almost exactly the same conditions at exactly the same moment. This example puts to rest the usual nonsense that the Canadian plains frontier was more peaceful than its American counterpart only because law preceded settlement, as if that was almost an accident.

One other small fact, which few have considered, bears thinking about. A great many Canadians cite the contrast between the racism and lynchings of the California gold strike and the orderly atmosphere of the Klondike to make the point that Canadians were, and are, far more orderly than Americans. But Dawson City, the heart of the Klondike, was essentially an American town. A large majority of gold seekers were Americans who followed the mining frontier up the spine of North America, from California and Nevada through Wyoming and Montana to the gold diggings in the Cariboo and Cassiar regions of British Columbia and, finally, to the Klondike and Nome gold strikes in the Yukon and Alaska. The vast majority of American miners in the Yukon welcomed Mountie law. It was institutions, not people, that made the difference, although that argument cannot be taken too far. Generally, Canadians were – and are – far more willing to accept control over their lives and their civil liberties than are Americans. These national qualities contributed to the making of the laws.

There is the story of the Dodge City gunfighter who was bounced out of Dawson City for "talking too loudly." It is impossible to imagine said gunfighter putting up with that sort of officious authority in the American West, where personal freedom trumped all. And when the Mountie took his gun away, it was with the certitude that he didn't have to be quick on the draw, as was the case in just about any western American saloon, because the Mountie knew, and so did the gunman, that he represented a police force that would relentlessly hunt down the gunfighter if he dared question Mountie authority.[67]

* * * * *

The law brought west by the Mounted Police was one reason that the Canadian ranching frontier was so unlike its American counterpart. The other reason, and a reason just as important, was the difference in land law. As has been seen, American land law was chiefly responsible for the imbecility of the Johnson County War. Because of these differences, the emerging cattle frontier of western Canada developed in marked contrast to its southern counterpart. When prospective ranchers began to pour into what would become southwestern Alberta after the extinction of the buffalo in 1879, they found the area already constantly patrolled by the NWMP. There would be remarkably few serious incidents involving Natives in ranching country, although cattle killing in the early days after the extinction of the buffalo would cause numerous problems. The atmosphere of Fort Macleod, the earliest cattle centre, was much like that of small-town Ontario, despite the attempt of the *Macleod Gazette* to sell newspapers by indicating otherwise. The vagrancy law and forced sobriety stifled attempts to duplicate the freewheeling atmosphere of the American cattle towns.

The first attempts at ranching in Alberta began in the mid-1870s, but a cattle boom did not develop until the early 1880s, after the Native peoples were put aside on reserves. Although the Alberta ranching frontier developed at almost the same time as that in Wyoming and Montana, its character from the beginning was quite different. The first reason for this difference is that the majority of the early ranchers were retired Mounted Policemen who had served three years in the force, thus making them eligible for attractive land grants. These ex-policemen gave the area both stability and a distinctive tone. Their social attitudes were very much those of Ontario and the Maritimes, not Texas, and, though most of these Mountie ranchers had a genuine liking for the American cowboys who came north, they had a thorough contempt for American legal institutions. They consciously distanced themselves from the atmosphere of the American range.[68]

Then, in the early 1880s, Ottawa developed a land policy for the ranching country, which led, almost instantly, to a strong connection to the financial centres of eastern Canada and to a submerging of the initial influence of the American cowboys such as Johnson who had brought most of the early herds north to populate the Canadian ranching country. By the mid-1880s, Alberta ranching had become a mature extension of eastern and British financial interests, closely linked to the Canadian Pacific Railway and to the Conservative federal government of Sir John A. Macdonald.

Land policy for the ranching area was initially based on the Homestead Act of 1872, which was very similar to its American counterpart.[69] But, in 1881, Ottawa, paying little attention to democratic sentiments, shaped a policy for ranching country that was influenced by powerful forces within the Conservative government. The primary goal was to tie ranching interests to the federal Conservatives and to promote a ranching community that would act as a buffer to northward expansion of American cattlemen. It was still an age of acute Canadian anxiety toward American expansion; the echoes of manifest destiny could still spook Canadian politicians.

As has been seen, American western land policy was strongly influenced by the belief that western land was "public land." Out of this belief grew a strong conviction that the land was there for all Americans. Squatters' rights became enshrined in law. The opposite held on the western Canadian ranching frontier. These new lands being opened by the federal government were termed "Crown Land," the term suggesting a very different philosophy, and it was the duty of the Mounties to summarily turf any squatters who attempted to settle on ranching leases. Later, when the Conservatives gave way to a Liberal federal government in the 1890s, squatters on ranching leases did gain some rights. By then, however, the Canadian ranching frontier had become stable, and there was little danger of violence.

The 1881 lease policy essentially followed that of Australia, which had huge tracts of land unsuited to agriculture. The Canadian government opted for stability over democracy, guaranteeing a sure supply of beef for the western Native reserves and for the export market to Britain. By 1885, huge leases had been taken up in southwestern Alberta, encompassing more than two million acres, 50,000 head of cattle, and 5,000 horses.[70]

The main force behind the development of a Canadian ranching policy was Conservative senator Matthew H. Cochrane, a close friend of Sir John A. Macdonald, who had built an internationally respected herd of Shorthorns, Herefords, and Aberdeen Angus cattle in the eastern townships of Quebec. He focused his interest in the early eighties on the prospect of the mass production of good beef on the limitless and cheap grazing lands of Alberta. The availability of the railway, refrigeration, and the British market pointed toward substantial profits. Senator Cochrane approached Macdonald with an argument that became the basis for Canadian land policy for southern Alberta's ranching country. First, he assured Macdonald that a most successful export trade in cattle could be developed given the right conditions. Also, a properly constructed ranching community would bring stability to the West. If the goals of stability, improvement in the quality of cattle, and a safe investment climate were to be established, then the chaos of the open range system in the US must be avoided. That system was attractive at first, but was fraught with insecurity of investment, the total inability to prevent overstocking, and the unresolvable tensions between those competing for the "free range." Instead, Cochrane argued, large-scale investors in the cattle business needed the security of long-term leases at reasonable rates and the right to purchase enough land for buildings and hay land. After mulling these arguments over, Macdonald's cabinet introduced its grazing lease policy late in 1881. The government would grant leases of up to 100,000 acres for a period of up to twenty-one years. The rental fee was set at one cent per acre per year and, in order to deter speculation on these leases, the lessee had to place one head of cattle on every ten acres and was not allowed to go beyond this limit. Thus overgrazing, it was argued, would be avoided. (It was subsequently found that ten acres per head was not nearly enough.) Land could be purchased within the lease at two dollars an acre.[71] Certainly, this system was not very democratic, but it would avoid the overgrazing and violent competition of the American range.

Senator Cochrane was also very influential in the federal government's policy for sheep ranching in the West. After initially being opposed to sheep, he changed his mind and exerted great influence on the government's decision in 1884 to allow sheep north of a line formed by the Bow and Highwood rivers, but not south of that line. So, in one rather arbitrary act, the federal government, in dictating that sheep would be allowed only north of the line of the Bow and Highwood, prevented the kind of sheep wars that ignited the "free land" of the American West.[72] A significant difference can be perceived in the terminology of the two systems. In Canada, this lease land was called "Crown land"; in the American West the term "public land" was used. The different terms suggest an important difference in the philosophies of western land holding.

This federal policy immediately led to the era of the big cattle companies in the Canadian West, with Senator Cochrane leading the field. In the next half decade, much of the choice grazing land of southern Alberta found its way into the hands of friends of the Conservative federal government. Rich eastern Canadians and Britons with the right credentials soon dominated the Alberta ranching frontier of the 1880s. They saw to it that the ranching community would look to eastern Canada, not to south of the border. By 1887, over 4.4 million acres were under lease, and sixteen of these leases were for the maximum 100,000 acres.[73]

When the inevitable howl was raised against the control of choice grazing land by a privileged few, Ottawa, at first, blandly ignored these populist outbursts. Western stability and Conservative fortunes were better served by alignment with these powerful interests. The federal ranching policy guaranteed that at least southern Alberta would be controlled by a group who were right-thinking: conservative in outlook, beholden to the government, steeped in the proper reverence for things British and colonial, and looking east rather than south economically and culturally. This was certainly not a cattle frontier of popular mythology![74]

But, by 1885, pressure from settlers became strong enough to force the federal government to amend the lease policy somewhat. Simon Evans argues, however, that even though the original lease law and its later variations caused minor clashes with settlers, these disputes were on a "dramatically different level" than those in Montana and Wyoming.[75] Settlement was to be allowed on the big leases, without waiting for the twenty-one year lease to expire.[76] Also, there would be no more twenty-one year leases, though the original ones were to be honoured.[77] By 1892, opposition to the big leases had reached a point that the federal government called a meeting with a number of prominent ranchers and informed them that the old leases would be cancelled by 1896 (six years short of the twenty-one years originally promised). In return, the ranchers could purchase up to 10 percent of their leases at two dollars per acre (later changed to $1.25 per acre) and apply for new leases, which would be open to settlement. And the government sweetened the deal with a promise of more water reserves that would not be open to settlement.[78]

In the election of 1896, Laurier's Liberal government came to power. At first, under Minister of the Interior Clifford Sifton, little changed. However, in 1905, Frank Oliver, an avowed foe of the ranchers, became the minister. He saw big ranchers as a pampered elite, which, of course, they were. Oliver almost immediately put a number of water reserves up for auction. In 1905, he also tightened lease regulations by inserting a two-year cancellation clause. As Max Foran argues, "The 1905 regulations promulgated by a government unsympathetic to ranching interests represented the death knell of the ranching industry as it had existed after 1881."[79] After 1905, the ranching industry retreated west into the foothills of Alberta where it was not in competition with agriculture. Oliver's regulations and the vicious winter of 1906–7 resulted in ranching increasingly becoming a cherished way of life, not an economic system.[80] Of that terrible winter of 1906–7, Wallace Stegner wrote: "The net effect of the winter of 1906–07 was to make stock farmers out of ranchers. Almost as suddenly as the disappearance of the buffalo, it changed the way of life of a region."[81]

Stegner has given us a compelling picture of that catastrophic winter of 1906 through the fictional eyes of a young greenhorn English cowboy, Rusty, desperately trying to prove his mettle and gain the acceptance of the old hands. He and his crew are caught by early storms as they attempt to bring in stray cattle missed in the spring roundup. In trying to head some cattle, Rusty's horse stumbles, and Rusty is over his head "like a rock from a slingshot, clawing at nothing." As he lies there, more dead than alive, one of his mates rides over and asks, "Bust anythin'?" That's his only comment.

Another cowboy, who has seen Rusty flying through the air, says, "You should have seen old Rusty get piled today. You was up in the air long enough to grow feathers." Another adds, "When he see his horse was too slow, he took off and flew." This is the end of the discussion. No commiseration! The cowboy code dictated that Rusty make light of his condition, although he could hardly walk or see straight.

Stegner gives one of the most haunting descriptions of that terrible winter, when cattle died in the thousands, and the cowhands occasionally risked their lives for what was left of the herd:

> [Rusty] is furious at their violent, futile effort. ... Inhuman labor, desperate chances, the risk of death itself, for what? For a bunch of cattle who would be better off where their instinct told them to go, drifting with the storm until they found shelter. For owners off in Aberdeen or Toronto or Calgary or Butte who would never come out themselves and risk what they demanded of any cowboy for twenty dollars a month and found.

But those cowboys stayed loyal to the outfit. At the height of the blizzard, as the crew are trying to find a line shack before they die of exposure and cold, one of them [Spurlock], who is completely played out, begs to stop for a moment. Rusty takes over and somehow coaxes and bullies him to keep going for the few more miles to the shack, thus saving his life, though he can hardly stand himself. Soon, men recently on the point of freezing to death are joking with each other. One cowboy's evil-smelling feet are the only ones not frozen because "Cold couldn't get through that crust. ... I think you shouldn't make any mistake and wash them feet till spring. We'll need somebody around to do the chores while we get well." Another comments, "I tell you," as he lifted his left foot out of the bucket [of snow] and raised his right one tenderly in, "there's no business like the cow business to make a man healthy and active. There's hardly a job you can work at that'll keep you more in the open air."

> The Rusty Cullen who sat among them was a different boy, outside and inside, from the one who had set out with them two weeks before. ... The notion insinuated itself into his head, not for the first time, that his sticking with Spurlock ... was an act of special excellence, that the others must look upon him with a new respect because of it. But the tempting thought did not stand up under the examination he gave it. Special excellence? Why hadn't anyone

praised him for it then? He knew why: because it was what anyone of them would have done. To have done less would have been cowardice and disgrace. It was probably a step in the making of a cowhand when he learned what would pass for heroics in a softer world was only chores around here.[82]

Federal lease policies for the western Canadian ranching frontier were announced, as one might guess, just before the federal election of 1882. Senator Cochrane, of course, was first in line, followed by a who's-who of eastern society. Montreal, then the financial centre of Canada, was well represented by the Allan family of the Allan Steamship Lines, who were the principal investors in the Bar U (the North-West Cattle Company), and by William Winder, an ex-Mounted Policeman, principal investor in the Winder Ranche Company.

British interests were among the first to take advantage of the initial 1881 lease policy. They were led by Alexander Stavely Hill, a British Conservative MP, and Lord Latham, Britain's Lord Chamberlain, who were major investors in the Oxley Ranche Company, and by Sir John Walrond-Walrond, founder of the Walrond Ranche Company. The Marquis of Lorne, Canada's governor general, was a shareholder, together with his A.D.C., Sir Francis de Winton, in the Alberta Ranche Company.[83] The list goes on. As has been seen, this situation was very similar to the Wyoming range in the 1880s. The difference is that there was a far greater acceptance of these people in the Canadian West. After all, Canada was still, in mentality, a British colony. Although there was certainly some animosity toward the rich and toward the titled English, and a certain spoofing of upper-class ineptitude on the range, there was a far deeper English community than in the American West. The presence of both ex-Mounties who had taken up ranching and a large number of English farmers and small-scale ranchers created a very different atmosphere than that in Wyoming, with its deep resentment for rich foreigners who were grabbing the American people's birthright. This class structure in Alberta was strengthened by the ranching managerial class, which, with very few exceptions, consisted of eastern Canadians or Britons of financial consequence. As David Breen who, together with his mentor L. G. Thomas, is one of the leading experts on the early Canadian range, has pointed out:

> The Canadian range was never in the hands of "wild and woolly" westerners, either American or Canadian. The ranch country was instead under the supervision of middle and upper class

easterners. ... Power in the Canadian West was exercised not by men carrying six-shooters and wearing chaps but rather by men in well-tailored waist coats. ... Unlike the American West, early management did not arise from the indigenous frontier population. ... American influence, contrary to popular belief, was restricted to the few American foremen and cowboys. ... Moreover, after 1885 the number of Americans constantly diminished and by 1890 even most cowboys were Canadian or British.[84]

Thus, the atmosphere of the Canadian range soon took on a somewhat colonial cast that almost eclipsed the initial atmosphere established by American cowboys and trail bosses such as Johnson who first stocked the Canadian range.

Max Foran has recently argued in his authoritative study of the early Alberta ranching industry that the Canadian leasehold system introduced in 1881 resulted in an absolute contrast with the American cattle frontier. Formal leaseholds "precluded rangeland violence in western Canada." Foran adds, "In sharp contrast to the American experience, the survival of the leasehold system [in Alberta] helped consolidate the ranchers' privileged position."[85] And as David Breen has argued, the presence of the Mounted Police to enforce federal lease policy meant that overgrazing was not the severe problem that it became south of the border, where competition for cattle range often led to violence. Also, the Mounted Police regularly removed squatters from the big leases. In the American West, squatter sovereignty was a sacred principle; in the Canadian West, the opposite held.

There was, however, one celebrated case of threatened violence on the Canadian range that occurred when the Mounted Police attempted to remove a squatter, Dave Cochrane (no relation to Senator Cochrane), from the Walrond Ranche lease. Cochrane, a former member of the Mounted Police, allegedly asked the manager of the ranch, Duncan McEachran, for $5,000 for his improvements before he would leave. McEachran, outraged, refused. Thereupon, Cochrane lit a match to light his pipe, with the comment that it took only one small match to burn the entire range. McEachran paid up! Subsequently, in 1891, fire destroyed three hundred tons of hay at the Walrond Ranche in what was probably a case of arson. This case has been used to demonstrate Canadian range violence. Actually, it indicates the opposite. The Cochrane episode was an isolated one; when fire destroyed the hay on the Walrond Ranche, the Mounted Police provided the ranch with special protection for a year and a half.[86]

Simon Evans' recent study of the Alberta range, *The Bar U and Canadian Ranching History*, a magnificent achievement that now sets the standard for the history of the Alberta ranching frontier, complements the work of Thomas, Breen, and Foran. On the issue of government policies, Evans states, "No more stark contrast exists between the cattleman's frontier in Canada and in the United States than in the differing roles played by the central governments of the two countries in the management of their western lands."[87] In striking contrast to Canadian lease legislation, the American cattle empire was "outside the protection afforded by the law," leading to illegal fencing, the violent defence of "accustomed range," and range wars such as the Lincoln County and Johnson County wars. As discussed earlier, western American ranchers rejected legislative proposals similar to the Canadian lease arrangements of 1881 because they thought they could dominate the public land and wouldn't have to fence it or pay taxes.

It has generally been argued by leading historians of the Canadian range – L. G. Thomas, David Breen, Hugh Dempsey, Simon Evans, Max Foran, and Edward Brado, as well as by Paul Sharp, the American historian of the Canadian–American western frontier – that the combination of land law and the protection of the Mounted Police resulted in a ranching frontier significantly more peaceful than its counterpart to the south. Hugh Dempsey gets it exactly right in his book *The Golden Age of the Canadian Cowboy*:

> But the Canadian West was not like the American West – either the real one or the imaginary one of pulp fiction. Canada had no lynching of horse thieves, gunfights at the OK Corral, crooked sheriffs, or gunfighters travelling from town to town looking for trouble. On the other hand, the Canadian West was not entirely docile; it had its share of horse stealing, cattle rustling, boot legging, theft, general mayhem and murder.
>
> There was a noticeable difference in the presence of the law in the American and Canadian West. Americans were not essentially a lawless people, but if they found themselves in a situation where the law was ineffectual or nonexistent, they had no hesitation in making their own rules. ... This is what happened on the frontier. In some areas, the only jurisdiction was the army, and its mandate was limited. As the ranching industry became established, marshals and sheriffs were elected, but there was no way they could control the flotsam and jetsam of a disrupted society that spread across the American frontier after the Civil War. As a result, horse thieves were lynched and cowboys settled their differences with

six-shooters. Men were governed more by their attitude of right and wrong than by the dictates of the law. The Canadian West was entirely different.[88]

One historian of the Canadian–American ranching frontier, however, vehemently disagrees with these other historians of the Canadian range. Warren Elofson argues in three recent books, two of which are on the Canadian–American ranching frontier, that the peaceful Canadian ranching frontier was a myth; not only was there more violence on the Canadian side than most historians acknowledge, but he even mounts a provocative, if very questionable, argument that American vigilante law was more effective than Mounted Police law.[89] He also accuses many in the Mounted Police of being both inept and corrupt. His major charges are important enough to answer in some detail since his books are the first major scholarly studies of comparative law on the Canadian–American ranching frontier in two generations, since Paul Sharp's *Whoop-Up Country* published forty years ago.[90] If he is right, Canadian historians –including the present author – have been seriously misleading their readers!

Elofson's general arguments are supported by a small group of historians centred at the University of Calgary, who back his theme that the western Canadian frontier was far more violent than usually pictured, and the western American frontier far less so. However, their evidence is meagre and far from convincing. For instance, Louis Knafla has argued that there was, indeed, vigilantism on the western Canadian frontier, but his evidence is minimal and unconvincing.[91] Knafla has also accused early Canadian anglophone political leaders of promoting Canada as a far more peaceful and law-abiding society than the aggressive and dynamic American society in order to attract immigrants and steer them away from the US.[92]

Certainly, these revisionist historians are right on two counts. The level of violence and lawlessness on the American frontier is often exaggerated; as well, there was lots of petty crime on the western Canadian frontier. My disagreement with them – and it is a fundamental one – is their claim that the western Canadian frontier was lawless and, by inference, not that different from the western American frontier. That argument is categorically wrong.

It is probably true that many Canadian historians have gone too far in stressing the peacefulness of both Canadian society in general and western Canadian society in particular in order to draw a sharp contrast with American society. The sharpest contrast has been drawn usually between the shoot-'em-up American West and the rigid colonial West under Mounted

Police control. And it is certainly true that a number of early Mounties wrote memoirs that were more than a little self-serving. The Mounties came west with a determination to show the Americans how to run a frontier; in places, their writings verge on propaganda in stressing how peaceful the Canadian West was under their jurisdiction. There was, in fact, lots of minor crime in the Canadian West on the level of drunkenness, assaults, and petty theft. But there was a marked absence of serious crime. Thanks to the Mounted Police and to the code of law they brought with them, it was almost non-existent. The Mounties, of course, didn't always get their man, but they certainly tried their best. Their determination and perseverance were legendary. If they had been inept and corrupt, the western Canadian population surely would have reacted by forming vigilante groups. This never came close to happening.

Typical of the tone of this revisionist writing is that of Lesley Erickson's *Westward Bound*, which argues that new research has exposed the "mild vs the wild West paradigm of the Canadian vs the American West as a false dichotomy."[93] But these revisionist historians do not make their case. Erickson, for example, is writing in the field of social crime. She finds many examples of the ill-treatment of Native women by frontier courts or of hired men who compromised the boss's wife behind the barn. These are important issues, but they hardly constitute grounds for calling the Canadian West lawless. Those of us who argue that there was a dramatic difference in the levels of endemic violence and lawlessness on the two frontiers acknowledge that there was considerable petty or social crime on the western Canadian frontier. But these revisionists cannot find examples on the western Canadian frontier of persistent Indian wars, the violent persecution of minorities by uncontrolled mobs, range wars, lynchings, shoot-ups in cattle town saloons, or the presence of professional gunmen. How do those who so categorically state that they have dispelled the myth of the peaceful Canadian western frontier account for the almost total absence on their supposedly lawless Canadian frontier of boot hills, lynchings, and barroom shootouts?[94]

Some revisionist historians have relied heavily on local newspapers to argue that there were much higher crime rates on the western Canadian frontier than usually acknowledged. But these newspapers are an extremely doubtful source. It is all too easy to find lurid accounts of crime in these papers, but the accounts are usually not to be trusted. R. C. Macleod, a leading historian of the western Canadian frontier and of Mounted Police history, and Heather Rollason Driscoll have shown decisively in two important articles how biased and unreliable some of these early papers were, especially the *Calgary Herald* and *Macleod Gazette*, and particularly when it came to the reporting of Native issues. For instance, they point out that one study of crime in early Calgary, Tom Thorner's article "The Not So Peaceable Kingdom: Crime and Criminal Justice in Frontier Calgary," the subject of his University of Calgary master's thesis, was based largely on the *Calgary Herald*.[95] As Macleod and Rollason Driscoll point out, Tom Thorner's use of the *Calgary Herald*, which was "full of vitriolic descriptions of Native people," as a basis for his assessment of crime rates is very suspect. He concluded that most of the cattle killing and horse stealing were being done by Natives. "Thorner does not appear to have considered issues of reliability such as whether or not the paper selectively reported cases. Nor does he consider how the attitudes of the editor and the lobby groups affected how crime was reported."[96] Macleod and Rollason Driscoll came to a very different conclusion.

They have clearly shown that the *Macleod Gazette* and the *Calgary Herald*, the two newspapers of the Alberta ranching frontier, were seriously biased when reporting Native crime. These papers made it seem that there was far more Native than white crime, while the statistics show conclusively that the reverse was the case.

> Our evidence showed that Natives were significantly under-represented in the jails compared to whites in the population and were often treated with a degree of leniency not shown to any other group. This generalization holds true for all kinds of crime from simple assaults to murder. The only partial divergence from the pattern concerns livestock theft where Native crime rates were higher than for other categories of offences, but even here the rates for Natives were lower than for the rest of the population.[97]

It is important to realize that today's high rate of Native incarceration was not always so. At a time when the Cree, Blackfoot, and Assiniboine populations were reeling from the extinction of the buffalo, their forced subjugation to reserve life, and the overwhelming onslaught of disease, they were clearly the most law-abiding element on the frontier.[98] Their forbearance in the face of starvation and the end of their way of life was astonishing. And the meticulous work of Macleod and Rollason Driscoll, based on the court records of the Mounted Police and the reporting of the leading frontier newspapers, directly contradicts the loose claims of those who argue that these Native groups were responsible for widespread violence and crime.[99]

Readers of the *Macleod Gazette* in particular would conclude that Natives figured very prominently in crime. The paper made it seem that Natives were the major source of crime on the frontier; court records showed clearly that the opposite was the case.[100] For the period 1878 to 1885, there were only forty-five cases of violent crime in the entire area under Mounted Police control for Natives and whites combined. These mostly involved threats with firearms. This amounts to six cases a year! There were only five homicide cases for the entire period, and only two involved Natives.[101] That leaves three white homicide cases in eight years, a rather pathetic statistic to confront for those intent on arguing that the western Canadian frontier was seething with murder and mayhem.

The evidence of Macleod and Rollason Driscoll is very strongly substantiated by the first in-depth study of the relationship between Native groups in Saskatchewan and the Canadian legal system in the last quarter of the nineteenth century. Shelley Gavigan's recent book *Hunger, Horses, and Government Men: Criminal Law and the Aboriginal Plains, 1870–1905*, published by the Osgoode Society for Canadian Legal History, is a very impressive and detailed study of Mounted Police law and relations with Native peoples. Although the book does not cover the Alberta ranching frontier, its conclusions are equally applicable for that region. Gavigan's purpose was to expose the Native side of the legal relationship. Her conclusion is very close to that of Macleod and Rollason Driscoll: crime was very rare in Native society, with the exception of horse stealing, which was not a crime under Native law, and cattle killing, which was probably inevitable given the semi-starving state of Native peoples.[102] Gavigan found very few cases of Native drinking, and she actually made little mention of Native horse stealing and cattle killing.

Gavigan's most startling conclusion is that the court system treated Native defendants with scrupulous fairness, and, most surprising of all, these defendants learned to use the court system to their benefit. Contrary to the findings of Lesley Erickson, who claimed much ill-treatment of Native women by frontier courts, Gavigan found practically none, arguing that the defence of Native women in the Saskatchewan court system was especially impressive.[103] This is clearly an area for further investigation. And she provided convincing evidence that when a Mountie did abuse his authority, he was treated very harshly.[104]

Certainly, the Native peoples of the plains had every reason to descend into lawlessness as the buffalo vanished, as did their whole way of life, to be traded for the soul-destroying atmosphere of the Indian reserves. That they did not become lawless and vindictive is a remarkable testament to their strength of character and the resilience of their culture. As ranches took root, Native peoples were in the process of being retooled into wards of the state, without any say in the matter. They were told by overbearing missionaries, teachers, and farm instructors that everything they had believed in for millennia was wrong. Instead, they were to renounce paganism and the nomadic way of life for the civilizing influence of farming. Their souls would be redeemed from the everlasting fires of hell by Christianity. Under these conditions, all the old certainties evaporated, as their chiefs – the holders of the old ways – were ridiculed by these upholders of the new order and Indian agents replaced the chiefs as figures of authority. Braves in the making, with hormones raging, were now told that horse stealing would lead to jail; they must, instead, impress their intended sweethearts with how many potatoes they could hoe!

Government officials, armed with the insufferable certainty of late nineteenth-century zeal to save the Native peoples from themselves, predicted that the old ways would be gone in a generation. A new generation, properly Christian and embracing the new agriculture, would rise from the ashes. Actually, it could be argued that there was a surprising lack of racism in this outlook, but the officials more than made up for it in their cultural arrogance and in their astounding blindness toward Native culture. There should be no surprise that, under these conditions, Native society became unhinged. The real surprise is that these Native groups did not lash out more than they did at their oppressors.

The careful work of Gavigan and Macleod and Rollason Driscoll is a much-needed corrective to the overheated contentions of Warren Elofson that the western Canadian frontier was violent, that many Mounted Policemen were both ineffective and corrupt, that there was "a great deal of [Native] bitterness and racial animosity that often manifested itself in violence and death," that Montana vigilante law was more effective than Mountie law, that there was vigilantism and lynching on the Canadian frontier, contrary to the assertions of Canadian historians, and, finally, that the Canadian West saw a number of gunfights.[105] This, indeed, is a riveting list of accusations that, if true, essentially overturns the established interpretation of important parts of western Canadian history. If his charges are left unchallenged, general readers and historians alike will assume that his views are acknowledged to be the new "truth."

Thus far, Elofson is the only historian to make such charges. The importance of his otherwise impressive books requires a reply, since one of the fundamental arguments of this work is that the two frontiers were very dissimilar precisely because of the very marked differences in the levels of violence. More to the point, the very different legal institutions and cultural attitudes toward violence and crime on the two frontiers accounted for much of these marked differences.

For a start, in *Cowboys, Gentlemen, and Cattle Thieves: Ranching on the Western Frontier*, Elofson argues: "While Canada saw no large-scale Indian/white massacres on the ranching frontier of the type glorified by American film, there was a great deal of bitterness and racial animosity that often manifested itself in violence and death."[106] This, indeed, is a startling charge, if true, and a dramatic departure from established wisdom. There are two issues here. Elofson implies, first, that the theme of extreme violence on the American frontier was the product of American films, not responsible historical research. Well, highly regarded historians have provided overwhelming evidence to the contrary, of pervasive violence, whether cattle town barroom shootings, lynch mobs, Indian wars, racial violence against Mexicans and Chinese on the mining frontier, persistent labour violence, or the range wars of the Lincoln and Johnson counties and Pleasant Valley variety. There is a vast amount of carefully documented material on western American violence. The Canadian Plains frontier was singularly free of virtually all that sort of violence.

A key part of Elofson's evidence for this claim of violence and death is the lynching by Canmore, Alberta, residents of two members of the Kootenai tribe in 1888.[107] But Hugh Dempsey, one of the Canadian West's most respected historians and the foremost historian of western Canadian Native history, has pointed out in a review of Elofson's book that the lynching did not take place in the Canadian West, as Elofson implies, but in Montana, near Flathead Lake.[108] And Dempsey pointed out that there is no evidence that Canmore settlers were involved in this lynching.[109] "It was purely an American affair." In fact, Dempsey states, there is no evidence of any lynching at any time in the Canadian ranching country, or anywhere else in the Canadian West.

Elofson also cites two famous Native murder cases to indicate the prevalence of racial "violence and death" on the western Canadian frontier, those of Charcoal and Almighty Voice. Both killed several people, including Mounties. Hugh Dempsey again has questioned Elofson's findings, pointing out that Charcoal's killing of Sergeant Wilde of the Mounted Police was a special case that did not demonstrate a trend. Dempsey contends in his biography of Charcoal that Charcoal first killed a fellow Native whom he caught messing with his wife and then killed Wilde because he intended to commit suicide and needed someone important to precede him to the Spirit World to announce his coming and to be his emissary, a custom common to the Native peoples of the plains. And Charcoal was apprehended in 1897 by his own two brothers.[110] So the example of Charcoal hardly makes Elofson's case.

Nor does Almighty Voice, who was not, as Elofson states, a Stoney, nor was he hanged. Almighty Voice was also a special case and had nothing to do with ranching country. He was a Cree, not a Stoney, the grandson of Chief One Arrow, whose reserve was at Batoche, the focal point of the 1885 Métis Rebellion in Saskatchewan. Almighty Voice was a product of that rebellion; he created a sensation in the 1890s because his case was so unusual. He was arrested for killing a settler's cow. His father, John Sounding Sky, was also in jail at the time for stealing a coat and some money. Almighty Voice escaped jail and almost immediately killed a Mountie who attempted to arrest him. There followed a spectacular manhunt, during which Almighty Voice wounded several more. He was finally surrounded in a wooded area by the Mounted Police, who brought in two field guns, one of which blew him up, contrary to Elofson's contention that he was hanged. Thus ended perhaps the most tragic moment in the relations between the NWMP and the peoples of the Canadian Plains, whose world was undergoing "the dying of the light."[111] Almighty Voice's anger was not directed toward the settlers and ranchers but, instead, the desperate atmosphere of the reserve. His was the ultimate defiance; he had eluded capture for over eighteen months and killed four people – all without a pass from his agent![112]

There was only one other Mounted Policeman killed by a Native during the nineteenth century. In 1879, five years after the arrival of the NWMP, Marmaduke Graburn was mysteriously murdered while out on patrol. The presumed killer, a Blackfoot named Starchild, was acquitted for lack of evidence by a jury made up mostly of ex-Mounties, even though the jury thought he was probably guilty.[113] One of the jury members, E. H. Maunsell, a rancher and former Mountie, had this to say: "As a matter of fact it required greater courage to acquit Starchild than to convict him. ... There is no doubt the verdict we gave was not a popular one. The whole country was crying out for vengeance."[114] Starchild was later put in jail for bringing stolen horses into Canada. In jail, he learned English and, when released, became a scout for the NWMP. The killing of three Police in twenty-five years by Natives does not seem to justify a verdict that racial "violence and death" "often" manifested itself on the Canadian frontier.

But what about friction and violence between ranchers and the Cree and Blackfoot? Virtually all historians of the Canadian ranching frontier have emphasized the lack of hostility in the relationship. But, once again, Elofson differs. In *Cowboys, Gentlemen, and Cattle Thieves* he recounts an incident in 1887 near High River in which a rancher shot at and killed a

Blackfoot and fatally wounded another for killing cattle.[115] He uses this incident to claim that there was an atmosphere of "general" hostility and violence between ranchers and Native people. Consistently, Elofson takes a solitary incident and elevates it to a general principle. In fact, this incident demonstrates the exact opposite. Throughout the period of the ranching frontier, this was the only incident recorded by the Mounted Police of a rancher shooting a Native. And again Elofson gets his facts wrong. Only one Blackfoot was killed, not two, and the Blackfoot had not been killing cattle.[116] In 1887, a rancher named Thompson followed a group of Blackfoot who had broken into his house and stolen a few things. When Thompson and a friend, Tucker Peach, approached the Blackfoot camp, they were fired on. They retaliated and fatally wounded Trembling Man. According to the *Calgary Herald*, Peach was also wounded.[117] The killing of Trembling Man caused a great state of excitement among the Blackfoot, and the NWMP had a hard time calming them down.[118] This incident was exactly the sort of Native-white clash that frequently resulted in reprisals or war in the American West. As already stated, this was the only incident of its kind, but the *Calgary Herald* was convinced that the country would soon be aflame in an Indian war. The newspaper used the incident to call for "Indian removal!"[119]

Elofson's other example of poisonous relations with Native people on the ranching frontier includes a charge of vigilantism, a practice supposedly absent from the Canadian frontier. He states that, in 1894, a man named Skinner on the Blackfoot reserve was killed by an irate father for refusing food for his sick child. For a start, Elofson has both the spelling of the name and the date wrong. This, perhaps, is being picky, but it doesn't inspire confidence. On April 3, 1895, the ration issuer on the reserve, Skynner, was shot and killed by Scraping High after his son died of tuberculosis. An investigation disclosed that another Blackfoot had threatened to shoot Skynner for hurting his wife. And there were other complaints. It appears that Skynner had it coming.[120] After killing Skynner, Scraping High took up a position in the burial ground and held off the NWMP and a group of civilian volunteers for two days. He was finally killed by Constable Magnus Rogers.[121] This episode does not reflect murder and mayhem in ranching country; it instead reflected a situation exclusive to the reserve system at a time when the reserve population was in a state of semi-starvation.

Elofson claims that this "trigger-happy" group of citizens was executing vigilante justice on Scraping High. How can this be vigilantism if these citizens were helping the NWMP? The whole point of vigilantism was that it was extra-legal. Also, the three Blackfoot chiefs who sat on the inquest into Scraping High's death absolved the Police and citizens of all blame. Instead, their wrath was directed toward the Indian Department and the reserve school system.[122] If, as Elofson contends, there had been a "trigger-happy" shootout, the three chiefs would certainly not have acted as they did. The Mounted Police looked into this case very carefully. There is a large file, which gives no indication that there was any vigilante activity whatever.[123] There were, in fact, only two Native attacks on Indian reserve employees during the entire frontier period, an extraordinary testimony to Native forbearance, given their desperate situation.[124]

Although vigilantism never gained a foothold in the Canadian West, there were several cases of what might be called vigilantism that are revealing. In 1892, a man named Skallent was murdered near Edmonton. Almost immediately, suspicion pointed to a man named Ole Mickelson. He disappeared, and Inspector Piercy, in charge of the Edmonton Mounted Police detachment, took charge and had posters printed offering a reward of $200 for assistance in his capture. Mickelson was seen near Red Deer (halfway between Edmonton and Calgary), and a group of armed citizens gave chase. Mickelson fired on the group and, in returning the fire, one of the group, William Bell, killed him. This killing touched off a major debate over law and order in the North-West Territories. Newspapers saw Bell as a hero; the Mounted Police were horrified. Bell was tried in the Supreme Court of the North-West Territories for killing Mickelson when he might have been arrested alive. The jury found Bell not guilty; locally, he was elevated to the status of a hero. Inspector Piercy was severely chastised by the commissioner of the Mounted Police for lack of judgment in offering a reward without the sanction of the lieutenant-governor and involving civilians. Inspector Piercy, sternly reprimanded for instigating what might be considered vigilante justice, committed suicide.[125]

Shortly after this incident, in 1895, the town of Lethbridge became embroiled in another incident involving one James Donaldson, who was openly having an affair with the wife of his landlord, Charles Gillies. Gillies committed suicide, whereupon a group of seven or eight masked men, including Sergeant Hare of the Mounted Police, ambushed Donaldson, tarred and feathered him, and dragged him through Lethbridge to the Lethbridge House, a local saloon. It appeared that this punishment was universally popular with all save Mounted Police officialdom. Superintendent R. Burton Deane referred to the incident as an "unprecedented occurrence of lynch law."

It proved impossible to prosecute the masked men. Donaldson would not give evidence. Sergeant Hare gave evidence, but then escaped across the US border, as did another key witness. Despite Commissioner Herchmer's insistence that the guilty parties must be convicted, the jury could not reach a verdict. The case was a fiasco, but the relentless attempt of the Mounties to bring the guilty parties to justice did send the message that this sort of action would not be condoned. There are no other cases like this on record.[126]

Elofson also contends that there were several lynchings on the Canadian frontier. His evidence is anecdotal and very meagre. He claims, for instance, that in 1882 a man named Bowles was lynched because he didn't help put out a prairie fire near Fort Macleod. His evidence? The *Macleod Gazette*, a notoriously unreliable source. Paul Sharp has alluded to this same lynching and one other in the Canadian West, also citing the *Gazette* for the lynching of Bowles. The second lynching Sharp mentions was that of the driver of the Macleod stage, who allegedly made his passengers get out and push the stage up a steep hill. His evidence? Absolutely none! The fact that there is no mention of either of these supposed lynchings in Mounted Police files means that they almost certainly did not happen. In both cases, the reasons for the lynchings seem very unconvincing. Also, the NWMP were under very strict orders to investigate any rumours of lynchings. There is nothing in Mounted Police records to suggest that they even *might* have happened.[127]

There has been, in fact, only one properly verified lynching in the Canadian West. In 1884, a group of American vigilantes crossed into British Columbia from Washington Territory and lynched a Native boy, Louie Sam, a fourteen-year-old Sto:lo boy, whom they accused of killing a shopkeeper in Nooksack, Washington Territory. The vigilantes hanged him from a tree near Sumas, BC, after forcibly taking him from the custody of a special deputy who was transporting him to Canadian officials. Canadian undercover police officers went to Nooksack and found evidence that the boy had been wrongly accused. In fact, some of the members of the lynch party had profited from the murder of the storekeeper. In 2006, the Washington senate offered an official apology to the Sto:lo Nation in a ceremony in the Washington state legislative building.[128]

Did the western Canadian ranching frontier have the sort of gunfights and barroom shootups usually associated with a raw frontier? In a word, no! Hugh Dempsey in *The Golden Age of the Canadian Cowboy* could find only three gunfights in cattle country in all of the frontier period and only one death. Even if there were a few more, they would hardly justify the charge that there was "considerable gunfighting." There just wasn't![129] In Beahen and Horrall's history of the Mounted Police, their discussion of murders, which would have included lethal gunfights, found that from 1892 (when liquor was first allowed in the North-West Territories) to 1900, there were fifteen murders in the Territories, and ten of them were family affairs. That leaves five in eight years – hardly a number that would be found on any self-respecting gunslinger frontier.[130]

There were two areas of crime that did cause the Mounties a huge headache – Native cattle killing and both Native and white horse stealing. On the open range, it was extremely difficult to detect cattle killing. For Native people who had just watched the buffalo disappear, cattle killing was an irresistible temptation. With the border so close, cross-border horse stealing was relatively easy. Together, these two categories accounted for the majority of the Mounted Police's work.

Most of the cross-border horse stealing was concentrated in the area from the Cypress Hills, just north of the Alberta-Saskatchewan border with the US, and east to the Big Muddy Valley, south of present-day Regina. This was far from the Alberta ranching frontier. The badlands of the Big Muddy, into which horse thieves could disappear without a trace, was the northern end of the Outlaw Trail, which stretched from Mexico to the badlands of Saskatchewan. In this area of the Cypress Hills and the Big Muddy, the only serious gangs of Canadian-American cattle country were concentrated. It was perfect horse-stealing country. If pursued by the Mounties, they just slipped across the border into American territory, and vice versa, if chased by American authorities.

Beth LaDow has written about the area just below the Canadian border from the Cypress Hills to the Bug Muddy. The American community of Havre, just south of the Cypress Hills, was the Dodge City of the North, notorious for its drinking, gambling, and general lawlessness. It was the bootleg capital of the northern plains.[131] And then there was Landusky, Montana, described by the western artist Charlie Russell, only partly tongue-in-cheek:

> The leadin' industries is saloons and gamblin' houses … the shootin's remarkably accurate an' almost anybody serves as a target. … Funerals in Landusky is held at night under a white flag, so that business ain't interrupted in the daytime.[132]

This area from Havre and Landusky to the Cypress Hills and the Big Muddy gained the reputation of being the most lawless area of the northern plains, ideal for hiding stolen horses. Here the famous Nelson-Jones gang held sway. Frank Jones was an American, and Charles "Red" Nelson a Canadian. The gang even included an ex-Mountie, Frank Carlyle.[133] When Jones was killed in a shootout in the US with law officers, he was replaced by Dutch Henry Leuch (pronounced Youch!). The gang then became the Dutch Henry Gang, and was very unusual on the frontier in having three Canadian members.

They were operating in the only corner of the Canadian/American frontier where they could function as they did.[134]

The Big Muddy Valley was very close to the small settlement of Willow Bunch, whose historical claim rests on its French Canadian trader Jean Louis Legare, who was chiefly responsible for returning Sitting Bull to the American authorities in the spring of 1881. In the fall of 1876, thousands of Sioux crossed into Canada as political refugees after the Custer fight. Sitting Bull joined them the next spring with 135 lodges, swelling Sioux numbers to a peak of 5,600.[135] These Sioux settled in a region from the Cypress Hills to the area around Willow Bunch. These are largely forgotten years in the history of the Sioux because Sitting Bull was a great disappointment to those who saw him as the scourge of the West. He behaved in Canada as a model citizen. Much of the information about him in these years from 1877 to 1881 lies in the field of diplomatic relations between the US, Canada, and Britain. The issue of the Sioux refugees in Canada was the first one that tested the Treaty of Washington in 1866, the new accord between the three countries that was meant to clear the air after the Civil War.

For the next four years, the Sioux remained in Canada. They were remarkably peaceful, but Canadian authorities viewed them as a potential powder keg. Their presence in the Cypress Hills, a disputed area between the Cree and Blackfoot and the last refuge of the buffalo on the Canadian plains, upset the balance significantly. They hastened the end of the buffalo, so that by 1879, they were in a state of starvation, killing their horses and trapping gophers to keep alive.

Finally, it seems that the one who convinced Sitting Bull to return was the Willow Bunch trader, Jean Louis Legare. He offered to escort the Sioux south to Fort Buford. When he turned up at their camp with wagons loaded with food and started south, the starving Sioux had no option but to follow the food. Sitting Bull arrived at Fort Buford at the end of July 1881. He handed his gun to his young son to surrender; he couldn't bring himself to do it. Then, contrary to the government's promises, Sitting Bull was arrested and taken to Fort Randolph to be imprisoned for two years, after being stripped of all his authority.[136]

It would seem that most of the crime in the Canadian West was centred in the Cypress Hills–Big Muddy region, but one would reach a very different conclusion from reading the newspapers of the Alberta ranching country. It is very clear from reading the *Macleod Gazette* and the *Calgary Herald* that order would not have prevailed between the new settlers and the Native groups if the settlers, as in the American West, had been in control of the law. An editorial in the *Macleod Gazette* in 1883 gives a glimpse of what would have been, at a time when, according to the Mounted Police, the Native peoples were showing extraordinary restraint in the face of starvation and the end of their way of life:

> It has just come to this, these Indians must be kept on their reserves, else the indignant stockmen will some day catch the red rascals and make such an example of them that the noble red man will think h_ll's a poppin, besides a probable attack of kink in the back of the neck [hanging] and we can't say that we should greatly blame them either. That a lot of dirty, thieving, lazy ruffians should be allowed to go where they will, carrying the latest improved weapons, when there is no game in the country, seems absurd.[137]

Two months later, the *Gazette* added a footnote, "If we are obliged to fight these Indians to stop their depredations, let the entertainment commence."[138]

As the *Calgary Herald* replaced the *Macleod Gazette* for the title of the leading newspaper of ranching country, it, too, took up the cry. The paper made it clear that it didn't really care what happened to its Native neighbours, as long as they didn't "infest our streets." A Native dog that killed a Calgarian's chicken warranted front-page coverage, an example of the evils of allowing Indians off their reserves.

> If these Indians and their dogs are not kept on their reserves, there is liable to be trouble with them presently in Calgary. A stray shot at an Indian or his dog is a very little thing with an angry man, but might lead to no end of trouble.[139]

The tempo of anti-Native sentiment in these newspapers escalated as a result of the 1885 Rebellion. By 1887, a bumper year for anti-Native bile, there were many references to "thieving redskins" and warnings that if a few were shot, it would have a good effect on the others. The same year, shrill editorials in the *Calgary Herald* were complaining that Canadian Indian policy was an utter failure because Indians were allowed to roam through settlements. The solution was to remove them to an Indian territory some distance from Calgary and open their reserves to white settlement.

> The country is rapidly filling up, and it is unreasonable that a large tract of the very best of it should remain idle and unproductive. The interests of Calgary demand that steps be taken to induce

the Indians to give up their present reserve and accept one that will not be so much in the way of our development.[140]

Two years later, the paper proposed a law preventing Natives from coming into Calgary. Directly under this editorial was another, entitled "Bigotry on the Rampage," accusing Ontario of small-mindedness and injustice on the Jesuit Estates question![141] The *Macleod Gazette* and the *Calgary Herald* served as constant reminders of what would have been if the federal government had loosened its grip on the law.

Wallace Stegner addressed the typical settlers' attitude toward their Native neighbours in southern Saskatchewan: "Most of the [settlers] were immigrants from sections of the United States and Canada where Indians were part of a lurid past ... they brought fully developed prejudices with them which we inherited without question or thought." If not for the Mounted Police, law and order on the western Canadian frontier would probably have been far closer to that of the American West in its treatment of Native peoples![142]

There was also a constant barrage of complaints and editorials in the *Gazette* and the *Herald* about rustling and cattle killing by both Natives and whites. If not for the iron control of the Mounties, vigilantism might have taken hold and settler friction with Native groups might have erupted into war as in the American West. But the simple fact is that white settlers on the Canadian plains, for all their threats, did not dare to take the law into their own hands. And in fairness to the ranchers, most of the silly and inflated talk came from urban communities. It is clear that the Mounties protected the Native population from the sort of prejudice that is reflected in western newspapers on both sides of the border.

There was, however, a dark side to the lack of serious crime in the Canadian West. Apartheid came to the Canadian West in 1882, as the reserve system came into effect. The Mounted Police, that year, under pressure from the Indian Affairs department, introduced the pass system, which was at first an informal system that required Natives to have a pass from the Indian agent if they wanted to leave the reserve. The system was initially implemented in an attempt to stop cross-border horse stealing and cattle killing on the open range, but this policy was in flagrant violation of the treaties, which promised the Native peoples free access to all land that was not in private hands. It also had no basis in law, as the NWMP were acutely aware. At first, many Mounted Police were extremely reluctant to enforce the system. But there is no getting around the fact that the Canadian government, through the Mounted Police, instituted a policy of apartheid in the Canadian West. Peace and order trumped human rights and treaty obligations. The government feared that exaggerated newspaper reports of rampant horse stealing and cattle killing might lead to settlers taking the law into their own hands and decided it must sacrifice principles for order.[143] Here was the first instance of the Mounted Police's use of repression and dishonesty in the name of peace and order. Increasingly, the Mounted Police used the pass system to force a separation of races as the railway brought a flood of settlers to the Canadian West.

In 1884, the superintendent of Indian Affairs suggested the use of the pass system to prevent Natives from camping near white communities. At this point, the commissioner of the Mounted Police argued that a pass system would be "tantamount to a breach of confidence with Natives generally."[144] Such a system would be an act of bad faith with those chiefs who had been reluctant to sign the treaties; they had been reassured by promises of freedom to hunt and to travel for purposes of trade. When Indian Affairs complained that Natives were camping around towns for immoral purposes, the Mounted Police retorted that they had learned their immorality from the whites.

Indian Affairs kept up its pressure to make the policy official and, finally, as a result of the Rebellion, Sir John A. Macdonald gave in. The Indian Affairs department sent him a list of recommendations for the post-Rebellion handling of Native tribes in August 1885, with the comment that a pass system would be beneficial for the Natives' "own good and morality." Scribbled in the margins of this document are the initials JAMD – (John A. Macdonald). Here was the official sanction for the first breach of trust with the Native peoples of the plains.[145]

Behind the implementation of this pass system, too, lay a fierce disagreement between the Mounted Police and the new Indian Affairs establishment. The NWMP argued that the Natives on reserves, with the buffalo now gone, must be better fed so that they would not resort to cattle killing. The Indian Affairs officials, in the 1880s, were increasingly alarmed that they were creating Canada's first welfare system and demanded that no food be given without work in return. The Native peoples of the Canadian plains were given the stark choice: work or starve. In reality, the only work possible on these new reserves was European-style agriculture, something very foreign to the Native hunting cultures of the plains. It was in this atmosphere that the Mounted Police had to handle a potentially explosive situation. Native cattle killing continued, as did ranchers' complaints, but the pass system undoubtedly kept the situation from boiling over. As settlers poured in, complaints mounted, reaching a crescendo in 1894. After years of few Native arrests for cattle killing, in 1894 there were forty-nine.[146] In June 1894, a group of Bloods went to the Mounted Police and admitted that they were killing cattle because they were starving; their crops had failed, and their agent had cut back their rations. They admitted to killing as many as thirty head a month.[147] This situation led to the greatest number of arrests for cattle killing in the nineteenth century – eighteen arrested and sixteen convicted.[148]

Clearly the presence of the Mounted Police kept Native-white animosity from erupting into open hostility. And their patrol system kept rustling on the open range from spilling over into vigilante action. There were, of course, hotheaded ranchers who complained vociferously about stolen stock and threatened vigilante action. But they did not take action, largely because most cattlemen realized that the Mounted Police were doing the best job they could with limited manpower. As well, the hotheads were warned very bluntly that any vigilante action would be dealt with strictly. Lynching would be considered murder!

Most historians writing on the pass system have argued that the 1885 Rebellion caused the government to impose it, but the system appeared informally as early as 1882. Though unstated by the NWMP, probably the most compelling argument for their finally agreeing to use the pass system was their conviction that Native cattle killing and horse stealing might result in ranchers resorting to vigilante action. The Mounted Police were so determined that there would be no vigilantism in their jurisdiction that they finally, though reluctantly, decided that good faith with the Native peoples of the plains was less important than preventing the possible rise of vigilantism. So they agreed to a policy that would reduce Native cattle killing and horse stealing, despite its glaring illegality.

There is one more very important consideration. Most frontier Americans were not going around shooting each other. Most were just as law-abiding as Canadians. The myth of the lawless American is just as distorted as the myth of the completely peaceful Canadian. The critical difference between the frontiers was that the small minority of Americans in the West who were causing most of the trouble could not easily be controlled because American legal institutions were largely ineffectual in doing so. In the Canadian West, the opposite was the case. The Mounties had tight control of the lawless white element through legislation related to liquor, guns, and vagrancy. And now they had equal control of the Native population through the pass system. Peace and order trumped liberty and individual rights. The NWMP regularly sent American troublemakers packing back across the border using the Vagrancy Act, if they were found loitering in towns without proof of employment. It took only a small minority to give the American West its overheated reputation for lawlessness. And blame it, too, on the outlaws' publicists. They did a magnificent job of magnifying the badness of the American West.

What is most striking in these circumstances is how easily and happily Americans who emigrated to Canada adapted to Canadian customs and institutions when they came north. The vast majority who came to the early Canadian West welcomed the security provided by the Mounties' police state, as did, too, the thousands of American prospectors who came to the Klondike gold diggings in 1898 – to the point of producing a very large petition of thanks to the Mounties for making the Klondike diggings so safe. It is interesting, too, that an acknowledged Indian killer, gunfighter, and vigilante like Johnson in one setting became a quiet citizen in Alberta with many good friends among the Blackfoot and Stoney peoples. And he had no need for his six-guns. They were stowed away at the back of a cupboard. It is all about institutions.

A standard explanation for this difference of law and order on the two frontiers is that, in Canada, the Mounties arrived before settlement; in the American West, the law arrived somewhat later. This difference explains almost nothing, except that the Canadian philosophy put a very large emphasis on prevention. But, in Canada, when the law arrived, it was very different to that south of the border. That is the key point. The law of the Mounties and that of the Texas Rangers, for instance, were worlds apart. A study of these two institutions says much about the legal ethos that the wider societies created.

The first comparative study of the Mounted Police and the Texas Rangers, Andrew Graybill's *Policing the Great Plains*, appeared recently.[149] In many ways, Texas and Alberta are the bookends of the cattle frontier, and the Texas Rangers and the Mounties have acquired a similar national mythology. Also, the North-West Mounted Police came west in 1874, the same year that the Texas Rangers, after a long and picturesque career, were finally officially institutionalized. It is therefore most fitting that a comprehensive study of the world's two most famous police forces should finally be written. Graybill's book is both timely and thoroughly researched. It fits with what seems to be the new wave of focusing more on similarities than differences. This causes certain difficulties when comparing Rangers to Mounties, who were in their most significant aspects diametrically opposite. They were products of their cultures, and the culture of Texas was dramatically different from that of eastern Canada, where the Mounties originated. Their mandates, too, were vastly different; the Rangers, in their early days, were essentially a loose militia whose central purpose was to rid Texas of Indians and Mexicans, using considerable violence if necessary. The Rangers brought with them an enormous pride as fighting men; their photographs bristle with armaments and the look of tough, trigger-ready frontiersmen. The Mounted Police were a completely different sort of force, a professional force who saw themselves as the inheritors of the military traditions of the British Empire. They represented an Anglo-Canadian Victorian culture that was completely at odds with the ethos of Texas. In their early years, they were chiefly concerned with bringing stability and order to the frontier and with establishing harmonious relations with Native peoples.

There is the saying in Alberta that Texans and Albertans are the same, except that Albertans like Americans better. Texas cowmen were certainly welcomed in Alberta, as long as they kept their revolvers holstered. And there is much evidence that Americans coming up the cattle trails to Alberta soon felt at home. Despite the perception that all Americans were fascinated by guns and violence, a fascination shared by many Canadians in a voyeuristic way, when Americans moved north and lived under very different legal institutions, the evidence indicates that the vast majority grew to see these differences in a positive light. A somewhat incongruous situation developed in the Canadian ranching community whereby Americans themselves were enthusiastically welcomed, but not some of their ideas. American cowboys, with their infectious openness and easy humour, provided a much-needed contrast to the tight formality of Victorian Canada. Any anti-Americanism directed at these cowboys was almost bound to be motivated by the conviction that all Americans were lacking in discipline and were thus innately lawless. There were, of course, just enough boisterous American cowboys on the Canadian range to feed the prejudice.

* * * * *

The early Alberta ranching community, as already indicated, at first developed into a unique enclave of eastern and British privilege. Most of those who established ranches in the 1880s shared similar backgrounds and attitudes. Most were well educated and came west with enough capital to establish themselves comfortably. Their style, in most cases, bore no resemblance to the harsh struggle for bare subsistence of the homesteaders. By the 1880s, the English with enough money to do so flocked to Alberta's ranching country more than to any other part of the British Empire.[150]

Scores of historians have already pointed out Frederick Jackson Turner's oversimplifications. It is enough to say that there is no better example of the inadequacies of the Turner thesis than the Alberta ranching frontier. These ranchers were almost as determined as the Mounted Police to impose their beliefs on this raw frontier and to recreate the sorts of communities they had left. The values that came with them from eastern Canada or Britain – reverence for the monarchy, belief in a conservative type of democracy, respect for property, and a strong link with the church – were essentially unaltered by the frontier environment.[151] They failed dismally, however, in trying to persuade their cowboys to dress for dinner.

At first, this ranching frontier had an overwhelming English atmosphere. Many of the eastern Canadians who pioneered the ranching country shared the English belief that all things English were best. This was not just a case of a lingering and pathetic colonialism. The Alberta ranching frontier was developing at a time when, as Sir John A. Macdonald observed, Canada's gristle had not yet hardened to bone. Canada did not have the luxury of being truly independent. She was caught between two great powers, Britain and America, and Canadians of the period were still all too conscious of American manifest destiny. Britain was Canada's protector, a counterbalance to American domination and expansionist tendencies. It was also a period when Britain was at the height of her power; Canadians could feel superior in being part of an empire that bestrode the world – the greatest civilization, so most Anglo-Canadians believed, the world had yet produced. Canadians believed they were the inheritors of political, legal, and social institutions that had evolved through centuries and were tried and true. But a funny twist to this Anglo-Canadian mentality was that while many Canadians were prepared to lay down their lives for British ideals – as many did in the First World War – they detested nothing more than pompous Britons! They could not abide British condescension.

Turner's environmental imperative fades before this early Alberta ranching community. Certainly, the English ranchers were besotted with the landscape of the Alberta foothills, just as Wister was with the Eden he found in Wyoming, but the English ranchers, to the annoyance of many, preserved their Englishness and tried very hard to fashion an English colonial enclave in the Canadian West.

Yet, that said, one of the most striking features of Alberta ranching literature is how deeply affected these people were by the country they settled, by the foothills country of the Rockies, so different in its emotional appeal than the seeming endless flatness of the prairies. There is an excitement in the early writings of the ranching community that is rarely seen in other homesteading literature. With few exceptions, these early ranchers loved their life. The rhythms of ranch life were far more appealing than the subsistence drudgery of the pioneer farmer. There was no literature of dark ennui, so typical of the sod-house prairies, or the images of dust and drudgery found in a novel like Sinclair Ross's *As For Me and My House*. Perhaps, more than anything else, the feeling of freedom and exhilaration that the horse gave to this life explains the special nature of ranching life.

The existence of the rancher revolved around horses, both for work and sport. Many of the early English ranchers brought with them a passion for racing horses and riding to hounds, with the coyote pinch-hitting for the fox, and neighbourhood dogs substituting for a proper pack of hounds. When the new sport of polo was introduced to the ranching community, it instantly became popular. And local gymkhanas were almost weekly affairs.

The other focal points of ranching life, of course, were the frequent dances, very much as Wister described the Bear Creek barbeque at the Searight Goose Egg Ranch. In the early days it was a community affair, involving ranchers, Mounted Police, Métis, and Natives.[152] The most important institution in ranching country was the annual Mounted Police New Year's Ball, to which all were invited. Col. Macleod, the second commissioner of the Mounted Police, but the one who is rightly famous for establishing the basic character of the force in the West, set the tone very early on when he opened the ball by asking a Native woman to dance. Sadly, that tradition did not last.

Women, too, generally shared their men's love of ranching life, in contrast to their homesteading sisters. The note of resigned bitterness so often encountered in the writings of farming women who settled the prairies is conspicuously absent from ranching literature. It undoubtedly helped that they came to the West with money – otherwise ranching was an impossibility. And they were generally held in high esteem, especially by the cowboys. Though many of them worked very hard, they were seen as the mistresses of their ranches, not as the drudges of the subsistence homestead and the sod hut. The women of ranching country were usually as passionate about horses as were their husbands and often accompanied them on coyote hunts or shooting parties, riding side-saddle and sometimes in riding habit.[153] I knew an early horse buyer, Lou Chambers, who had great fun seeing the expressions on other people's faces when he would arrive to try out a rank horse and would put his wife's side-saddle on the horse and then buck it out. With a rider's legs crossed and locked, it takes a very good bucking horse to unseat a side-saddle rider.

Monica Hopkins, who ranched with her husband Billie in the very English ranching community around Priddis and Millarville, said that she loved every minute of her life there. After a crash course in domestic science before leaving Ireland, which included the "intricacies of ironing," she joined her husband in the West and, though she wrote of long hours of hard work on the ranch, she saw her new life as a great adventure.[154] Undoubtedly, her love of this new land was partly based on its non-threatening nature. She had a degree of financial security, was surrounded by her beloved books, and was part of a like-minded community that had imported and planted its beliefs and customs almost unaltered. Monica Hopkins was part of a ranching community that worked hard but still found plenty of time to indulge its love of sport and parties.

Almost every town had its horse-racing track, and there were at least half a dozen ranchers' polo teams in the period before the First World War. It has been said that the first polo in North America was played in southern Alberta in 1886. Before long, there were ranching teams at Pincher Creek, Macleod, High River, Millarville, and Cochrane. Polo had come to England only a decade earlier.[155]

However, as more Americans came north to establish smaller, mostly mixed-ranching and farming properties and more came from eastern Canada to establish comparatively modest ranches, the tone of ranching country changed from the earlier very English atmosphere. The most obvious manifestation of this change was seen in the institution of the rodeo, which was an echo of the open range and included activities such as roping and riding horses "meaner 'n cat piss," as well as later additions such as bulldogging and chuckwagon racing. The American influence was clearly seen in the creation of the first Calgary Stampede in 1912 by American entrepreneur Guy Weadick.

An intriguing aspect of this rodeo world was that it was, perhaps, the only place where Native competitors could compete as equals with white cowboys and escape the Indian reserves. Starting with Cody's Wild West, the Sioux were introduced to the rodeo and took to it instantly; it allowed them to reclaim their position as one of the great equestrian people of history. But Native enthusiasm for the rodeo was not without irony. The rodeo was not in their heritage. In fact, their customary handling of horses was usually the antithesis of the rough, often brutal, treatment of green horses on the open range. A customary Native way of gentling a young horse was to lead it beside an older, wiser horse to waist-deep water, with two riders seated on the older horse. Then one rider would gently ease himself onto the green horse, which was incapable, because of the deep water, of much more than a few crow-hops.[156] These were the original horse whisperers! Native participants in the rodeo were clearly reclaiming an important part of their heritage of superb horsemanship, but they were also adopting a culture of the rodeo which was not part of their past.

Another Native training method seems terribly cruel, but there was a good reason for it. A horse would be tethered and left almost to die of hunger and thirst. Then, the owner would, with elaborate affection, bring it food and water. Ever after, the horse would return to that spot and to that person. On the plains, before fences, it was critical to be able to catch your horse easily. In an era of tribal raids and counting coup on the enemy, it could mean the difference between life and death.

The rodeo was just as eagerly embraced by the English ranchers of the Alberta foothills. It just goes to show that both the Native peoples and the English did have the capability to change and to come to a meeting of minds. In a very real way, the rodeo can be seen as the extension of the rendezvous, initiated in the fur trade of French colonial times, which meshed the traditions of medieval European trade fairs and the gatherings of Native groups to trade and gossip at traditional locations. The institution of the rendezvous spread across the continent to find its most picturesque setting in the gatherings of Native traders and American mountain men in the shadow of the Rockies. Roughly three-quarters of these fabled American mountain men were actually of French extraction.[157]

The American influence, brought up the cattle trails, also included a brand of humour that only works with the right accent and lazy delivery. Cowboy humour is unique and distinctive. One form, made famous in Wister's frog story, is the long, drawn-out story, with the ending turned on its head once the listener is thoroughly sucked in. More often it was the pithy saying, such as the old-timer commenting on one particular winter that was so cold his nose froze solid, "Damned if it ain't. Hard enough to peck holes in a board." Or the well-known cowboy saying, "I had a bath last week and I don't feel so good anymore."

A cowboy friend of mine, and later a well-known sculptor in the tradition of Remington, Doug Stephens, told me of being on a spring round-up in the foothills when a freak snowstorm hit. He and one other cowboy had expected to get the cattle back to home base by nightfall, but were delayed getting coy steers out of the bush. They had nothing to eat, no warm clothes, and couldn't leave the cattle. By nightfall, they got the cattle as far as a fenced field where they could hold them. There was nothing for it but to hunker down under some old straw stooks that had been discarded. As Doug was finally drifting off to sleep, with melting snow dripping down his back, his companion gave him a big whack on his shoulder and said, "Doug, did you close that gate back there? I feel a breeze on the back of my neck."

My father loved to tell about a horse-buying trip to Colorado. He was staying in quite a decent hotel in Denver. As he was checking out, he saw a huge cockroach advancing across the foyer. It caused quite a stir and a very flustered manager was trying to deal with the situation when a bandy-legged old cowboy got off the elevator. He took one look, gave a great war whoop and yelled at his companions, "Grab her, boys, and ear her down til I throw a saddle on her!"

* * * * *

After establishing the Two Bar Ranch for Gordon and Ironside in 1893, Johnson's days as a ranch foreman ended for unknown reasons, though he later stayed on with Gordon and Ironside as a cattle buyer. But he was still very much a part of the ranching community. Shortly after leaving the Two Bar, an old friend from Wyoming, Blue Osborne, with Johnson's help, picked a site for a ranch about six miles from the Bar U in the Wintering Hills. Osborne had married Maggie Laycock, a cousin of Mary Johnson. It was Osborne who brought Bill Piggott, the great Black cowboy, from Texas to Calgary. Piggott is credited with originating bulldogging. He gave an exhibition of this art in front of the grandstand at Victoria Park, riding Blue's pinto cow pony. Johnson recalled that at one point in the proceedings, while Piggott was watching the steer roping, a steer got loose, jumped the fence in front of the grandstand, and took off after one of the spectators, Eneas McCormick. In a flash, Piggott grabbed the steer and bulldogged him down with his trademark method of sinking his teeth in the steer's nose and then letting go of the horns. As he stood up, he reached into his mouth and pulled out a tooth.

In the 1890s, Johnson began to concentrate more on raising horses than cattle. For a start, they were much more capable of rustling for their feed in the winter since their feet were better suited for pawing through crusted snow, something cattle have great difficulty doing. And prices were good. Johnson hired his old friend from Wyoming, Shorty Niar, to break the horses. Shorty, for a time, had been with Bill Cody's Wild West and delighted in telling that, when he was performing in England, whenever one of Cody's cowboys was bucked off, the King would shout, "Give him to Shorty! He'll ride him." No one wanted to point out to Shorty that the reigning monarch, Queen Victoria, was not a king! Johnson's friendship with Shorty was no doubt tested somewhat when Shorty, through carelessness, burned down the house.

In 1895, with prices for horses dropping in Canada, Johnson decided to take a few carloads of horses to Europe, hoping to find a better market. He spent a year in Europe, selling horses in France, Germany, and Belgium for prices that made the gamble worthwhile. While in Antwerp, sitting at a sidewalk café, he saw a man he knew from Wyoming days strolling by, "dressed to the nines." Johnson called him by name, which caused the man to whirl around, with his hand reaching for his concealed pistol. When he realized who it was, the man sat down and chatted about old days. He had robbed a train in Montana and escaped to Europe with a great deal of money. They parted, the man knowing that a perverse article of the cowboy code would keep him safe from discovery. Johnson last heard of him in Cairo, where he had set himself up under the name Harrison Pasha.

When Johnson returned from Europe, it seemed that he might be willing to settle down. He went into partnership with a Captain d'Eyncourt, who had bought a ranch from Harry Critchley on Beddington Creek, about eighteen miles northwest of Calgary. Johnson had a log house built and then hired Tom and Ed Marshall to break horses. Their brother, Lee, was one of the best bucking-horse riders of the time. Four miles from the ranch was the Gibson's Cup of Tea Ranch. One of the Gibson boys, Tom, was to win the Canadian Championship for bucking-horse riding at the 1912 Calgary Stampede. Later, in the 1919 Calgary Stampede, Tom was injured, and his brother Guy was allowed to sub for him. He distinguished himself by putting in a top performance on the great bucking horse Fox. Both Tom and Guy worked for Johnson from time to time.

The other great bucking-horse rider who turned up in the neighbourhood was Shorty Niar, who was breaking horses for R. G. Robinson on the Big Spring Ranch. Johnson said, with a certain tone in his voice, that after Shorty moved into the neighbourhood, he kept a close guard on the matches. Shorty did turn up one day at the Johnson ranch for repairs after a run-in with the Robinson's Coach-horse stallion. The horse had Shorty down in the manger, chewing him up pretty badly. Shorty was heard to say, "You son-of-a-bitch, you had better make a good job of it. If ever I get out of here, you'll catch it." Luckily, Mary Johnson, the trained nurse, was nearby to patch him up.

This was a good time to be in the horse business. Johnson's first love was always for horses, and business was good, especially after the Boer War began in 1899, creating a large demand for remounts. By now, Johnson's sons, Laurie and Bert, were able to help. They were still light enough to back the young horses when they first started into training.

BRONCO BUSTERS SADDLING
Century, February 1888

Frederic Remington, "Bronco Busters Saddling," *Century*, February 1888. Rough methods of horse breaking were often necessary on the open range.

Good horsemen now wince at the frontier term "horse breaking." It evokes all the roughness and cruelty that were so common in the treatment of range horses. Many of the cowboys were not good horsemen, and the good ones often had to ride horses that had been broken in a hurry, often from a wild state. So there is no question that many of the early western training methods don't bear close scrutiny – they called for the use of savage bits, spurs, and quirts. One positive aspect of fencing the range was that cowboys could now spend more time gentling young horses, and they did not have to re-establish basics each time with half-wild mustangs roped from the herd.

Horses and dogs are perhaps the only animals with a natural generosity of spirit toward humans. In the case of horses, this quality has allowed humans to create a special bond or – all too often – to take terrible advantage of these gentle and trusting creatures. As ranching became more settled, there was a very important place for the gentle side of horse training, and people like Johnson and his sons Laurie and Bert were greatly admired; Laurie and Bert were in great demand to bring on young stock.

Happily, the cruel side of the horse business receded as ranches became established. But the old brutal traditions are sometimes still on display on the rodeo circuit or in the high-stakes world of show jumping. I once watched a friend almost killed in a national three-day event championship (cross-country jumping) because a team coach had made her practice with a wire attached to a tractor battery that was placed along the top rail of the training jump. Another wire was tied to the horse's tail. When the two wires touched, the horse got a hell of a jolt. This made the terrified horse try to jump beyond its capabilities. The horse clearly had something wrong with its back, which accounted for its sloppy jumping. In a national championship event, this terrified horse turned upside down over a jump and landed on top of its rider, who was in hospital for months. Anything for the country's greater glory!

And then there is the Calgary Stampede's chuckwagon race. It seems that every year or so a few more horses are killed, and every year or so a few more band-aid rules are added. But rules are not the issue. These rules cannot control the brutal training methods that sometimes take place behind the scenes. You just have to observe the wild look in the eyes of some of the chuckwagon horses as they are waiting for their heat to know that something bad is likely to happen. Fifty chuckwagon horses have died since 1986 at the Calgary Stampede. But the event is so popular and, more to the point, so lucrative that it remains. Fifty horses in twenty-five years is just considered "acceptable collateral damage!" It is truly sickening.

At the other end of the spectrum, I have watched Laurie Johnson on one of his superbly trained polo ponies, and it was clear to me that the best in western equestrian traditions had come down to him from his father – trust and partnership, and the understanding that the horse's mouth is sacred. For those who follow these principles, there is an extraordinary return – the lightness and confidence of a horse ridden by seat and legs, not hands, and liberated by the snaffle bit from the implements of torture that should be found only in museums.

Johnson took enormous pride in the smoothness of the horses he trained and the confidence of these horses in their riders. Johnson's horses were especially known for their gentle mouths, the ultimate testament to a good horseman. One of his cut horses was the top horse in its day in Alberta. But it wasn't all horses. Like many other ranchers, he loved shooting. He kept a setter and retriever and a pack of coyote hounds for hunting. One of his treasures was an English shotgun that Captain d'Eyncourt brought him from England.

Wolves at the time had moved south from their usual habitat and were a menace to young stock. One of Johnson's greyhounds, Sweep, caused quite a stir by catching and killing single-handed a strikingly large white female wolf. On the other hand, Edward Brado tells of an Alberta rancher who imported six Russian wolfhounds to deal with the wolf problem. He turned them loose on a large wolf, who sped off with the wolfhounds in hot pursuit. When the rancher caught up with the kill, the wolf had disappeared. Four of his dogs lay dead, a fifth was dying, and the sixth had a severed leg. Wolves don't grab and hold; they dart in and slash with teeth that cut like a knife.[158]

Though Johnson was happy on the d'Eyncourt ranch and settled easily into Alberta ranching society, he always felt like a sojourner in his new country, an exile from his own. He would always remain, deep down, a Virginian and an American. And perhaps, like so many others who had known the frontier before fences, he found it impossible to settle completely into the quiet, fenced life of Alberta ranching. The d'Eyncourt ranch was the first place since leaving Minnesota forty years earlier that he could truly call home. But the restlessness persisted. Partly, perhaps, to get this restlessness out of his system, he made one last visit to Wyoming in the summer of 1900. The main purpose of the visit was to see Fred Hesse, who, after the failure of the Powder River company, had located a ranch on the middle fork of the Crazy Woman River. They had much to talk about, and Johnson returned home with an acute wistfulness for the old days, but glowing from the parting words of the reticent Fred Hesse. "You," Hesse told him, "were the best cowhand that ever worked for the Powder River outfit." It was a compliment that Johnson would never forget, coming from someone he considered one of the great cowmen of the American West. Hesse repeated these words about Johnson to others, so Johnson knew they were not just the parting words of a friend.

That same year, Mary went back to England to visit family, just in time to witness the pageantry surrounding the death of Queen Victoria and the mourning of an empire at its height. While she was away, Laurie and Bert moved their beds into their father's bedroom, and Laurie remembered his father's last words every night, "First one asleep, whistle!"

When Mary returned from England, she was accompanied by her youngest sister, Emily, who had met on the ship a dashing young soldier, Cecil Rice-Jones, returning from the Boer War and heading for the Canadian West to try his hand at ranching. He located in the Cypress Hills in southwestern Saskatchewan. He and Emily were married the next year, around the same time that the Johnsons had their next child, Frances Olive.

In 1901, the Duke and Duchess of Cornwall and York (the future King George V and Queen Mary) paid a visit to Canada and other parts of the Empire. The Royal entourage, which included the Canadian prime minister, Sir Wilfrid Laurier, and the governor general and his wife, Lord and Lady Minto, arrived in Calgary on September 29. They were given a typical Calgary welcome: a parade of cowboys and cowgirls, Native horsemen in full regalia, a Mounted Police honour guard on their matched black horses, and the obligatory gift of Stetson cowboy hats. The first order of business was a meeting on horseback between the Duke and three chiefs of the Stoney nation, located halfway between Calgary and Banff. The chiefs, Jacob Bearspaw, John Chiniki, and Jonas Big Stoney, reminded the future monarch with great ceremony of the ancient promises to their people, and the Duke replied with the equally ancient and hollow promise of honouring the treaties "as long as the sun shall shine and waters flow."

The party then proceeded to Victoria Park, future site of the annual Calgary Stampede, where the Duke received the Mounted Police honour guard and presented medals to veterans of the Boer War. Then the royal party settled in to watch a rodeo, the horses first being blindfolded and saddled and then ridden from a standstill. Johnson had been asked to give a demonstration of roping, which he did on his favourite cut horse, Sailor. He roped, threw, and tied two steers, and then was presented to the Duke and Duchess. By this point in his life, he had left competition behind, but he still gave demonstrations and judged numerous competitions. Roping was not for the effete. As one old cowboy remarked about his roping hand, "It used to blister, but now it just smokes a bit."[159]

Johnson's friend, Frank Ricks, who had a large reputation as a bucking-horse rider, was to ride against John Ware, the Black cowboy of early Alberta fame. He let Ware ride first and then declared Ware the winner; he said that no one could make a better ride. Many attempts had been made over the years to have a roping competition between Johnson and Ware. Johnson refused to compete against a Black man; Ricks was far more diplomatic! Ware was considered by many to be the best bucking-horse rider in Canada at the time of the 1893 Calgary Rodeo. But there was a question of style. According to L. V. Kelly, Ware rode by brute strength; Frank Ricks rode more by balance.[160]

A frequent visitor to the ranch was Kathleen Parslow, daughter of the man who had bought the d'Eyncourt ranch. Kathleen greatly fancied Mary's violin and spent many hours playing it, with Mary accompanying her on the piano. Kathleen, at this point in her mid-teens, had made her public debut in San Francisco at the age of six and, through the generosity of Lord

Strathcona, went on to study the violin at the Saint Petersburg Conservatory under the great Leopold Auer (the teacher of Jascha Heifetz). Kathleen Parslow undoubtedly became the most famous of Calgary's home-grown daughters. She went on to perform with great success in both North America and Europe. She taught at the Toronto Royal Conservatory and founded the Parslow String Quartet.

Shortly before the disastrous winter of 1906–7, Alberta's equivalent of the Great Die-Up in Wyoming, the d'Eyncourt ranch was sold to the company of Parslow and Hamilton, who moved cattle onto the ranch just in time to lose 1,000 head in that catastrophic winter. Now, for the second time, Johnson avoided having cattle under his care during another "storm of the century." When Captain d'Eyncourt sold the ranch, the Johnson family moved into Calgary, and Johnson began buying cattle for Gordon, Ironside and Fares, a job that kept him away from home for long stretches. Mary did most of the bringing up of the boys.

In 1904, shortly after Johnson moved to Calgary, *The Book* arrived by mail. Laurie and Bert remembered their father's excitement as he began to read the copy of *The Virginian*, sent to him by Owen Wister, with the inscription, "To the hero from the author." He was overcome with emotion. Laurie recalled watching his father reading the book, springing to his feet and pacing the room, muttering, "I'll be damned," or "The old so-and-so. Fancy remembering that."

Johnson did not say, then or later, that he was the Virginian. As the fame of the book spread, it was others who voiced the theory that the book was based on him. One of these was Loronzo (Ren) Smith, who had worked at Wolcott's VR Ranch that summer of 1885 when Wister and Johnson were there.

G. J. Fuller, the Alberta cowboy artist, worked at one time for Ren Smith, and wrote to Jean Johnson:

> Ren was no slouch with a rope, but he often remarked that Ebb Johnson was the best all round cowboy he had ever known. It would seem to be more than just a coincidence that throughout Wister's book, from catching the rope-wise pony to killing Trampas, he should portray the birthplace, the mannerisms, accent, character and personality of a man he knew as well as he knew Ebb Johnson and not be aware of the fact.

7: The Book (1891–1904)

With the publication of *The Virginian* in 1902, Wister transformed the cowboy. Before its publication, the image of the cowboy was essentially that of the dime novel – a rough, violent, one-dimensional drifter, or the stage cowboy of Buffalo Bill's Wild West variety. Wister's novel was to transform this early image of the cowboy almost overnight.

It would be difficult to find a more unlikely bard of the West. Everything in Wister's upbringing and temperament predisposed him to find these uncouth westerners rather contemptible or, at most, only quaintly interesting. Wister was born and raised a snob. His life began in Philadelphia's upper crust and, until his trip to Wyoming in 1885, he exerted considerable energy in avoiding unwashed democracy. He was born, in 1860, to a caste preoccupied with antecedents, social hierarchy, and literary pursuits.

His mother, Sarah Wister, came from a distinguished acting family and was herself a literary force, greatly admired, for instance, by Henry James. She was beautiful and charming, but cold and haughty; she spoke French and Italian fluently and played several instruments. Her poetry and essays on music, art, literature, and education found their way into some of America's leading literary journals. She was also described as being utterly domineering and overbearing and having "a remarkable incapacity to maintain tolerable relations with individuals beneath her station."[1] Her influence on her son was profound; he wrote to her every week until her death.

She was the daughter of Fanny Kemble, the famed British Shakespearean actress, and Pierce Butler, a prominent Philadelphian with strong roots in Georgian plantation society. Kemble was a great beauty who had published six volumes of poetry and a journal about her time on a Southern

The young Owen Wister, an unlikely bard of the West. His mother kept a diary about his activities entitled "A Child of Promise." His was a hothouse childhood. American Heritage Center, University of Wyoming.

plantation, which was credited by some with helping to sway British opinion against intervening on the side of the South in the Civil War.[2] Owen was also not unconscious that one of his forebears, the original Pierce Butler of Georgia, a man of great vanity and vehemence about the rights of Southern slaveholders, had been a delegate to the Constitutional Convention.[3] The vast gulf between Fanny and Pierce over the issue of slavery doomed their marriage; their very public divorce surely contributed to their daughter Sarah's emotional brittleness. It would seem, too, that Owen inherited the Butler arrogance and disdain.[4] The deep difference of opinion between Fanny and Pierce over slavery was also to have a profound effect on the extended family during the Civil War, a split that Wister would later attempt to reconcile in his writing.[5]

Wister grew up in the shadow of his beautiful, brilliant, and cold mother, desperate to please and impress her and acutely conscious both of her critical view of his achievements and of her lack of affection toward him. Wister's father, a prominent Philadelphia physician, seems less important in Wister's life. By all accounts, Dr. Wister adored his wife and gave her free rein in her literary and social pursuits. He worked very hard and mostly accepted his wife's blueprint for the upbringing of Owen, their only child.

Wister's was a strictly regulated and rather precious upbringing. His father suffered a nervous breakdown, and the family spent three years in Europe, where Wister first went to school in Switzerland and then for a year in England. In 1873, at the impressionable age of thirteen, Wister was sent to St. Paul's School in Concord, New Hampshire, one of America's most exclusive boarding schools. There Wister could indulge both his sense of being very special and also his passion for literature, drama, and music.[6] He graduated in 1878 and followed the natural path of so many St. Paul's graduates to Harvard. Earlier, while in Switzerland, he had begun to be afflicted with the problem that would send him west in 1885: a paralysis of one side of his face and serious eye problems.

Harvard in the 1870s had perhaps fifty faculty members and a student body of a thousand. Harvard's intimate atmosphere allowed Wister to form a friendship with a student two years his senior – Theodore Roosevelt. The two were to become lifelong friends. Their friendship first took root in Harvard's Porcellion Club, one of the country's most prestigious and exclusive clubs. Here Wister formed many lasting friendships with students who were to become the political and business leaders of America. And, undoubtedly, other important friendships were formed in Count Lorenzo Papanti's dancing classes. Harvard also gave Wister the opportunity to become a solid member of Boston society, allowing him to mingle with the Cabots and

Saltonstalls and the literary and intellectual leaders of American society, such as Parkman, Longfellow, and Holmes.

When Wister graduated summa cum laude in 1882 with a double major in music and philosophy, he was confidently ensconced among the most privileged in American society. And there is no indication that he would have had it any other way. His focus was steadfastly on upper-class America and the culture of Europe.

On graduating from Harvard, he was at last able to indulge his first love – music. In the summer of 1882, armed with a letter of introduction from his grandmother Fanny Kemble to her friend Franz Liszt at Wagner's house in Bayreuth – now the great shrine to Wagnerian opera – Wister sought out the great man and was given an audition. Wister's father was most unenthusiastic about the prospect of his son devoting his life to music, but was prepared to foot the bills if his son showed great talent – something, it was thought, that could only be determined in Europe. So Wister performed, and Liszt judged him to have "un talent prononcé."[7] There followed a period at the Paris Conservatoire, studying under Ernest Guiraud, but it all came to naught. Dr. Wister rejected Liszt's opinion on the grounds that he knew nothing about what was appropriate for a well-bred American. "Liszt is a damn Jew and I am an American gentleman."[8] Though Wister's father appears to have relented and agreed to musical training in Europe, Wister decided to give in to his father's true wishes and returned to the United States to begin a career in business.

Through family connections, Wister was given a position at the Union Safety Deposit Vaults with the brokerage firm of Lee, Higginson, headed by Henry Lee Higginson, a man of great wealth and taste who had single-handedly founded the Boston Symphony Orchestra. Soon Wister was immersed in Boston society and, being fresh from Europe, was in great demand among those who avoided "low and common topics" – which included most American subjects. Wister was clearly enjoying himself, but found some of Boston's society contrived and superficial. He was especially scathing toward Boston's eligible young women, whom he found "often ignorant of all things in Heaven and Earth except what their first cousins were doing and saying."[9]

But Wister soon tired of the brokerage world, developed a lifelong distaste for bankers, and increasingly sought an outlet for his artistic side – spurred on, it appears, by the writer William Dean Howells, who befriended him during this period. In the fall of 1884, Wister began work on a novel entitled *A Wise Man's Son*, but the project seems to have fizzled. About the same time, Wister got his father to agree to a new career – the law.

> I would go to Harvard Law School, since American respectability accepted lawyers, no matter how bad, which I was likely to be, and rejected composers, even if they were very good, which I might possibly be.[10]

Wister was to begin law school in the fall of 1885. But, in the meantime, his health collapsed. He complained increasingly of bad headaches, vertigo, and even an occasional hallucination. His father, a physician, even spoke of Wister as having a "mental illness."[11]

It seems that, at this point in his life, fate intervened in the form of Dr. S. Weir Mitchell, one of Philadelphia's most prominent physicians, who specialized in treating the nervous disorders of Boston's and Philadelphia's upper class. He was a psychiatrist, author of a dozen novels, and conversationalist par excellence. He was also Philadelphia's First Citizen, as no man had been since Benjamin Franklin and Benjamin Rush.[12] He was a distant relation of the Wisters. He was probably America's leading specialist at the time in the treatment of nervous disorders, and also Philadelphia's leading literary figure in the late nineteenth century.[13] His specialty, the "Weir Mitchell treatment," called for rest, massage, diet, and exercise, and, most importantly, an extended visit to Europe for relaxation. In Wister's case, Dr. Mitchell suggested that the cure should be sought in the opposite direction. Dr. Mitchell's prescription was for Wister to go west and live outdoors, a notion that had probably never crossed Wister's mind. In the light of Wister's later literary development, the rest of Dr. Mitchell's prescription is more than a little ironic. He urged Wister to "see more new people":

> Learn to sympathize with your fellow man a little more than you are inclined to. You don't feel kindly to your race, you know. There are lots of humble folks in the fields you'd be the better for knowing.[14]

So it would seem that the birth of the cowboy mystique owes a lot to Weir Mitchell. Would Wister, the consummate snob firmly focused on Europe, ever have discovered the West and his calling as the Kipling of the common folk if Dr. Mitchell had not intervened at this moment in his life? Wister might just as easily have become a prosperous Boston or Philadelphia lawyer and a failed author.

But, fortunately for American literature, Wister followed Dr. Mitchell's advice and, as outlined in chapter 5, found himself boarding a train for the West at the end of June 1885, accompanied by two of his mother's spinster friends, who were there partly to look after the somewhat neurotic Owen. Their destination was the Wyoming ranch of Major Frank Wolcott, a friend of Weir Mitchell, in the Big Horn Basin.[15]

At this point in Wister's life, there is no hint whatever that he was destined to become besotted with the West. If anything, one could expect him to have the same attitude toward the West that his mother persisted in all her life; the West was in the wrong direction, it was uncouth, vulgar, uncomfortable, and peopled by the wrong sort. Yet, in 1885, Wister was at his most vulnerable; he was unhappy in the direction of his life, thwarted in his dream of a musical career – the only area thus far in which he had shown any real talent – and greatly bothered by his sense of inferiority in a family of great achievement. In retrospect, it is clear that Wister in 1885, at the age of twenty-five, was open to a new direction and obsessed with the question of how he was to leave his mark on the world.

How Wister discovered Wyoming and found his calling was the main subject of a previous chapter. He was instantly and profoundly moved by what he saw, and the germ was then planted in his mind that was to mature during later trips to the West, resulting in his western writing of the 1890s and finally culminating in 1902 with his vision of the West expressed in *The Virginian*.

Darwin Payne, in his splendid biography of Wister, is surely right when he states that the trip to Wyoming in 1885 was the pivotal point in Wister's life.[16] In Wyoming, Wister underwent a spiritual awakening – that is not too strong a term. And, as has been argued earlier, Wister's friendship with Everett Johnson was the starting point for what would later emerge as the character of the Virginian. In years to come, Wister would record his impressions of the West while actually travelling in the region. But in his "Notes on Wyoming 1885," which actually was written at some later point when Wister was back East, he commented,

> I have been hearing a wonderful lot of good stories. I mean typical & characteristic stories from ranchers and cattlemen – gamblers and cowboys. ... A finer lot of men than the cowboys & ranch foreman of the region I have seen nowhere. Their virtues – courage, reckless generosity and a certain kind of "tenderness bred of a wild life." Five or six of them coming 100 miles on the stage with me

> were all as attentive and gentle & careful with an old woman who was a passenger – as I fear few gentlemen would have been.[17]

Wister again visited Wyoming, in 1887 and 1889, to hunt in the Wind River and Yellowstone country. On both occasions George West guided the trip, and Wister befriended him to the extent that West later became a serious contender for the distinction of being the Virginian. Meanwhile, after his Wyoming trip in 1885, Wister finished his law degree, settled into life in Philadelphia, made other trips to Wyoming in 1888 and 1891, and tried several times to write a comic opera. These attempts came to nothing. Then, in 1890, as his journal makes clear, Wister's literary ambitions began to turn to western themes. By 1891, he consciously began to record western impressions and anecdotes during his stay at a ranch on the south fork of Powder River, just south of Buffalo, Wyoming, and then on a hunting trip with George West. On his return to the East, Wister later claimed, the idea of becoming the Kipling of the American West materialized during dinner in autumn 1891 at the Philadelphia Club with a friend, Walter Furness. Much later, in *Roosevelt: The Story of a Friendship*, Wister described the moment when he became a western writer:

> And so one Autumn evening of 1891, fresh from Wyoming and its wild glories, I sat in the club dining room with a man as enamoured of the West as I was. This was Walter Furness. ... From oysters to coffee we compared experiences. Why wasn't some Kipling saving the sage-brush for American literature, before the sage-brush and all that it signified went the way of California forty-niner, went the way of the Mississippi steam-boat, went the way of everything? Roosevelt had seen the sage-brush true, had felt its poetry; and Remington, who illustrated his articles so well. But what was fiction doing, fiction, the only thing that has always outlived fact? Must it be perpetual teacups? Was Alkali Ike in the comic papers the one figure which the jejune American imagination, always at full-cock to banter or brag, could discern in that epic which was being lived at the gallop out in the sage-brush. To hell with the tea-cups and the great American laugh! We two said, as we sat dining at the club. The claret had been excellent. "Walter, I'm going to try it myself!" I exclaimed to Walter Furness. "I'm going to start this minute." "Go to it – you ought to have started long ago." I wished him goodnight, he wished me good luck. I went up to the library; and by midnight or so, a good slice of Hank's Woman was down in the rough.[18]

Wister, in western clothes, poses sometime during the 1890s. He was then in his thirties and was becoming a well-known western writer. American Heritage Center, University of Wyoming.

Well, it makes a good story, but Wister was being less than candid. It was probably true that he began "Hank's Woman" that night, but the story was not his first attempt at a western theme. His first western manuscript, *The Story of Chalkeye: A Wind River Romance*, which was not published during his lifetime, bears the inscription on the front, "This was a first essay – begun in early 1891 and never finished."[19] Wister's western writing did not start with a flash of inspiration, a sudden recognition of a calling. It began with a rather uninspired story which Wister never published. *The Story of Chalkeye* was based on a real cowboy of that name who had worked with Johnson on the 76 Ranch. It is important to note that Wister was writing about real people in the form of Lin McLean, whose real name was Jim Drummond, and Chalkeye, both of whom, according to Johnson, were known to Wister in Wyoming. But both plots obviously came from his imagination.

"Hank's Woman," though third rate, is intriguing because Wister's wonderful ability to catch the westerners' rhythms of speech and peculiar expressions is clearly evident. The cowboy theme first appears in this story, but there is no hint of the epic cowboy hero who later emerges in his writing. His cowboys are rough, primitive underlings; however, there is just a trace of the emerging theme of western superiority.

Once again, Weir Mitchell gave destiny a prod. Two manuscripts, "Hank's Woman" and "How Lin McLean Went East," gathered dust until Mitchell urged Wister to send them to Henry Mills Alden at Harper and Brothers, promising to provide a letter of introduction. Alden accepted the manuscripts, and Wister was launched as a minor western author. Though Wister had probably been thinking of western themes for some time, 1892 marked his emergence as a western author.

It is perhaps a bit odd that Wister should rather suddenly come to his new calling, work feverishly on his first effort, and then produce a story, "Hank's Woman," that is both excessively sombre and unflattering to the West – a very un-Kiplingesque little story. After Wister's euphoric view of Wyoming in 1885, he recorded in his diary at the time of writing "Hank's Woman," "I begin to conclude from five seasons of observation that life in this negligent irresponsible wilderness tends to turn people shiftless, cruel and incompetent."[20]

However, in his second attempt, "How Lin McLean Went East," published in the December 1892 issue of *Harper's New Monthly Magazine*, there is the first glimpse of the theme that would make him famous – eastern artificiality and false values evaporating before the openness and spontaneity of the West.[21] But there was a vast gulf between the footloose and womanizing

Lin McLean and the quiet and gentle cowboy figure who later, in the form of the Virginian, would capture the nation.

Wister's cowboys of 1892 had only one thing in common – utter irresponsibility. "They gallop over the face of the empty earth for a little while, and those whom rheumatism or gunpowder do not overtake, are blotted out by the course of empire, leaving no trace behind. … A few … take a squaw to wife and supinely draw her rations from the government while she cuts the wood, digs the irrigation ditches, and bears them half-breeds with regularity."[22] Wister's initial cowboy was charming and refreshing in his directness and lack of artifice, but was essentially a philandering and dissolute drifter. What does come through Wister's early western writing in a clear and striking way, however, is an acute ear for dialogue and a sense of realism. But there is no evidence at this early stage of an attempt to create a cowboy legend.

Wister was also busy in 1892 in a different direction. He published a story, "The Dragon of Wantley," a parody of the King Arthur legend. It met with enthusiasm, certainly from Mark Twain, who wrote Wister, "I have taken *The Dragon of Wantley* away from my wife and daughter – by violence – I am reading it with a delicate and tingling enjoyment."[23]

It would seem that there was little to connect the Arthurian legend to Wister's western writing, but perhaps even now a link was forming in Wister's mind between the chivalrous world of Arthur's England and the shadowy figure, the Virginian, who would first appear in 1892 in "Balaam and Pedro," a story of shocking cruelty to a horse, avenged by the silent cowboy from Virginia.[24] Certainly, by 1895, the link between the legend of Arthur and the American cowboy would be very clear in Wister's article "Evolution of the Cow-Puncher."

"Balaam and Pedro," like his two previous western articles, was based on actual events in Wyoming. In this case, the theme came from an incident of terrible cruelty to a horse that Wister had witnessed while staying on the TTT Ranch. The owner, Bob Tisdale, became so infuriated with a played-out horse that, after beating it unmercifully, he reached forward and gouged out one of its eyes, leaving a "sinkhole of blood." This incident clearly preyed greatly on Wister's mind, partly because he did not have the courage to intervene. By exposing Tisdale in this story and having him severely beaten by the Virginian, he was making amends for his own lack of courage.

When Roosevelt read the story, he wrote Wister to tell him how much he liked the piece, but argued very strongly that the description of the eye gouging was too graphic. Wister took his advice and toned down the description of the incident considerably in the later novel.

So, exactly a decade before the publication of *The Virginian*, Wister had begun to introduce some of the characters and themes that were to become central to the novel. Besides the Virginian, Wister introduced Balaam (Tisdale); Trampas, the arch-villain of the later novel, with the inappropriate first name Sorgy for someone so thoroughly wicked; Judge Henny (who eventually became Henry); and Shorty, the initial owner of Pedro. At the end of the story, Balaam and the Virginian are attacked by Indians, as also happens in the novel. Balaam is saved by Pedro, who senses the presence of the Indians. The fate of the Virginian is not clear; it is presumed that he has been killed. This so upset a law office clerk who worked on the piece that he wrote Wister to tell him that he must not let the Virginian die.

And Wister, most importantly, had begun to reshape his image of the cowboy. In his new character, the Virginian, Wister had begun to develop a different sort of cowboy – soft-spoken and gentle with horses and women, but terrible in his righteous fury. In "Balaam and Pedro," a large part of which was to become a chapter in the novel, the evolution of the cowboy who was to make Wister famous began.

Wister sent "Balaam and Pedro" to the *Atlantic Monthly* and to *Cosmopolitan*, but was rejected at both publishing houses. The story was eventually published by *Harper's New Monthly Magazine* in January 1894. Wister seems to have been at least partially conscious of the turning point this story represented: "I know I have never done anything so good, or that contains such a big swallow of Wyoming."[25]

1892 was a busy year for Wister. He was now writing regularly and had more or less abandoned the law. He also began performing publicly in a piano quartet, one of whose members was a distant cousin, Mary Channing Wister. He would later marry "Molly" Wister in 1898. Also, in 1892, Wister made a trip to Texas in search of western themes. There he found a number of interesting subjects, but Texas was certainly no Wyoming in his estimation. He found Texans generally hypocritically moralistic, murderous, and of the "poor white trash" calibre.[26] Wister's enduring cowboy hero would not be a Texan, the most representative cowboy of the time; instead, he would consciously choose another type – a Tidewater Virginian with the very un-Texan gentlemanly code of the Old South.

After "Balaam and Pedro," illustrated by a man he had heard of but not yet met – Frederic Remington – Wister was delighted when *Harper's Monthly* asked for a series of eight articles on the West. Actually Wister was *Harper's* second choice; Rudyard Kipling had declined. In July 1893, Henry Alden of *Harper's* wrote to Wister with his offer. "Each must be a thrilling story having its ground in real incident, though you are left free for imaginative treatment." Of all the topics "not the least striking ... is that of the appeal to Lynch Law, which ought to give a capital subject for one of your stories."[27]

One of these articles, which appeared in the November 1893 issue of *Harper's New Monthly Magazine*, was about a deranged hen by the name of Em'ly, but it marked a very important stage in the development of Wister's Virginian.[28] The setting was Judge Henny's ranch on Sunk Creek, and the story introduces the relationship between Wister and the Virginian, which was to be so central to the later novel.

The story marks the first time that Wister would write in the first person, a literary device that is central to the novel. And, of great importance for the theme of this book, Wister set the story in 1885, the year he first came to Wyoming and was chaperoned for the summer by Johnson.

> It was my first taste of Wyoming and I was justly called the tenderfoot. ... I was known simply as the "tenderfoot," and a special cowboy was assigned to guide me in my rambles and prevent my calamitously passing into the next world. ... I am sure he cursed this novel job that had fallen to him, although he betrayed no feelings whatever. A more silent man than he was at first I have never seen. During his odious duty of companioning me over the trackless country ... he would not speak an unnecessary syllable. ... In his eyes I must have appeared a truly abominable thing.

Here for the first time is Wister's acknowledgment that he spent much of his first summer in the company of a cowboy who was ordered to look after him, much as Johnson described the situation to Jean. And it was the first time that Wister had written with candour about his rather humiliating condition in the summer of 1885.

The article and the later chapter of the novel are very similar; they both do two important things. They establish the theme of eastern incompetence through contrasting Wister's constant bungling with the Virginian's quiet competence, and they establish the close friendship that grows between them through their shared sentiments toward the antics of the poor deranged Em'ly.

There is one seemingly insignificant change in wording from the earlier to the later version. In describing the chicken that takes off for parts unknown, the Virginian in the novel refers to her as a "right elegant" Dominicker. In the earlier version, the Virginian uses the expression a "right smart" Dominicker. One of Johnson's favourite expressions throughout his life, to make a special point, was that something was "a right smart of...." Perhaps it was an expression that Wister remembered from riding with Johnson that summer of 1885. In Johnson's vocabulary, the word "smart" did not mean intelligent. The expression is used throughout the novel by the Virginian, and it is entirely plausible that Wister used it because he associated it with Johnson's way of speaking.

A month later, in December 1893, Wister had another of his western stories published. "The Winning of the Biscuit-Shooter" included a shadowy Virginian and Judge Henny, and also features the first appearance of Molly Wood, the new school marm. However, the story's central theme involved Lin McLean and his courting of Miss Peck, the biscuit-shooter, a woman of "thick waist" and "brutal comeliness." Lin McLean's courting of Miss Peck is the opposite of the hero's courteous wooing of the refined eastern schoolteacher in *The Virginian*. At one point in "The Winning of the Biscuit-Shooter," Miss Peck is heard to shout "Quit, now, Lin McLean, or I'll put yur through that window, and it shut." The story ends with the two of them off to the justice of the peace to be married, and Wister makes it plain that the easygoing and somewhat dissolute Lin does not deserve to be permanently attached to this plain and unpromising woman.[29] (In a later story she kills herself with a drug overdose.) Here is not the stuff of a Kiplingesque saga!

In September 1893 came a critical moment in the history of the cowboy legend. Quite by accident, while escaping an early winter storm in the Yellowstone country, Wister took shelter at North's Inn and found, to his delight, Frederic Remington, who was similarly taking refuge. The two men immediately took to each other and spent long hours swapping visions of the West. Both were deeply conservative in their political views, and, though Remington was far more unromantic and realistic in his outlook, he shared Wister's excitement for the West. Here began what was shortly to become a critical collaboration to invent what was to become the popular image of the cowboy. Remington had been commissioned by *Harper's* to illustrate western stories, but the two men had not yet met. Remington by now was a very well-known artist of the American West and, in 1889, had published his first significant article on the West in *Century Magazine* – "The Horses of the Plains."[30] Wister, in 1893, was in the West on assignment to *Harper's Magazine*, writing his series of western stories. *Harper's* would send Wister to the West again in 1894 in search of more real western stories.

Remington, like Wister, would make many trips to the West in search of themes for his writing and illustrations. His great purpose was to record what he considered to be the passing of the frontier in a realistic and

Theodore Roosevelt first went west in 1883 and was captivated by the ranching country of the Great Plains. He established a ranch in the Dakota Badlands and collaborated with Wister and Roosevelt in a new vision of the cowboy. Here he poses with this favorite horse, Manitou. Library of Congress, LC-USI 62-91139.

unromantic fashion. His work focused on the early explorers, Native interaction with frontiersmen, pioneers, soldiers, and, finally, cowboys.

Wister and Remington independently knew Theodore Roosevelt, who had already begun writing on western themes and had established a ranch in the Dakotas.[31] Remington, since the mid-1880s, had been a well-known illustrator of the West and by the late 1880s was a regular illustrator for such magazines as *Harper's*, *Outing*, and *Century* and was very busy producing illustrations for Roosevelt's *Ranch Life and the Hunting Trail*, published first in serial form by *Century*. Now Wister and Remington, with Roosevelt's advice from the wings, began very self-consciously to develop an image of the American cowboy that was to be a blend of realism and wishful thinking. All three shared a profound love of the West and revered the rugged life that seemed to have been lost in the East. But it went far beyond this. All three came from old American stock and shared a deeply conservative outlook. And, most importantly, they all thought that something was profoundly wrong with America.

1893 was a significant moment for this collaboration to take root. The United States had just plunged into one of the worst depressions of the century and, as already discussed, Frederick Jackson Turner was to announce, in a paper that year to the American Historical Association, the closing of the American frontier, with all that this fact implied. In this atmosphere of economic depression, old-guard Americans became increasingly alarmed by massive European immigration. As Richard Hofstadter has so brilliantly argued in *The Age of Reform* and elsewhere, America was going through a psychic crisis in the 1890s. Americans like Wister, Remington, and Roosevelt, products of a quickly disappearing caste, were disturbed to the core.

With selective nostalgia, they looked back to an era of simple virtues and racial homogeneity (conveniently ignoring, of course, those of African and Native ancestry). Now, at the height of the era of the robber barons, America, they were convinced, was losing her soul. The America of Jefferson was being replaced, on the one hand, by a polyglot immigrant society and, on the other, by an urban and effete society that had forgotten the moral principles that had made the country great. Remington saw industrial America as a cancerous growth spreading across the continent.[32]

As they looked at their country with a bitter wistfulness, they wondered if there was any salvation. So it was in this frame of mind that the three looked at America's last, rapidly disappearing frontier and found there a type of American that, they thought, was no longer to be found elsewhere. Unconsciously or not, they were Turnerians in their belief that the frontier imparted moral qualities not to be found in the rest of the country. And they began to look on the cowboy as the last "type" of free American, unadulterated by the decadent influences pervading the rest of the country.

So the three set about to enshrine the cowboy in the image of American qualities that they believed to be in danger of extinction. It will no doubt come as a shock to the casual reader of cowboy literature to learn that the transformation of the cowboy type was motivated by a deep pessimism about American society and an equally deep racism; certainly Wister and Remington were pronounced bigots, even if the same cannot quite be said of Roosevelt. The cowboy they created was Anglo-Saxon, with well-defined racial characteristics; they invented him as a counterbalance to the new multiracial society that was emerging through massive new immigration in the 1880s and 1890s.

Remington's influence on Wister's vision of the cowboy is clear, direct, and well documented; that of Roosevelt is more indirect and not as easy to document. Roosevelt, who was a voracious reader, was very aware of Wister's western writing before his cowboy theme emerged in the mid-1890s. Roosevelt knew him well enough to invite him in 1894 to be an associate member of the Boone and Crockett Club, which he had founded in 1887 largely to interest influential men in protecting wildlife. The club was

Frederic Remington, "The Cowboy." Remington's horses were very realistic; he was also one of America's foremost painters of horse movement – he and Charlie Russell. Remington's cowboy exudes all the "Anglo-Saxon" qualities of toughness and virility that Wister and Remington wished to convey. Amon Carter Museum.

named for his two heroes who would feature in his *The Winning of the West*, Daniel Boone and Davy Crockett.[33]

The fact that Roosevelt included Wister in his prestigious club indicates that he believed that Wister shared the same beliefs about the western wilderness and its endangered wildlife. Douglas Brinkley, author of *The Wilderness Warrior*, a very impressive and thorough study of Roosevelt's crusade to preserve America's wildlife and wilderness, goes so far as to argue that Roosevelt had a significant influence on Wister's writing about western wilderness and its wildlife.[34] Wister and Roosevelt had many discussions about the role of the West in revitalizing American society; it is plausible that Roosevelt's influence can be seen in Wister's shaping of part of the Virginian's character. The Virginian does not have the typical rough attitude toward animals; his concerns for the depraved chicken Em'ly and his towering rage at the mistreatment of a horse are not those of your average cowboy. And his love of the unspoiled wilderness, so wonderfully expressed at the end of the novel when the Virginian takes Molly to his special wilderness retreat for their honeymoon, could come straight out of Roosevelt's writing.

When Roosevelt first went west in 1883 and 1884, he described the Badlands of Dakota in much the same way as would Wister soon after. The land seemed "hardly proper to belong to this earth." He found a sacredness to this land "that exuded a cosmic sense of God's Creation as described in Genesis."[35] This was in 1883, two years before Wister's almost identical description of Wyoming. And when Roosevelt first went west, he held the same romantic view of cowboys as Wister did somewhat later, likening them to the knights of England.[36] Was it mere coincidence that both men saw these things in such a strikingly similar way?

The fact that Roosevelt was the first of the two to discover the West, buy into a ranch and establish another, and to write about cowboys and ranching indicates strongly that it was Roosevelt who probably influenced Wister's thinking about the West, and not the other way around. By the time that Wister began to write about the West in the early 1890s, Roosevelt had already established himself as an important writer on the West and was emerging as the most important American conservationist of the late nineteenth century.

In 1884, Roosevelt collected his experiences on hunting and ranching in his first book on the West, *Hunting Trips of a Ranchman*, published in 1885. His main theme: the importance of the vigorous life as an antidote to the artificial and feminizing life of the eastern city. His core message was that hunting and the western life was good for the American soul; it awakened

Theodore Roosevelt in a very posed studio portrait in 1895, his Winchester 1876 Delux model at the ready, and his silver-mounted Bowie knife designed by Tiffany's of New York in his belt. Significantly, he has shed his glasses; in the West he was known as "Old Four Eyes." Over the years, he was to capitalize on his western image with great success. Harvard College Library, Thoedore Roosevelt Collection, R500P69a-001.

the primitive man, a theme that would pervade his writing. American democracy required a return to the savage.[37]

Certainly, it took some time for Roosevelt to acquire the look of a savage. When he first went west, it was as a squeaky-voiced, "four-eyed" easterner. The cover illustration for *Hunting Trips of a Ranchman* did not help matters – it featured a studio portrait of Roosevelt in buckskins, gun at the ready. It exuded a distinct air of phoniness and caused much hilarity back in the Dakotas.[38] But Roosevelt soon won respect in the West for his enthusiasm and tenacity and his willingness to pull his weight at roundups.

Next came his book, in 1887, on the western expansionist Thomas Hart Benton, father-in-law of John Charles Fremont, the western "pathfinder." His theme here was an ode to American expansionism and manifest destiny; the US had the *right* to "swallow up the land of adjoining nations who were too weak to withstand us." These nations included Great Britain; her colonial possessions in North America should belong to the US! His bullying attitudes in international relations were matched by his acceptance of western attitudes toward law. Western pioneers were "a race of masterful spirit [who were] accustomed to regard with easy tolerance any but the most flagrant violations of law."[39] What emerges from Roosevelt's western writing is a rather alarming sense of flouting the law and an American exceptionalism in foreign relations. Might makes right!

In 1886, Roosevelt wrote six articles for *Outing Magazine* and noticed elsewhere in the magazine the illustrations of an artist new to him. He was greatly impressed by the freshness and honesty of Frederic Remington's work; on the spot he decided that his next book must be illustrated by Remington.[40] Two years later, in 1888, Roosevelt's *Ranch Life and the Hunting Trail* appeared, illustrated by Remington. This was followed in 1893 by *The Wilderness Hunter*. Despite this, they did not become close friends until later. But it is clear that Roosevelt had great admiration for Remington's art. For instance, he wrote him in 1895 to say, "I never so wish to be a millionaire ... as when you have pictures for sale. It seems to me that you in your line, and Wister in his, are doing the best work in America today."[41] Roosevelt, for instance, would not have considered Remington suitable for membership in his Boone and Crockett Club; Remington was just a bit too coarse and bumptious – and he associated with sheep! For his part, Remington did not take greatly to Roosevelt at first. Inherited wealth grated on him, as did Roosevelt's imperious manner. Just as Wister would later hold Remington at arm's length, after the initial euphoria of collaborating on western themes, so, too, did Roosevelt. Yet, at the end of 1897, Roosevelt wrote Remington, "You come closer to the real thing with the pen than any other man in the western business. And I include Hough, Grinnell and Wister. ... I don't know how you do it any more than I know how Kipling does it."[42]

Somewhat later, in 1898, when Roosevelt was presented with a special gift by his regiment at the end of the war with Spain, he broke down with emotion when he unveiled Remington's first and perhaps greatest sculpture – the Bronco Buster. It was the perfect gift, so completely representing Roosevelt's feelings for the cowboy and the West. Roosevelt wrote Remington in September 1898, "It [the Bronco Buster] was the most appropriate gift the Regiment could possibly have given me, and the one I would have valued most. I have long looked hungrily at that bronze, to have it come to me in this precise way seemed almost too good."[43] Roosevelt again wrote to Remington in 1908 to say, "I do not think that any bronze you will ever make will appeal to me more than the one of the broncho-buster, which you know my regiment gave me."[44] That sculpture now resides as a permanent fixture in the Oval Office of the White House.[45]

Roosevelt's next western writing, *The Winning of the West*, occupied him from 1888 to 1896.[46] He had been urged to write on this theme by his good friend and mentor, Henry Cabot Lodge, then America's leading imperialist. This multivolume work was a history of western American expansion from Boone to Crockett. It was an ode to western expansionism, its central theme being the triumph over those who blocked the way. In the introduction to the first volume of *The Winning of the West*, Roosevelt traced the history of Anglo-Saxons from Alfred the Great to George Washington. He argued that the most important part of world history in the last three centuries was the spread of English-speaking peoples over the "waste spaces" of the globe. The remorseless advance of Anglo-Saxon civilization was merely destiny, and the winning of the American West was the "crowning achievement" of that mighty movement. Of course, the "warped, perverse and silly morality" that would preserve the American continent "for the use of a few scattered savage tribes, whose life was but a few degrees less meaningless, squalid and ferocious than that of the wild beasts with whom they hold joint ownership" was beyond contempt.[47] With the publication of these four volumes, Roosevelt became America's leading propagandist of Anglo-Saxon frontier conquest and, as well, the country's leading proponent of social Darwinism. And then, in a passage that would come back to haunt him:

> The most ultimately righteous of all wars is a war with savages, though it is apt to be also the most terrible and inhumane. The rude, fierce settler who drove the savage from the land lays civilized mankind under a debt to him. ... It is of incalculable importance

that America, Australia and Siberia should pass out of the hands of their red, black and yellow aboriginal owners, and become the heritage of the dominant world races.[48]

Somewhat later, and unlike Wister, Roosevelt would show a change of heart toward Native peoples, especially after a visit to the Sioux reservation at Pine Ridge. He came away with a great compassion for the western tribes who had been herded literally at bayonet point onto reservations.[49]

The first volumes of the *Winning of the West* were published just as Wister was developing his cowboy themes for *The Virginian*. It would seem clear that he was influenced by Roosevelt's views, both in print and in conversation. Roosevelt's view of the cowboy certainly came close to that of Wister's in his 1895 essay "The Evolution of the Cow-Puncher," discussed in more detail below, which fused all his significant beliefs on that figure. Wister's article would give to the country a completely fresh and far more sophisticated image of the cowboy. But it is important to realize just how important Roosevelt was to this process.

In *Ranch Life and the Hunting Trail* (1888), which first appeared as a series of articles in *Century Magazine*, Roosevelt had this to say about the Dakota cowboy: he faced life with a "quiet, uncomplaining fortitude," brave, hospitable, hardy, adventurous,

> ... he is the grim pioneer of our race; he prepares the way for the civilization from before whose face he himself must disappear. Hard and dangerous though his existence is, it has yet a wild attraction that strongly draws to it his bold, free spirit. ... The moral tone of the cow camp, indeed, is rather high than otherwise. Meanness, cowardice and dishonesty are not tolerated. There is a high regard for truthfulness and keeping one's word, intense contempt for any kind of hypocrisy, and a hearty dislike for a man who shirks his work. ... A cowboy will not submit tamely to an insult, and is ever ready to avenge his own wrongs; nor has he an overwrought fear of shedding blood. He possesses, in fact, few of the emasculated, milk-and-water moralities admired by the pseudophilanthropists; but he does possess, to a very high degree, the stern, manly qualities that are necessary to a nation.[50]

Nothing like this had been written previously about the American cowboy. Roosevelt and Wister also clearly shared a strong belief in the cowboy as an antidote to milk-and-water, limp-wristed easterners.

More than six months before Frederick Jackson Turner would deliver his famous address at the Chicago World's Fair on the importance of the frontier, Roosevelt, in January 1893, gave the biennial address before the State Historical Society of Wisconsin at Madison. His thesis: the Old Northwest was the "heart of the country." Turner, who was in the audience taking notes, later quoted Roosevelt's address in his 1920 book *The Frontier in American History*. After Turner gave his address in Chicago, Roosevelt stated that Turner had "put into definite shape a good deal of thought which [had] been floating around rather loosely."[51]

The link between Roosevelt's early volumes of *The Winning of the West* and Turner's paper on the significance of the frontier in American history is very clear. Turner demonstrated his admiration for Roosevelt's first two volumes in a review in 1889 and had marked Roosevelt's passage describing "the significance" of the vast movement that conquered the West.[52] Wilbur Jacobs has argued in *The Historical World of Frederick Jackson Turner* that Roosevelt's *The Winning of the West* gave Turner the inspiration for his thesis. In turn, Roosevelt praised Turner's 1893 paper and wrote to him that he intended to use his theme in the later volumes of *The Winning of the West*.[53]

Roosevelt in a popular venue, and Turner in an academic one, were saying similar things. Roosevelt stressed conquest and unabashed triumphalism; Turner put his emphasis on the quiet conquest of the axe and plough, but both were celebrating the Anglo-Saxon male conquest of nature and the Indian barrier, although Turner said very little about Indians. Both found the focal point of American development in the frontier and in the unique character it fostered.[54] Neither one had anything to say about the "frontier of sewing" or the "frontier of laundry."[55] Today, Roosevelt's *Winning of the West*, whose final volume came out in 1896, is hard reading with its trumpeting of manifest destiny and the glorification of violence against both Native peoples and neighbours to north and south.

As Turner was giving his now-famous address in Chicago at the 1893 World's Columbian Exposition, celebrating America's four hundred years since Columbus, close by were Buffalo Bill Cody and his Buffalo Bill's Wild West and Congress of Rough Riders of the World, fresh from the triumphs of London and Paris. In his own way, Cody, too, had his frontier thesis, one that came much closer to Roosevelt's version than it did to Turner's. Turner stressed settlement, not conquest; Cody's theme of violent conquest and the taming of the Indian was actually closer to what really happened. Cody's genius was to popularize Roosevelt's theme of triumphant conquest.

Turner's frontier statement has become unquestionably one of the most quoted and controversial sentences in American historical literature: "The existence of an area of free land, its continuous recession, and the advance of American settlement westward, explains American development."[56] Historians are still fighting over Turner. Turner's emphasis on the peaceful occupation of a largely empty continent is obviously open to criticism.[57] Because of the way that Roosevelt, Cody, and many others emphasized conquest, Turner was consciously looking for another tack: "I have refrained from dwelling on the lawless characteristics of the frontier because they are sufficiently well known. The gambler and the desperado, the Regulators of the Carolinas and the vigilantes of California, are types of that line of scum that the waves of advancing civilization bore before them, and of the growth of spontaneous organs of authority where legal authority was absent."[58] Above all, Turner studiously avoided Cody's Wild West and its central theme, the unabashed conquest of a continent bristling with Indians. Instead, Turner attempted to counter in his writing what he considered Cody's grossly exaggerated picture of the West, along with other equally lurid and sensational literature about the West.[59]

Turner must be seen in the context of his time. To present-day historians, he appears to downplay the blood and gore of the frontier and has been accused of giving a false picture of the western frontier. However, he was doing so to bring a more academic, balanced interpretation to an overheated literature. But, as Patricia Nelson Limerick has pointed out in *The Legacy of Conquest* and elsewhere, no amount of careful historical research seems to be able to influence the popular mind on the issue of the West. As a prime example, Cody's carefully honed mix of excitement, violence, competition, and dramatic narrative were just too powerful. Even today, most people want to believe in the likes of Billy the Kid and Jesse James. In the heyday of the dime novel, a small, self-appointed group wielded an enormous and rather dangerous power over the public mind – and this holds true today in regard to the movie industry. History is manipulated in the most callous, and sometimes insidious, way. The truth gives way to what sells! Scrupulous historians can try as they might to change this, but to no avail; for most, Billy the Kid and Jesse James, both products of the dime-novel industry, remain heroes, and Yellow Hand died in a hand-to-hand duel.

Turner stressed the progressive nature of American society, claiming that this unique American style of progress was very much the result of an enduring frontier legacy, not the product of a European heritage. But, paradoxically, Turner argued that this American culture was achieved by a continual retreat to the primitive simplicity of the frontier.[60]

Meanwhile, Wister, almost a decade before Turner's frontier paper, began to think in a similar way in 1885 when he enthused that the atmosphere of Wyoming was "unvarnished by Europe." Roosevelt, Wister, and Cody all saw the West as the nucleus of a new Americanism. So, it can be argued that Turner was almost a latecomer to arguments that others were already expressing. On one level, Wister's belief that the hope of the country resided in the cowboy appears absurd. But, especially in the crass and ugly era of the Gilded Age, there was something very refreshing in the honest simplicity of the western outlook, in the directness and lack of artifice, and in the lack of adulation for money in a period of intense greed and unchecked capitalism. Surely Turner was also onto something when he argued that progress required the stripping away of false and shallow values that tended to encrust "sophisticated" society. Sadly, after Wister's moment of revelation, he reverted to kind and became among the worst offenders in upholding the values of an impossible eastern caste of snobs and racists. But Wister's legacy from his moment of revelation still reverberates strongly in American society. Wister's other writings are now long forgotten, and he is remembered only for the one great work that he so soon rejected. More than any other writer of the West, he stirred the American imagination with the image of a frontier figure that remains an icon for much of what is best in American society.

* * * * *

However, in 1893, the year of Chicago, Wister's western beliefs were just beginning to jell. The first collaboration between Wister and Remington developed with Wister's story "Baalam and Pedro," but the new image of the cowboy first emerged in force in a pivotal article in 1895, written by Wister and illustrated by Remington, "The Evolution of the Cow-Puncher." The story was Wister's, but the writing was clearly a collaboration of beliefs. The idea for the article took root in January 1894 when Wister was visiting Remington, and Remington urged him to tell the story of the cowboy – his rise and decline. Then Remington began sending regular suggestions by mail.

1895 was the high point of Wister's writing on the West. He wrote five western essays that year, including his most important thus far, "The Evolution of the Cow-Puncher." He also published in January 1896 his first collection of western stories, *Red Men and White*, which was a compilation of previously published stories. This collection has been called his "law and order" stories. It is interesting to note that several of his stories portray lynch mobs in very negative terms. His attitude changed as the Johnson County

Frederic Remington sketch, sent to Wister in 1895 when Wister was writing "The Evolution of the Cow-Puncher." The caption read, "Great and rising demand for - a cowboy article - "The Evolution and the Survival of the Cowboy" - by O. Wister with 25 illustrations by the eminent artist Frederico Remintonio - just out." Library of Congress, Owen Wister Papers, box 33.

War approached, and he became an apologist for the vigilante tactics of the big ranchers in Wyoming.

"The Evolution of the Cow-Puncher" appeared in *Harper's New Monthly Magazine* in September 1895; Wister wasted no time getting to his theme:

> Our first hundred years will grow to be only the mythological beginnings in the time to come ... it won't be a century before the West is simply the true America with thought, type, and life of its own. ... No rood of modern ground is more debased and mongrel [than the East] with its hordes of encroaching alien vermin, that turn our cities to Babels and our citizenship to a hybrid farce, who

degrade our commonwealth from a nation into something half pawn-shop, half broker's office. But to survive in the clean cattle country requires a spirit of adventure, courage, and self-sufficiency; you will not find many Poles or Huns or Russian Jews in that district. ... Even in the cattle country the respectable Swedes settle chiefly to farming, and are seldom horsemen. ... The Frenchman to-day is seen at his best inside a house; he can paint and he can play comedy. ... The Italian has forgotten Columbus and sells fruit. Among the Spaniards and Portuguese no Cortez or Magellan is to be found to-day. Except in Prussia, the Teuton is a tame slippered animal. ... But the Anglo-Saxon is still forever homesick for out-of-doors. ... It is not the dollars that played first fiddle with him, else our Hebrew friends would pioneer the whole lot of us. Adventure, to be out of doors, to find some new place far away from the postman, to enjoy independence of spirit or mind or body ... this is the cardinal surviving fittest instinct that makes the Saxon through the centuries conqueror, invader, navigator, buccaneer, explorer, colonist, tiger-shooter.[61]

Sir Lancelot, Drake, Raleigh, Hawkins, Boone – "from the tournament at Camelot to the round-up at Abilene," the Anglo-Saxon had maintained the spirit of adventure as had no other race and, as often as not, had done so in the company of a good horse.

The cowboy had taken from the Mexican vaquero – that "small, deceitful alien" – his customs and accoutrements, and the Anglo-Saxon spirit burned afresh:

> Thus late in the nineteenth century, was the race once again subjected to battles and darkness, rain and shine. ... Destiny tried her latest experiment upon the Saxon, and plucking him from the library, the haystack, and the gutter, set him upon his horse; then it was that, face to face with the eternal simplicity of death, his modern guise fell away and he showed once again the medieval man. It was no new type, no product of the frontier, but just the original kernel. ... The cow-puncher took wild pleasure in existing. No soldier of fortune ever adventured with bolder carelessness, no fiercer blood ever stained a border. If his raids, his triumphs, and his reverses have inspired no minstrel to sing of him ... it is not so much the Rob Roy as the Walter Scott who is missing. ... These wild men ... begot no sons to continue their hardihood. War they made in

> plenty, but not love; for the woman they saw was not the woman a man can take into his heart. ... Grim lean men of few topics and not many words concerning these ... indifferent to death, but disconcerted by a good woman, some with violent Old Testament religion, some avowing none. ...
>
> And what has become of them? Where is this latest outcropping of the Saxon gone? ... he has been dispersed, as the elk, as the buffalo, as all wild animals most inevitably will be dispersed. Three things swept him away – the exhausting of the virgin pastures, the coming of the wire fence, and Mr. Amour of Chicago, who set the price of beef to suit himself. But all this may be summed up in the word Progress.[62]

The sense of lament is palpable, both for a type that is quickly disappearing and for the lack of a poet "to connect him with the eternal" – there has not yet been "distance to lend him enchantment."

> We have no Sir Thomas Mallory! Since Hawthorne, Longfellow, and Cooper were taken from us, our flippant and impoverished imagination has ceased to be national, and the rider among Indians and cattle, the frontiersman, the American who replaces Miles Standish and the Pathfinder, is now beneath the notice of polite writers.[63]

Here certainly is the first serious treatment of the cowboy in American literature. There is no question that Wister took the cowboy of the dime novel and turned him into a respectable subject. But Wister's cowboy of 1895, who leaps off the page at the reader, has, as yet, none of the charm and subtlety of his eventual cowboy hero. "The Evolution of the Cow-Puncher" marks a midpoint in Wister's own evolution on the subject of the cowboy.

Wister's cow-punchers of 1895 populate a West that is fast disappearing; the essay is a lament for a time that is quickly passing. Barbed wire and the beef trusts are changing everything. The true cowboy type will soon fade away. One of the characteristics that is most striking about Wister's cowboy is that he without question embodied the Anglo-Saxon. This cowboy was not a Mexican, and certainly not a Black. The West, for Wister, is the testing ground for Anglo-Saxon qualities. Here is the last refuge of the "true American," not yet polluted by European immigration.

Remington's first (of five) illustrations for this article fits the theme exactly: a mounted cowboy rampant, with a host of Anglo-Saxon knights, crusaders, cavaliers, frontiersmen, explorers, and soldiers of the Raj, receding into the misty past. The painting is entitled "The Last Cavalier." The final illustration is equally evocative – a cowboy closing a gate in a barbed wire fence that stretches to the horizon. The free range, and with it the American frontier, are no more. A chapter in American history had ended. The illustration gives no hope for the future.

Wister had consulted closely with Remington over the five illustrations for the article. It is not too much to call it a creative collaboration. The visual impact of Remington's drawings was as important as Wister's words. Wister was delighted with the result. He wrote to Remington,

> ... nothing I know of yours seems to reach what you have done this time. And other people seem as enthusiastic as I am. The "Last Cavalier" though it brought tears very nearly to my eyes, is not quite so good as you intended, not quite so good as its idea: I'm not sure the idea can be adequately stated short of a big canvas – But "what an unbranded cow has done" is not only vast, but states itself utterly. So much has never been put on any page of Harper – that I've seen, ... The level of the whole five is up in the air – away up. To me personally, the Last Cavalier comes home hardest, and I love it & look at it. It's so very sad and so very near my private heart. But you must do it again – you must get that idea expressed with the same perfection that the unbranded cow is done with. Then we shall have a poem much better and more national than Hiawatha or Evangeline. There ought to be music for the Last Cavalier. Only you couldn't understand it ... the Last Cavalier will haunt me forever. He inhabits a Past into which I withdraw and mourn.[64]

In crafting this pivotal depiction of the cowboy, Wister also was strongly influenced by Roosevelt's article "What Americanism Means," which invoked the rugged individualism, the "strength, integrity and learned equality" of the frontier, in order to counter the hyphenated Americanism of mass immigration. The western frontier would rid America of these hyphenated Americans. The old frontier had turned early American immigrants into true Americans, and it would continue to do so.[65] In addition, Roosevelt's essay lashed out, as did Wister, at effete eastern society, comprised of "base, low, silly, despicable, flaccid weaklings." One of the most contemptible in Roosevelt's view was Henry James, Sarah Wister's great friend. Roosevelt referred to him as that "miserable little snob" who preferred English society and literature to his own. He accused James of fleeing America because he

Frederic Remington, "The Last Cavalier" (1895), the first of five illustrations for Wister's article "The Evolution of the Cow-Puncher." Remington's painting caught Wister's theme exactly – the cowboy as the last in a long line of romantic horsemen: crusaders, knights of the age of chivalry, cavalry of the Raj, buckskin-clad plains men. Courtesy of Lawerence H. Kyte, Jr.

"cannot play a man's part among men."[66] He also charged him with writing "polished, pointless, uninteresting stories about upper social classes of England [which] make one blush to think he was once an American."[67] James privately responded to Roosevelt's charge, calling him a "dangerous and ominous jingo" and the "monstrous embodiment of unprecedented and resounding noise."[68]

Remington's 1889 essay "Horses of the Plains" also had a pivotal influence on Wister's cowboy article, while Roosevelt's 1895 article "True American Ideals," in which he railed against the state of America's economic and political life, had a strong effect on Remington's thinking about the frontier. In turn, Wister's 1894 article "The National Guard of Pennsylvania" (illustrated by Remington), which contrasted the Americanism of the National Guard to the un-Americanism of the labour agitators, influenced Roosevelt's article on American ideals. All three were profoundly upset by the Panic of 1893, the crippling labour strikes, anarchism, and the "disease" of immigrant socialism. They clearly fed off each other in a very significant way.[69]

During the late 1880s and 1890s, Remington was not only the leading artist and illustrator of the American West, but also an extraordinarily

Frederic Remington, "The Fall of the Cowboy" (1895), the last of his illustrations for Wister's article "The Evolution of the Cow-Puncher." The unmounted cowboy is closing the gate on the open range. Barbed wire has imposed a new era on the western range. Even the horses are sad! Amon Carter Museum, 1961-230.

prolific writer. In the two decades between 1887 and 1906, he produced 111 short stories and articles and seven novels and collections of short stories, mostly on western subjects.[70] In this period, since both Wister and Remington did most of their writing for *Harper's*, they were very aware of each other's writing, even when they were not in close communication.

Wister's linking of the cowboy to the cavalier of Sir Walter Scott and to a far wider Anglo-Saxon mythology was compelling but not completely original. The germ of the idea surely came from Roosevelt's introduction to *The Winning of the West*. This was also the period of Anglo-Saxon adventurers who sacrificed themselves to duty and empire in darkest Africa, the Arctic, and the Antarctic. The belief in Anglo-Saxon superiority suffused Captain Scott's race to the South Pole, his first attempt falling in the year of the publication of *The Virginian*. Americans, too, were caught up in the theme of Kipling's "white man's burden," which was actually addressed to Americans, urging them to their duty of taking civilization to the "lesser breeds," in this case the Filipinos. The brass plaques in Westminster Abbey, honouring explorers for their "signal intrepidity" spoke, as well, to Americans about the sacred duties of race. It is no surprise that Wister wrote three passionate books during the period of the First World War and the early 1920s pressing his countrymen to support the Anglo-Saxon against the Hun.

It was in this period, just prior to the First World War, that Roosevelt would explore one of the most remote rivers on the planet, the River of Doubt, a tributary of the Amazon, which would later be named for him. He was attacked by Natives, and even the frogs were poisonous. As Roosevelt was descending the river, Ernest Shackleton was attempting to cross the Antarctic.[71]

Wister's conspicuously Anglo-Saxon cowboy, however, was more than a little fraudulent. Like it or not, the real cowboy owed a great debt to Wister's "small, deceitful alien," the Mexican *vaquero* – as well as to the gaucho of Argentina, the *huaso* of Chile, *llanero* of Venezuela and Columbia, and the *vaqueiro* of Brazil. Richard Slatta, in his magisterial book *Cowboys of the Americas*, brings to light both the huge debt owed by the American cowboy to his southern cousins and, also, the striking similarity in these other cowboy cultures to the American idolization of the cowboy. With great authority, Slatta tells the story of the spread of horses and cattle throughout the Western Hemisphere, from Patagonia to Alberta. Charles Darwin could be describing one of Wister's cavaliers in this depiction of the Spanish gaucho of Argentina: "they are generally tall and handsome. ... Their politeness is excessive."[72] As Slatta points out, "the gaucho has become the epitome of Argentine national virtue: 'obedience, patriotism, honesty, trustworthiness.'"[73]

Remington urged Wister to include other cowboy types in "The Evolution of the Cow-Puncher," but Wister was clearly intent on promoting the Anglo-Saxon, not any other inferior race. Nonetheless, this was the high point of Wister's and Remington's collaboration and close friendship. Considering how soon Wister withdrew to an aloof reserve with Remington, his letters of the period to Remington display a surprising warmth and informality. "Why the L _ Oh Bear don't you write to me?" And, in obvious reference to Remington's first sculpture, the Bronco Buster of 1895, Wister addressed him "Dear Mud."[74] (Remington had just written to Wister in high excitement that he had been playing with mud. He had produced in his first effort what many consider his greatest sculpture.[75])

Yet, even while writing his article on the Anglo-Saxon cowboy, Wister was working on other western articles that would eventually be incorporated into *The Virginian* and developed into the character of his Virginian cowboy. It would seem that Wister by the mid-1890s was developing both

Frederic Remington, *The Bronco Buster*, 1895, Remington's first attempt at "playing with mud." At this stage, he was virtually untutored in scuplture. The result is astonishing - the balance and raw energy jump from the sculpture. This version of the Bronco Buster was created using the cumbersome sand-cast method.

Remington's 1909 version of the Bronco Buster. It was almost his last sculpture. It was slightly larger than the original 1895 sculpture and exuded even more energy and raw power. Remington was now using the more satisfactory lost-wax technique, which allowed the sculptor to put more detail into the sculpture.

Frederic Remington, *The Rattlesnake* (1905). Both horse and rider are in complete balance. The cowboy is concerned only with keeping his hat! This is perhaps Remington's greatest cowboy sculpture – the harmony between horse and rider is extraordinary. Remington produced a number of cowboy sculptures: *The Stampede, Coming Through the Rye,* and *The Wicked Pony.* All of them exude power and vitality; they epitomize Remington's, Wister's and Roosevelt's vision of the West.

a general, archetypal cowboy and his own special cowboy, who was unique and was meant to stand out from the herd.

By 1895, with the publication of "The Evolution of the Cow-Puncher," Wister had his cowboy "type" clearly in mind. Then, between 1895 and 1902, he would refine his story and add the romance. Much of this was done while he lived in Charleston, beginning in 1898, when he was starting to think of the themes of the book he would write after *The Virginian*, a study of Charleston society titled *Lady Baltimore,* after a special kind of cake! This book would stress the bleakness of the American political, economic, and cultural landscape and lament the fact that there were only pockets of true gentility left in the country. Already, by 1902, even before the publication of *The Virginian*, Wister was beginning to retreat into his bitter little enclave of Butler Place and the "right sort" of people in Charleston.

After completing the story of Em'ly, Wister's next theme involving his Virginian appeared in March 1896. "Where Fancy Was Bred" recounts the famous baby-swapping incident at the Goose Egg Ranch. Judge Henny has now become Judge Henry, and Trampas has lost the rather silly name Sorgy. Shorty, Lin McLean, and Jim Westfall are also front and centre at the Swinton Brothers' barbeque. Now, many of the main characters of *The Virginian* are present, and the story includes some of the main themes of the novel – the rescue of Molly from the bogged-down stagecoach; the beginning of the lethal feud with arch-villain Trampas; the baby swapping, abetted by Lin McLean, which was a famous story from Texas to Montana; and, finally, the beginning of the Virginian's courting of Molly. By the final writing of the novel, these themes were spread over three chapters. And it is clear that this story marks the emergence of an important literary figure. Wister was no longer just writing squalid tales of local western colour.

But what is so fascinating in this period of Wister's writing is that he was juggling three very dissimilar themes at once – the ugly and vulgar West of Lin McLean, the upper-crust world of aristocratic post–Civil War Charleston, and the highly romantic parts of *The Virginian* that would create an instant national sensation. An extraordinary tour de force!

In March and September of 1897, two more Lin McLean stories appeared: "Separ's Vigilante" and "Destiny at Drybones," both published by *Harper's*. Both stories were again of the squalid variety and very different in quality to the parts of *The Virginian* that were about to be created to fill in the gaps between the Virginian episodes already written. Between these two stories, there emerged another Virginian story, "Grandmother Stark," that was to become, almost unchanged, another chapter of the novel. This story would become one of the key sections of the novel – Molly's finding of the Virginian, left to die by hostile Indians; her nursing him back to health; her decision not to leave the West for Vermont; and her final capitulation to his wooing. One question emerges. By this point, it is clear that Wister had much of the eventual shape of the novel in his mind. The main themes were there, and it was now a matter of creating the links between episodes that would produce a novel. But, with the novel now clearly in mind, why would he give away one of the most important themes of the novel – the circumstances that led Molly to change her mind and decide that her future was with the West – and with the Virginian?

There is one important difference between the article and the later chapter. Although the two are almost identical, one vital theme was added between 1897 and 1902 – the issue of lynching. While the Virginian is delirious after the Indian attack, he refers to the lynching of his good friend

Steve. In the novel, but not in the article, the Virginian murmurs, "Steve … it ain't so … Steve, I have lied for you." As has been seen, Wister was referring to a real incident in Johnson's life over which he agonized greatly. Several authors have read utterly absurd implications into these few words, coupled with Steve's use of a private nickname for the Virginian, to speculate about a very intimate relationship between the Virginian and Steve. Their speculations are totally spurious and without any basis whatever.

In 1897, Wister completed his first cowboy book, *Lin McLean*, which was published later that year. This book, which was really a collection of six stories based on some of his real experiences in the West, was well received as "perhaps the truest representation of an actual cowboy that American fiction has given us."[76] But the book was not a literary success. It was too episodic, and, more to the point, the rough Texas cowboy that Wister depicted did not catch the public imagination. The story was rescued from its rather silly plot by effective descriptive writing, a wonderful eye for detail, and an ear for dialogue. The book was illustrated by Remington.

From 1897 until 1902, after finishing *Lin McLean*, Wister started concentrating on his second cowboy, the Virginian. He also married Mary Channing Wister, a distant cousin, in 1898 and embarked on a six-month honeymoon, starting in Charleston and including a prolonged visit to his old friend George Waring from Harvard days, who was still living in the Methow Valley of Washington State (see chapter 5). Oddly, this was his first visit to Charleston, and it seemed to hit him in a fashion reminiscent of his first visit to Wyoming. He had found an oasis in "our great American desert of mongrel din and waste." Here he found the old gentility, whose disappearance he so lamented.[77] His mother urged him to write about the unique society of Charleston, as he had done with Wyoming.

After returning from his marathon honeymoon, Wister got back to his writing, producing a little book, *Padre Ignazio*, about an Indian mission in California, and an essay about the Virginian, "The Game and the Nation," in which the Virginian humiliates the villain Trampas with his frog story. He also wrote a two-part series on Richard Wagner's operas. In the next year, 1900, he published a collection of western short stories, *The Jimmyjohn Boss and Other Stories*, in which *Hank's Woman* appeared, but this time featuring the Virginian, not Lin McLean. He also wrote some poetry and a short biography of President Ulysses Grant. So this was a prolific period for Wister, and it is clear that he was no longer obsessed with becoming the Kipling of the West. The intensity of the period of writing "The Evolution of the Cow-Puncher" seems to have dissipated, and the close relationship with Remington also seems to have faded. None of these writings caused much of a stir; Wister said that he made enough money to keep one horse in hay, but not two. And he had ballooned somewhat, to almost two hundred pounds, causing him to hire a fitness trainer. It is not clear what credentials the trainer claimed; he advised Wister that his delicate health was caused by taking too many baths.[78]

Remington, too, had ballooned – to over three hundred pounds – and the spark between the two, which their collaboration on the cowboy had ignited, was now extinguished for good. They had been drifting apart after the heady days of collaboration over Wister's essay on the cow-puncher, but the rift became permanent in 1899. They had arranged to meet in New York but, at the last minute, Remington had wired that he couldn't make the appointment. Wister didn't get the message. He waited, with increasing annoyance, and, later, when Remington brushed off the incident in his usual casual way, Wister was deeply offended and ended the friendship. After that, their relationship became formal and professional. There were to be no Remington illustrations in *The Virginian*.[78a]

Wister spent much of 1901 developing the *Virginian* manuscript and writing a short book, *Philosophy 4*, based on a real incident at Harvard when two rich and lazy students hired a Jewish tutor to help them swat up for an exam, and then did better on the exam than the tutor. *Philosophy 4* is a truly nasty little book, showing Wister at his worst. It is full of anti-Semitism and extols the natural superiority of the Anglo-Saxon – the chosen ones who, by right of birth, should be at Harvard, and the ones who, by natural right, should go on to be America's leaders. Later, in *Roosevelt: The Story of a Friendship*, Wister would reminisce about his student days at Harvard, "Not a musical show had yet been concocted by the Broadway Jew for the American moron."[79]

Wister paid a visit to the White House that year, on the invitation of the new vice president, Theodore Roosevelt, who had vaulted into the position on the public adulation following his Rough Riders' charge up San Juan Hill during the Spanish-American War. The two had kept in fairly regular touch in the last decade, Wister sending Roosevelt his western stories, and Roosevelt commenting on them, always with considerable adulation. Wister now had a contract for *The Virginian* with Macmillan, and he was spending considerable time turning his series of Virginian stories written since 1891 into a cohesive novel. He must have been very conscious, as he developed *The Virginian*, that his first cowboy book had been roundly criticized as interesting but disjointed and episodic. By the time the final novel appeared, eight stories that would become part of *The Virginian* had already appeared, leading some critics to say that the book was mostly a collection of stories cobbled together in a "scissors-and-paste" fashion. Certainly Wister was aware of this criticism; at one point, he had considered calling the book *The Virginian, A Tale of Sundry Adventures*. However, these criticisms are only partly just. What the novel clearly has is a compelling vision of early Wyoming and, although a number of the early chapters are episodic, based on earlier short stories, there is a clear narrative flowing through half the chapters.[80]

In 1902 the book came out with the title *The Virginian: A Horseman of the Plains*. In the preface, Wister declared his mission: to write about the "last romantic figure" in America. On the issue that was already causing considerable speculation and pestering, he wrote, "Sometimes readers inquire, Did you know the Virginian?" His answer, "As well, I hope, as a father should know his son." This was the only clue he was willing to give. Obviously, one of the great strengths of the novel was that its hero could not be identified with any real person.

The book was instantly one of the great triumphs of American literature. Within two months, 50,000 copies were printed; within three months, 100,000. In the first eight months, the book was reprinted fourteen times; by 1911, when the next edition was published, forty times.[81] Even Henry James, the most elevated American author of the period, called the book "a rare and remarkable feat." Only Wister's mother could find little to admire. Her cold appraisal of her son's greatest triumph leaves one stunned. For her, popularity was a strike against the book. A novel that the common people could admire was clearly a failure.

The reaction of Wister's mother is, perhaps, not surprising. For all his life, she had held a suffocating and utterly domineering control over him. In his childhood, she kept a journal entitled "The Early Years of a Child of Promise." Almost everything he did she criticized. When he went to Wyoming in 1885, she ensured that two of her women friends were looking after him. Even in the moment of his great triumph with the tremendous success of *The Virginian*, she sent him a long letter outlining in detail all that was wrong with the book. Perhaps what upset her most was the dominant theme of masculine escape from feminine control. Wyoming was a man's world; some have argued that the depraved hen Em'ly represented domineering feminine reformers who are made to look ridiculous; a central theme in the book is the triumph of the untutored western aristocrat over the feminine manners and social position of Bennington. Above all, when Molly tells the Virginian that she will leave him if he fights Trampas, and he ignores her, the pathos of that scene can be seen as liberation for Wister from his mother's suffocating control. No wonder she hated the book!

In the Wister papers at the Library of Congress, there is a huge outpouring of letters to Wister from all parts of the United States in the immediate aftermath of the publication of the book. East and West, North and South, from westerners who closely related to the book, to the eastern literary set who admired the book as literature, *The Virginian* was an immediate and stunning success. Especially surprising was the very large number of letters from women saying that it was their favourite novel.[82] This instant and uniformly enthusiastic response to the book must have been overwhelming to Wister, especially after the very muted response to his earlier book-length attempts. There was also, according to a Montana newspaper at the time, an "avalanche" of applications from young women in New England for teaching positions in the West.[83] Two years later, *The Virginian* became a play and in 1914 the first movie came out, the first of four movie versions. The 1914 movie was produced by Cecil B. DeMille, followed by new versions in 1923, 1929, and 1946. The 1929 version featured Gary Cooper as the Virginian, a performance that essentially launched his career. In the 1960s, *The Virginian* would also become a TV series, running from 1962 to 1970.

Without question, *The Virginian* launched the outpouring of western cowboy literature that began with Zane Grey and seems to have ended, for the moment at least, with Louis L'Amour and Larry McMurtry. In-between have been hundreds, if not thousands, of cowboy novels, movies, and TV programs. It is safe to say that Wister launched the foremost popular mythology in American history. Even the White House invokes cowboy imagery on special occasions. Perhaps just one example will suffice to demonstrate the power of what Wister started – an example that Wister's mother would have hated most. Gene Autry's Cowboy Commandments aptly demonstrate the place of the cowboy in the American firmament:

> The good cowboy never takes unfair advantage, keeps his word, tells the truth, is gentle with children, the elderly and animals, is tolerant, helps those in distress, works hard, respects women, his parents, and the law, does not drink or smoke, and is patriotic.[84]

There have been only two persistent criticisms of *The Virginian*: that there is little about cattle, and that the character of Molly is not a success. What a dull story it might have been if filled with cows! The criticism of Molly is more just, but she does play a very important part in the novel as the easterner who has to be brought around very grudgingly to an appreciation of the West. In a way, Molly is a victim of this theme, a theme vital to Wister's purpose. And the end of the book is very powerful when Molly's great-aunt shows the Virginian the likeness of General Stark and comments wistfully that there used to be men like that in Vermont, but they have gone west. The book ends with Molly understanding that the West is the future of the country. A very powerful theme if you don't know that Wister had already rejected it for a far tamer and more odious one!

Wister had created a western masterpiece that endures to the present, but, even before the publication of *The Virginian*, Wister was already abandoning the West. His Kipling-of-the-West period was over. The president of Macmillan, the company that had published *The Virginian*, asked him to write another western book, but Wister wanted to write something quite different. The West had lost its allure, and he had become besotted with what he considered the last true enclave of aristocracy in America, the close little society of Charleston. There he had found his spiritual home.[85] By 1902, he was already retreating into an increasingly misanthropic view of American society and into his early extreme snobbery. His next book, *Lady Baltimore*, published in 1906, would be full of pessimism regarding America and nastiness toward new Americans. He was especially bitter about "uppity" Blacks in positions of political importance during Reconstruction, and he argued that Reconstruction was a dismal failure. As one critic, John Lukacs, wrote, "Its pessimism is as pervasive as anything written by Herman Melville or Henry Adams."[86]

Lady Baltimore was centred in Charleston, for Wister "the most appealing, the most lovely" city in America, encompassing "a high society of distinguished men and women who exist no more. ... Nowhere in America such charm, such character, such true elegance as here." In Charleston, Wister revelled in a genteel society protected from "our sullen welter of democracy" and "the commercial deluge of the wrong sort ... the lower class, with dollars and no grandparents." A greater contrast with Wyoming and cowboys could not be imagined!

The "Lady Baltimore" was a wedding cake, made from the Lady Baltimore recipe and ordered for a wedding that never took place because the bride-to-be has allied herself to the decadent and money-grubbing nouveaux riches of the North. These "Replacers" have elbowed aside the old Southern aristocracy of Charleston and created a new and ugly society. The story is essentially a lament for the old South before the Civil War, when Blacks knew their place and a wise and cultured elite ruled the South. *Lady Baltimore* is essentially a Jamesian novel of manners with little plot, an "unabashed homage to aristocratic traditions and class distinction."[87] The narrator, Augustus (Wister), lets it be known that he would be happy if all the Blacks were deported; Blacks, after all, are a "menial race" – whose skulls are more like those of apes. Southern lynching is objectionable only on aesthetic grounds! Even for the time, *Lady Baltimore* is shockingly virulent on the subject of Blacks and Jews. The book "represents an unabashed outpouring of racist attitudes unmatched in the fiction of any other major American writer of the twentieth century."[88] The book had modest sales before it "lapsed into popular and critical obscurity."[89]

In 1909 and 1910, Wister and his wife spent two consecutive summers on the Wyoming dude ranch of Struthers Burt. In the introduction to the 1951 Heritage Press edition of *The Virginian*, Burt recounted an incident that occurred during the second summer. Molly Wister's father, also a Wister, died while Owen and Molly were out of communication on the Burt ranch. It took several days for the news of his death to reach them. In the meantime, the newspapers of the country somehow assumed that it was Owen Wister who had died, and the obituaries poured forth. Many were long and critical. One in particular called him a "first-rate second-rate writer." According to Burt, Wister was devastated and never really recovered.[90] He wrote very little fiction after that.

So, hardly before the ink was dry on *The Virginian*, Wister had returned to his privileged set, eulogizing an era before the "sweeping folly of the Fifteenth Amendment" (the Constitutional Amendment that gave the vote to African-Americans), when Negro servants were properly attentive – "like an old family dog." *Lady Baltimore* conjures up the image of the old South, so much a part of Wister's heritage on his mother's side, as the last citadel of good breeding, an enclave not yet destroyed by "the invasion of the proletariat." Where was Weir Mitchell when he was needed to remind Wister once again: "Learn to sympathize with your fellow man a little more than you are inclined to. You don't feel kindly to your race, you know. There are a lot of humble folks in the fields you'd be better for knowing." Weir Mitchell showed in his lifetime that he was a man of great wisdom and generosity of spirit; Wister, for all his talent, was possessed of a mean and gnarled soul. It is more than a little ironic that Wister dedicated *Lady Baltimore* to Weir Mitchell!

Wister had long ago lost the friendship of Remington through neglect and distaste for Remington's tiggerish ways. Now he ran the risk of losing Roosevelt as well over his disdain for the unwashed. Roosevelt had always been full of enthusiasm for Wister's western writing, and over the years had given him much encouragement and advice on western subjects. But Roosevelt did not like *Lady Baltimore* when it appeared in 1906 and told Wister so bluntly.

While Wister found his spiritual home in the society of Charleston, "the most civilized in America," Roosevelt accused Wister of creating far too dark a picture of the hopeless depravity of northern society and of being far too uncritical of southern aristocratic society. In a long letter to Wister in April 1906, Roosevelt argued that northerners were not as lacking in virtue as Wister argued and southerners not nearly so virtuous. After all, they had clung to slavery long after the civilized world had given it up. Wister's Charleston aristocrats

> offer as melancholy an example as I know of people whose whole life for generations has been warped by their own wilful perversity. ... They drank and duelled and made speeches, but they contributed very, very little toward anything of which we as Americans are now proud. At the time of the Civil War they were still trying to reopen the slave trade; during Reconstruction they brought their punishment absolutely on themselves.[91]

Wister could still argue, fifty years after the Civil War, that giving Blacks the vote was a mistake because they were intellectually and morally inferior, and he defended white southerners' attempts to keep the vote away from them. He even criticized Roosevelt, now the president, for appointing a Black to the important post of collector of customs for the port of Charleston. Wister pointed out that the appointment had caused great consternation among the "right" people in Charleston; Roosevelt countered that Wister was condoning an aristocratic class that was attempting to replace slavery with a system of peonage. He accused Wister of giving strength to those in the South who were doing everything in their power to prevent Blacks from gaining equality and made it clear that he thought that Wister's friends were extreme reactionaries who would do the country great harm. Wister simply could not agree with Roosevelt's main point: progressive and educated Blacks, such as the man he had appointed to an important position in Charleston, must be given a chance, "the very type ... about which [Charleston aristocrats] lie so unblushingly."[92] To Wister's credit, in his *Collected Works* in 1928, he prefaced *Lady Baltimore* by printing Roosevelt's letter in full, and he revised some of the more negative passages.[93]

Here was a clear intellectual parting of the ways between Wister and Roosevelt. And there is a large irony in this parting, for Wister was arguing against one of his own most powerful arguments in *The Virginian*, that a natural aristocracy of talent should be able to rise to the top. After his youthful discovery of Wyoming and its cowboys in the mid-1880s, he had soon returned to his very conservative and malevolent view of mankind. Added to his pronounced anti-Semitism and utter disdain for immigrants was an even greater disdain for Native peoples. In his preface to Remington's 1898 publication *Done in the Open*, he wrote of how accurately Remington had drawn "this inferior race which our conquering race has dispossessed ... ending with its squalid degeneration under the influence of our civilized manners." Actually, Remington's art did not match Wister's words!

One of the main themes of *The Virginian* – which is implicit throughout the novel, but stated explicitly in five central chapters – is that quality will prevail over equality.[94] The theme is first stated when the Virginian says to Molly, "equality is a great big bluff." The comment is at the centre of his courting; he is telling her that he can rise above his roots and that, one day, he will be worthy of her. The theme becomes, perhaps, the central message of the book in the next chapter: "The Game and the Nation – Act First."

> All America is divided into two classes – the quality and the equality. ... It was through the Declaration of Independence that we Americans acknowledged the *eternal inequality* [Wister's emphasis] of man. For by it we abolished a cut-and-dried aristocracy. We had seen little men artificially held up in high places, and great men artificially held down in low places. ... Therefore, we decreed that every man should henceforth have equal liberty to find his own level. By this very decree we acknowledged and gave freedom to true aristocracy. ... Let the best man win! That is America's word. That is true democracy. And true democracy and true aristocracy are one and the same thing. If anybody cannot see this, so much the worse for his eyesight.

Stirring words. And for a time, Wister really did believe that true American democracy was to be found in the egalitarian air of Wyoming. His Virginian cowboy was America's true aristocrat, capable of rising from humble roots to marry into one of America's most revered families. But it was a passing phase. Even before *The Virginian* was published, Wister had recanted. Now it was the old aristocracy of Charleston – the ultimate inequality, a caste who based their importance on who their grandfathers were – that counted with Wister. Clearly he had soon rejected the innate nobility of the cowboy and had essentially given up on the possibility of the West's ability to reform the nation. Immigrants, especially Jews, were scum; Indians were little better than vermin; the debate with Roosevelt over the ability of a Black to preside over the port of Charleston demonstrated clearly Wister's belief that *all* Blacks were too inferior to hold such a post. He was wholly unmoved by Roosevelt's argument that you can't shut the door on an entire race.

Did his own words come back to haunt him in later life – that *every* man should have equal liberty to find his own level, thus giving freedom to true aristocracy? Perhaps his complete disillusionment with these sentiments in later life accounts for his general disillusionment with the West.

Each of his "natural aristocrats" – George West, Charles Skirdin, Everett Johnson – had proven a disappointment. His youthful optimism about America was clearly misplaced, and he increasingly retreated to what was bred in the bone, a belief in the reliability of old families and old values. Like his old friend and fellow grump, Henry Adams, who looked at his country with a "profound world-weary cynicism" and presided over his tight little circle, the most exclusive in Washington, Wister could only lament the passing of America. He had slipped back very comfortably into that inward-looking and inbred little word that Henry Cabot Lodge described so well in his memoir *Early Days*: "Everybody knew everybody else and all about everybody's family. Most people were related." It was a caste utterly set in its ways, "clipping coupons from Granny's trust fund," but with "a sense, even in the best households, of living on borrowed time."[95]

Surely here lies a great irony. As Wister rejected his creation, the whole nation became caught up in what he had wrought. Wister's Virginian became an instant inspiration for the nation, one that is still deeply embedded in the character of the West. And at the centre of that character is Wister's notion of "quality." As Wister was being lionized across the nation, he entered a grumpy, unproductive period in which he wrote only *Lady Baltimore* and two other small works, a short biography of President Grant in 1901 and, in 1907, *The Seven Ages of Washington*.

Roosevelt could not shake Wister from his misanthropic views, but certainly the strong friendship persisted. Again, in the 1911 edition of *The Virginian*, the dedication to Roosevelt was even more fulsome than in the original edition. In that year also, Wister published a collection of western short stories, *Members of the Family*.

Even before the publication of *The Virginian*, Wister was becoming pessimistic about the future of the West. Like the East, it was filling with the wrong sort. Now, he could only find comfort in the lost world of Charleston gentility. In retrospect, it is indeed ironic that one of the greatest attractions of *The Virginian* is that the cowboy is not a rough Texan. Instead, he came from the old Tidewater society of Virginia and embodied that culture, even though he is given humble roots. Despite the terrible war to rid the country of the southern slaveholding mentality that had ended less than forty years before, the entire country was drawn, perhaps unwittingly, to that southern code of honour and the gentle but iron code of manners that lay at the foundation of slaveholding southern society. And now Wister was retreating into an extreme form of that old southern mentality. *Lady Baltimore*, when it was published in 1906, was only a minor success, which probably pleased his mother greatly.

In 1912, Wister did seek Roosevelt's advice on a proposed western book to be titled *The Marriages of Scipio*. The theme: Scipio Le Moyne, a character in *The Virginian*, was to be the main character in "the tragedy of the cowpuncher who survives his own era and cannot adjust himself to the more civilized era which succeeds it."[96] Roosevelt's answer – "Why, my dear Dan ... when you come to your cowboy tragedy, why – don't leave it in such an unrelieved blackness. Let in some sunlight." Undoubtedly, if Wister had written the book, he would have let in very little light. Probably, by this point in his life, Wister was incapable of optimism or a generosity of spirit. It seems that after the period of *The Virginian*, Wister descended into an outlook of very selective nostalgia and bitterness. When his book on General Washington appeared in 1907, the review in the influential *American Historical Review* accused him of "crude historical knowledge" and added that the book was unreliable and "idealized beyond reality."[97]

Actually, Wister had asked Roosevelt about three possible books, and Roosevelt had advised him to write all three. Wister decided on *Romney*, a thinly disguised book about Philadelphia's passing from the old to the new order. He never finished the book, but it was clearly meant to be the last of a trilogy connecting the three regions of America. Again, as with *The Virginian* and *Lady Baltimore*, a narrator tells the story. In *Romney*, it is once again Augustus, the narrator of *Lady Baltimore*.

The central theme of *Romney* is very similar to that of *Lady Baltimore*; a study of manners among the old guard of late nineteenth-century Philadelphia. *Romney* and *Lady Baltimore* share a great many similarities; both lament the death of civility, manners, and a ruling caste of education and taste. Certainly Wister was on safe ground in his descriptions of aristocratic Philadelphia. He was born there near his ancestral mansions of Vernon, Grumblethorpe, and Butler Place, and grew up amid family portraits by Thomas Sully, Sir Thomas Lawrence, and Sir Joshua Reynolds.[98]

Wister began work on *Romney* in 1912 and stopped abruptly in 1913 when his wife Molly died in childbirth. After her death, it seems that he couldn't bring himself to continue. And then the war came, and Wister became obsessively caught up in making the case for an Anglo-American alliance in three books: *The Pentecost of Calamity* (1915), *A Straight Deal* (1920), and *Neighbours Henceforth* (1922).

Romney begins with a lament for the demise of the old Philadelphia aristocracy and the "economic destruction of the old American family, and the invasion of the Hun, the Vandal, the Croat, and all the rest of the steerage." It is perhaps just as well that *Romney* was not completed, since the plot is rather ridiculous and implausible, centred on an Austrian family of great wealth, with a regal "great lady" of a mother and two oafish sons, Mort and Dug, who couldn't possibly have been the sons of that well-bred mother. Wister created an untenable plot. Mort and Dug represent the new, vulgar rich, whom Wister so detested. Yet the mother is pictured in imperious and cultured old world colours, which Wister so admired. He and his caste, which included Henry James and Henry Adams, looked to Europe for all that was best in music, taste, and culture. But Wister so hated the new immigration from Europe that he used Dug and Mort – two extremely unlikely names for European immigrants – to flail at his pet hate. *Romney* is badly muddled!

In *Romney*, as with his other writing, Wister has moments of wicked genius in his descriptions of character, but the overall theme is contrived; vulgarity is equated with immigration. Wister in this period became the vice president of the Immigration Restriction League; *Romney* appears to be a platform for Wister to vent his beliefs about the destruction of his beloved country by the alien hordes. A minor theme in *The Virginian* had taken over his writing. Wister probably realized that the book wasn't working and simply abandoned it.

Wister's last western writing was published in 1928. *When West Was West* is a collection of short stories full of nostalgia, pessimism, and disillusionment. Of the nine stories, seven are very dark, featuring degenerate and abused Indians, aging pioneers whose Garden of Eden has become a junkyard, towns that have been taken over by whores and pimps, and cowboys who are now pathetic relics. The great promise of the West at the end of *The Virginian* has become a lament for the region that has sold its soul to the same "Replacers" who inhabit *Lady Baltimore* and *Romney*. Wister's daughter commented that Wister never spoke of the West later in life. It's as if the West that he had built up to be the regeneration of the country had played false with him.

So, in the end, Wister became a great writer for the creation of one character, a character who brilliantly caught the American imagination. That cannot be taken away from him, but Wister cannot be considered in the first rank of American writers, nor, except for one brief moment, with the great western American writers: Willa Cather, John Steinbeck, Walter Van Tilburg Clark, or Wallace Stegner. His heart was too small, and, in the end, he

Wister in his seventies. By then, he was disillusioned with the West and had retreated into his little world of "the right people." He had become bitter and xenophobic. American Heritage Center, University of Wyoming.

returned to the society and ways of thought that he had parodied in *The Virginian*. He could never overcome his upbringing. Roosevelt tried to chide him out of some of his extreme pessimism and spleenfulness, but without success. In the end, it seems that Wister had given up on the West. When he died in 1938, he had long since emotionally left the West behind and was writing a book on French wines! It probably no longer mattered to him who his Virginian was. Perhaps that explains his odd response to the Calgary newspaperman – to be found in the Postscript of this work – shortly before his death. The man was trying, once again, to pry out of Wister whether Johnson was, in fact, his Virginian. Wister was now in a different world; his West no longer existed, and those on whom he had based his Virginian had all proven to be disappointments, West demonstrating his moral failings, Skirdin a night watchman sweeping floors, and now Johnson running a butcher shop. His world now encompassed only the few who mattered in Charleston, Boston, and Philadelphia. So why not reveal his western hero? He was old and tired and sick – and disillusioned with the West. How else to understand his response to the Alberta reporter – "Everett Johnson seemed to be the one."[99]

8: Afterword (1904–1946)

The terrible winter of 1906-7 effectively ended the old days of the open range. For some time, it had been clear that the ranching industry had to change. Even with the chinook winds of Alberta, the big ranchers could not count on bringing their cattle through the winter without extra feed. The open range was giving way to a combination of smaller ranches and mixed farming. The tame, fenced West had little appeal for Johnson; he found it hard to settle down to the new ranching life of the twentieth century.

The winter of 1906-7, too, marked the end of Johnson's life as a cowboy and cattleman. At the relatively young age of forty-seven his life changed. The drama and excitement of the Wyoming range became a receding memory. For the rest of his life he was to feed on those memories, grasping every opportunity to relive the old days with those who had known them. An incurable restlessness prevented him from taking up a ranch of his own. Instead, he was to be a frequent visitor on the ranch that his son Laurie and daughter-in-law Jean homesteaded up the Ghost Valley west of Cochrane. In most ways, the rest of his life was an anticlimax, but he still had his memories and some old friends from Wyoming who came to live in Alberta or just came for a visit. Although there was no longer a strong path to his life, the vignettes that Jean recorded of his later years still give an important insight into the character of the early Alberta ranching community after the Alberta die-up, especially pointing to the mingling of Americans, Canadians, and English in the ranching country in the years between the two world wars. Many of these Americans had come north to avoid the continuation of the range violence in Wyoming and Montana. They gave the Alberta ranching community a unique colour as they mingled with and

Studio portrait of Everett Johnson, Calgary, Alberta.

tutored the many eastern Canadians and English ranchers who, unlike the English in Wyoming, had come to stay.

It is not known what alternatives he wrestled with or what pressures might have come from Mary, but in 1910, Johnson, now fifty years old, established a butcher shop in Cochrane, a small town just west of Calgary on the Bow River with a stunning panorama of ranchland and mountains.[1] The town of Cochrane, named for Senator Matthew H. Cochrane, who established the first large ranch in the Canadian West, was a typical bustling ranching town boasting two livery stables and several stone quarries. Tending a butcher shop was certainly a step down in the world after managing some of Alberta's biggest early ranches, but at least it allowed Johnson lots of time to gossip with the many cowboys who frequented Cochrane.

One of those whom Johnson had known in earlier days was Frank Ricks, a well-known bronc rider who had been born in California in the late 1850s. Johnson may have been the only one north of the line who knew that Ricks was Jesse James' cousin. He had brought a large sum of money to Alberta and bought a hotel in Banff and a ranch south of the Bow River, west of Cochrane. There he even built a dance hall and used to hire orchestras for his popular parties. He often visited Johnson in Cochrane, and the two would sit outside the butcher shop talking about the old days. When people came near, the two old friends would lapse into silence.

In 1911, Wister and Johnson met for the last time. Wister discovered that Johnson lived near Calgary and sent him a telegram suggesting that they meet there. Johnson did not talk much to Jean about this meeting; he was certainly glad to see Wister again. For his part, Wister was probably disappointed to find that Johnson had traded his saddle and gun belt for a butcher shop in exactly the sort of little cowtown that he so despised. After their visit, Wister never wrote Johnson again.

It is easy to speculate that Wister left Calgary disillusioned with much of what had so excited him earlier about the West. Everything had changed, and now he found that his most important inspiration was in trade! It must have seemed an almost deliberate affront.

In September 1912, the Duke of Connaught and his daughter, Princess Patricia, visited Alberta. While attending the first Calgary Stampede, they stayed with Senator James Lougheed, the son-in-law of Richard Hardisty. Hardisty had been an important figure in the early fur trade of the Canadian West; his grandson, Peter Lougheed, would become premier of Alberta in the 1970s. After the Stampede, a camp, guarded by the Mounties, was set up on the Ghost River, halfway from Calgary to Banff. From the camp, the Duke and Princess Patricia fished and rode into the glorious foothill country of the Stoneys. During their stay, a big parade of cowboys was organized at Cochrane, led by Mary Johnson riding her husband's big black 7D horse side-saddle. Laurie was riding his favourite cow pony, Billy, a small flea-bitten grey with great cow sense. The Duke was greatly taken with Billy, as was Princess Patricia, who asked if she might try a real cow pony. She put Billy through his paces and came away much impressed with the soft mouth and amazing anticipation of a good cow pony.

In 1919, Calgary held its first real Stampede since the famous one of 1912. This time it was Charlie Russell's exhibition of paintings that drew Johnson. He went to visit his old acquaintance and took Laurie with him to the King George Hotel on Calgary's Ninth Avenue where Russell was staying. Laurie recalled the two old friends reminiscing about Montana days and about the time when Johnson had brought the 76 herd north. Russell kidded Johnson a bit about "the book," for which he had provided the illustrations, and commented, "I noticed you always rode a double-rigged Macheer saddle so I put you on one when I did the illustrations." Russell described the Macheer saddle as the old-time bronc rider's saddle of the 1880s. "I've seen bronc riders use the old macheer saddle with a Texas tree. It had two cinches an' was called a rim-fire. The horn was low and flat … The macheer was one piece of leather that fit over the cantle and horn makin' a covering for the whole rig." For Russell, "an old time rim-fire man was the real cowboy."[2] Laurie recalled that Russell did not think much of the book, but his father stood up for Wister and said that he generally did a good job of recreating a time, even if he got some things wrong. A lot of old cowboys drifted into the room as they were talking – Jack Miller, Tommy Chapman – and the talk turned to long-gone broncs and long horns.

A cowboy's saddle was his most important possession – next to his horse. I have seen Johnson's saddle, or at least one he rode in Alberta. I don't know if it was a Macheer, but it was the proper working stock saddle of range days that put the rider in the middle of the saddle, not at the back on the horse's loins, as so many modern western saddles do. Richard Slatta quotes Robert Cunninghame Graham, author of the classic *Horses of the Conquest*, describing the seat of the South American llanero as "so straight and upright that a plummet dropped from his shoulder would touch his heel." Slatta also quotes Theodore Dodge:

> The cowboy rides what is well-known as the cowboy's saddle, or Brazos tree. It is adapted from the old Spanish saddle. . . . The line of its seat from cantle to horn, viewed sidewise, is a semicircle; there is no flat place to sit on. This shape gives the cowboy, seen

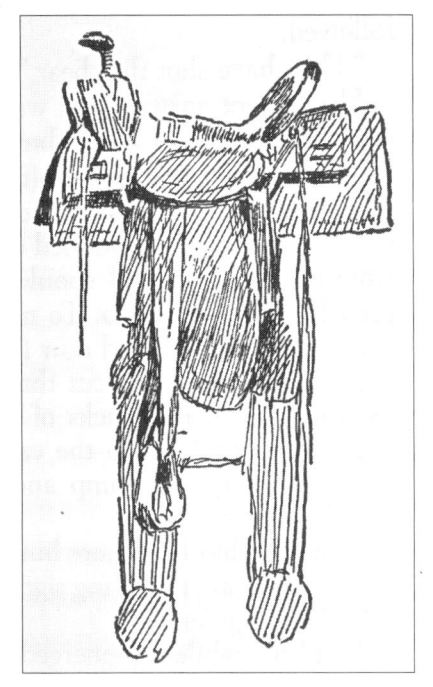

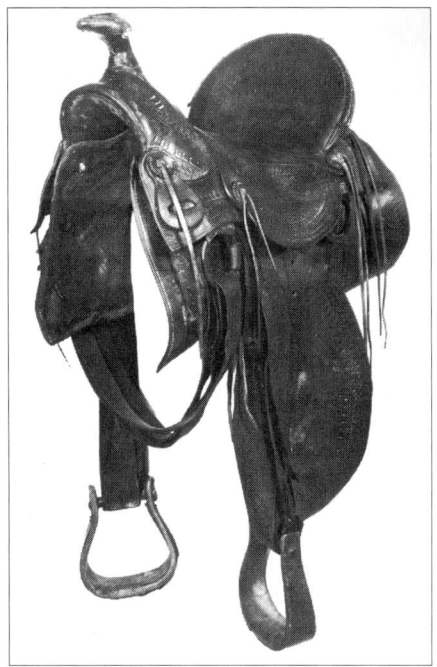

L: Charlie Russell's sketch of Johnson's Macheer saddle, which he drew for the 1911 edition of *The Virginian*.

R: A typical Texas stock saddle of the post Civil War era, the type used by most cowboys coming up the cattle trails from Texas. The saddle put the rider's legs in the proper position to influence the horse effectively.

from the side, all but as perpendicular a seat in the saddle as the old knight in armour.[3]

In Alberta, Burt Sheppard, a well-known cowboy from Longview, described the old double-rigged saddles used by Canadian cowboys during the late nineteenth century: "The old saddles had very little leather in the seat and were built to tip a rider into the middle of the saddle."[4] This is the classic international seat, as important for a good western rider as for jumping, dressage, or polo. The better the rider, the more the seat and legs are used, and the less the hands are used. In many modern western saddles, the seat slopes to the back, placing the rider too far back with legs stuck forward in a useless position and with too much weight on the horse's loins. Only with the heels in a straight line down from the back of the shoulders, as described by Cunninghame Graham, can the rider properly influence the horse with seat and legs – and not ride on the horse's mouth!

Laurie said that many cowboys from the South came to visit Johnson in Cochrane, some with pasts that did not bear scrutiny. Laurie remembered being helped by a stranger from the South with a bucking horse that was giving him difficulty. Laurie introduced him to his father, who took an instant and strong dislike. Johnson, from beneath the brim of his hat, fixed the stranger with a penetrating look; beneath the deceptive gentleness and courtesy, he had his number. Not long after he arrived in Cochrane, the stranger disappeared, along with one of his employer's horses. What bothered Johnson was not exactly the stranger's dubious morality. Johnson had a number of friends from the early days who had found themselves on the wrong side of the law. But there was a subtle and sometimes ambiguous code from the days of mavericks and the open range that did not include stealing from your employer.

Johnson liked to tell a story of a cowboy friend, George Forgey, who had little respect for the law. After spending a year in a Montana jail, George headed north with a friend, Griffiths, and a bunch of someone else's horses. They were apprehended by a sheriff just short of the border, and the three started back south. The sheriff's horse played out so he asked Forgey to catch a gentle horse from the bunch. Forgey roped a good-looking horse and they were on their way again. As they were riding along quietly, Griffiths saw his chance and slipped his quirt under the tail of the sheriff's horse. The horse's reaction was not at all gentle! The sheriff was very quickly on the ground and Forgey and Griffiths were again headed north, now with the sheriff's horse and saddle.

Forgey had originally come to Alberta in 1905 with one of Johnson's good friends, Ed (Boney) Thompson, who was recognized as one of the greatest riders on either side of the border. Johnson told Jean that one of his Montana neighbours coveted his land and tried, in a number of ways, to do him out of it. Thompson was known to be very fond of rice pudding. So he was not surprised to see a dish of it on his table, partly eaten – or so it seemed. Boney ate some and became violently ill; the pudding had been poisoned. Boney shortly left for Alberta, after ensuring that the man he suspected would never again try to poison anyone. For several years after arriving in Alberta, Boney made a point of never sitting with his back to a door or window. He took up a homestead, which became part of the Rhodes Ranch (now known as the Grand Valley Ranch), but like so many other cowboys from the open range days – Johnson included – he was unable to settle down and eventually sold it. With his friend Forgey, he broke horses for G. E. Goddard at the Bow Valley Horse Ranch. Johnson introduced Boney to his son Laurie, and the two soon became fast friends, both breaking horses at the Bar C, a horse ranch that at one time had almost a thousand horses. Thompson competed in the 1912 Calgary Stampede; he was considered by many to be the greatest bucking rider that year but, to his utter disgust, he failed to draw a horse that could keep up to his talents.

In 1921, Boney and Laurie were breaking horses near Dog Pound Creek, northwest of Cochrane. Boney, then forty-eight and suffering from ulcers, offered to ride a rough horse that was causing considerable trouble for one of the other horse breakers. He mounted without changing to his own saddle. Although the stirrups were too long, he bucked the horse to a standstill after a pile-driving ride. The others could see that something was wrong, and when the horse came to a stop, Boney slumped to the ground in agony. He begged for his gun to end the excruciating pain. After a long, agonizing ride, Laurie got Boney to a road and then to hospital in Calgary. But Boney's pelvis was shattered and his bladder punctured. He died shortly after in hospital. Johnson made all the arrangements for a proper cowboy funeral. The church was packed with mourners, including several chiefs from the Stoney nation at Morley. A wreath of wildflowers was put on the coffin, and a group of mounted cowboys followed Boney's horse, Big Sis, to the cemetery.

One of Johnson's closest friends in Alberta was an Ontarian, Wheeler Mickle, who had come west during the Cariboo gold rush in 1862 to drive stagecoach. In 1881 he had come to Alberta and was employed by the Mounted Police freighting between Fort Walsh and Calgary. In the spring of 1885, when the North-West Rebellion erupted, he signed on as a teamster with General Strange's Alberta Field Force. He was one of the first to come upon those murdered in the Frog Lake Massacre. On May 26, 1885, he wrote to his wife Julia, "We have found and buried 8 bodies at Frog Lake. The troops are searching the ruins for more bodies while I am writing. If we come up to the Indians we will not leave one to tell the tale, or there will be none of us left." In the fall of 1885, he took up land west of Cochrane. When he retired to Cochrane in 1913, he spent many happy hours with Johnson, sitting outside his butcher shop and swapping memories.

Another very close friend with a dubious past was Hank Smith, a tall, slim Texan about Johnson's age who settled in Alberta, married, and took up land. When Johnson knew him in Wyoming, Smith had a reputation for being over-quick to settle matters with a gun and was known to have killed a sheriff in Texas who had tried to arrest him. Johnson told one story of a new dentist in Buffalo, Wyoming, who was in his office when Smith walked in, suitably drunk, and sat down in the dentist's chair. He announced that he wanted a tooth pulled. After examining him carefully, the dentist said all his teeth looked good and asked him which one was causing trouble. Smith replied, "Any damn one you choose." When the dentist said he couldn't do that, Smith pulled his gun, prodded the dentist in the stomach and said, "Pull a tooth."

Even in Alberta, Johnson still considered Smith dangerous and cited the case of one young man who left the country and did not return until he knew that Smith was dead. Smith died while plowing a field, something Johnson found hard to reconcile with his past life. And Johnson gave thanks that he had never done anything as foolish as to go into farming.

Johnson told Jean that Henry Smith, as he was known in Wyoming, was the hardest man he had ever known. He had certainly gained a reputation in Wyoming and, during the period of the Invasion of 1892, was accused of ambushing George Wellman, a US deputy marshal, and shooting him in the back. Smith, as a member of the Black Sash Gang, was blamed and arrested, but nothing could be proven and he was released. Jean believed that Johnson knew who fired the shot that killed Wellman, but he would never say.

Certainly Wister was fascinated by Smith in Wyoming, considering him thoroughly bad, hard, and cruel, and left a very thorough description of him in the character of Trampas (see chapter 5). Johnson, though, valued Smith's friendship and admired his uncompromising hardness. It is very ironic, indeed, that Wister's model for Trampas should end his life in Alberta as a good friend of Johnson.

A very different sort of friend, "Gentleman Charlie Parks," had grown up in Montana and came to Alberta in about 1900 as a horse breaker. He was open and generous, but a heavy drinker and, when drunk, a ferocious fighter who loved to scrap. He mixed a pronounced chivalry toward women with an eccentric courtesy, even in the midst of his legendary fights. He would preface a blow by saying, "I'm sorry, but I have to hit you." Then, jerking his adversary to his feet, "Excuse me, you Son of a Bitch, but I have to hit you again."

In 1925, Jean was teaching east of Crossfield (a town slightly north of Calgary) when there appeared at the door of the house where she was staying a young cowboy on a good-looking chestnut horse, its coat and silver-mounted bridle gleaming in the sun. "I thought I had never seen anything so beautiful." The cowboy was Laurie Johnson, who Jean soon learned was making his living breaking horses and was widely considered to be one of Alberta's finest horsemen. He was shorter than his father, but had inherited his grace and gentleness with horses, as well as his quiet southern courtesy. Thus began Laurie's courting of Jean.

Shortly, she was to meet her future father-in-law at the Calgary Stampede, where Johnson was leading the pioneer section of the parade. And the next spring, the Johnsons moved to a place several miles from where Jean was boarding. Jean remembered Johnson when she first knew him in the spring of 1926, at the age of sixty-six, as tall and straight and still remarkably handsome, but somewhat stout. What struck her most were his eyes, the eyes that had so fascinated Wister – shrewd and penetrating, sometimes inscrutable, and of the same shifting colour that Wister had described.

After Laurie and Jean were engaged, and Johnson was at ease with his future daughter-in-law, Johnson brought up the subject of education. Usually they talked about horses, but this day he brought up a subject much on his mind.

> "Laurie is worried about his lack of education. I told him he best do some practice writing to improve his penmanship." He paused and I could see that he was hesitant to speak what was on his mind. His thoughts seemed far away. Finally, he said, "That is what I did, under what you might call similar circumstances." And he changed the subject abruptly.

Soon he was talking of Wyoming, of Buffalo Bill and Yellow Hand, of Hesse and the 76. Jean felt that she had passed her probation.

Laurie and Jean were married on February 14, 1927. At the time, Laurie was foreman of the Rhodes Ranch in Grand Valley, west of Calgary. B. F. Rhodes, a wealthy Englishman, raised thoroughbreds for the track and thoroughbred crosses for polo, a sport first played in North America in the Pincher Creek region of southern Alberta, brought there in the 1880s by early English ranchers. Here was history repeating itself, with Laurie, like his father, working for an English outfit, although this situation was far more usual in Alberta than it had been in Wyoming.

Polo was strong in early Alberta because of the English ranching influence, and Laurie, while working for Rhodes, became hooked on the game. Ranchers in his area trailed their horses into Cochrane, where a very high level of polo had developed, with players such as Archie Kerfoot, Bill Wooly-Dod, and Jim Cross, grandson of Col. Macleod of Mounted Police fame. Fierce rivalry existed between the Cochrane and Calgary teams.[5]

Shortly after Jean and Laurie married, Johnson came to live with them. He and Mary had decided to part ways. It is not at all clear from Jean's

Laurie Johnson on one of his favorite polo ponies in 1931. Captain Edmund Wilmot is credited with introducing polo to the Canadian West in the 1880s. The game became an instant passion with western ranchers. Glenbow Archives, NA 2924-13.

manuscript whether this was sudden or the culmination of a long process. Whatever the case, Johnson was always happiest when he was at the ranch, with the open country and a good horse under him. However, Jean remarked that not all was smooth sailing. If he liked their friends, Johnson could be extremely charming; if he did not like them, he glared them out of the house. He could be aloof to the point of disdain and so remote that he was unreachable.

It was during these years that Johnson forged a special bond with Jean, and began to tell her things from the past that he was reluctant to talk about with others. A natural ritual developed that began with the cleaning and stoking of his favourite pipe, and then, as he gazed out toward the wooded hills and the mountains to the West, "I mind one time…" Most of his stories were humorous anecdotes about Wyoming and old friends or notorious westerners he had known. Often he would comment on how distorted some of the stories of the early West had become. "Some of the stuff you read about Wild Bill Hickok sounds like it was written by Mrs. Custer!" There was only one bitter memory – the events surrounding the Johnson County War. This part of his past became almost an obsession with him.

Johnson came from a musical family, and he loved to sing. Often when he was riding, he would get a misty, far-off look and his deep baritone would make the soothing sounds of the cattle drive. Jean remembered that a few of his songs were more than a little ribald.

> *Beans in the pot and a hotcake and bacon*
> *Sally in the bed and the bed clothes a'shakin...*

In 1928, Laurie and Jean rented the Clarkson Ranch west of Cochrane and ran about a hundred head of horses on Dog Pound Creek, including a stallion for breeding polo ponies. Laurie traded this horse for a beautiful imported Thoroughbred stud named Forcett. Laurie was able to make an even trade because Forcett had some age on him, and, more to the point, he had a reputation as a man-killer. At one point, Laurie was told, Forcett had stood on several feet of manure because no one was brave enough to go into his stall. His current owners had been afraid of him and only led him out of his stall with a groom holding a rope on either side. Naturally, the horse was half out of his mind.

When Laurie got him home, he turned him out every day in a large corral, and he was soon a different horse. But the first day he was out, Johnson walked out into the corral. Forcett made a rush at him, ears back, eyes rolling and teeth bared. Johnson stopped, faced him, and just stood there, his hands at his sides. Forcett went up to him, stopped, sniffed him, and then looked off into the distance almost sheepishly. Shortly after that, Laurie was chosen, along with Archie Kerfoot, Billy Dean-Freeman, and Claude Londale, to represent Alberta in a polo tournament, and while they were away, Jean looked out the window one morning to see Johnson riding away on Forcett. The man-killer was on a loose rein and both of them seemed to be enjoying themselves immensely.

The next spring, Forcett caused the only quarrel that Jean ever had with her father-in-law. Times were starting to be very tough, and Jean had begun raising chickens to help make ends meet. Jean bought a precious sack of wheat, and every morning would grind some in the coffee grinder for the baby chicks. Johnson stole the sack of wheat for Forcett and hid it deep down in a manger, covered with hay. Jean looked everywhere and when she finally found the sack, she let Johnson know that she was mad – but she left the sack in the manger for Forcett.

The Great Depression hit the Canadian West more severely than any other area of the world. The bottom fell out of the horse market, but many people in the ranching community made it through those years with very little money by resorting to a barter system. At least those in the ranching area of the Alberta foothills didn't have to contend with the extreme drought of the farming country to the east. One of the Johnson's neighbours approached Jean to see if she would buy his sheep – four young ewes heavy with lamb. He was heading for the city to try his luck. Jean was proud of her new flock, especially as it doubled in short order. But she had not calculated Johnson's reaction. When the sheep had arrived, he had been away visiting friends. When he returned, he took one look at the sheep and saddled up his horse Spoke and left the contaminated ranch. A week later, Jean sold the sheep. Only then would Johnson return. His prejudice against sheep from Wyoming days was too ingrained.

Shortly after the sheep incident, a truck driver working on the Ghost River Dam on the Bow River, which was being built by Calgary Power, stopped in and stayed for dinner. Talk somehow turned to the Black Hills, and the man said that his father had worked in the Hills in the early days under the name "Bigfoot Charlie." As he was leaving, he turned to Johnson and asked him, "Who shall I tell my father I was talking to?" Johnson answered, "Tell him you were talking to 'the Pretty Kid.'" Johnson was quiet for a while after he left, with a far-off look, and then said to Jean and Laurie, "I reckon that man doesn't know that his daddy was an outlaw."

It was that evening that Johnson talked long into the evening about driving stagecoach into Deadwood as a kid of sixteen, of Johnny Slaughter and the outlaw Sam Bass, of the popular Slaughter killed in the first holdup of the Deadwood stage in the spring of 1877 and of the driverless stagecoach careening into Deadwood. From this moment, Johnson began to tell Jean more and more about the early days. Jean listened and wrote. Later, she wished that she had asked more questions and also had known what questions to ask; much was implied and little divulged on a number of subjects.

In one of his musings on people he had known, he told Jean that the highest praise he could give someone was that he had never backed down from any man. He was talking about courage, not pugnaciousness. He then started reminiscing about a fellow Virginian who had come to Alberta in the early days and shared Johnson's code of southern honour. The man had a reputation for fighting; his fights were legion, sparked by his prickly southern sensibilities. Johnson told Jean that he was relieved that he never had to fight him, but he had come close. He was walking along a street in Calgary, carrying his fighting cock, Dewey, and heading for Billy Elliott's livery stable, when he met him. The man stopped him and said, "Well! A fighting bird and a fighting man," in a way that Johnson found offensive and challenging. Johnson said, "I just stood there and looked at him and he dropped his eyes." Jean asked, "Do you think you could have licked him, Dad?" For a moment he didn't speak. Then he said quietly, "I would have killed him – and he knew it. I would have had to kill him." Even in Alberta, this antebellum southern code never left these men.

In 1933, Jean and Laurie, with Johnson, moved from the Bow Valley to the Coleman Ranch north of the Stoney Indian Reservation at Morley. Here their first daughter, Donna Carroll, was born, to be followed by Margaret Jean. Now, in the worst depths of the Depression, most waking thoughts were centred on somehow making do – trading milk and butter for groceries at the Morley Trading Post, or selling six horses for twenty-five dollars apiece, a windfall that kept them going for six months.

Ranchers in the Alberta foothills during these terrible days of the mid-1930s looked at the condition of their drought-plagued farming neighbours and considered themselves lucky. They did not have to contend with shifting soil that covered fence lines or swarms of locusts that could eat the seat off a John Deere tractor. Game was plentiful, and game laws were very loosely enforced. Firewood was everywhere and, even in the driest years, a vegetable patch kept them in necessities. Food and warmth were the only absolute requirements. Beyond that, people just made do. No one needed a car; they were not going anywhere that a horse couldn't take them. With a degree of hindsight, many who have reminisced about the Great Depression have argued that it was a positive time – if you were not a prairie farmer or riding the rails looking for work. Things became simpler, and people made their own fun. Many communities came closer together, and people looked after each other.

Laurie made good money for the times by hiring out himself and his team for construction work along the highway being built west of Banff from Lake Louise to Jasper. Jean regularly rode to her homestead on Jean's Creek, fifteen miles north of where they were living. Johnson, now badly stove up with rheumatism, made himself useful around the ranch, especially looking after Donna, who was already, at the age of four, a terror on horseback. He did much of the cooking, which was very reminiscent of the roundup!

In 1936, they moved to Laurie's homestead on Robinson Creek, situated in a high valley north of the Ghost River, with the Rabbit Lake Stoney Indian Reserve on the north and east and the Forest Reserve on the west. Finally, this was home, the Lazy JL – as it still is today for Donna, her two sons, and their children. Guy Gibson put up the logs for the house and built the big fieldstone fireplace. Laurie and Jean finished the house, while Johnson cooked and kept an eye on the two girls.

Looking west toward the Rocky Mountains from the ranching country of the Ghost River, where Laurie and Jean Johnson established their Lazy J L Ranch. Here Johnson spent the last years of his life. Author's photo.

Shortly after they settled in, Jean saw a strange horse coming up from the south one day, and as the horse and rider got closer, she realized that the rider was Johnson. As he reined up, looking very pleased with himself, he asked, "How do you like my new horse?" Rattler was a beautiful, good-moving chestnut, and Johnson, now in his seventies, rode him many hundreds of miles each year. His favourite route was into Cochrane and then down to Turner Valley to visit his other daughter Dot. He could always find friends along the way for a visit and a place to stay the night. When he got sleepy as he rode along, he would just find a shady spot for a nap, while Rattler grazed nearby. After spending a week or two with Dot's family, the Clarksons, he would often move on to Tip Johnson's ranch west of Millarville and stay a night or two. And then to Charlie Mickle's, and Jappie and Lulu Rogers' at Bottrel, and so, leisurely, back to the Lazy JL – just a few hundred miles' round trip.

Once back at the ranch, Johnson's main purpose in life was to ensure that his granddaughters would carry on a tradition of horsemanship, first instilled by his Virginia father, and then overlaid with the West. And he was

Everett Johnson on his favourite horse Rattler near the end of his life. Even in his 80s, he still rode hundreds of miles to visit friends.

obviously delighted to see that both Donna and Peggy were natural horsewomen. He took great pride in watching them breaking their own colts at the age of nine and ten. When they started winning trophies in local horse shows, no one could have been prouder.

Both girls had much of their education by correspondence. Music, too, was very important; they rode ten miles for music lessons from Norma Piper Pocaterra, an Alberta woman who earlier had a meteoric opera career in Italy managed by her husband, George Pocaterra, who was a legend in the Kananaskis region of southern Alberta. George came to Canada from Italy in 1903, became a cowboy, and homesteaded the Buffalo Head Ranch in the Highwood Valley, next to what would become Guy Weadick's Stampede Ranch. Weadick was the force behind the creation of the Calgary Stampede in 1912. Pocaterra, who in addition to Italian spoke English, German, and Spanish, added Stoney to that list, as he explored much of the Kananaskis country and trapped there with his Stoney friends, especially Spotted Wolf, who became his blood brother. Pocaterra Creek, Dam, and Power House are now named for him, though he would have been distressed by the damming of his beloved Kananaskis country.

In 1933, he sold the Buffalo Head to R. M. Patterson, the author of a number of western and northern Canadian classics, including his most famous book, *Dangerous River,* about the fabled Nahanni River in today's Northwest Territories. Raymond Patterson and his wife Marigold were very good friends of my parents, and it is through R.M., as he was known, that three friends and I canoed the Nahanni in 1972, when very few people had been on the river. Before we canoed the river, I remember Raymond Patterson taking me to his study after a very good dinner and showing me his map of the Nahanni, with an X where he thought the Nahanni gold was: up the Flat River (which is anything but flat), where Albert Faille – the Legend of the Nahanni – had his cabin. Rumours abounded for years that Faille had found gold up the Flat, but nothing has ever been found.

Pocaterra, after selling his ranch to Patterson, returned to Italy and met Norma Piper, who was studying opera in Milan. They married in 1936, and he took over her opera career, with huge success, until the war intervened. They returned to Canada and bought a ranch in the Ghost Valley, down the steepest hill I have ever driven. For many years the Pocaterras had a Second World War vintage jeep that barely navigated the hill to the ranch house.

Jean remembered one moment of horsemanship that stuck in her mind. When Johnson was in his mid-seventies, some bachelor neighbours gave him one of their horses to ride. Their horses were noted for their iron mouths, and this particular horse was one of the worst. It also had the attractive habit of whirling and bolting for the barn on the least provocation. This it did and galloped full tilt straight for a very steep ravine. Johnson just leaned forward, grabbed the side of the bit, pulling the horse's head around, and threw him. At the same moment, he rolled off, got up. and dusted himself off. Even at seventy-five, he made it look easy.

By the early years of the Second World War, Johnson, now in his early eighties and suffering increasingly from rheumatism, could still amaze his daughter-in-law.

> One day I noticed him spinning Laurie's six-shooter, a single-action 38 Colt. I asked him to show me his draw. He said that ordinarily he carried his gun in the holster at his side; but when he knew he might have to use it, he stuck it in the front of his trousers. It seemed to me that this was an awkward position from which to draw – until he demonstrated it. He placed the gun in the top of his trousers, in front, and let the hammer down on the edge of the

material. A flash of movement and the gun was pointing. I hardly saw the motion of his hand – swift and deadly as a rattlesnake striking. I cannot say how a rattlesnake strikes; I cannot say how he drew. His eyesight was still so remarkably keen that he could read good print without his glasses.

After watching this demonstration, an earlier comment of his came back to her. She looked at her father-in-law's intense blue eyes and remembered him saying that he was never concerned about gunmen with brown eyes; it was the hard blue eyes you had to watch for if you were going up against someone in a gunfight. It wasn't just the speed that counted in a gunfight; it was the cool intent.

And he hadn't lost his eye for a pretty woman. When a friend who had just returned from studying in England, Marion MacKay, came out to the ranch to stay for Easter, Johnson was smitten. Marion was a very talented artist, tall, strikingly handsome, and had a wonderful sense of humour that delighted Johnson. For some reason, he called her Mary, and he would gaze after her and say to Jean, "I love that Mary harder than a mule can kick downhill." And after she left, he would ask, "Have you had a letter from Mary? I would admire to hear what she has to say." Although still a romantic in his eighties, he was skeptical about marriage, especially regarding the restraints it put on a man. While on that subject, he blurted out that marriage to a wrong woman was just about the worst fate that could befall a man. "He'd be better off in Hell with his back broke."

One by one, his old friends died. Finally, the only ones left were the sons of Bill Reid of the Wagon Box Fight – George and Jack. They had come to Canada in 1910, and in 1914 both had joined the Royal North-West Mounted Police. George remained with the force for many years, as did his younger brother Jack.

The Reid family may be unique in having four sons who were law officers, and two, George and Jack, who were officers on both sides of the border. Jack Reid was first a deputy sheriff at the age of sixteen under an older brother at Medora, North Dakota, where the family ranched. Jack moved to Canada in 1909 and, at the beginning of the First World War, helped the Mounted Police with a difficult case of rustling, which required Jack to fish out the incriminating evidence from a particularly ripe privy. The Mounties were so impressed by his evidence in court that they hired him on the spot as a stock detective, with the rank of special constable. In 1916, he was promoted to the rank of staff sergeant, responsible mostly for cases of stolen stock, both horses and cattle. From 1921 to 1929, he served with the Alberta

(From left) Jean Johnson, Harry Snyder, John Oldfield and my father, Harry Jennings, with the log ranchhouse that Jean and Laurie built.

Provincial Police. He then went on to become one of western Canada's most renowned gunsmiths, with a large reputation south of the border. In his reminiscences, he stressed that rustling in ranching country was always an issue, but only a serious problem near the American border.[6]

It was through Jack Reid that Johnson met my father and his long-standing hunting partner, Col. Harry Snyder. Jack was a very close friend of my father. And it was Jack who first told my father and mother about the link between Wister and Johnson, and about his own father's part in the Wagon Box Fight. Sadly, I was too young to remember the many evenings Johnson spent with my parents talking about hunting, my father's passion, and about the early West, another of his passions. At some point, probably quite early on, my father became Johnson's doctor. But that was an easy job. I can remember my father saying that Ed, as he called him, was still tough as nails – though by now in his eighties.

Jack Reid also introduced Johnson to Col. Snyder. Harry Snyder came from an old Virginia family, and he, too, was besotted with the early West. He had hunted all over the world, written a book on big-game hunting, and, in Africa, killed the largest elephant on record and outfitted and led several geographical expeditions to the Canadian North. After an expedition to the

Col. Harry Snyder (left) and Johnson at the Tipi, Snyder's baronial retreat in the Rocky Mountains. The main room had much in common with Theodore Roosevelt's Gallery at Sagamore Hill.

fabled Nahanni River country, the mountain range now called the Ragged Range was named for him. He also had an encyclopedic knowledge of the old West. He and Johnson had much to talk about. Col. Snyder's wife, Louise, told my mother that when the two men "discovered" each other, they sat in two big chairs in front of the mammoth fireplace at the "Tipi," Col. Snyder's baronial retreat in the mountains west of Sundre, Alberta, on the Red Deer River, and talked non-stop for several days without going to bed, surrounded by Col. Snyder's impressive collection of Russell paintings and Remington bronzes. Louise periodically brought them food and took away the dirty dishes. They slept in the big chairs and then just took up where they had stopped.

During all the years that Johnson used his son's ranch as his anchor, Jean did periodically wonder why he had never taken up land. She never asked him outright, but from a number of things he said she concluded that

Col. Snyder's main room at the Tipi, featuring his world-record elephant tusks. It is clear from this picture and the following one that he and Roosevelt would have been soul mates.

he had a different set of values. Material things meant nothing to him, and he hated fences, both literally and as a reminder of a West that was gone. When he was reminiscing, his far-off look was for the days before fences and rules and government people. He demanded freedom; in Wyoming the land had been his – he did not want to own it and be held down by it. When Wyoming became peopled and fenced, he moved on. The real Wyoming would live on in his memory, and nothing after would be the same. As with many who've had intense wartime experiences, the rest of life became an epilogue. In a way, Johnson was a victim of the same Wyoming that rendered Wister breathless and euphoric when he first saw it. Just as Wister would never write anything first-rate after *The Virginian*, once his Genesis was tamed, life for Johnson could not be the same after the open range was gone. Increasingly, he retreated to the untamed landscape of his imagination. He would often ride north into the Forest Reserve – to the high ridges looking

Theodore Roosevelt's gallery at Sagamore Hill, Oyster Bay, New York. Courtesy of Sagamore Hill National Historic Site, National Parks Service, Oyster Bay, NY. SAHI-9300, IMG 1348.

down on the Ghost River country, but as he gazed out over this rugged, unfenced country, Jean thought he was seeing Wyoming, not Alberta.

In 1941, at the age of eighty-one, Johnson made his last trip by horseback to Turner Valley to visit his daughter and her husband, Bob Clarkson. His Clarkson grandchildren were now both in the army, Patricia with the WACs, and Bob and Donald with the Canadian Army. Bob became middleweight boxing champion of the Canadian Army and went on to train commandos during the war.[7]

Shortly after he returned from Turner Valley, Johnson rather suddenly bent down and kissed Jean on the cheek, an unusual gesture for him! "Jeannie, I want you to have Rattler. I reckon my riding days are over." After he stopped riding, a change came over him. It was as if giving his horse to Jean was an admission that his life was winding down. After escaping on a trip to Fairbanks, Alaska, with Dot's husband, Chappie, who was working on the building of the Alaska Highway, a new tone entered his conversations with

Jean. He now told her stories of dark events that he had told no one else, first making her promise that she would never disclose any of what he told her. She never did. But in none of the stories that he told her did he ever betray a friend.

In the spring of 1946, Johnson spent several weeks at Col. Snyder's ranch, and the two laid great plans for a trip to Wyoming. Johnson was on his way back to the ranch when he stopped in on an old friend near Gleichen – close to General Strange's Colonization Ranche, where he had been foreman. He suddenly took ill and fell into a coma. My father was called and he arranged for an ambulance to take him to the Holy Cross Hospital in Calgary, where my father was chief of staff. Ebb Johnson died before he could reach the hospital.

He was buried in Queen's Park Cemetery in Calgary. Under his name on the headstone are the words "The Virginian." I think he would have preferred simply, "A Virginian Cowboy."

POSTSCRIPT

One final note regarding Johnson's connection to Wister. In April 1969, Jean Johnson wrote to James McCook, formerly city editor of *The Albertan*, one of the two Calgary dailies of the time, regarding the newspaper's correspondence with Wister in the early 1930s when the first "talkie" version of *The Virginian* came out. McCook had contacted Wister at that time because of rumours in Calgary that Johnson was the Virginian. McCook had not kept detailed notes, but told Jean that Wister had replied to his telegram, saying that "Johnson seemed to be the man, although he had not been in touch with him for many years." On the strength of this reply, *The Albertan* had invited Johnson to go to the movie with a reporter from the paper. McCook remembered that Johnson was extremely reluctant to go to the movie, which made *The Albertan* believe that Johnson was no "put-up job." Johnson did not enjoy the movie!

Wister's ambiguous reply to *The Albertan* is very puzzling. His response appears to be the only time that he acknowledged who the Virginian was. The closest he had come previously was to state that Corporal Skirdin was the "type" that he had in mind when he wrote the novel. But why would he say that Johnson *"seemed"* to be the man? Who knows what was going on in Wister's mind in the early 1930s? By then he was in his mid-seventies and was not at all well; he had also become disillusioned with the West. Perhaps he just thought it was time to stop being coy. After all, what did it matter anymore? He died in 1938 at the age of seventy-eight. It is a great shame that no one at the time had the understanding to follow up on Wister's comment.

Notes

PREFACE

1. Sidney Freifeld, *Undiplomatic Notes: Tales From the Canadian Foreign Service* (Toronto: Hounslow Press, 1990), 20–22.

INTRODUCTION: AMERICA'S GUN CULTURE AND THE VIGILANTE TRADITION

1. Ashraf H.A. Rushdy, *American Lynching* (New Haven: Yale University Press, 2012), 1.
2. The word "lynch" originated in Bedford County, Virginia in 1780, during the Revolutionary War. The leader of the Bedford Militia, Colonel Charles Lynch, became known for his sometimes abrupt way of dealing with the enemy. Rushdy, *American Lynching*, 23-25. The Oxford Dictionary defines lynching: "To kill someone for an alleged crime without legal trial, especially by hanging." However, the word lynch is sometimes used to describe the act of tarring and feathering or whipping. In the nineteenth century in the South, lynching could also include torture, skinning, burning alive and beheading. In this study, the word is used essentially as the Oxford Dictionary defines it.
3. The more that is known about the Loyalists, the more it is realized that they represented all levels of society and all political persuasions. But the Loyalists who were to have a large political and legal influence in Canada were almost exclusively conservative. They believed devoutly in maintaining ties with the British monarchy and ensuring that society was not changed by revolution.
4. John N. Jennings, "The North West Mounted Police and Indian Policy, 1874-1896" (PhD diss., University of Toronto, 1979), 99–104.
5. J. Edward Chamberlin, *If This Is Your Land, Where Are Your Stories? Finding Common Ground* (Toronto: Knopf Canada, 2003), 29–30
6. Jennings, "The North West Mounted Police," 287–97.

7   In J. S. Moir, ed., *Character and Circumstance* (Toronto: Macmillan, 1970).

8   The English common law dictated that it was only as a very last resort that a threatened person had the right to resist with deadly force.

9   Richard M. Brown, "Violence," in *The Oxford History of the American West*, ed. Clyde A. Milner, Carol A. O'Connor, and Martha A. Sandweiss (New York: Knopf, 1994), 393–94.

10 See Simon Schama, *The American Future: A History* (Toronto: Penguin Canada, 2008).

11 An oft-quoted line from Hilaire Belloc's poem for children, "Jim, Who Ran Away From His Nurse, and Was Eaten by a Lion."

12 Jennings, "The North West Mounted Police," 113.

13 See L. H. Thomas, *The Struggle for Responsible Government in the North-West Territories, 1870–1897* (Toronto: University of Toronto Press, 1956).

14 Schama, *The American Future*, 326.

15 Ibid., 264.

16 Ibid., 268–69.

17 See Jean Pfaelzer, *Driven Out: The Forgotten War Against the Chinese Americans* (New York: Random House, 2007), and Alexander Saxton, *The Indispensible Enemy: Labor and the Anti-Chinese Movement in California* (Berkeley: University of California Press, 1975).

18 See J. Brian Dawson, "The Chinese Experience in Frontier Calgary," in *Frontier Calgary, 1875–1914*, ed. A. W. Rasporich and Henry Klassen (Calgary: McClelland & Stewart West, 1975).

19 John McLaren, "The Early British Columbia Judges, the Rule of Law and the Chinese Question: The California and Oregon Connection" in John McLaren, Hamar Foster and Chet Orloff, *Law For the Elephant, Law For the Beaver: Essays in the Legal History of the North American West* (Regina: Canadian Plains Research Center, 1992), 237.

20 Ibid., 263–64.

21 See especially Joe E. Franz, "The Frontier Tradition: An Invitation to Violence" and Richard Maxwell Brown, "The American Vigilante Tradition," in *The History of Violence in America*, ed. Hugh Davis Graham and Ted Robert Gurr (New York: Bantam, 1969); and Brown, "Violence," in *The Oxford History of the American West*.

22 See Robert Dykstra, *The Cattle Towns* (New York: Knopf, 1971); Frank Richard Prassel, *The Western Peace Officer* (Norman: University of Oklahoma Press, 1972); and Eugene Hollon, *Frontier Violence* (New York: Oxford University Press, 1974).

23 Prassel, *Western Peace Officer*, 22.

24 Hollon, *Frontier Violence*, 97.

25 Ibid., 88, 97.

26 Roger D. McGrath, *Gunfighters, Highwaymen and Vigilantes: Violence on the Frontier* (Berkeley: University of California Press, 1984), 84–85, 185.

27 See McGrath, *Gunfighters*; Franz, "The Frontier Tradition"; Harry Sinclair Drago, *The Great Range Wars: Violence on the Grasslands* (Lincoln: University of Nebraska Press, 1970); Joseph G. Rosa, *The Gunfighter: Man or Myth?* (Norman: University of Nebraska Press, 1969); Philip D. Jordan, *Frontier Law and Order* (Lincoln: University of Nebraska Press, 1970); and Brown, "Violence," in

The Oxford History of the American West.

28 See Richard Hofstadter and Michael Wallace, eds., *American Violence: A Documentary History* (New York: Knopf, 1970).

29 See Franz, "The Frontier Tradition."

30 Drago, *Great Range Wars*, 48–49.

31 Jordan, *Frontier Law and Order*, ix, 13.

32 Rosa, *Gunfighters*, 264.

33 Brown, "Violence," in *The Oxford History of the American West*, 423.

34 Ibid.

35 Ibid.

36 See Richard Maxwell Brown, "Law and Order on the American Frontier: The Western Civil War of Incorporation," in *Law For the Elephant, Law For the Beaver*, 74–76.

37 See William D. Corrigan and Christopher Waldrep, eds., *Swift to Wrath: Lynching in Global Historical Perspective* (Charlottesville: University of Virginia Press, 2013).

38 Richard Maxwell Brown, " Historical Patterns of Violence in America," in Hugh Davis Graham and Ted Robert Gurr, *A History of Violence in America*, (New York: Bantam, 1969), 67–68.

39 Ibid., 68–69.

40 See Ida B. Wells-Barnett, On Lynching (Amherst, New York: Humanity Books, 2002).

41 J. H. Chadbourn, *Lynching and the Law* (Chapel Hill: University of North Carolina Press, 1933), 3.

42 Toronto *Globe and Mail*, June 14, 2005. The Senate seems to have changed its mind after viewing the graphic horrors of lynching in James Allen et al., *Without Sanctuary: Lynching Photography in America* (Santa Fe: Twin Palms, 2000).

43 Brown, "Violence," 154. As would be expected, Texas had more vigilante movements – 52 – than any other state or territory. Brown traces 116 eastern and 210 western movements.

44 John G. Cawalti, *The Six Gun Mystique* (Bowling Green, OH: Bowling Green University Popular Press, 1971), 58–61.

45 Keith Walden, *Visions of Order* (Toronto: Butterworth, 1982), 62.

46 Michael Dawson, "That Nice Red Coat Goes To My Head Like Champagne: Gender, Antimodernism and the Mountie Image, 1880–1960," *Journal of Canadian Studies* 32, no. 3 (Fall 1979): 119-39. The red colour of the Mountie uniform was actually called "Hunting Pink," named for a tailor of that name who specialized in making coats for the fox-hunting crowd.

47 Ibid., 129.

48 Ibid., 130.

49 Jill Lapore, "Battleground America: One nation under the gun." *New Yorker* (April 23, 2012), 40.

50 Quoted in the *Peterborough Examiner*, July 18, 2013.

51 Yemen is second, with a rate half that of the United States. Lepore, "Battleground," 39.

52 April 21, 2007. This figure is close to the FBI estimate for 2000: 250 million firearms in private hands and 5 million new ones added every year. See Michael A. Bellesiles, *Arming America: The Origins of a National Gun Culture* (New York: Knopf, 2000). Cook and Ludwig estimate that there are 200 million firearms in private hands. Paul M. Barrett, *Glock: The Rise of America's Gun* (New York:

Crown, 2012), 258–59, estimates that there are between 200 and 300 million guns in private hands in the US. This works out to roughly one firearm per adult. It is estimated that 40% of American handguns are acquired without a background check. Despite leading the world in gun ownership, only one-third of American households own any guns, down from half of American households forty years ago. Lepore, "Battleground," 39, citing the National Policy Opinion Center, University of Chicago. Gun ownership is higher among white and rural Americans.

53   Lepore, "Battleground," 39–40. Of these 300 million firearms, 106 million are handguns, 105 million are rifles, and 83 million are shotguns. 40% of guns purchased are from private sellers at gun shows.

54   See Wikipedia for FBI statistics. In 1992, for instance, there were 13,220 murders in the US using handguns; in Canada there were 128 – and that number was well above the average.

55   New York Times, February 14, 2015. The film was based on Kyle's book *American Sniper: The Autobiography of the Most Lethal Sniper in U.S. Military History* (New York: William Morrow, 2012). Kyle also wrote *American Gun* (New York: William Morrow, 2013), a history of the United States seen through ten of her most famous guns.

56   Toronto *Globe and Mail*, July 1994, article by Geoffrey Simpson. Wikipedia, obviously a somewhat doubtful source for scrupulous accuracy, compares some national homicide rates per hundred thousand people in 2010 and 2011: US 4.8; Canada 1.6; U.K. and Australia 1.2; Western Europe 1.3; France 1.6; Germany 1.1; Russia 25.5. According to Barrett, *Glock*, 257, the general homicide rate in the US is roughly five times that of Canada, Britain, Australia, and Western Europe.

57   Lepore, "Battleground," 47.

58   Philip J. Cook and Jens Ludwick, *Gun Violence: The Real Cost* (New York: Oxford University Press, 2000), 15. These authors calculate that the cost of gun violence per year in the United States is $100 billion. They state: "Among developed countries, the U.S. is distinctive not for the high volume of violent crime, but for the high percentage of those crimes that involve a gun and the main consequence – a homicide rate far in excess of any developed country."

59   Ibid.

60   A CBS News survey, January 2012, in *Vanity Fair*, April 2012. The survey polled approximately 1,200 people, certainly not a definitive number, but a number not to be ignored.

61   Martin Friedland, *A Century of Criminal Justice* (Toronto: Carswell, 1984), 129.

62   Ibid., 113–14. The Canadian handgun rate in these years was about 10 percent of all homicides. In the US, it was 50 percent. In the US, 90 percent of firearm robberies were carried out with handguns. Friedland, *Century of Criminal Justice*, 117.

63   A special permit is required to carry a handgun. Very few permits are issued, especially for protection. Friedland, *Century of Criminal Justice*, 118–19.

64   See chapter 6.

65 Hofstadter and Wallace, *American Violence*, 24.
66 Ibid., 6.
67 Ibid., 26.
68 Ibid., 4, 12.
69 Ibid., 25.
70 Leslie A. Pal, "Between the Sights: Gun Control in Canada and the United States," in *Canada and the United States: The Differences that Count*, 71. For two contradictory opinions on the Second Amendment, see Warren Freeman, *The Privilege to Keep and Bear Arms: The Second Amendment and its Interpretation* (New York: Quorum Books, 1999), and Stephen P. Halbrook, *The Every Man Be Armed: The Evolution of a Constitutional Right* (Albuquerque: University of New Mexico Press, 1984). Adam Winkler, in *Gunfight: The Battle over the Right to Bear Arms in America* (New York: Norton, 2011), points out the legal complexities surrounding the Second Amendment. In 2008, the US Supreme Court, in a 5–4 decision, ruled that the Second Amendment does, in fact, protect the right of private citizens to have a gun at home. Barrett, *Glock*, 258.
71 Lepore, "Battleground," 42.
72 Gordon Wood, *The Creation of the American Republic* (Chapel Hill: University of North Carolina Press, 1969); and Bernard Bailyn, *The Ideological Origins of the American Revolution* (Cambridge, MA: Harvard University Press, 1967).
73 Michael Waldman, *The Second Amendment: A Biography* (New Haven: Yale University Press, 2014), xii, 7, 27, 97.
74 It is ironic that the Dominion of Canada Rifle Association preceded the NRA by three years and gave it some guidance in its early years. But the DCRA was created for almost opposite reasons. Its primary purpose was, first, to train Canadians for a possible invasion from the United States in the tense years following the Civil War and then to train Canadians to kill for the Empire, as war in Europe loomed. R. Blake Brown, *Arming and Disarming: A History of Gun Control in Canada* (Toronto: University of Toronto Press, 2012), chapters 2 and 3.
75 During the Clinton era, two gun laws were passed: the 1993 Brady Handgun Control Act, which required federally licensed gun dealers to conduct background checks, but with no such requirement for unlicensed dealers, and the Violent Crime Control and Enforcement Act of 1994, which banned nineteen military-style assault weapons and certain high-capacity magazines of more than ten rounds. *Globe and Mail*, Dec. 18, 2012.
76 Lapore, 46.
77 *The Economist*, Dec. 22, 2012.
78 *Globe and Mail*, Dec. 17, 2012.
79 *Harper's Magazine*, June, 2013.
80 Four presidents, Lincoln, Garfield, McKinley and Kennedy have been killed; six more have had assassination attempts: Jackson, both Roosevelts, Truman, Ford and Reagan. As well, Kennedy's brother, Robert, and Martin Luther King Jr. could top a list of important Americans who have been killed or had attempts on their lives.
81 April 21, 2007, 11; Barrett, *Glock*, 253.
82 In 2007, a semi-automatic rifle was used to kill seven and wound four at the Westwoods Mall in Omaha, Nebraska. And the next

year at a house party in a suburb of Los Angeles, four semi-automatic pistols were used to kill an ex-wife and her family. The decade ended with the Glock 9 killing of five and the wounding of sixteen at Northern Illinois University by a student who had gone off his medication (Barrett, *Glock*, 22), and, finally, the killing of thirteen and wounding of twenty-nine by a radical Muslim at Fort Hood, Texas.

83 Eight were killed and one wounded at a California hair salon in 2011. And then, of course, came the attempt at political assassination at a rally in Tucson, Arizona. Six were killed and fourteen wounded by Jared Loughner using a semi-automatic Glock 19 pistol with a special oversized magazine that took thirty-three rounds (Barrett, *Glock*, 253). He was found incompetent to stand trial, but he had had no trouble getting his hands on a Glock (Barrett, *Glock*, 259). The day after the Tucson killings, there was a huge rush of Glock 19 sales at gun stores in Tucson, but no call for a debate on guns (Barrett, *Glock*, 264). 2011 also saw the killing of seven and the wounding of three with a 9 mm Glock at Grand Rapids, Michigan.

84 Toronto *Globe and Mail*, July 21, 2012. The M&P 15 has a detachable ten or thirty round box magazine.

85 Pew Research Center poll, reported in the *Globe and Mail*, Jan. 17, 2013.

86 In April 2013, President Obama's bill was defeated in the Senate by a narrow margin. Obama called the failure of the bill "shameful" and added that Republicans had "willfully lied" about the consequences of the bill.

87 *Globe and Mail*, Feb. 26, 2013.

88 *New York Times*, Dec. 30, 2012.

89 *Globe and Mail*, Dec. 18, 2012. In 2011, Britain (including Scotland) had sixty-five gun homicides. The US had more than half that number (thirty-four) every day! At first, the handgun ban did not have the desired effect, but in the long run, gun violence in Britain dropped considerably. More than 200,000 weapons and 700 tons of ammunition were confiscated by police in the last fifteen years. Andy Marsh, the firearms director for Britain's Association of Chief Police Officers, stated recently that Britain now has "significantly lower levels of gun crime, levels that continue to fall." In 2011, firearms killed fifty-nine people in Britain, which has a population of 63 million. *Washington Post*, Feb. 1, 2013.

90 From 1996 to 1998, 700,000 rifles were turned in. A study by the *American Journal of Law and Economics* in 2010 stated that, between 1995 and 2006, gun-related homicides in Australia dropped 59% and the firearm-suicide rate dropped 65%. *Time*, Dec. 15, 2012.

91 Ibid., Feb. 15, 2013.

92 *Globe and Mail*, Jan. 19, 2013.

93 *Fifth Estate*, Jan. 10, 2013.

94 *Peterborough Examiner*, Dec. 20, 2012. In 2012, a Johns Hopkins University gun policy center study concluded, "Although there is little difference in the overall crime rates between the U.S. and other high-income countries, the homicide rate in the U.S. is seven times higher than the combined homicide rates of 22 other high-income countries." Waldman, *Second Amendment*, 162.

95 Walter Prescott Webb, *The Great Plains* (New York: Grosset & Dunlap, 1931), 496–98.

96   Friedland, *Century of Criminal Justice*, 131. Because of this divided jurisdiction, for instance, the 1968 Gun Control Act has had little effect on handgun policies.
97   Ibid., 125. S. C. 1885, c. 51, s. 14.
98   Brown, *Arming and Disarming*, 47.
99   Ibid., p. 7. Beginning in the 1860s, the federal government largely banned people from carrying revolvers and required retailers to keep records of handgun purchases.
100 Ibid., 126.
101 Ibid., 132–33.
102 Ibid., 151–54.
103 The RCMP has a central handgun registry, making it easier than in the US to track handguns. Friedland, *Century of Criminal Justice*, 132.
104 Brown, *Arming and Disarming*, 190.
105 "Gun Control: The Options."
106 Friedland, *Century of Criminal Justice*, 114–16.
107 Brown, *Arming and Disarming*, 211.
108 Ibid., 214.
109 Pal, *Between the Sights*, 68–70.
110 This law is in the process of being repealed, but the point is that the federal government was able to pass a law that was extremely unpopular in large parts of rural Canada.
111 Friedland, *Century of Criminal Justice*, 137.

1: BEGINNINGS

1   All references to Everett Johnson, unless otherwise indicated, come from his daughter-in-law Jean Johnson's manuscript about his life, "A Virginian Cowboy: His Life and Friends," which she deposited with the Glenbow Archives in Calgary, Alberta.
2   Robert M. Utley, *The Indian Frontier of the American West, 1846–1890* (Albuquerque: University of New Mexico Press, 1984), 76. Myrick stated, "As far as I am concerned, if they are hungry let them eat grass or their own dung."
3   T. R. Fehrenbach, *Lone Star: A History of Texas and the Texans* (New York: Macmillan, 1985), 571.
4   See Walter Prescott Webb, *The Texas Rangers: A Century of Frontier Defense* (Austin: University of Texas Press, 1935); Fehrenbach, *Lone Star*; Robert M. Utley, *Lone Star Justice: The First Century of the Texas Rangers* (New York: Berkley Books, 2002); Andrew R. Graybill, *Policing the Great Plains: Rangers, Mounties, and the North American Frontier, 1875–1910* (Lincoln: University of Nebraska Press, 2007).
5   Ted Grant and Andy Russell, *Men of the Saddle: Working Cowboys of Canada* (Toronto: Van Nostrand, 1978), 39.
6   Wallace Stegner, *Wolf Willow: A History, a Story, and a Memory of the Last Plains Frontier* (New York: Viking Compass, 1966), 136.
7   Ibid., 135–36.
8   Ibid.
9   James H. Cook, *Fifty Years on the Old Frontier* (Norman: University of Oklahoma Press, 1963), 26–27.
10 Cited in Grant and Russell, *Men of the Saddle*, 26.
11 Cook, *Fifty Years*, 99–100.
12 Fehrenbach, *Lone Star*, 545.
13 Nyle H. Miller and Joseph W. Snell, *Great Gunfighters of the Kansas Cowtowns, 1867–1886* (Lincoln: University of Nebraska Press, 1963), 249–50.

14 Fehrenbach, *Lone Star*, 536–37.
15 W. Eugene Hollon, *Frontier Violence* (New York: Oxford University Press, 1974), 210.
16 Robert R. Dykstra, *The Cattle Towns* (New York: Knopf, 1968), 58.
17 Joseph G. Rosa, *The Gunfighter: Man or Myth?* (Norman: University of Oklahoma Press, 1969), 106–7.
18 Stanley Vestal, *Dodge City, Queen of the Cowtowns* (London: Nevill, 1955), 35–37.
19 Mari Sandoz, *The Cattlemen* (New York: Hastings House, 1958), 146. Boot Hill Cemetery was originally created to bury the casualties of the clashes between the track layers, troops, and buffalo hide men.
20 Dykstra, *The Cattle Towns*, 113, 143–44. Dykstra claims that there were 45 killings in the Kansas cattle towns from 1870 to 1885, fifteen of them in Dodge City. He states that the first killing in Dodge did not occur until 1878. However, Rosa, *The Gunfighter*, 113, claims that there were 25 killings in Dodge in 1872 alone. He provides convincing evidence for at least one of them. Stuart Lake, admittedly a doubtful source, claimed that there were 80 killings in Dodge before Wyatt Earp arrived there in May 1876. Stuart Lake, *Wyatt Earp, Frontier Marshal* (New York: Houghton Mifflin, 1931), 138.
21 Dee Brown and Martin Schmitt, *Trail Driving Days* (New York: Scribner's, 1952), 94.
22 Dykstra, *The Cattle Towns*, 119–21.
23 Lake, *Wyatt Earp*, 70.

2: THE BLACK HILLS

1 R. M. Utley, *Cavalier in Buckskins: George Armstrong Custer and the Western Military Frontier* (Norman: University of Oklahoma Press, 1988), 136–37.
2 Ibid., 133. The rumours would, indeed, prove true. In the hundred years after 1875, one single gold mine in the Black Hills produced a billion dollars in gold. Nathaniel Philbrick, *The Last Stand: Custer, Sitting Bull, and the Battle of the Little Bighorn* (New York: Viking, 2010), 4.
3 Utley, *Cavalier in Buckskins*, 139.
4 Philbrick, *The Last Stand*, 64–65.
5 Patricia Nelson Limerick, *The Legacy of Conquest: The Unbroken Past of the American West* (New York: Norton, 1987), 334.
6 Robert K. DeArment, *Assault on the Deadwood Stage: Road Agents and Shotgun Messengers* (Norman: University of Oklahoma Press, 2011), 8.
7 Ibid., 42, 51. Sam Bass, after his many stagecoach robberies around Deadwood, left for Texas and formed a new gang. In 1878, the Texas Rangers cornered him near Round Rock and killed him in a shootout. "Persimmon Bill" Chambers, whose reputation rested on stealing Native horses, as well as holding up stagecoaches, was wanted for the cold-blooded murder of an army sergeant in 1876. He saw the man with a large wad of money, so "I just plugged him in the back." He laughed as he related the story. Persimmon Bill simply vanished, and his subsequent history is unknown. DeArment, *Assault on the Deadwood Stage*, 132, 207.
8 See Harry N. Scheiber, *Abbott-Downing and the Concord Coach*

(Concord: New Hampshire Historical Society, 1989).

9. Agnes Wright Spring, *The Cheyenne and Black Hills Stage and Express Routes* (Lincoln: University of Nebraska Press, 1948), 88–91.
10. Watson Parker, *Deadwood, the Golden Years* (Lincoln: University of Nebraska Press, 1981), 59. By October, the population of Deadwood was estimated to be 3,000.
11. Ibid., 207.
12. Ibid.; Estelline Bennett, *Old Deadwood Days* (Lincoln: University of Nebraska Press, 1982), 112.
13. Paul Trachtman, *The Gunfighters* (New York: Time-Life Books, 1974), 170.
14. DeArment, *Assault on the Deadwood Stage*, 59.
15. Parker, *Deadwood*, 210.
16. Bennett, *Old Deadwood Days*, 253–55.
17. DeArment, *Assault on the Deadwood Stage*, 182.
18. Ibid., 91.
19. Ibid., 180.
20. Ibid., 144.
21. Ibid., 95.
22. Parker, *Deadwood*, 193.
23. W. Eugene Hollon, *Frontier Violence: Another Look* (London: Oxford University Press, 1974), 116.
24. Joe B. Franz and Julian E. Choate, *The American Cowboy: Myth and Reality* (Norman: University of Oklahoma Press, 1955), 90.
25. Kent L. Steckmesser, *The Western Hero in History and Legend* (Norman: University of Oklahoma Press, 1965), 118–20; Eugene Hollon, "Frontier Violence: Another Look," in *People of the Plains and Mountains*, ed. Ray Allen Billington (Westport, CT: Greenwood, 1973), 87.
26. Trachtman, *Gunfighters*, 16.
27. Nyle H. Miller and Joseph W. Snell, *Great Gunfighters of the Kansas Cowtowns* (Lincoln: University of Nebraska Press, 1963), 78.
28. Stuart N. Lake, *Wyatt Earp: Frontier Marshal* (New York: Houghton Mifflin, 1931), 157.
29. Allen Barra, *Inventing Wyatt Earp: His Life and Many Legends* (New York: Carroll, 1998), 69.
30. Ibid., 70.
31. Ibid.
32. DeArment, *Assault on the Deadwood Stage*, 205. Lee A. Silva, in his huge multivolume biography of Earp, goes into excruciating detail on the issue of whether Earp was ever a shotgun messenger while in Deadwood. He concludes that he was – probably! Lee A. Silva, *Wyatt Earp: A Biography of a Legend: The Cowtown Years* (Santa Ana, CA: Graphic Publishers, 2002), 400–432.
33. Lake, *Wyatt Earp*, 157.
34. Frank Richard Prassel, *The Western Peace Officer* (Norman: University of Oklahoma Press, 1972), 51.
35. DeArment, *Assault on the Deadwood Stage*, 32.
36. See Christine Bold, *Selling the Wild West: Popular Western Fiction, 1860 to 1960* (Bloomington: Indiana University Press, 1987). Wheeler wrote thirty-three Deadwood Dick novels, and when he died in 1885, the Beadle company kept his death a secret and churned out another ninety-seven stories under his name.
37. DeArment, *Assault on the Deadwood Stage*, 138–42.
38. Ibid.
39. Ibid., 101–4, 205.

3: BILL CODY

1. Agnes Wright Spring, *The Cheyenne and Black Hills Stage and Express Routes* (Lincoln: University of Nebraska Press, 1948), 180.
2. Don Russell, *The Lives and Legends of Buffalo Bill* (Norman: University of Oklahoma Press, 1988), 50.
3. Louis S. Warren, *Buffalo Bill's America: William Cody and the Wild West Show* (New York: Knopf, 2005), 18–20.
4. Ibid., 18.
5. Russell, *Lives and Legends*, 103, 123–24; Warren, *Buffalo Bill's America*, 86, 89.
6. Warren, *Buffalo Bill's America*, 55–56.
7. Russell L. Barsh, "The Substitution of Cattle for Bison on the Great Plains," in *The Struggle for the Land: Indigenous Insight and Industrial Empire in the Semiarid World*, ed. Paul A. Olson (Lincoln: University of Nebraska Press, 1990), 107–8.
8. Warren, *Buffalo Bill's America*, 57.
9. Barsh, "The Substitution of Cattle," 108.
10. Russell, *Lives and Legends*, 86, 94.
11. Warren, *Buffalo Bill's America*, 127.
12. Ibid., 116, 146.
13. Ibid., 158.
14. Russell, *Lives and Legends*, 170–73.
15. Ibid., 178.
16. Warren, *Buffalo Bill's America*, 149.
17. Russell, *Lives and Legends*, 156, 179. Cody was also notably casual about spelling. Bill Reid appears as "Reed" in his writing.
18. The battle of Summit Springs, on July 11, 1869, was in retaliation for Cheyenne raids. Cody was a scout for Col. Eugene Carr's Fifth Cavalry.
19. Richard W. Etulain, *Telling Western Stories: From Buffalo Bill to Larry McMurtry* (Albuquerque: University of New Mexico Press, 1999), 18.
20. Russell, *Lives and Legends*, 192–94, 196.
21. Ibid., 199.
22. Ibid., 207.
23. Paul L. Hedren, *First Scalp For Custer: The Skirmish at Warbonnet Creek, Nebraska, July 17, 1876* (Lincoln: University of Nebraska Press, 1980), 61.
24. Russell, *Lives and Legends*, 225.
25. Warren, *Buffalo Bill's America*, 118.
26. Nathaniel Philbrick, *The Last Stand: Custer, Sitting Bull, and the Battle of the Little Big Horn* (New York: Viking, 2010), 59. This claim of Custer's parenthood has been met with scorn by other historians.
27. Russell, *Lives and Legends*, 230.
28. William F. Cody, *The Life of Hon. William F. Cody* (Lincoln: University of Nebraska Press, 1978), 342–44.
29. Warren, *Buffalo Bill's America*, 118.
30. See Richard White, "Frederick Jackson Turner and Buffalo Bill," in *The Frontier in American Culture: Essays by Richard White and Patricia Nelson Limerick*, ed. James R. Grossman (Berkeley: University of California Press, 1994).
31. Warren, *Buffalo Bill's America*, 218.
32. Russell, *Lives and Legends*, 227. For Madsen's account, see Don Russell Collection, Buffalo Bill Historic Center, Chris Madsen, "Buffalo Bill Fight."
33. Hedren, *First Scalp For Custer*, 66; Russell, *Lives and Legends*, 225. Russell includes one other scout named Tate.
34. Russell, *Lives and Legends*, 226, 235.

35 Hedren, *First Scalp For Custer*, 67.
36 Russell, *Lives and Legends*, 226.
37 Ibid. See also Johnny Backer Collection, MS 6, Series IV, W. F. Cody Collection, Buffalo Bill Historical Center, Cody, Wyoming, for the testimony of Chris Madsen, Louis V. Cooke, and Sgt. John Hamilton.
38 In the mid-1950s, a vigorous debate was carried on in the pages of *The Westerner's New York Posse Brand Book* concerning Captain King's credibility (vol. 2, no. 4, 1955; vol. 3, no. 1, 1956; vol. 4, no. 2, 1957). Both Mari Sandoz and Art Woodward accused King of falsifying facts concerning the Yellow Hair incident in his *Campaigning with Crook*. See Mari Sandoz, "Captain Charles King as Portrayer of the West," *The Westerner's New York Posse Brand Book* 2, no. 4 (1955), pt. 84, and Art Woodward, "More on Captain Charles King – A Defense," *The Westerner's New York Posse Brand Book* 3, no. 1 (1956).
39 Russell, *Lives and Legends*, 229, 232–33.
40 Don Russell, "Captain Charles King," *The Westerner's New York Posse Brand Book* 4, no. 2 (1957), 39–40.
41 Warren, *Buffalo Bill's America*, 171.
42 Ibid., 120; Robert Utley in *Frontier Regulars* states that 800 Cheyennes left the Red Cloud Agency for the Powder River country, but he is probably speaking in more general terms. Robert M. Utley, *Frontier Regulars: The United States Army and the Indian, 1866–1891* (New York: Macmillan, 1973), 268.
43 Warren, *Buffalo Bill's America*, 120. Warren mentions that there is considerable material on the Yellow Hair incident at the Nebraska State Historical Society in Lincoln.
44 A. E. Brininstool, "Who Killed Yellow Hand?," *Outdoor Life – Outdoor Recreation*, Feb. 1930, cited in Warren, *Buffalo Bill's America*, 119.
45 Warren, *Buffalo Bill's America*, 122–23.
46 Ibid.
47 Ibid., 138–39.
48 Russell, *Lives and Legends*, 231.
49 Philbrick, *Last Stand*, 40, 48.
50 Russell, *Lives and Legends*, 298.
51 Ibid., 314.
52 Ibid., 315–16.
53 Warren, *Buffalo Bill's America*, 191, 195.
54 Ibid., 359–60.
55 Ibid., 282.
56 Ibid., 305.
57 Ibid., 284.
58 Ibid., 305.
59 Jill Jonnes, *Eiffel's Tower: And the World's Fair Where Buffalo Bill Beguiled Paris, the Artists Quarreled, and Thomas Edison Became a Count* (New York: Viking, 2009), 112.
60 Ibid., 132.
61 Russell, *Lives and Legends*, 350.
62 Richard Slotkin, *Gunfighter Nation: The Myth of the Frontier in the Twentieth Century* (Norman: University of Oklahoma Press, 1998), 73.
63 Jonnes, *Eiffel's Tower*, 267.
64 Russell, *Lives and Legends*, 358–59.
65 Etulain, *Telling Western Stories*, 15. Sitting Bull's cabin was purchased from his heirs, set up on the midway of the Chicago fairgrounds, and manned by Sioux who pointed out the bullet holes for visitors. Philbrick, *Last Stand*, 308.

66 Eric Larson, *The Devil in the White City: Murder, Magic, and Madness at the Fair That Changed America* (New York: Vintage, 2003), 250.

67 Russell, *Lives and Legends*, 313.

68 This has not been verified. But as Mary Lou Pence has stated in her study of Nat Boswell, the most difficult obstacle in her study was to verify the names of those associated with him. Many were referred to only by first name. And newspaper accounts of the time are very sketchy. Mary Lou Pence, *Boswell, the Story of a Frontier Lawman* (Cheyenne, WY: Pioneer Printing, 1978).

69 See Pence, *Boswell*.

70 Robert K. DeArment, *Assault on the Deadwood Stage: Road Agents and Shotgun Messengers* (Norman: University of Oklahoma Press, 2011), 147–50.

71 Pence, *Boswell*, 147; Richard Maxwell Brown, *Strain of Violence: Historical Studies of American Violence and Vigilantism* (New York: Oxford University Press, 1975), 108.

72 DeArment, *Assault on the Deadwood Stage*, 206–7.

4: WYOMING

1 T. A. Larson, *History of Wyoming* (Lincoln: University of Nebraska Press, 1978), 194.

2 Andy Russell, *The Canadian Cowboy* (Toronto: McClelland & Stewart, 1993), 48–49.

3 John D. McDermott, *Red Cloud's War: The Bozeman Trail, 1866–1868*, vol. 1 (Norman: Arthur H. Clark, 2010), 4–10.

4 Robert A. Murray, *The Bozeman Trail* (Boulder, CO: Pruett, 1988), 5.

5 See Robert M. Utley, *The Indian Frontier of the American West, 1846–1890* (Albuquerque: University of New Mexico Press, 1984), 92–93.

6 US War Department, *The War of the Rebellion*, series 1, vol. 48, pt. 2, 356.

7 Kingsley Bray, *Crazy Horse: A Life* (Norman: University of Oklahoma Press, 2006), 86.

8 Murray, *Bozeman Trail*, 7.

9 Robert M. Utley, *Frontier Regulars: The United States Army and the Indian, 1866–1891* (New York: Macmillan, 1974), 11–14.

10 Ibid., 59–67.

11 Louis S. Warren, *Buffalo Bill's America: William Cody and the Wild West Show* (New York: Knopf, 2005), 106.

12 Grace R. Heberd and A. E. Brininstool, *The Bozeman Trail* (Cleveland: A. H. Clark, 1922), vol. 1, 307; Bray, *Crazy Horse*, 96, states that there were 1,500 warriors involved in the Fetterman fight and Utley, *Frontier Regulars*, 105, put the number at 1,500–2,000.

13 Heberd and Brininstool, vol. 1, 305–6; Utley, *Frontier Regulars*, 105, stated that the cavalry under Lieut. Grummond were armed with Spencer repeating carbines and the two civilians, James Wheatly and Isaac Fisher, were armed with Henry repeating rifles.

14 Bray, *Crazy Horse*, 95.

15 Ibid., 101.

16 Ibid.

17 Dee Brown, *The Fetterman Massacre* (Lincoln: University of Nebraska Press, 1962), 188.

18 Ibid., 198.

19 Heberd and Brininstool, *Bozeman Trail*, vol. 2, 21.

20 Brown, *Fetterman Massacre*, 194.
21 Quoted in Utley, *Frontier Regulars*, 111 (Senate Executive Documents, 40th Congress, 1867).
22 Bray, *Crazy Horse*, 78.
23 Russell, *The Canadian Cowboy*, 49.
24 Utley, *Frontier Regulars*, 123–25.
25 Bray, *Crazy Horse*, 108.
26 Heberd and Brininstool, *Bozeman Trail*, 223.
27 Ibid., 51–52.
28 Bray, *Crazy Horse*, 109–10.
29 Heberd and Brininstool, *Bozeman Trail*, 66–68.
30 Utley, *Frontier Regulars*, 125–29. George E. Hyde, *Red Cloud's Folk: A History of the Oglala Sioux Indians*, stated that there were 1,000 warriors at the battle, and six were killed and six wounded, clearly an absurd tally for a battle of this magnitude.
31 Robert A. Murray, *Military Posts in the Powder River Country of Wyoming, 1865–1894* (Lincoln: University of Nebraska Press, 1968), 53.
32 Utley, *Frontier Regulars*, 69.
33 Robert M. Utley, *Cavalier in Buckskin* (Norman: University of Oklahoma Press, 1988), 177, 189–90; H. F. Williamson, *Winchester: The Gun That Won the West* (Washington, DC: Combat Forces Press, 1952), 43, 51–52; Lee Kennett and James L. Anderson, *The Gun in America: The Origins of a National Dilemma* (Westport, CT: Greenwood, 1975), 117.
34 Douglas D. Scott and Richard A. Fox Jr., *Archaeological Insights into the Custer Battle* (Norman: University of Oklahoma Press, 1987), 112; Utley, *Cavalier in Buckskins*, 190, states that many Sioux at the battle were armed with repeating rifles and many with trade muskets and bows and arrows.
35 Scott and Fox, *Archaeological Insights*, citing the US Army Ordinance Report of 1879, 112–13.
36 Jerry Keenan, *The Wagon Box Fight* (Buffalo, WY: Bozeman Trail Association, 1988), 2.
37 William Murphy, "The Forgotten Battalion," *Annals of Wyoming* 7, no. 2 (October 1930): 395.
38 Robert A. Murray, "The Wagon Box Fight: A Centennial Appraisal," *Annals of Wyoming* 39, no. 1 (April 1967): 105.
39 James S. Hutchins, ed., *Boots and Saddles at the Little Big Horn* (Fort Collins, CO: Old Army Press, 1976), 33–35.
40 Roy A. Appleman, "The Wagon Box Fight," in *Great Western Indian Fight*, ed. Members of the Potomac Corral of the Westerners (Lincoln: University of Nebraska Press, 1960), 155. Murray, "The Wagon Box Fight," 45, states that "a few civilians were armed with seven shot Spencers."
41 George Madis, *The Winchester Book* (Lancaster, Texas: Art and Reference House, 1971), 167. The .44-calibre Henry was designed by B. Tyler Henry in 1860 and produced at the New Haven Arms Company. It was modified in 1866 and again in 1873.
42 William B. Edwards, *Civil War Guns* (Harrisburg, PA: Stackpole, 1962), 158–62; Charles E. Chapel, *Guns of the Old West* (New York: Coward-McCann, 1961), 247. The Henry rifle was a 16-shot .44-calibre lever action rifle with a 24-inch octagonal barrel, weighing nine and a quarter pounds. It was the forerunner of the Winchester repeating rifle.

43 Louise Barnett, *Touched By Fire: The Life, Death, and Mythic Afterlife of George Armstrong Custer* (New York: Henry Holt, 1996), 297.
44 Utley, *Frontier Regulars*, 70.
45 Chapel, *Guns of the Old West*, 257.
46 Keenan, *Wagon Box Fight*, 8, states that there were two officers, twenty-four enlisted men, and six civilians at the fight.
47 Information on George Reid's part in the Wagon Box Fight comes from Jean Johnson's manuscript "A Virginian Cowboy" in the Glenbow Archives.
48 Heberd and Brininstool, *Bozeman Trail*, vol. 2, 85.
49 Ibid., 162–68. Utley, *Frontier Regulars*, 124, states that when Lt. Sigismund Sturnberg was killed, Al Colvin, a civilian, took charge of the engagement. At the Hayfield Fight, Lt. Sturnberg and nineteen soldiers were guarding twelve civilian hay cutters.
50 Ibid., 70, 81.
51 Utley, *Frontier Regulars*, 148.
52 Bray, *Crazy Horse*, 167.
53 Glenbow Archives, John Henry Reid, "Biography of a Cardston Poineer," D 920, R 356, 1958.
54 Russell, *The Canadian Cowboy*, 49.
55 The 76 would establish line camps on Salt Creek, Crazy Woman Creek, Buffalo Creek and one on the middle fork of the Powder River, which became the KC Ranch, where the shootout took place during the Johnson County War.
56 Terry G. Jordan, *North American Cattle-Ranching Frontiers: Origins, Diffusion, and Differentiation* (Albuquerque: University of New Mexico Press, 1993), 8.
57 Emerson Hough, *The Passing of the Frontier* (New Haven, CT: Yale University Press, 1918), 43.
58 Andy Adams, *Log of a Cowboy* (New York: Airmont, 1969).
59 Allen Andrews, *The Splendid Pauper* (New York: Lippincot, 1968), 82; Lawrence Woods, *British Gentlemen in the Wild West: The Era of the Intensely English Cowboy* (New York: Free Press, 1989), 58.
60 Woods, *British Gentlemen*, 57.
61 Lawrence Woods, *Moreton Frewen's Western Adventures* (Boulder, CO: Roberts Rinehart, 1993), 73.
62 Maurice Frink, *Cow Country Cavalcade* (Denver, CO: Old West Publishing, 1954), 241; Woods, *Frewen's Western Adventures* put the return for 1883 at 5 percent, 84.
63 Agnes Wright Spring, *The Cheyenne Club: Mecca of the Aristocrats of the Old Time Cattle Range* (Kansas City: Ornduff, 1961), 19.
64 Hesse was foreman of the 76 from 1882 to 1890. After that, he operated his own ranch, the 28 Ranch, on Crazy Woman Creek. In the 76 account ledger, Johnson's salary from 1886 to 1888 is listed at $40 per month. He is no longer listed after the summer of 1888. Jim Drummond was also listed on the ledger in 1887 and 1888. University of Wyoming, Western Heritage Center, Fred G. S. Hesse Papers, Coll. 240.
65 Spring, *The Cheyenne Club*, 19.
66 Moreton Frewen, *Melton Mowbray and Other Memories* (London: Herbert Jenkins, 1924), 96–97.
67 Ibid., 142.
68 Ibid., 166–67.
69 Ibid., 212; Andrews, *Splendid Pauper*, 75.

70 Anita Leslie, *Mr. Frewen of England* (London: Hutchinson, 1966), 64–65.
71 Andrews, *Splendid Pauper*, 31.
72 Leslie, *Mr. Frewen*, 61.
73 Woods, *British Gentlemen*, 194–95.
74 Frink, *Cow Country Cavalcade*, 119.
75 Woods, *Frewen's Western Adventures*, 73.
76 Andrews, 89; Woods, *Frewen's Western Adventures* claimed that the 76's return in 1883 was 5 percent and in 1884 it was 3 percent, at the back of the pack! The Swan ranch had a return of 10 percent. The average for the big ranches in 1884 was 6 percent (117–18).
77 Woods, *Frewen's Western Adventures*, 131
78 John Clay, *My Life on the Range* (Norman: University of Oklahoma Press, 1962), 180.
79 Mari Sandoz, *The Cattlemen* (New York: Hastings House, 1958), 99.
80 Ibid., 236.
81 Ibid., 244.
82 The principle of refrigeration was first demonstrated in Scotland in 1756. In 1758, Benjamin Franklin was experimenting with its principles. By 1820 the British scientist Michael Faraday liquefied ammonia and other gasses using high pressures and low temperatures. In 1842, an American physician designed the first system to produce ice. Alexander Twining is credited with the first commercial use of refrigeration in 1856. By the 1870s, commercial refrigeration units were in use. Refrigerated railway cars started in the 1840s and by 1900, Chicago, the centre of the meat packing industry, had adopted ammonia-cycle commercial refrigeration.
83 Clay, *My Life on the Range*, xii–xiii.
84 Ibid., 3.
85 Sandoz, *The Cattlemen*, 247.
86 Frink, *Cow Country Cavalcade*, 197.
87 Ibid., 249.
88 Ibid., 71.
89 Deborah Donahue, *The Western Range Revisited* (Norman: University of Oklahoma Press, 2000), 13.
90 See Wallace Stegner, *Beyond the Hundredth Meridian: John Wesley Powell and the Second Opening of the American West* (Boston: Houghton Mifflin, 1954) and Donald Worster, *A River Running West: The Life of John Wesley Powell* (New York: Oxford University Press, 2001). For a discussion of earlier western American land legislation, see Roy M. Robbins, "Preemption – A Frontier Triumph" in *Essays on the History of the American West*, ed. Stephen Salsbury (New York: Holt Rinehart, 1975).
91 Donahue, *Western Range*, 15.
92 Ibid., 19.
93 Ibid., 30. The Taylor Grazing Act of 1934 turned eighty million acres into grazing districts, with ten-year renewable leases. Edward E. Taylor was a congressman from Colorado.
94 Christopher Ketcham, "The Ruin of the West: How Republicans are Plundering our Public Lands," *Harper's Magazine*, February 2015, 23–31.
95 Larson, *History of Wyoming*, 175.
96 Ibid., 181.
97 Ibid., 177.
98 Frink, *Cow Country Cavalcade*, 10.
99 Hough, *Passing of the Frontier*, 43.
100 Larson, *History of Wyoming*, 167.

101 Russell L. Barsh, "The Substitution of Cattle for Bison on the Great Plains" in *The Struggle For the Land: Indigenous Insight and Industrial Empire in the Semiarid World*, ed. Paul A. Olson (Lincoln: University of Nebraska Press, 1990), 117.

102 Ibid., 112.

103 Robert H. Fletcher, *Free Grass to Fences: The Montana Cattle Range Story* (New York: University Publishers, 1960), 117–18.

104 Frink, *Cow Country Cavalcade*, 6.

105 Andrews, *Splendid Pauper*, 82.

106 Woods, *Frewen's Western Adventures*, 127.

107 Woods, *British Gentlemen*, 168.

108 American Heritage Society Archives, Frewen Papers, MC 9529.

109 Andrews, *Splendid Pauper*, 225.

110 Woods, *Frewen's Western Adventures*, 197.

111 Leslie, *Mr. Frewen*, 201–2.

112 In 1928, Aaron Copland wrote the music for the ballet *Billy the Kid*, which was choreographed by Eugene Loring. The ballet was based on Walter Noble Burns' 1926 novel *The Saga of Billy the Kid*, which turned Billy into a folk hero for the downtrodden, a latter-day Robin Hood, a champion of the little people battling corrupt and powerful politicians. During the Depression, when the ballet was produced, the mythology of Billy the Kid was at its zenith. Copland admitted that he didn't really know much about the real Billy the Kid when he composed the music.

113 Donna A. Ernst, *The Sundance Kid: The Life of Harry Alonzo Longabaugh* (Norman: University of Oklahoma Press, 2011), 28.

114 Ibid., 30–32.

115 Ibid., 33.

116 Anne Meadows, *Digging Up Butch and Sundance* (Lincoln: University of Nebraska Press, 1996), 89.

117 Richard Patterson, *Butch Cassidy: A Biography* (Lincoln: University of Nebraska Press, 1998), 113.

118 See Daniel Buck, "Surprising Development: The Sundance Kid's Unusual – and Unknown – Life in Canada," *Journal of the Western Outlaw – Lawman History Association* (Winter 1993), 34.

119 Meadows, *Digging Up Butch*, 33.

120 Patterson, *Butch Cassidy*, 160.

121 Ibid., 193.

122 Paul Trachtman, *The Gunfighters* (New York: Time–Life Books, 1974), 92.

123 Ibid., 215.

124 Toronto *Globe and Mail*, Feb. 15, 1992.

125 Patterson, *Butch Cassidy*, 245.

126 Larry Pointer, *In Search of Butch Cassidy* (Norman: University of Oklahoma Press, 1977), 219.

127 Patterson, *Butch Cassidy*, 250–51.

128 See Pointer, *In Search of Butch Cassidy*.

129 John W. Davis, *Wyoming Range War: The Infamous Invasion of Johnson County* (Norman: University of Oklahoma Press, 2010), 13, 44.

130 Clay, *My Life on the Range*, 269.

131 Ibid., 117–18.

132 Larson, *History of Wyoming*, 176.

133 Ibid., 179.

134 Davis, *Wyoming Range War*, 36; Henry Sinclair Drago, *The Great Range Wars: Violence on the Grasslands* (Lincoln: University of Nebraska Press, 1970), 171, states that in the Texas Panhandle, ranchers in the 1880s hired gunmen to protect their illegal fences.

135. Larson, *History of Wyoming*, 273.
136. Davis, *Wyoming Range War*, 19.
137. *Big Horn Sentinel*, Nov. 2, 1884.
138. Emerson Hough, *The Story of the Cowboy* (New York: Appleton, 1897), 273–77.
139. Ibid., 311.
140. *Big Horn Sentinel*, June 5, 1885.
141. Helena Huntington Smith, *War on Powder River: The History of an Insurrection* (Lincoln: University of Nebraska Press, 1966), 76, 117.
142. Ibid.
143. Clay, *My Life on the Range*, 274–75. The term drygulching refers to a form of ambush. In the West, trails often went through dry gulches where water courses had dried up, making them an ideal location for ambush.
144. W. Turrentine Jackson, "The Wyoming Stock Growers' Association: Political Power in Wyoming Territory, 1883–1890," *MVHR*, March 1947, 589.
145. Larson, *History of Wyoming*, 230.
146. Ibid., 182.
147. Sandoz, *Cattlemen*, 59.
148. Davis, *Wyoming Range War*, 76–80.
149. Robert K. DeArment, *Alias Frank Canton* (Norman: University of Oklahoma Press, 1996), 83–86.
150. See DeArment, *Alias Frank Canton*.
151. Fanny Kemble Wister Stokes, ed., *Owen Wister Out West: His Journals and Letters* (Lincoln: University of Nebraska Press, 1972), 116.
152. Clay, *My Life On the Range*, 278–79.
153. Frederick Allen, *A Decent, Orderly Lynching: The Montana Vigilantes* (Norman: University of Oklahoma Press, 2004), xvii.
154. Philip D. Jordan, "The Town Marshal and the Police," in *People of the Plains and Mountains*, ed. Ray Allen Billington (Westport, CT: Greenwood, 1973), 102–4.
155. Allen, *A Decent, Orderly Lynching*, 212.
156. Ibid., 230–32.
157. Ibid., 250.
158. Ibid., 305.
159. Thomas J. Dimsdale, *The Vigilantes of Montana* (Norman: University of Oklahoma Press, 1953), 211.
160. Clyde A. Milner and Carol O'Connor, *As Big As the West: The Pioneer Life of Granville Stuart* (New York: Oxford University Press, 2009), 220.
161. Sessional Papers, 1884, Report of Commissioner A. G. Irvine.
162. Cited in Hugh Dempsey, *The Golden Age of the Cowboy* (Calgary: Fifth House, 1995), 86.
163. Ibid., 237.
164. Granville Stuart, *Forty Years on the Frontier* (Lincoln: University of Nebraska Press, 2004), vol. 2, 197.
165. Ibid., 209.
166. Warren Elofson, *Cowboys, Gentlemen, and Cattle Thieves* (Montreal: McGill-Queen's University Press, 2000), 153.
167. Warren Elofson, *Frontier Cattle Ranching in the Land and Time of Charlie Russell* (Montreal: McGill-Queen's University Press, 2004), 87.
168. Granville Stuart, *Forty Years on the Frontier* (Glendale, CA: Arthur H. Clark, 1967), 209.
169. Milner and O'Connor, *As Big as the West*, 247.
170. Elofson, *Frontier Cattle Ranching*, 82.
171. Allen, *A Decent, Orderly Lynching*, 359–60.
172. Warren Elofson, "Law and Disorder in the Ranching Frontiers of Montana and Alberta/

173 See Casey Tefertiller, *Wyatt Earp: The Life Behind the Legend* (New York: John Wiley, 1997).
174 Davis, *Wyoming Range War*, 58.
175 Ibid., 283.
176 Clay, *My Life on the Range*, 270.
177 Trachtman, *Gunfighters*, 194–98.
178 Clay, *My Life on the Range*, 283.
179 Larson, *History of Wyoming*, 273.
180 See Smith, *War on Powder River*; Sandoz, *The Cattlemen*; A. S. Mercer, *The Banditti of the Plains: Or the Cattlemen's Invasion of Wyoming, 1892* (Norman: University of Oklahoma Press, 1983); Davis, *Wyoming Range War*.
181 Larson, *History of Wyoming*, 275.
182 Ibid., 281.
183 Ibid., 276.
184 Darwin Payne, *Owen Wister: Chronicler of the West, Gentleman of the East* (Dallas: Southern Methodist University Press), 1985, 117–26. After the eye-gouging incident, Wister rode with a friend to Fort McKinney, where he met "Black Henry" Smith, the model for Trampas.
185 Smith, *War on Powder River*, 242.
186 See Dean F. Krakel, *The Saga of Tom Horn: The Story of a Cattleman's War* (Lincoln: University of Nebraska Press, 1954).

5: OWEN WISTER AND WYOMING

1 Proof of Johnson's presence at the VR Ranch can be found scratched on one of the ranch's barn walls. Among many initials is "Buckeye, Slim, Eb" – the name that Johnson went by in Wyoming.

Assiniboia, 1870–1914." *Journal of the West* 42, no. 1 (Winter 2003): 41–47.

2 Darwin Payne, *Owen Wister: Chronicler of the West, Gentleman of the East* (Dallas: Southern Methodist University Press, 1985), 77. The school was the West Pennsylvania Square Seminary for Young Ladies.
3 Agnes Wright Spring, *The Cheyenne Club: Mecca of the Aristocrats of the Old Time Cattle Range* (Kansas City: Ornduff, 1961), 25.
4 Ibid., 17.
5 Ibid., 19.
6 American Heritage Center, University of Wyoming, Wister Diary.
7 F. K. W. Stokes, *My Father, Owen Wister: and Ten Letters Written by Owen Wister to his Mother during His First Trip to Wyoming in 1885* (Laramie: University of Wyoming Press, 1952).
8 Darwin Payne, "Owen Wister Discovers Wyoming," *Persimmon Hill* 12, no. 1 (1982): 29.
9 See "The 88 Centennial," *Casper Magazine*, Feb.–March 1979. The ranch is now run by the fourth generation of Henrys, with the fifth in the wings. Currently the 88 is owned by Bill Henry, the grandson of Mike Henry, and his wife Pat. Bill Henry is also the head of the life science department at Casper College. The 88, which now covers 30,000 acres along nineteen miles of the Cheyenne River, is run by Mike Henry's great-grandson, Mike, and his wife Susan.

By the end of his life in 1923, at the age of eighty-three, the original Mike Henry had become one of Wyoming's leading citizens, a successful rancher, a major stockholder in the Poposia Coal Company, the first president of the Bank of Hudson, the president of an oil company, and a major holder of real estate. In fact, he fits the picture of the future that Wister had staked out for his Virginian! Biography of Mike Henry, Wyoming State Historical Research and Publication Division; *Torrington Telegram*, June 17, 1915.

10   "88 Centennial," *Casper Magazine*, Feb.–March 1979, 5.

11   W. P. Ricketts, *Fifty Years in the Saddle* (Sheridan: Star Publishing, 1942), 68. The Searights ran 20,000 head of cattle on either side of the Platte River for eighty miles. Ricketts worked on the Goose Egg for a few years and left in 1885. He made no mention of baby swapping.

12   Ibid.

13   See "88 Centennial," *Casper Magazine* (Feb.–March 1979); *Torrington Telegram*, June 17, 1915; Profile of "Mike" Henry by Agnes R. Wright, Wyoming State Librarian, in the Wyoming State Archives; Interviews with Mike Henry's grandson, Bill Henry, who is head of the Life Science Department at Casper College.

14   In 1892, the year in which Wolcott led the "Invasion" of Johnson County, he owed the estate of Thomas Nelson $131,427. Wolcott was forced to give up his shares in the VR to pay the debt. The VR was bought in 1983 by Dave True. The ranch by then encompassed 61,000 acres, half deeded and half lease land. The ranch ran 2,000 head of cattle and ninety horses. The VR Ranch tour pamphlet, June 10, 1989. See also Payne, *Owen Wister*, 90.

15   John Clay, *My Life on the Range* (New York: Antiquarian Press, 1961), 142.

16   T. A. Larson, *History of Wyoming* (Lincoln: University of Nebraska Press, 1978), 124.

17   American Heritage Center, File B-W 83-f, an anonymous article, "Major Frank Wolcott, alias Jack of Spades," written in September 1886.

18   Ibid.

19   Library of Congress (hereafter LC), Wister Journal, October 12, 1889.

20   Larson, *History of Wyoming*, 269–70; See also Glenda Riley, *Wild Women of the Old West* (Golden, CO: Fulcrum, 2003); George W. Hufsmith, *The Wyoming Lynching of Cattle Kate, 1889* (Glendo, WY: High Plains Press, 1993). Hufsmith also wrote an opera on the subject of Cattle Kate.

21   Moreton Frewen, *Melton Mowbray and Other Memories* (London: Herbert Jenkins, 1924), 212.

22   Joel Williamson, *A Rage for Order: Black/White Relations in the American South Since Emancipation* (New York: Oxford University Press, 1986), 96.

23   W. Eugene Hollon, *Frontier Violence* (New York: Oxford University Press, 1974), 51.

24   Williamson, *Rage for Order*, 122–24.

25   See Alice M. Hadley, *Where the Winds Blow Free* (Caanan, NH: Phoenix, 1976). The original Stark, Archibald, came to America from Scotland in 1720. The Stark mansion that Wister knew was built by General John Stark's eldest son, Major Caleb Stark. Elizabeth "Molly" Stark was a Page, also from Dunbarton. Charlotte Stark died in 1889. It is claimed that General Lafayette was entertained at the Stark house on his last trip to America.

26 Elsewhere, in a Calgary newspaper interview, Johnson said that the real Trampas, the one he killed in the bar of the Occidental Hotel in Buffalo, was named Frank Bull, not White Clay George. It is quite possible that the man went by both names, as many did who wanted to keep their identity private.

27 LC, Wister Journal, June 26, 1891.

28 Payne, *Wister: Chronicler of the West*, 120, 125; Helena Huntington Smith, *The War on Powder River: The History of the Insurrection* (Lincoln: University of Nebraska Press, 1967), 253–58.

29 Fanny Kemble Wister Stokes, *Owen Wister Out West: His Journals and Letters* (Lincoln: University of Nebraska Press, 1972), 20.

30 Payne, *Wister: Chronicler of the West*, 143.

31 LC, Wister Journal, May 23, 1894.

32 Payne, *Wister: Chronicler of the West*, 264.

33 Owen Wister, *Roosevelt: The Story of a Friendship, 1880–1919* (New York: Macmillan, 1930), 355.

34 Ibid., 124, 164.

35 LC, Wister Papers, Box 9, Wister to his mother, August 4, 1887, from Fort Washakie.

36 Payne, *Wister: Chronicler of the West*, 134.

37 Ibid., 197.

38 LC, Wister Journal, 1895, 16.

39 LC, Wister Journal, June 8, 1895.

40 Payne, *Wister: Chronicler of the West*, 156.

41 Ibid., 65, 129–30.

42 Richard W. Slatta, *The Cowboy Encyclopedia* (Santa Barbara, CA: ABC Press, 1994), 374.

43 Payne, *Wister: Chronicler of the West*, 314.

44 Ibid., 197.

45 LC, Wister Journal, 1893, February–March.

46 Ibid., Letters to Wister.

6: ALBERTA

1 Lawrence M. Woods, *Moreton Frewen's Western Adventures* (Boulder, CO: Roberts Rinehart, 1993), 112.

2 Ibid., 131.

3 Ibid., 127, 131.

4 Ibid., 134.

5 Ibid., 142.

6 Ibid., 159.

7 American Heritage Center, Frewen Papers, MC 9529-2-11.

8 Woods, *Frewen's Western Adventures*, 162.

9 Ibid.

10 Ibid., 158.

11 Ibid., 187.

12 Edward Brado, *Cattle Kingdom: Early Ranching in Alberta* (Vancouver: Douglas & McIntyre, 1984), 157; Hugh Dempsey, *The Golden Age of the Canadian Cowboy* (Calgary: Fifth House, 1995), 78.

13 Woods, *Frewen's Western Adventures*, 187.

14 Ibid., 194.

15 Ibid., 180, 187–88, 194–95.

16 Warren M. Elofson, *Frontier Cattle Ranching in the Land and Times of Charlie Russell* (Montreal: McGill-Queen's University Press, 2004), 139.

17 Brado, *Cattle Kingdom*, 262–65.

18 The Quorn Ranch, south of present-day Okotoks, had a 66,000-acre lease. It never did break into the British remount market. The ranch folded after the 1906–7 winter. Brado, *Cattle Kingdom*, 146.

19. See Grant McEwan, *John Ware's Cow Country* (Edmonton: Institute of Applied Arts, 1960).

20. Alan B. McCullough, "Not an Old Cow-Hand: Fred Stimson and the Bar U Ranch," in *Cowboys, Ranchers and the Cattle Business: Cross-Border Perspectives on Ranching History*, eds. Simon Evans, Sarah Carter, and Bill Yeo (Calgary: University of Calgary Press, 2000), 31.

21. Lachlin McKinnon, *Autobiography* (Calgary, Glenbow Archives, nd).

22. Simon M. Evans, *The Bar U and Canadian Ranching History* (Calgary: University of Calgary Press, 2005), 72.

23. Evans, *Bar U*, 105.

24. Ibid., 18.

25. McCullough, "Not an Old Cow Hand," 34.

26. Evans, *Bar U*, 32.

27. See Vicky Kelly, "Butch and the Kid," *Glenbow* 3, no. 6 (Nov. 1970); Simon Evans, "The Bar U Community during the 1890s," *Research Links, Parks Canada Service, Western Region* 1, no. 1 (Spring 1993).

28. Gerald Friesen, *The Canadian Prairies: A History* (Toronto: University of Toronto Press, 1984), 276. Fares joined the partnership in 1897.

29. Evans, *Bar U*, 76–77.

30. Ibid., 85.

31. Simon M. Evans, "Some Observations on the Labour Force of the Canadian Ranching Frontier during Its Golden Age, 1882–1901," paper presented to the Canadian Historical Association, June 1994, 10. This census of 1901 confirms David Breen's findings that, after 1885, the number of the Americans on the Canadian range constantly diminished.

32. Robert Utley, *The Indian Frontier of the American West, 1846-1890* (Albuquerque: University of New Mexico Press, 1984), xix.

33. See John Jennings, *The Canoe: A Living Tradition* (Toronto: Firefly Books, 2002) and *Bark Canoes: The Art and Obsession of Tappan Adney* (Toronto: Firefly Books, 2004). The Native birch bark canoe is clearly Canada's most important historical symbol.

34. Donald Creighton, *The Road to Confederation* (Toronto: Macmillan, 1964), 141–42.

35. For relations between fur traders and Native peoples and Sir George Simpson's role in the fur trade, see James Raffan, *Emperor of the North: Sir George Simpson and the Remarkable Story of the Hudson's Bay Company* (Toronto: HarperCollins, 2007); John S. Galbraith, *The Little Emperor: Governor Simpson of the Hudson's Bay Company* (Toronto: Macmillan, 1976); E. E. Rich, *The Fur Trade and the Northwest to 1857* (Toronto: McClelland and Stewart, 1967); Olive Patricia Dickason, *Canada's First Nations: A History of Founding Peoples From Earliest Times* (Toronto: McClelland and Stewart, 1992); Arthur J. Ray, *Indians in the Fur Trade: Their Role as Trappers, Hunters, and Middlemen in the Lands Southwest of Hudson Bay, 1660–1870* (Toronto: University of Toronto Press, 1974); Arthur J. Ray, *I Have Lived Here Since the World Began: An Illustrated History of Canada's Native People* (Toronto: Key Porter, 1996); Robin Fisher, *Contact and Conflict: Indian-European Relations in British Columbia, 1774–1890* (Vancouver: University of British Columbia Press, 1992).

36 See John Jennings, "The Plains Indian and the Law," in *Men in Scarlet*, ed. Hugh Dempsey (Calgary: Historical Society of Alberta/McClelland & Stewart West, 1974).

37 Wallace Stegner, *Wolf Willow: A History, a Story, and a Memory of the Last Plains Frontier* (New York: Viking Compass, 1966), 100–102.

38 Shelley A. M. Gavigan, *Hunger, Horses, and Government Men: Criminal Law on the Aboriginal Plains, 1870–1905* (Vancouver: UBC Press, 2012), 39–40. The act creating the NWMP was titled An Act Respecting the Administration of Justice, and for the Establishment of a Police Force in the North-West Territories, 1873, 36 Vict., c. 35, s. 3.

39 Ibid., 40.

40 See North-West Territories Act, 1875, 38 Vict., c. 49, s. 61. This was an omnibus legislation, which included "the prohibition of manufacture, import, distribution and sale, and possession of intoxicants." It also authorized the Lieutenant-Governor in Council to appoint stipendiary magistrates, who could preside over a broad range of cases. By 1877, all criminal cases could be tried in the North-West Territories except those involving the death penalty, which were still tried in Manitoba.

41 Philip D. Jordan, "The Pistol Packin' Cowboy," in *The Cowboy: Six-Shooters, Songs, and Sex*, ed. Charles W. Harris and Buck Rainy (Norman: University of Oklahoma Press, 1976), 64.

42 Ibid., 69.

43 Floyd Bard (as told to Agnes Wright Spring), *Horse Wrangler* (Norman: University of Oklahoma Press, 1960), 198.

44 Frederick Ings, *Before the Fences: Tales from the Midway Ranch* (Calgary: McAra Printing, 1980), 48.

45 Stegner, *Wolf Willow*, 5.

46 Ibid., 134.

47 Sessional Papers, Report of the Commissioner of the NWMP, 1885 and 1886, 119, 130.

48 LAC (Library Archives Canada), RG (Record Group) 18 (Mounted Police records), A-1, vol. 126, no. 3, Fort Macleod monthly report, Jan. 1897.

49 Martin L. Friedland, *A Century of Criminal Justice: Perspectives on the Development of Canadian Law* (Toronto: Carswell, 1984), 125; R. Blake Brown, *Arming and Disarming: A History of Gun Control in Canada* (Toronto: Osgoode Society for Canadian Legal History, 2012), 68–72; See also Lee Kennett and James L. Anderson, *The Gun in America: The Origins of a National Dilemma* (Westport, CT: Greenwood, 1975), chapter 5, "Firearms and the Frontier Experience." Blake Brown points out that the Liberal government of Alexander Mackenzie passed two important pieces of gun regulation in 1877 and 1878. The 1877 bill limited the use of pistols, adding them to the list of "offensive weapons" that were not allowed to be carried. The 1877 act represented the first time in Canada that handguns began to be regulated on a national level. The act banned the carrying of handguns unless there was reasonable cause to fear assault. A jail term of thirty days could be imposed. Anyone committing an offence with a handgun could be sent to jail for six months. In 1878, the Blake Act, The Better Prevention of Crime Act, 1878,

S.C. 1878, c. 17, allowed for the search of persons suspected of carrying weapons and of homes believed to contain guns kept for illegal purposes. People could still buy handguns and gun dealers did not need to keep records. This changed in 1892. The Criminal Code of 1892 introduced a nationwide permit system for handguns; it imposed a severe penalty, up to five years in jail, for carrying an offensive weapon for a purpose dangerous to the public peace; it raised the penalty for carrying a pistol "without justification." A person could carry a handgun only with a certificate of exemption from a Justice of the Peace, and the J.P. had to vouch for that person's "discretion and good character." The Code also stipulated that the J.P. had to record these certificates and, most importantly, gun sellers must record all handgun sales. As well, no one under sixteen could buy a handgun. Collectively, the handgun legislation of 1877, 1878 and 1892 "represented the beginning of permanent regulation of handguns. This early legislation began to differentiate the firearm laws of Canada and the United States and became the cornerstone of a regulatory framework that, over time, encouraged a substantially lower level of pistol ownership in Canada than in the United States and also, perhaps, different attitudes to handguns in the two nations. Brown, *Arming and Disarming*, 72–79.

50 Friedland, *A Century of Criminal Justice*, 132

51 Ibid., 133.

52 Dempsey, *Golden Age*, 106–11.

53 Ibid., 113–14.

54 R. C. Macleod. "The North-West Mounted Police and Minority Groups" in *The Mounted Police and Prairie Society, 1873–1919*, ed. William M. Baker (Regina: Great Plains Research Center, 1998), 129.

55 David Breen, *The Canadian Prairie West and the Ranching Frontier, 1874–1924* (Toronto: University of Toronto Press, 1983), 82–85. The thoroughness of this patrol system is clear from the numerous reports in NWMP files, some of them very thick. The extent of these patrols can be seen, for instance, in the statistics from the Calgary division in 1889. In that year alone, the Calgary division sent out more than 2,000 patrols.

56 Carl Betke, "Pioneers and Police on the Canadian Prairies, 1885–1914" in *The Mounted Police and Prairie Society*, ed. William M. Baker (Regina: Great Plains Research Center, 1998), 223–24.

57 John Jennings, "The North West Mounted Police and Indian Policy After the 1885 Rebellion," in *1885 and After: Native Society in Transition*, ed. F. Laurie Barron and James B. Waldram (Regina: Canadian Plains Research Center, 1986), 232.

58 John Jennings, "Policemen and Poachers: Indian Relations on the Ranching Frontier," in *Frontier Calgary: Town, City and Region*, ed. A.W. Rasporich (Calgary: McClelland and Stewart West, 1975), 89.

59 SP, Mounted Police Report, 1884, 15.

60 Brian Hubner, "Horse Stealing and the Borderline: The NWMP and the Control of Indian Movement, 1874–1900," in *The Mounted Police and Prairie Society, 1873–1919*, ed. William M. Baker (Regina: Canadian Plains Research Center, 1998), 55–69; Mounted Police *Annual Report*, 1888, 9 and

1889, 1–2; Department of Indian Affairs, *Annual Report*, 1891, 82; Department of Indian Affairs, *Annual Report*, 1895, 75, 154; Mounted Police *Annual Report*, 1898, 3.

61   Jennings, "North West Mounted Police," 208.

62   Ken S. Coates and William R. Morrison, *Strange Things Done: Murder in Yukon History* (Montreal: McGill-Queen's University Press, 2004), 5.

63   See William R. Morrison, *Showing the Flag: The Mounted Police and Sovereignty in the North, 1894–1925* (Vancouver: UBC Press, 1985); Howard Blum, *The Floor of Heaven: A True Tale of the Last Frontier and the Yukon Gold Rush* (New York: Broadway, 2011); Edward Lester, *Guarding the Goldfields: The Story of the Yukon Field Force* (Toronto: Dundurn, 1987).

64   Coates and Morrison, *Strange Things Done*, 6–9.

65   Blum, *Floor of Heaven*, 395.

66   Coates and Morrison, *Strange Things Done*, xiii.

67   Pierre Berton, *Why We Act Like Canadians: A Personal Exploration of Our National Character* (Toronto: McClelland and Stewart, 1982), 22.

68   See Breen, *Canadian Prairie West*.

69   The Dominion Lands Act of 1872 was essentially the same as the American Homestead Act of 1862, except that it stipulated three years for "proving up" rather than five. At first, women were allowed access to homestead land, but this changed in 1876. Single women were then barred from claiming homesteads.

70   Sheila McManus, *The Line Which Separates: Race, Gender, and the Making of the Alberta–Montana Borderlands* (Lincoln: University of Nebraska Press, 2005), 46.

71   Breen, *Canadian Prairie West*, 15–19.

72   Brado, *Cattle Kingdom*, 74.

73   Max Foran, *Trails and Trials: Markets and Land Use in the Alberta Beef Cattle Industry* (Calgary: University of Calgary Press, 2003), 4.

74   Breen, *Canadian Prairie West*, 20–22.

75   Evans, *Bar U*, 121.

76   McManus, *Line Which Separates*, 51.

77   Brado, *Cattle Kingdom*, 176–91.

78   Ibid., 189.

79   Foran, *Trails and Trials*, 6.

80   Ibid., 29.

81   Stegner, *Wolf Willow*, 137. After the winter of 1906, 85 percent of leasehold cattle were in herds of under 500 head. When the Conservative Party returned to power in 1911, it formulated a new lease policy, which was introduced in 1914. Ten-year closed leases were introduced of up to 12,000 acres at two cents per acre, to be stocked at a rate of 35 acres per head. Two years after the introduction of the new legislation, 3,352 leaseholders were in control of over five million acres. Foran, *Trails and Trials*, 49–55.

82   Stegner, *Wolf Willow*, 139–219.

83   Breen, *Canadian Prairie West*, 27–29.

84   Ibid., 30.

85   Foran, *Trails and Trials*, 1–2.

86   Brado, *Cattle Kingdom*, 188.

87   Evans, *Bar U*, 35.

88   Dempsey, *Golden Age*, 104.

89   See Warren M. Elofson, *Cowboys, Gentlemen, and Cattle Thieves* (Montreal: McGill-Queen's

University Press, 2000); *Frontier Cattle Ranching in the Land and Times of Charlie Russell* (Montreal: McGill-Queen's University Press, 2004); *Somebody Else's Money* (Calgary: University of Calgary Press, 2009).

90 Paul Sharp, *Whoop-Up Country: The Canadian-American West, 1865–1885* (Norman: University of Oklahoma Press, 1973).

91 Knafla, in an article on violence on the western Canadian frontier, has stated that the claim that there was no vigilantism on that frontier "is not supported by the evidence." See Louis A. Knafla, "Violence on the Western Canadian Frontier," in *Violence in Canada: Sociopolitical Perspectives*, ed. Jeffrey Ian Ross (Somorset, NJ: Transaction Publications, 2004), 29. His evidence for that statement? An article by Paul Sharp and a printed lecture by Robin Winks. Paul Sharp's evidence, discussed elsewhere, is minimal and unconvincing. Robin Winks' paper, in arguing the exact opposite of Knafla, states that there was "little vigilante justice" in the Canadian West. Winks provides no evidence whatever that there was any vigilantism in western Canada. See Robin Winks, *The Myth of the American Frontier: Its Relevance to America, Canada and Australia* (Leicester, UK: Leicester University Press, 1971), 26. Winks argues that Americans, unlike Canadians, are a violent people "given to quick solutions to immediate problems."

92 Knafla, "Violence," 11.

93 Lesley Erickson, *Westward Bound: Sex, Violence, the Law, and the Making of a Settler Society* (Vancouver: UBC Press, 2011), 33. Terry Chapman, in an essay in Louis A. Knafla's *Crime and Justice in Europe and Canada* (Waterloo: Wilfrid Laurier University Press, 1981) entitled "The Measurement of Crime in Nineteenth-Century Canada: Some Methodological and Philosophical Problems," argues that the theme of a peaceful Canadian West is a "time-worn" and "hapless" cliché. She then accuses traditional Canadian historians of manufacturing the myth of a peaceful society "in an attempt to give Canadians a sense of identity and a much-needed sense of superiority" over Americans.

94 The term "Boot Hill" originated in Dodge City and refers to cemeteries where they buried men who had been shot or lynched with their boots on.

95 Tom Thorner, "The Not So Peaceable Kingdom: Crime and Criminal Justice in Frontier Calgary" in *Frontier Calgary: Town, City and Region*, eds. A. W. Rasporich and Henry Klassen (Calgary: University of Calgary, 1975).

96 R. C. Macleod and Heather Rollason Driscoll, "Natives, Newspapers and Crime Rates in the North-West Territories, 1878–1885," in *From Rupert's Land to Canada*, eds. Theodore Binnema, Gerhard E. Ens, and R. C. Macleod (Edmonton: University of Alberta Press, 2001), 250.

97 R. C. Macleod and Heather Rollason, "Restrain the Lawless Savages: Native Defendants in the Criminal Courts of the North West Territories, 1878–1885," *Journal of Historical Sociology* 10, no. 2 (June 1997): 157-83. The same point is also made in John Jennings, "The North West Mounted Police and Indian Policy, 1873–1896" (PhD diss., University of Toronto, 1979).

98 See James Daschuk, *Clearing the Plains: Disease, the Politics of Starvation, and the Loss of Aboriginal Life* (Regina: University of Regina Press, 2013). This book is a well-researched and devastating account of both the effects of European diseases on Aboriginal Plains cultures and the added loss of life in these communities because of malnutrition.

99 Macleod and Rollason Driscoll can argue with authority because of the surprisingly good records at their disposal. In 1873, the year that the Mounted Police were formed, the federal parliament passed legislation extending most Canadian criminal law to the North-West Territories and made provisions for a court system. Within four years, the Territories had a "fully functioning criminal justice system." The authors point out (157, 159) that their study of Native crime in this period rests on "unusually good" records: the North-West Mounted Police criminal court records, yearly summaries of Indian agents, beginning in 1878, the decennial census of 1881, a special census of the NWT in 1885, and four regional newspapers: the *Saskatchewan Herald*, the *Edmonton Bulletin*, the *Calgary Herald*, and the *Macleod Gazette*. These newspapers were especially important for a qualitative analysis and to study white perceptions of Native crime.

100 In an eight-year period, Macleod and Rollason Driscoll documented 1,355 criminal cases. Of these, only 242 cases (18 percent) involved Native defendants. And the conviction rate for Natives was much lower than for whites. Ibid., 163.

101 Ibid., 166. Liquor offences constituted the largest single category – almost 500 cases. Only 4 percent of the defendants were Native. Eleven percent of cases involved livestock theft. This was the only category where Natives outstripped whites.

102 Gavigan, *Hunger, Horses, and Government Men*, 86. In the first decades of Mounted Police law, Natives, according to court files, accounted for less than one-third of those accused of crimes. And most were accused of petty crimes.

103 See Gavigan, *Hunger, Horses, and Government Men*, chapter 3.

104 Ibid., 105. One constable was sentenced to three months in jail for being drunk and disorderly and was jailed again for exhorting money from a Native woman.

105 See Elofson, *Cowboys, Gentlemen, and Cattle Thieves*.

106 Ibid., 114.

107 Ibid.

108 Hugh Dempsey's review is found in *Alberta History* 49, no. 2 (Spring 2001), 27.

109 Hugh Dempsey, in *Alberta History* 50, no. 1 (Winter 2002): 28, refuted Elofson's claim that anyone from Canmore was involved in the lynching at Flathead Lake, Montana.

110 R. C. Macleod, *The North-West Mounted Police and Law Enforcement, 1873–1905* (Toronto: University of Toronto Press, 1976), 150; Jennings, "The North West Mounted Police," 327.

111 See Jennings, "The North West Mounted Police," chapter 8: "The Almighty Voice Affair."

112 Ibid., 347.

113 Ibid., 176–81.

114 Glenbow Archives, Elizabeth Bailey Price Correspondence, E. H. Maunsell to Mrs. Price, May 29, 1922. After leaving the Mounted Police, Maunsell became one of the biggest ranchers in the Canadian West and a successful banker.

115 Elofson, *Cowboys, Gentlemen, and Cattle Thieves*, 114.

116 Jennings, "The North West Mounted Police," 193.

117 *Calgary Herald*, August 26, 1887.

118 LAC, RG 18, vol. 1085, file 544.

119 Jennings, "North West Mounted Police," 193-94. Elofson concludes from this incident that the fact that there was so little "shock and dismay" in the media about the death "suggests that there was a general and widespread value system that inclined cattlemen to use the gun to protect their stock from Natives whenever necessary." Elofson, *Cowboys, Gentlemen, and Cattle Thieves*, 114. A single incident in the entire frontier period does not "suggest a value system" of violent retribution for Native stealing. It demonstrates the exact opposite! And the *Calgary Herald*, in calling for Indian removal, was certainly "suggesting" shock and dismay.

120 LAC, Record Group (RG) 10, Indian Affairs, vol. 3912, file 111,762; RG 18, Mounted Police Records, vol. 1329, file 76.

121 Jennings, "North West Mounted Police," 306-7; SP, Mounted Police Report, 1895, 6, 129; SP, Department of Indian Affairs, *Annual Report*, 1895, xviii.

122 LAC, RG 18, Mounted Police Records, vol. 105, file 147.

123 LAC, RG 18, vol. 1329, file 76; RG 10, vol. 3912, file 762; SP, 1895, xvii.

124 LAC, RG 18, vol. 78, file 233, Report of Inspector Sanders, March 5, 1893; RG 18, vol. 1281, file 296. In later life, Inspector Sanders was a patient of my father in Calgary. My father told me that he was one of those stiff-backed soldiers who was incapable of telling a lie.

125 William Beahen and Stan Horrall, *The Red Coats on the Prairies* (Regina: Centax, 1998), 99-100.

126 Anna-Maria Mavromichalis, "Tar and Feathers: The Mounted Police and Frontier Justice," in *The Mounted Police and Prairie Society, 1873-1919*, ed. William M. Baker (Regina: Great Plains Research Center, 1998), 109-15.

127 Elofson cites one other lynching in Alberta ranching country. A trail herd allegedly picked up someone else's stock as they passed through. A posse of ranchers was formed, and when they returned with the missing stock, "they were all missing their ropes." The evidence for this supposed lynching? Someone named Drew, in his reminiscences. This sort of vague evidence cannot be taken seriously without corroborating evidence. Elofson, *Frontier Cattle Ranching*, 79.

128 Toronto *Globe and Mail*, March 2, 2006.

129 Elofson (*Cowboys, Gentlemen, and Cattle Thieves*, 111) claims that an episode in 1891 "suggests that barroom gunfighting was entwined in the popular culture of the cowboy." One incident hardly "suggests" a popular culture of gunfighting. In this period, there was practically no mention of gunfights in Mounted Police reports. When there was a gunfight, it was taken very seriously. Again, Elofson has taken one solitary incident and turned it into a "frequent means of dispute resolution."

130 Beahen and Horrall, *Red Coats*, 98.

131 Beth LaDow, *The Medicine Line: Life and Death on the North American Borderland* (New York: Routledge, 2002), 128.

132 Ibid., 123.

133 Dempsey, *Golden Age*, 89.

134 Ibid., 91.

135 SP, Mounted Police Report, 1877, #18, 3.

136 See Jennings, "North West Mounted Police," chapter 4, "Sitting Bull in Canada." In 1882, Legare filed a claim with the Canadian government for $48,891 for providing for 500 Sioux on the trek south, thus keeping them peaceful. The Canadian government gave him $2,000. Finally, after years of court battles in the US, Legare received $5,000 from the American government.

137 *Macleod Gazette*, May 14, 1883.

138 Ibid., July 14, 1883.

139 *Calgary Herald*, Jan. 29, 1885.

140 Ibid., Feb. 11, 1887.

141 Ibid., March 6, 1889. The Jesuit Estates question resulted from the Papacy's suppression of the order in the new world in 1773. The order's extensive landholdings in Canada became the property of the British government. Revenues from Jesuit lands were to go toward educational programs. The society was restored in 1814, and in 1842 a number of Jesuits returned to Canada. Subsequently, the issue of restitution became a major issue. The Jesuit Estates Act of 1888 gave the order $400,000 in compensation. This aroused intense anti-Catholic feelings in Protestant Ontario and an unsuccessful attempt in Parliament to disallow the act.

142 Stegner, *Wolf Willow*, 50.

143 Jennings, "North West Mounted Police," 219.

144 SP, Mounted Police Report, 1884, 6.

145 Jennings, "North West Mounted Police," 287–91.

146 LAC, RG 18, vol. 101, file 38; SP, Mounted Police Report, 1895, 194–247.

147 Ibid., Superintendent Steele to Commissioner, June 9, 1894.

148 Jennings, "North West Mounted Police," 304.

149 Andrew R. Graybill, *Policing the Great Plains: Rangers, Mounties, and the North American Frontier, 1875–1910* (Lincoln: University of Nebraska Press, 2007).

150 Patrick Dunae, *Gentlemen Immigrants: From the British Public Schools to the Canadian Frontier* (Vancouver: Douglas & McIntyre, 1981), 92.

151 Ibid., xxi.

152 Brado, *Cattle Kingdom*, 241.

153 Dunae, *Gentlemen Immigrants*, 53.

154 Monica Hopkins, *Letters from a Lady Rancher* (Calgary: Glenbow Museum, 1981), ix–xi.

155 See Tony Rees, *The Galloping Game: An Illustrated History of Polo in Western Canada* (Cochrane, AB: Western Heritage Centre Society, 2000).

156 John C. Ewers, *The Horse in Blackfoot Indian Culture* (Washington: U.S. Government Printing Office, 1955), 60–64. Blackfoot informants told Ewers that they used several horse-breaking methods, but the one described was the best and most popular. The method was also used by other Plains peoples, including the Sioux, Comanche, Apache and Assiniboine. Horses were usually broken when they were two or three years old, by young boys from

12 to 18. Ewers was told by one informant that water breaking was so successful because most horses don't like to get their heads wet and would soon stop bucking in deep water. A good buffalo horse was trained to respond to pressure from the legs and a shifting of weight, not dissimilar to the training of a dressage horse! The hands were busy with bow or gun. And the Plains buffalo hunters rode with a short stirrup, similar to modern jump riders and Three Day Eventers.

157 For a good discussion of Native rodeo, see Morgan Baillargeon and Leslie Tepper, eds., *Legends of Our Times: Native Cowboy Life* (Vancouver: UBC Press, 1998).

158 Brado, *Cattle Kingdom*, 154.

159 Ted Grant and Andy Russell, *Men of the Saddle: Working Cowboys of Canada* (Toronto: Van Nostrand, 1978), 83.

160 L. V. Kelly, *The Range Men* (Toronto: Briggs, 1913).

7: THE BOOK

1 John L. Cobbs, *Owen Wister* (Boston: Twyne, 1984), 2.

2 Malcolm Bell Jr., *Major Butler's Legacy: Five Generations of a Slaveholding Family* (Athens: University of Georgia Press, 1987), 374–76. Fanny Kemble's *Journal of a Residence on a Georgian Plantation, 1838-1839* was published in London in early 1863, as British opinion was switching from being generally pro-Southern to being more critical of Southern obstinacy on the subject of slavery.

3 Ibid., 87. Wister grew up on one of Pierce Butler's estates: Butler Place in Germantown, near Philadelphia.

4 Bell, *Major Butler's Legacy*, 75.

5 Ibid.

6 See August Heckschur, *St. Paul's: The Life of a New England School* (New York: Scribner's, 1980).

7 Darwin Payne, *Owen Wister: Chronicler of the West, Gentleman of the East* (Dallas: Southern Methodist University Press, 1985), 5. Wister played for Liszt in Richard Wagner's house at Bayreuth. As Wister recalled later, he played his own composition, Merlin and Vivien, for him. "He jumped up in the middle and stood behind me muttering approval, and now and then he stopped me and put his hands over my shoulders onto the keys, struck a bar or two and said: I should do that here if I were you." Owen Wister, *Roosevelt: The Story of a Friendship* (New York: Macmillan, 1930), 22.

8 Fanny Kemble Wister, *That I May Tell You: Journals and Letters of the Owen Wister Family* (Wayne, PA: Haverford House, 1979), 110.

9 Ibid., 64.

10 Ibid., 73.

11 Cobbs, *Owen Wister*, 7.

12 E. Digby Baltzell, *Philadelphia Gentlemen: The Making of a National Upper Class* (Philadelphia: University of Pennsylvania Press, 1979), 126, 152–57.

13 John Lukacs, *Philadelphia: Patricians and Philistines, 1900-1950* (New York: Ferrar Straus Giroux, 1981), 39.

14 Payne, *Owen Wister*, 76.

15 Elsewhere, I have pointed out that this book resulted from the fact that my father was a doctor, and one of his patients was Everett Johnson. My father became a doctor in a very peculiar way. When he enlisted with the Canadian Expeditionary Force during the First World War and

landed in England, he immediately was ordered to report to the Canadian Army Red Cross hospital on the estate of Lord and Lady Astor at Clivedon. There, with no choice in the matter, he was told that he was to play baseball for the Astorias, the team assembled in honour of the Duchess of Connaught, the wife of the Duke of Connaught, Canada's governor general and Queen Victoria's third son, who was a good friend of the Astors. The military commander of the hospital was a baseball fanatic, and he grabbed any well-known baseball player who arrived in England with the Canadian Expeditionary Force. My father also played in the famous Canadian–American all-star baseball game at Lord's Cricket Grounds on Canada Day, 1917, which attracted 10,000 spectators. As luck would have it, the Clivedon hospital's chief consultant, who spent every Monday morning doing the rounds of the hospital, was Canada's most famous doctor, Sir William Osler, Regius Chair in Medicine at Oxford University. All the baseball players were given hospital duties, and my father had the great good fortune to be sent by Sir William to Oxford for several courses. My father revered Osler, and, as soon as the war ended, he left the Royal Flying Corps, where he had been a fighter pilot, and enrolled in medicine at the University of Toronto.

Before taking up his position at Oxford in 1905, Osler had made his international reputation first at the University of Pennsylvania's medical school and then at Johns Hopkins in Baltimore. He had been enticed to Philadelphia from McGill University in Montreal in 1884 by Dr. S. Weir Mitchell, and the two of them were later to become great friends. Osler recounted how Mitchell had taken him to dinner when he was being considered for the post in Philadelphia and, when dessert came, was given the all-important cherry pie test; fortunately Osler had heard of this test and was able to dispose of his cherry pits in the proper Philadelphia manner. If he had not passed the test, he could not possibly have been considered for the post!

After Philadelphia, Osler went on to a distinguished career at Johns Hopkins University. There one of his great friends was Professor H. A. Rowland, a pioneer in atomic spectroscopy, after whom the physics building at Johns Hopkins is named. Professor Rowland happened to be my mother's uncle. Small world!

16 Payne, *Owen Wister*, 90.
17 Library of Congress, Washington, DC (LC), Wister Papers, Box 89.
18 Wister, *Roosevelt*, 29.
19 American Heritage Center (AHC), Wister Collection.
20 Fanny Kemble Wister, *Owen Wister Out West* (Chicago: University of Chicago Press, 1958), 15; "Hank's Woman," *Harper's Weekly* 36 (Aug. 27, 1892), 821–23.
21 Owen Wister, "How Lin McLean Went East," *Harper's New Monthly Magazine* 86 (December 1892), 135–46.
22 Ibid., 135.
23 LC, Wister Papers, Clemens to Wister, Aug. 4, 1895, Box 45.
24 Published in *Harper's Monthly* 88 (January 1894). The story was illustrated by Remington.
25 Kemble Wister, *Owen Wister Out West*, 196; "Balaam and Pedro,"

26. *Harper's New Monthly Magazine* (Jan. 1894), 293–307.
26. Payne, *Owen Wister*, 133.
27. LC, Wister Papers, Box 45, H. M. Alden to Wister, July 14, 1893.
28. "Em'ly," *Harper's New Monthly Magazine* (Nov. 1893), 941–48.
29. "The Winning of the Biscuit-Shooter," *Harper's New Monthly Magazine* (Dec. 1893), 52–57.
30. Frederic Remington was born in 1861, a year after Wister, and died at forty-eight of a ruptured appendix, a common cause of death in an age before antibiotics. His father had been a newspaper publisher, a Civil War hero, and, later, a breeder of race horses. After graduating from Yale's school of fine arts, Remington first went west in 1881.
31. *Harper's Monthly*, September 1895.
32. G. Edward White, *The Eastern Establishment and the Western Experience: The West of Frederic Remington, Theodore Roosevelt, and Owen Wister* (New Haven: Yale University Press, 1968), 93.
33. The club began with a dinner organized by Roosevelt in December 1887. The club's twin aims were "to promote manly sport with a rifle" and "to work for the preservation of the large game of the country." The cofounder was George Bird Grinnell, a good friend who promoted the ideas of the club through the magazine he edited, *Forest and Stream*. In 1888, Roosevelt wrote six articles for *Century*, illustrated by Remington, on the conservation theme. When Roosevelt became president, the ideas of the club became national policy.
34. Douglas Brinkley, *The Wilderness Warrior: Theodore Roosevelt and the Crusade for America* (New York: Harper, 2009), 463–67.
35. Ibid., 156.
36. Ibid., 148.
37. Ibid., 184.
38. Edmund Morris, *The Rise of Theodore Roosevelt* (New York: Coward, McCann & Geoghegan, 1979), 298.
39. Ibid., 333.
40. Brinkley, *Wilderness Warrior*, 194–95.
41. Remington Museum, Ogdensburg, NY, Remington Papers, Roosevelt to Remington, Nov. 20, 1895.
42. Ibid., Dec. 28, 1897.
43. Ibid., Sept. 19, 1898.
44. Ibid., June 29, 1908.
45. Brinkley, *Wilderness Warrior*, 335.
46. *The Winning of the West: An Account of the Exploration and Settlement of Our Country From the Alleghanies to the Pacific*, 4 vols. (New York: Putnam's, vol. 1 and 2, 1889; vol. 3, 1894; vol. 4, 1896).
47. Morris, *Rise of Theodore Roosevelt*, 462–63.
48. Ibid., 464.
49. Ibid., 454.
50. Quoted from Owen Wister's foreword, "The Young Roosevelt," to the 1926 edition of Roosevelt's *Ranch Life and the Hunting Trail*.
51. Brinkley, *Wilderness Warrior*, 241.
52. Morris, *Rise of Theodore Roosevelt*, 465.
53. Ibid., 465–66. In *The Historical World of Frederick Jackson Turner*, Wilbur Jacobs noted that Turner wrote an unpublished essay, "The Hunter Type," in 1890, which was based almost entirely on the early volumes of Roosevelt's *The Winning of the West*. Morris, *Rise of Theodore Roosevelt*, 465.
54. Brinkley, *Wilderness Warrior*, 241.

55 Patricia Nelson Limerick, "The Adventures of the Frontier in the Twentieth Century," in *The Frontier in American Culture*, ed. James R. Grossman (Berkeley: University of California Press, 1994), 75.

56 Frederick Jackson Turner, "The Significance of the Frontier in American History," *Annual Report of the American Historical Association for the Year 1893* (Washington, DC: Government Printing Office, 1894), 199.

57 Richard White, "Frederick Jackson Turner and Buffalo Bill," in *The Frontier in American Culture*, ed. James R. Grossman (Berkeley: University of California Press, 1994), 9.

58 Richard W. Etulain, *Telling Western Stories: From Buffalo Bill to Larry McMurtry* (Albuquerque: University of New Mexico Press, 1999), 29.

59 Ibid.

60 White, "Frederick Jackson Turner and Buffalo Bill," 25.

61 *Harper's New Monthly Magazine* (September 1895), 602–17.

62 Ibid.

63 Ibid.

64 Remington Museum, Ogdensburg, NY, Remington Papers, Wister to Remington, n.d.

65 Theodore Roosevelt, "What Americanism Means," *Forum* (April 1894).

66 Morris, *Rise of Theodore Roosevelt*, 467–68.

67 Elting E. Morison, ed., *The Letters of Theodore Roosevelt*, 8 vols. (Cambridge, MA: Harvard University Press, 1951), 390.

68 Morris, *Rise of Theodore Roosevelt*, 468, quoting Leon Edel, *Henry James, The Master: 1901–1916* (Philadelphia: Lippincott, 1972).

69 Ben Merchant Vorpahl, *My Dear Wister: The Frederic Remington–Owen Wister Letters* (Palo Alto, CA: American West Publishing, 1973), 38, 116.

70 See Peggy Samuels and Samuel Samuels, eds., *The Collected Works of Frederic Remington* (Garden City, NY: Doubleday, 1979). Remington wrote for *Harper's Weekly* and *Monthly*, *Harper's Round Table*, *Outing*, *Century*, *Cosmopolitan*, *Collier's*, *McClure's*, and *Scribner's*.

71 See Candice Millard, *The River of Doubt: Theodore Roosevelt's Darkest Journey* (New York: Broadway Books, 2005).

72 Charles Darwin, *Journal of Researches into the Geology and Natural History of the Various Countries Visited by H.M.S. Beagle* (New York: Hafner, 1952), 48, cited in Richard W. Slatta, *Cowboys of the Americas* (Albuquerque: University of New Mexico Press, 1990), 32.

73 Ibid., 197.

74 Remington Museum, Ogdensburg, NY, Remington Papers, Wister to Remington, n.d.

75 According to Susan Meyer, Remington was later the first American artist to use the "lost wax" process to produce his sculptures, a process brought from Europe by Riccardo Bertelli. This method of casting allowed great delicacy and movement not possible with the sand casting process. He was also in the forefront in America in adopting European impressionism in his paintings. See Susan Meyer, *America's Great Illustrators* (New York: Abrams, 1978).

76 Payne, *Owen Wister*, 170.

77 Ibid., 173.

78   Ibid., 189.

78a Atwood Manley and Margaret Manley Mangum, *Frederic Remington and the North Country* (New York: E.P. Dutton, 1988), 159–60. Later, in the 1911 edition, the editor did include a few Remington illustrations, but they were unrelated to the story.

79   Wister, *Roosevelt*, 18.

80   Robert Murray Davis, *Playing Cowboys: Low Culture and High Art in the Western* (Norman: University of Oklahoma Press, 1992), 7, 11.

81   Owen Wister, *Romney*, ed. James A. Butler (University Park: Penn State University Press, 2001), xxxi.

82   LC, Wister Papers, Box 79.

83   Ibid.

84   Slatta, *Cowboys*, 195.

85   Wister, *Roosevelt*, 246–47.

86   Cited in Cobbs, *Owen Wister*, 27.

87   Ibid., 105.

88   Ibid., 104–7.

89   Ibid., 102.

90   Struthers Burt, introduction to the 1951 Heritage Press edition of *The Virginian*, xiv.

91   Wister, *Roosevelt*, 251–53.

92   Ibid., 259–61.

93   Wister, *Romney*, xxxiv.

94   See Wister, *The Virginian*, chapter 12: "Quality and Equality," to chapter 16: "The Game and the Nation: Last Act."

95   Evan Thomas, *War Lovers: Roosevelt, Lodge, Hearst, and the Rush to Empire, 1898* (New York: Little, Brown, 2010), 5, 38.

96   Wister, *Roosevelt*, 319.

97   Payne, *Owen Wister*, 262.

98   Wister, *Romney*, xxvii.

99   See chapter 8.

8: AFTERWORD

1   All the information for this chapter came from Jean Johnson's manuscript.

2   Charles M. Russell, *Trails Plowed Under: Tales of the Old West* (New York: Doubleday, 1927), 166.

3   Richard Slatta, Cowboys of the Americas (New Haven: Yale University Press, 1990), 90.

4   Ibid., 39, 90–91.

5   See Tony Rees, *Polo, The Galloping Game: An Illustrated History of Polo in Western Canada* (Cochrane, AB: Western Heritage Centre Society, 2000). A Pincher Creek, Alberta, rancher, E. M. Wilmot, is credited with introducing the game to his ranching community in 1889. He founded, perhaps, the first organized polo club in Canada. It may have been the first club in North America. Polo goes back to ancient Persia and was introduced to the British Army in India shortly after the Indian Mutiny of 1857.

6   See Glenbow Archives, John Henry Reid, "Biography of a Cardston Pioneer"; private manuscript, "Canadian Justice," which Jack Reid distributed to close friends. He had hoped to have the article published in a magazine, but he was told by several magazine publishers that it was not sufficiently exciting!

7   Johnson had four children: Jessie Lucretia, Robert Everett Poindexter, Laurence Branch, and Frances Olive (Dot). Frances married H. K. "Chappie" Clarkson from Pincher Creek. They had five children: Patricia, Robert, Donald, Laurie, and William. Robert held the middleweight boxing championship for the Canadian Army in Europe. He was also a commando instructor. In 1927,

Laurie married Jean Lamont while he was foreman of the Rhodes Ranch in the Grand Valley west of Cochrane. Their children were Donna Carroll, born in 1929, and Margaret Jean, born in 1931. Donna married Richard Butters, whose family came to Alberta in 1883. They had the adjoining ranch to the Johnson ranch. They had three children, Erik, Lamont, and Ian. Margaret Jean married Lt. Commander S. R. Wallace and had three children, Robert, Laurence, and Carolyn. Jessie Lucretia married John Annear, and Robert Everett Poindexter married Ona Patterson.

Bibliography

OWEN WISTER'S WRITING

NOVELS

Lin McLean (1897)
The Virginian: A Horseman of the Plains (1902)
Lady Baltimore (1906)

SHORT STORY COLLECTIONS

Red Men and White. New York: Harper's, 1895
The Jimmyjohn Boss and Other Stories. New York: Harper's, 1900
Members of the Family. New York: Macmillan, 1911
When West Was West. New York: Macmillan, 1928

WESTERN ESSAYS AND SHORT STORIES

"Hank's Woman." *Harper's Weekly*, Aug. 27, 1892, 821–23.
"How Lin McLean Went East." *Harper's New Monthly Magazine*, Dec. 1892, 135–46.
"Em'ly." *Harper's New Monthly Magazine*, Nov. 1893, 941–48.
"The Winning of the Biscuit Shooter." *Harper's New Monthly Magazine*, Dec. 1893, 52–57.

"Balaam and Pedro." *Harper's New Monthly Magazine*, Jan. 1894, 293–307.
"The Promised Land." *Harper's New Monthly Magazine*, April 1894, 781–96.
"A Kinsman of Red Cloud." *Harper's New Monthly Magazine*, May 1894, 907–17.
"Little Big Horn Medicine." *Harper's New Monthly Magazine*, June 1894, 118–32.
"Specimen Jones." *Harper's New Monthly Magazine*, July 1894, 204–16.
"The Serenade at Siskiyou." *Harper's New Monthly Magazine*, Aug. 1894, 383–89.
"Salvation Gap." *Harper's New Monthly Magazine*, Oct. 1894, 673–80.
"Lin McLean's Honey-Moon." *Harper's New Monthly Magazine*, Jan. 1895, 283–93.
"The Second Missouri Compromise." *Harper's New Monthly Magazine*, March 1895, 534–45.
"La Tinaja Bonita." *Harper's New Monthly Magazine*, May 1895, 859–79.
"Where Charity Begins." *Harper's New Monthly Magazine*, July 1895, 268–72.
"The Evolution of the Cow-Puncher." *Harper's New Monthly Magazine*, Sept. 1895, 602–17.
"A Pilgrim On the Gila." *Harper's New Monthly Magazine*, Nov. 1895, 837–64.
"Where Fancy Was Bred." *Harper's New Monthly Magazine*, March 1896, 574–85.
"Separ's Vigilante." *Harper's New Monthly Magazine*, March 1897, 517–40.
"Grandmother Stark." *Harper's New Monthly Magazine*, June 1897, 63–75.
"Sharon's Choice." *Harper's New Monthly Magazine*, Aug. 1897, 447–57.
"Destiny at Drybone." *Harper's New Monthly Magazine*, Dec. 1897, 60–81.
"Padre Ignazio." *Harper's New Monthly Magazine*, April 1900, 692–703.
"The Game and the Nation." *Harper's New Monthly Magazine*, May 1900, 884–905.
"Concerning Bad Men: The True Bad Man of the Frontier, and the Reasons For His Existence." *Everybody's Magazine*, April 1901.
"Superstition Trail." *Saturday Evening Post*, Oct. 26, Nov. 2, 1901.
"In a State of Sin." *Harper's New Monthly Magazine*, Feb. 1902.
" With Malice Aforethought." *Saturday Evening Post*, May 3, 10, 1902.
"At the Sign of the Last Chance." *Cosmopolitan*, Feb. 1928.
"The Right Honorable the Strawberries." *Cosmopolitan*, Feb. 1928.

PRIMARY SOURCES

Manuscripts Division, Library of Congress

Owen Wister Papers
Theodore Roosevelt Presidential Papers

Glenbow Archives, Ranching Papers

"Correspondence, reports, memos etc. re ranching in southern Alberta, 1880–1926."
Ings, Fred. "Tales from the Midway Ranch." Manuscript.
Johnson, Jean. Fonds.
Johnson, L. B. (Laurie). "Sketches of His Life."
McKinnon, Lachlin. *Autobiography*. Private publication, n.d.
Plunkett, Sir Horace. "Ranching Correspondence with Earl Grey, Ottawa and Moreton Frewen, Wyoming, 1881–1890."
Reid, Jack H. Personal papers, 1917–1949.
Tetro, Harry A. "Survey of Historic Ranches, 1974."

Houghton Library, Harvard University

Theodore Roosevelt Collection
Frederic Remington Papers

Historical Society of New Hampshire

Caleb Stark Papers

Historical Society of Pennsylvania

Owen Wister Papers
Ferdinand J. Dresser Collection

Remington Museum, Ogdensburg, NY

Frederic Remington Papers

American Heritage Center, Laramie, WY

Owen Wister Collection
Moreton Frewen Papers, 1870–1932
Fred Hesse Collection
Johnson County, Wyoming, Assessment Rolls, 1883–1885

Buffalo Bill History Center, Cody, WY

W. F. Cody Papers

University of Wyoming, Laramie

Western Stock Growers' Association Records

NEWSPAPERS

Black Hills Weekly Pioneer, 1876–77
Black Hills Daily Times, 1877–78
Calgary Albertan
Calgary Herald

SECONDARY SOURCES

Abbott, E. C., and Helena Huntington Smith. *We Pointed Them North: The Recollections of a Cowpuncher*. Norman: University of Oklahoma Press, 1954.

Adams, Andy. *Log of a Cowboy*. New York: Airmont, 1969.

Adams, Ramon F. *The Old-Time Cowhand*. New York: Macmillan, 1968.

Allen, Frederick. *A Decent, Orderly Lynching: The Montana Vigilantes*. Norman: University of Oklahoma Press, 2004.

Allen, Robert S. *His Majesty's Indian Allies, 1774–1815*. Toronto: Dundurn, 1992.

Andrews, Allen. *The Splendid Pauper*. New York: Lippincott, 1968.

Appleman, Roy E. *The Wagon Box Fight*. Lincoln: University of Nebraska Press, 1960.

———. "The Wagon Box Fight." In *Great Western Indian Fights*, ed. Members of the Potomac Corral of the Westerners, 149–62. Lincoln: University of Nebraska Press, 1960.

Armstrong, Margaret. *Fanny Kemble*. New York: Macmillan, 1938.
Athearn, Robert G. *High Country Empire: The High Plains and the Rockies*. Lincoln: University of Nebraska Press, 1965.
———. *Westward the Briton*. Lincoln: University of Nebraska Press, 1953.
Atherton, Lewis. *The Cattle Kings*. Lincoln: University of Nebraska Press, 1961.
Ayers, Edward L. *Vengeance and Justice: Crime and Punishment in the Nineteenth-Century American South*. New York: Oxford University Press, 1984.
Baigell, Matthew. *The Western Art of Frederic Remington*. New York: Ballantine, 1976.
Baillargeon, Morgan, and Leslie Tepper. *Legends of Our Times: Native Cowboy Life*. Vancouver: UBC Press, 1998.
Baillie-Groham, William A. *Camps in the Rockies*. London: Sampson Low, 1882.
Baker, William M., ed. *The Mounted Police and Prairie Society, 1873–1919*. Saskatoon: Canadian Plains Research Center, 1998.
Bakken, Gordon. *The Development of Law on the Rocky Mountain Frontier: Civil Law and Society, 1850–1912*. Westport, CT: Greenwood, 1983.
Ball, Larry D. *The United States Marshals of New Mexico and Arizona Territory, 1846–1912*. Albuquerque: University of New Mexico Press, 1978.
Baltzall, E. Digby. *Philadelphia Gentlemen: The Making of a National Upper Class*. Philadelphia: University of Pennsylvania Press, 1979.
———. *The Protestant Establishment: Aristocracy and Caste in America*. New York: Vintage, 1964.
Bard, Floyd C. (as told to Agnes Wright Spring). *Horse Wrangler*. Norman: University of Oklahoma Press, 1960.
Barnett, Louise. *Touched By Fire: The Life, Death, and Mythic Afterlife of George Armstrong Custer*. New York: Henry Holt, 1996.
Barra, Allen. *Inventing Wyatt Earp: His Life and Many Legends*. New York: Carroll and Graf, 1998.
Barrett, Glen. *The Virginian at Medicine Bow*. Caldwell, ID: Claxton, 1978.
Barrett, Paul. *Glock: The Rise of America's Gun*. New York: Crown Publishers, 2012.
Barron, Laurie, and James B. Waldram, eds. *1885 and After: Native Society in Transition*. Saskatoon: Canadian Plains Research Center, 1986.
Barsh, Russell L. "The Substitution of Cattle for Bison on the Great Plains." In *The Struggle for the Land*, ed. Paul A. Olson. Lincoln: University of Nebraska Press, 1990.
Bartholomew, Ed. *Wyatt Earp*. Toyahvale, TX: Frontier Books, 1964.
Bartlett, Richard A. *The New Country: A Social History of the American Frontier, 1776–1890*. London, UK: Oxford University Press, 1974.
Baum, Dan. *Gun Guys: A Road Trip*. New York: Knopf, 2013.

Beahen, William. "Mob Law Could Not Prevail." In *The Mounted Police and Prairie Society, 1873-1919*, ed. William M. Baker, 101-8. Regina: Canadian Plains Research Center, 1998.

Beahen, William, and Stan Horrall. *The Red Coats on the Prairies*. Regina: Centax, 1998.

Beatie, Russell H. *Saddles*. Norman: University of Oklahoma Press, 1982.

Beaulieu, Alain, and Roland Viau. *The Great Peace: Chronicle of a Diplomatic Saga*. Ottawa: Museum of Civilization, 2001.

Bell, Malcolm Jr. *Major Butler's Legacy: Five Generations of a Slaveholding Family*. Athens: University of Georgia Press, 1987.

Bellesiles, Michael A. *Arming America: The Origins of a National Gun Culture*. New York: Knopf, 2000.

Bennell, John W., and Seena B. Kohl. *Settling the Canadian-American West, 1890-1915*. Lincoln: University of Nebraska Press, 1995.

Bennett, Estelline. *Old Deadwood Days*. Lincoln: University of Nebraska Press, 1982.

Bercuson, D. J., and L. A. Knafla. *Law and Society in Canada in Historical Perspective*. Calgary: University of Calgary, 1979.

Betke, Carl. " Pioneers and Police on the Canadian Prairies, 1885-1914." In *Lawful Authority: Readings on the History of Criminal Justice in Canada*, ed. R. C. Macleod, 98-119. Toronto: Copp Clark Pitman, 1988.

Billington, Ray Allen. *Frederick Jackson Turner: Historian, Scholar, Teacher*. New York: Oxford University Press, 1973.

———. *Land of Savagery, Land of Promise: The European Image of the American Frontier*. New York: Norton, 1981.

———. *People of the Plains and Mountains*. Westport, CT: Greenwood, 1973.

———. "Origin of the Land Speculator as a Frontier Type." In *Essays on the History of the American West*, ed. Stephen Salsbury. New York: Holt Rinehart, 1975.

Bisha, Karel D. *The American Farmer and the Canadian West, 1896-1914*. Lawrence: Coronado Press, 1968.

Blackstone, Sarah J. *Buckskins, Bullets, and Business: A History of Buffalo Bill's Wild West*. Westport, CT: Greenwood, 1986.

Blake, James Carlos. *The Pistoleer: A Novel of John Wesley Hardin*. New York: Berkley, 1995.

Blasingame, Ike. *Dakota Cowboy: My Life in the Old Days*. New York: Putnam's, 1958.

Blum, Howard. *The Floor of Heaven: A True Tale of the Last Frontier and the Yukon Gold Rush*. New York: Broadway, 2011.

Bold, Christine. *Selling the Wild West: Popular Western Fiction, 1860–1960*. Bloomington: Indiana University Press, 1987.

Brado, Edward. *Cattle Kingdom: Early Ranching in Alberta*. Vancouver: Douglas & McIntyre, 1984.

Brady, Cyrus Townshend. *The Sioux Indian Wars*. New York: Indian Head Books, 1992.

Branch, Douglas. *The Cowboy and His Interpreters*. New York: Cooper Square, 1961.

Brandt, Ernie. *A Cowboy's Memoirs*. Lethbridge: Southern Printing, 1977.

Bray, Kingsley M. *Crazy Horse: A Life*. Norman: University of Oklahoma Press, 2006.

Breen, David. *The Canadian Prairie West and the Ranching Frontier, 1874–1924*. Toronto: University of Toronto Press, 1983.

———. "The Turner Thesis and the Canadian West: A Closer Look at the Ranching Frontier." In *Essays on Western History*, ed. Lewis H. Thomas. Edmonton: University of Alberta Press, 1976.

Brininstool, A. E. "Who Killed Yellow Hand?" *Outdoor Life-Outdoor Recreation*, 1930.

Brinkley, Douglas. *The Wilderness Warrior: Theodore Roosevelt and the Crusade for America*. New York: Harper Perennial, 2009.

Broadfoot, Barry. *The Pioneer Years: Memories of Settlers Who Opened the West*. Toronto: Doubleday, 1976.

Bronson, Edgar B. *Reminiscences of a Ranchman*. Lincoln: University of Nebraska Press, 1962.

Brown, Dee. *The Fetterman Massacre*. Lincoln: University of Nebraska Press, 1962.

———. *The Galvanized Yankees*. New York: University of Illinois Press, 1963.

———. *Wondrous Times on the Frontier*. New York: Harper Perennial, 1991.

Brown, Dee, and Martin Schmitt. *Trail Driving Days: The Golden Days of the Old Trail*. New York: Scribner's, 1952.

Brown, Jesse, and A. M. Willard. *The Black Hills Trails*. New York: Arno Press, 1975.

Brown, Mark H., and W. R. Felton. *Before Barbed Wire*. New York: Bramhall House, 1956.

Brown, R. Blake. *Arming and Disarming: The History of Gun Control in Canada*. Toronto: University of Toronto Press, 2012.

Brown, Richard Maxwell. *No Duty To Retreat: Violence and Values in American History and Society*. Norman: University of Oklahoma Press, 1994.

———. *Strain of Violence: Historical Studies of American Violence and Vigilantism*. New York: Oxford University Press, 1975.

———. "The American Vigilante Tradition." In *A History of Violence in America*, eds. Hugh Davis Graham and Ted Robert Gurr, 154–226. New York: Bantam, 1969.

———. "Historical Patterns of Violence in America." In *A History of Violence in America*, eds. Hugh Davis Graham and Ted Robert Gurr, 45–84. New York: Bantam, 1969.

———. "Law and Order on the American Frontier: The Western Civil War of Incorporation." In *Law For the Elephant, Law For the Beaver: Essays in the Legal History of the North American West*, eds. John Mclaren, Hamar Foster, and Chet Orloff, 74–89. Regina: Canadian Plains Research Center, 1992.

———. "Violence." In *The Oxford History of the American West*, eds. Clyde A. Miller, Carol A. O'Connor, and Martha A. Sandweiss, 393–425. New York: Oxford University Press, 1994.

Buck, Daniel. "Surprising Development: The Sundance Kid's Unusual – and Unknown – Life in Canada." *Journal of the Western Outlaw – Lawman History Association* (Winter 1993).

Buntline, Ned [E. Z. C. Judson]. *Buffalo Bill, the King of the Border Men!: The Wildest and Truest Story I Ever Wrote*. Sweet and Smith's New York Weekly, December 23 to March 10, 1870.

Burroughs, John Rolfe. *Guardian of the Grasslands: The First Hundred Years of the Wyoming Stock Growers Association*. Cheyenne: Pioneer Printing, 1971.

Burt, Struthers. *Powder River*. New York: Farrar & Rinehart, 1938.

Butala, Sharon. *The Garden of Eden*. Toronto: Harper Collins, 1998.

Butler, William Francis. *The Great Lone Land*. Edmonton: Hurtig, 1968.

Canton, Frank. *Frontier Tales: The Autobiography of Frank M. Canton*. New York: Houghton Mifflin, 1930.

Carrigan, William D. *The Making of a Lynching Culture: Violence and Vigilantism in Central Texas, 1836–1916*. Urbana: University of Illinois Press, 2004.

Carrigan, William D., and Christopher Waldrep, eds. *Swift to Wrath: Lynching in Global Historical Perspective*. Charlottesville: University of Virginia Press, 2013.

Carrington, Margaret Irwin. *Ab'Sa'Ra'Ka, Home of the Crows: Being the Experience of an Officer's Wife on the Plains*. Lincoln: University of Nebraska Press, 1983.

Cawalti, John G. *The Six-Gun Mystique*. Bowling Green, OH: Bowling Green University Popular Press, 1971.

———. *Adventure, Mystery, and Romance: Formula Stories as Art and Popular Culture*. Chicago: University of Chicago Press, 1976.

Chadbourn, J. H. *Lynching and the Law*. Chapel Hill: University of North Carolina Press, 1933.

Chapel, Charles Edward. *Guns of the Old West.* New York: Coward-McCann, 1961.

Chapman, Terry, "The Anti-Drug Crusade in Western Canada, 1885–1925." In *Law and Society in Canada in Historical Perspective,* eds. David Bercuson and Louis A. Knafla, 89–115. Calgary: University of Calgary Press, 1979.

———."The Measurement of Crime in Nineteenth-Century Canada: Some Methodological and Philosophical Problems." In *Crime and Criminal Justice in Europe and Canada,* ed. Louis A. Knafla, 147–55. Waterloo: Wilfrid Laurier University Press, 1981.

———. "Sex Crimes in the West, 1890–1920." *Alberta History* 35 (Autumn 1987): 6–21.

Christianson, Chris. *Early Rangemen.* Lethbridge: Southern Printing, 1973.

———. *My Life on the Range.* Lethbridge: Southern Printing, 1968.

Clark, Walter Van Tilburg. *The Ox-Bow Incident.* New York: Random House, 1940.

Clay, John. *My Life on the Range.* Norman: University of Oklahoma Press, 1962.

Coates, Ken S., and William R. Morrison. *Strange Things Done: Murder in Yukon History.* Montreal: McGill-Queen's University Press, 2004.

Cobbs, John L. *Owen Wister.* Boston: Twayne, 1984.

Coblentz, Stanton A. *Villains and Vigilantes: The Fabulous Story of James King of William and of Pioneer Justice in California.* New York: A. S. Barnes, 1961.

Cody, Col. W. F. *Buffalo Bill's Life Story.* Mineola, NY: Dover, 1920.

———. "My Duel With Yellow Hand." *Harper's Round Table* 2, no. 23 (1899): 521–25.

Cohen, Eliot A. *Conquered into Liberty: Two Centuries of Battles along the Great Warpath That Made the American Way of War.* New York: Free Press, 2011.

Collins, Ellsworth, and Alma M. England. *The 101 Ranch.* Norman: University of Oklahoma Press, 1938.

Collins, Michael L. *That Damned Cowboy: Theodore Roosevelt and the American West, 1883–1898.* New York: Peter Lang, 1989.

Cook, James H. *Fifty Years on the Old Frontier.* Norman: University of Oklahoma Press, 1963.

Cook, Philip J., and Jens Ludwig. *Gun Violence: The Real Cost.* New York: Oxford University Press, 2000.

Craig, John R. *Ranching With Lords and Commons.* Toronto: William Briggs, 1903.

Cramer, Clayton E. *Armed America: The Remarkable Story of How and Why Guns Became as American as Apple Pie.* Nashville, TN: Nelson Current, 2006.

Cronon, William, George Miles, and Jay Gitlin, eds. *Under an Open Sky: Rethinking America's Western Past.* New York: Norton, 1992.

Culberson, William. *Vigilantism: Political History of Private Power in America.* New York: Greenwood, 1990.

Curley, Edwin A. *Edwin A. Curley's Guide to the Black Hills.* Mitchell, SD: Dakota Wesleyan University Press, 1973. First published 1877.

Cutler, James E. *Lynch-Law: An Investigation into the History of Lynching in the United States.* New York: Negro Universities Press, 1969.

Dale, Edward Everett. *Cow Country.* Norman: University of Oklahoma Press, 1942.

———. *The Range Cattle Industry: Ranching on the Great Plains from 1865 to 1925.* Norman: University of Oklahoma Press, 1960.

Dary, David. *Cowboy Culture.* Lawrence: University Press of Kansas, 1981.

———. *Entrepreneurs of the Old West.* Lincoln: University of Nebraska Press, 1986.

Daschuk, James. *Clearing the Plains: Disease, Politics, and the Loss of Aboriginal Life.* Regina: University of Regina Press, 2013.

Davis, John W. *Wyoming Range War: The Infamous Invasion of Johnson County.* Norman: University of Oklahoma Press, 2010.

Davis, Robert Murray. *Owen Wister's West: Selected Articles.* Albuquerque: University of New Mexico Press, 1987.

———. *Playing Cowboys: Low Culture and High Art in the Western.* Norman: University of Oklahoma Press, 1992.

Dawson, Michael. "That Nice Red Coat Goes To My Head Like Champagne: Gender, Antimodernism and the Mountie Image, 1880–1960." *Journal of Canadian Studies* 32, no. 3 (Fall 1979): 119–39.

DeArment, Robert K. *Alias Frank Canton.* Norman: University of Oklahoma Press, 1996.

———. *Assault on the Deadwood Stage: Road Agents and Shotgun Messengers.* Norman: University of Oklahoma Press, 2011.

Dempsey, Hugh A. *The Golden Age of the Canadian Cowboy.* Calgary: Fifth House, 1995.

———, ed. *Men in Scarlet.* Calgary: McClelland & Stewart West, 1974.

Dimsdale, Thomas J. *The Vigilantes of Montana.* Norman: University of Oklahoma Press, 1953.

Dippie, Brian W. *Custer's Last Stand: The Anatomy of an American Myth.* Missoula: University of Montana Publications in History, 1976.

———, ed. *Paper Talk: Charlie Russell's American West.* New York: Knopf, 1979.

Dobie, J. Frank. *Cow People.* Boston: Little, Brown, 1964.

———. *The Longhorns.* New York: Grosset & Dunlop, 1941.

———. *Prefaces.* Boston: Little, Brown, 1975.

Donahue, Deborah. *The Western Range Revisited.* Norman: University of Oklahoma Press, 2000.

Drago, Harry Sinclair. *The Great Range Wars: Violence on the Grasslands*. Lincoln: University of Nebraska Press, 1970.

Dunae, Patrick A. *Gentleman Immigrants: From the British Public Schools to the Canadian Frontier*. Vancouver: Douglas & McIntyre, 1981.

Durham, Philip, and Everett Jones. *The Negro Cowboys*. Lincoln: University of Nebraska Press, 1965.

Dykstra, Robert R. *The Cattle Towns*. New York: Knopf, 1971.

East Longview Historical Society. *Tales and Trails: A History of Longview and Surrounding Area*. Calgary: Northwest Publishing, 1973.

Elofson, Warren M. *Cowboys, Gentlemen, and Cattle Thieves*. Montreal: McGill-Queen's University Press, 2000.

———. *Frontier Cattle Ranching in the Land and Time of Charlie Russell*. Montreal: McGill-Queen's University Press, 2004.

———. *Somebody Else's Money: The Walrond Ranch story, 1883-1907*. Calgary: University of Calgary Press, 2009.

———. "Law and Disorder on the Ranching Frontiers of Montana and Alberta/Assiniboia, 1870–1914." *Journal of the West* 42 (2003): 40–51.

———. "The Untamed Canadian Ranching Frontier, 1874-1914." In *Cowboys, Ranchers and the Cattle Business: Cross-Border Perspectives on Ranching History*, eds. Simon Evans, Sarah Carter, and Bill Yeo, 81–99. Calgary: University of Calgary Press, 2000.

Erickson, Lesley. *Westward Bound: Sex, Violence, the Law, and the Making of Settler Society*. Osgoode Society for Canadian Legal History Series. Vancouver: UBC Press, 2011.

Ernst, Donna. *The Sundance Kid: The Life of Harry Alonzo Longabaugh*. Norman: University of Oklahoma Press, 2011.

———. *Sundance, My Uncle*. College Station, TX: Creative Publishing, 1992.

Erisman, Fred. *Frederic Remington*. Boise, ID: Boise State University, 1975.

Estleman, Loren D. *The Wister Trace: Classic Novels of the American Frontier*. Ottawa, Illinois: Jameson Books, 1987.

Etulain, Richard W. *Owen Wister: The Western Writing*. Boise, ID: Boise State College, 1973.

———. *Telling Western Stories: From Buffalo Bill to Larry McMurtry*. Albuquerque: University of New Mexico Press, 1999.

———. "Frontier, Region, and Myth: Changing Perspectives of Western American Culture." *Journal of American Culture* 3, no. 2 (Summer 1980): 268–84.

———. "Western Fiction and History: A Reconsideration." In *The American West: New Perspectives, New Dimensions*, ed. Jerome O. Steffen, 152–74. Norman: University of Oklahoma Press, 1979.

Evans, Simon M. *The Bar U and Canadian Ranching History.* Calgary: University of Calgary Press, 2004.

———. *Prince Charming Goes West: The Story of the EP Ranch.* Calgary: University of Calgary Press, 1993.

———. "American Cattlemen on the Canadian Range, 1874–1914." *Prairie Forum* 4, no. 1 (1979): 121–35.

———. "The Origins of Ranching in Western Canada: American Diffusion or Victorian Transplant." *Great Plains Quarterly* 3, no. 2 (Spring 1983): 79–91.

———. "Some Observations on the Labour Force of the Canadian Ranching Frontier during Its Golden Age, 1882–1901." Paper presented to the Canadian Historical Association, June 1994, 3–17.

Evans, Simon, Sarah Carter, and Bill Yeo, eds. *Cowboys, Ranchers and the Cattle Business.* Calgary: University of Calgary Press, 2000.

Evans, Stirling, ed. *The Borderlands of the American and Canadian Wests: Essays on Regional History of the Forty-ninth Parallel.* Lincoln: University of Nebraska Press, 2006.

Ewers, John C. *The Horse in Blackfoot Indian Culture.* Washington: United States Government Printing Office, 1955.

Ewing, Sherm. *The Ranch: A Modern History of the North American Cattle Industry.* Missoula, MT: Mountain Press, 1995.

———. *The Range.* Missoula, MT: Mountain Press, 1990.

Fehrenbach, T. R. *Lone Star: A History of Texas and Texans.* New York: Macmillan, 1985.

Fenin, George N., and William K. Everson. *The Western: From Silents to Cinerama.* New York: Orian, 1962.

Fiedler, Leslie A. *The Return of the Vanishing American.* New York: Stein and Day, 1968.

Flaherty, David H. *Essays on the History of Canadian Law.* Toronto: Osgoode Society, 1981.

Fletcher, Robert H. *Free Grass to Fences: The Montana Cattle Range Story.* New York: University Publishers, 1960.

Folsom, James K. *The Western American Novel.* New Haven, CT: College and University Press, 1966.

———, ed. *The Western: A Collection of Critical Essays.* Englewood Cliffs, NJ: Prentice-Hall, 1979.

Foran, Max. *Trails and Trials: Markets and Land Use in the Alberta Beef Cattle Industry, 1881–1948.* Calgary; University of Calgary Press, 2003.

Fort, Adrian. *Nancy: The Story of Lady Astor.* New York: St. Martin's Press, 2012.

Francis, Douglas, and Howard Palmer. *The Prairie West: Historical Readings.* Edmonton: University of Alberta Press, 1992.

Franz, Joe B., and Julian E. Choate Jr. *The American Cowboy: The Myth and the Reality*. Norman: University of Oklahoma Press, 1955.

Freifeld, Sidney. *Undiplomatic Notes: Tales From the Canadian Foreign Service*. Toronto: Hounslow Press, 1990.

Frewen, Moreton. *Melton Mowbray and Other Memories*. London, UK: Herbert Jenkins, 1924.

Friedland, Martin L. *A Century of Criminal Justice: Perspectives on the Development of Canadian Law*. Toronto: Carswell, 1984.

Friesen, Gerald. *The Canadian Prairies: A History*. Toronto: University of Toronto Press, 1984.

Frink, Maurice. *Cow Country Cavalcade*. Denver: Old West Publishing, 1954.

Frink, Maurice, W. Turrentine Jackson, and Agnes Wright Spring. *When Grass Was King*. Boulder: University of Colorado Press, 1956.

Fromkin, David. *The King and the Cowboy: Theodore Roosevelt and Edward the Seventh, Secret Partners*. New York: Penguin, 2008.

Gage, Jack R. *The Johnson County War*. Cheyenne: Flintlock Publishing, 1967.

Garavaglia, Louis, and Charles G. Worman. *Firearms of the American West*. Vol. 2, 1865–1894. Albuquerque: University of New Mexico Press, 1985.

Garber, Vie Willits. "The Wagon Box Fight." *Annals of Wyoming* 36, no. 1 (April 1964): 61–63.

Gard, Wayne. *The Chisholm Trail*. Norman: University of Oklahoma Press, 1954.

———. *Frontier Justice*. Norman: University of Oklahoma Press, 1949.

Gardiner, Claude. *Letters From an English Rancher*. Calgary: Glenbow Museum, 1988.

Gardner, Mark Lee. *To Hell on a Fast Horse: Billy the Kid, Pat Garrett, and the Epic Chase to Justice in the Old West*. New York: William Morrow, 2010.

Gates, Paul W. *The History of Public Land Law Development*. Washington, DC: Gaunt and Sons, 1987.

Gavigan, Shelley A. M. *Hunger, Horses, and Government Men: Criminal Law on the Aboriginal Plains, 1870–1905*. Vancouver: UBC Press for the Osgoode Society for Canadian Legal History, 2012.

Goetzmann, William H., and William N. Goetzmann. *The West of the Imagination*. New York: Norton, 1986.

Gonzales-Day, Ken. *Lynching in the West, 1850–1935*. Durham: Duke University Press, 2006.

Graber, Stan. *The Last Roundup: Memories of a Canadian Cowboy*. Saskatoon: Fifth House, 1995.

Graham, Hugh Davis, and Ted Robert Gurr. *A History of Violence in America*. New York: Bantam, 1970.

Graham, Robert Bontine Cunninghame. *Horses of the Conquest*. Norman: University of Oklahoma Press, 1949. First published 1930.

Grant, Johnny. *Very Close to Trouble*, ed. Lyndel Meikle. Pullman: University of Washington State Press, 1996.

Grant, Ted, and Andy Russell. *Men of the Saddle: Working Cowboys of Canada*. Toronto: Van Nostrand Reinhold, 1978.

Graybill, Andrew R. *Policing the Great Plains: Rangers, Mounties, and the North American Frontier, 1875–1910*. Lincoln: University of Nebraska Press, 2007.

Gressley, Gene M. *Bankers and Cattlemen*. New York: Knopf, 1966.

Grossman, James R., ed. *The Frontier in American Culture: Essays by Richard White and Patricia Nelson Limerick*. Berkeley: University of California Press, 1994.

Guernsey, Charles A. *Wyoming Cowboy Days*. New York: Putnam's, 1936.

Hadley, Alice M. *Where the Winds Blow Free*. Canaan, NH: Phoenix, 1976.

Hafen, LeRoy R., and Francis Marion Young. *Fort Laramie and the Pageant of the West, 1834–1890*. Lincoln: University of Nebraska Press, 1984.

Hage, Wayne. *Storm Over Rangelands: Private Rights in Federal Lands*. 3rd ed. Belleview, WA: Free Enterprise, 1994.

Hagedorn, Hermann. *Roosevelt in the Bad Lands*. Boston: Houghton Mifflin, 1921.

———. *Theodore Roosevelt: A Biographical Sketch, and Excerpts From His Writings and Addresses*. New York: Roosevelt Memorial Association, 1923.

Haley, J. Evetts. *The XIT Ranch of Texas and the Early Days of the Llano Estacudo*. Norman: University of Oklahoma Press, 1953.

Hamilton, W. T. *My Sixty Years on the Plains*. Norman: University of Oklahoma Press, 1962.

Hanson, Charles E. Jr. *The Plains Rifle*. Harrisburg, PA: Stackpole, 1960.

Hanson, Margaret Brock. *Powder River Country: The Papers of J. Elmer Brock*. Cheyenne: Frontier Printing, 1981.

Harring, Sidney L. *White Man's Law: Native People in Nineteenth-Century Canadian Jurisprudence*. Toronto: University of Toronto Press, 1998.

Harris, Charles W., and Buck Rainey, eds. *The Cowboy: Six-Shooters, Songs, and Sex*. Norman: University of Oklahoma Press, 1976.

Harrison, Dick. *Crossing Frontiers: Papers in American and Canadian Western Literature*. Edmonton: University of Alberta Press, 1979.

Hassrick, Peter H. *Frederic Remington: Paintings, Drawings, and Sculpture in the Amon Carter Museum and the Sid W. Richardson Foundation Collections*. New York: Harry N. Abrams, 1973.

Havard, Gilles. *The Great Peace of Montreal of 1701: French–Native Diplomacy in the Seventeenth Century*. Montreal: McGill-Queen's University Press, 2001.

Heberd, Grace R., and A. E. Brininstool. *The Bozeman Trail*. Glendale, CA: Arthur H. Clark, 1922.

Heckscher, August. *St. Paul's: The Life of a New England School*. New York: Scribner's, 1980.

Hedron, Paul L. *First Scalp For Custer: The Skirmish at Warbonnet Creek, Nebraska, July 17, 1876*. Lincoln: University of Nebraska Press, 1980.

High River Pioneers' and Old Timers' Association. *Leaves From the Medicine Tree*. Lethbridge: Lethbridge Herald, 1960.

Higham, Carol, and Robert Thacker. *One West, Two Myths*. Calgary: University of Calgary Press, 2004.

Higinbotham, John D. *When the West Was Young: Historical Reminiscences of the Early Canadian West*. Toronto: Ryerson, 1933.

Hill, Alexander Staveley. *From Home to Home: Autumn Ramblings in the North-West in the Years 1881, 1882, 1883, 1884*. New York: Argonaut Press, 1966.

Hillerman, Tony. *The Best of the West: An Anthology of Classic Writing from the American West*. New York: Harper, 1991.

Hofstadter, Richard. *The Age of Reform*. New York: Knopf, 1985.

———. *The Paranoid Style in American Politics: And Other Essays*. New York: Knopf, 1965

———. "America as a Gun Culture" *American Heritage* 21 (October 1970).

———. "Reflections on Violence in the United States." In *American Violence: A Documentary History*, ed. Richard Hofstadter and Michael Wallace. New York: Knopf, 1970.

Hofstadter, Richard, and Michael Wallace, eds. *American Violence: A Documentary History*. New York: Knopf, 1970.

Hoig, Stan. *The Humor of the American Cowboy*. Lincoln: University of Nebraska Press, 1958.

Holliday, Barbara. *To Be a Cowboy: Oliver Christensen's Story*. Calgary: University of Calgary Press, 2003.

Hollon, W. Eugene, *Frontier Violence*. New York: Oxford University Press, 1974.

———. "Frontier Violence: Another Look." In *People of the Plains and Mountains*, ed. Ray Allen Billington, 86-100. Westport, CT: Greenwood, 1973.

Hopkins, Monica. *Letters From a Lady Rancher*. Calgary: Glenbow Museum, 1981.

Horan, James D. *The Pinkertons: The Detective Dynasty That Made History*. New York, 1968.

Hough, Emerson. *The Passing of the Frontier*. New Haven, CT: Yale University Press, 1918.

———. *The Story of the Cowboy*. New York: Appleton, 1897.

Hough, Robert L. *The West of Owen Wister: Selected Short Stories*. Lincoln: University of Nebraska Press, 1972.

Hubner, Brian. "Horse Stealing and the Border Line: The NWMP and the Control of Indian Movement, 1874–1900." In *The Mounted Police and Prairie Society, 1873–1919*, ed. William M. Baker, 53–70. Regina: Canadian Plains Research Center, 1998.

Hufsmith, George W. *The Wyoming Lynching of Cattle Kate, 1889*. Glendo, WY: High Plains Press, 1993.

Hutchins, James S., ed. *Boots and Saddles at the Little Bighorn*. Fort Collins, CO: Old Army Press, 1976.

Hutton, Harold. *Vigilante Days: Frontier Justice along the Niobrara*. Chicago: Sage, 1978.

Hyde, George E. *Red Cloud's Folk: A History of the Oglala Sioux Indians*. Norman: University of Oklahoma Press, 1937.

Ings, Frederick William. *Before the Fences: Tales from the Midway Ranch*. Calgary: McAra Printing, 1980.

Iverson, Peter. *When Indians Became Cowboys: Native Peoples and Cattle Ranching in the American West*. Norman: University of Oklahoma Press, 1994.

Jackel, Susan, ed. *A Flannel Shirt and Liberty: British Emigrant Gentlemen in the Canadian West, 1880–1914*. Vancouver: UBC Press, 1982.

Jackson, W. Turrentine. "The Wyoming Stock Growers' Association: Political Power in Wyoming Territory, 1873–1890." *Mississippi Valley Historical Review* 33, no. 4 (March 1947): 571–94.

Jameson, Sheilagh. *Ranchers, Cowboys, and Characters: Birth of Alberta's Western Heritage*. Calgary: Glenbow Museum, 1987.

———. "The Social Elite of the Ranching Community and Calgary." In *Frontier Calgary*, eds. Anthony W. Rasporich and Henry C. Klassen, 57–70. Calgary: McClelland & Stewart West, 1975.

Jameson, W. C., and Frederic Bean. *The Return of the Outlaw Billy the Kid*. Plano: Republic of Texas Press, 1998.

Jenkinson, Clay S. *A Free and Hardy Life: Theodore Roosevelt's Sojourn in the American West*. Washburn, ND: Dakota Institute Press, 2011.

Jennings, John N. "The North West Mounted Police and Indian Policy, 1874–1896." PhD diss., University of Toronto, 1979.

———. "The North West Mounted Police and Indian Policy after the 1885 Rebellion." In *1885 and After: Native Society in Transition*, eds. F. Laurie Barron and James B. Waldram, 225–39. Regina: Canadian Plains Research Center, 1986.

———. "The Plains Indian and the Law." In *Men in Scarlet*, ed. Hugh Dempsey, 50–65. McClelland & Stewart West, 1974.

———. "Policemen and Poachers: Indian Relations on the Ranching Frontier." In *Frontier Calgary*, eds. A. W. Rasporich and Henry Klassen, 87–99. Calgary: McClelland & Stewart West, 1975.

Jeremko, Gordon, and David Finch. *Legendary Horsemen: Images of the Canadian West*. Longview, AB: OH Ranch, 1996.

Jonnes, Jill. *Eiffel's Tower: And the World's Fair Where Buffalo Bill Beguiled Paris, the Artists Quarreled, and Thomas Edison Became a Count*. New York: Viking, 2009.

Jordan, Philip D. *Frontier Law and Order*. Lincoln: University of Nebraska Press, 1970.

———. "The Pistol Packin' Cowboy." In *The Cowboy: Six Shooters, Songs, and Sex*, ed. Charles W. Harris and Buck Rainy. Norman: University of Oklahoma Press, 1976.

———. "The Town Marshal and the Police." In *People of the Plains and Mountains*, ed. Ray Allen Billington. Westport, CT: Greenwood, 1973.

Jordan, Terry G. *North American Cattle Ranching Frontiers: Origins, Diffusion, and Differentiation*. Albuquerque: University of New Mexico Press, 1993.

Keenan, Jerry. *The Wagon Box Fight*. Sheridan, WY: Fort Phil Kearny/Bozeman Trail Association, 1988

Kelly, Charles. *The Outlaw Trail: The Story of Butch Cassidy and the Wild Bunch*. New York: Bonanza Books, 1959.

Kelly, L. V. *The Rangemen: The Story of the Ranchers and Indians of Alberta*. Toronto: Briggs, 1913.

Kelly, Vicky. "Butch and the Kid." *Glenbow* 3, no. 6 (Nov. 1970): 4–5.

Kemble, Frances Ann. *Journal of a Residence on a Georgian Plantation in 1838–1839*. New York: Knopf, 1961

Kennett, Lee, and James L. Anderson. *The Gun in America: The Origins of a National Dilemma*. Westport, CT: Greenwood, 1975.

Knafla, Louis A., ed. *Crime and Criminal Justice in Europe and Canada*. Waterloo, ON: Wilfrid Laurier University Press, 1981.

———. *Law and Justice in a New Land: Essays in Western Canadian Legal History*. Toronto: Carswell, 1986.

———. *Laws and Societies in the Canadian Prairie West, 1670–1940*. Vancouver: UBC Press, 2005.

———. *Violent Crime in North America*. Westport, CT: Greenwood, 2003.

———. "From Oral to Written Memory: The Common Law Tradition in Western Canada." Introduction to *Law and Justice in a New Land: Essays in Western Canadian Legal History*, ed. Louis Knafla, 31–77. Toronto: Carswell, 1986.

———. "Introduction: Laws and Societies in the Anglo-Canadian North-West Frontier and Prairie Provinces, 1670–1940." In *Laws and Societies in the*

Canadian Prairie West, 1670–1940, ed. Louis A. Knafla, 1–55. Vancouver: UBC Press, 2005.

———. "Violence on the Western Canadian Frontier: A Historical Perspective." In *Violence in Canada: Sociopolitical Perspectives*, ed. Jeffrey Ian Ross, 10–39. Somerset, NJ: Transaction Publishers, 2004.

Krakel, Dean F. *The Saga of Tom Horn: The Story of the Cattlemen's War*. Lincoln: University of Nebraska Press, 1954.

———. "Hell in Johnson County, Wyoming" *The Westerners New York Posse Brand Book* 3, no. 3 (1956): 59–60, 71.

Kyle, Chris. *American Gun: A History of the U.S. in Ten Firearms*. New York: HarperCollins, 2013.

LaDow, Beth. *The Medicine Line: Life and Death on the North American Borderland*. New York: Routledge, 2002.

Lake, Stuart. *Wyatt Earp: Frontier Marshall*. New York: Houghton Mifflin, 1931.

Lamar, Howard. *The Frontier in History*. New Haven, CT: Yale University Press, 1981.

Lamb, F. Bruce. *Kid Curry: The Life and Times of Harvey Logan and the Wild Bunch*. Boulder, CO: Johnson Books, 1991.

Lambert, Neil. "Owen Wister's Hank's Woman: The Writer and his Comment." *Western American Literature* 4 (1969): 39–50.

———. "Owen Wister's Lin McLean: The Failure of a Vernacular Hero." *Western American Literature* 5 (Fall 1970): 219–32.

———. "Owen Wister's Virginian: The Genesis of a Cultural Hero." *Western American Literature* 6 (1971): 99–107.

Larson, T. A. *History of Wyoming*. Lincoln: University of Nebraska Press, 1978.

LeFors, Joe. *Wyoming Peace Officer*. Laramie, WY: Laramie Printing, 1953.

Lepore, Jill. "Battleground America: One nation, under the gun." *The New Yorker*, April 23, 2012, 39–47.

Leslie, Anita. *Mr. Frewen of England*. London, UK: Hutchinson, 1966.

———. *The Remarkable Mr. Jerome*. New York: Holt, 1954.

Limerick, Patricia N. *Legacy of Conquest: The Unbroken Past of the American West*. New York: Norton, 1987.

———. "The Adventures of the Frontier in the Twentieth Century." In *The Frontier in American Culture*, ed. James R. Grossman, 67–102. Berkeley: University of California Press, 1994.

Limerick, Patricia Nelson, Clyde A. Milner II, and Charles E. Rankin, eds. *Trails: Toward a New Western History*. Lawrence: University of Kansas Press, 1991.

Livingstone, Donna. *Cowboy Spirit: Guy Weadick and the Calgary Stampede*. Vancouver: Douglas & McIntyre, 1996.

Long, Philip S. *The Great Canadian Range*. Toronto: Ryerson, 1963.

———. *Seventy Years a Cowboy*. Billings, MT: Cypress Books, 1976.

Loo, Tina. *Making Law, Order, and Authority in British Columbia, 1821–1871*. Toronto: University of Toronto Press, 1994.

Lovering, Joseph P. *S. Weir Mitchell*. Boston: Twayne, 1971.

Lukacs, John. *Philadelphians: Patricians and Philistines, 1900–1950*. New York: Farrar Straus Giroux, 1981.

———. "From Camelot to Abilene." *American Heritage* 32, no. 2 (Feb./March 1981): 52–57.

MacEwan, Grant. *Blazing the Old Cattle Trails*. Saskatoon: Modern Press, 1962.

———. *Frederick Haultain: Frontier Statesman of the Canadian Northwest*. Saskatoon: Western Producer Prairie Books, 1985.

———. *John Ware's Cow Country*. Edmonton: Institute of Applied Art. 1960.

———. *Pat Burns: Cattle King*. Saskatoon: Western Producer Prairie Books, 1979.

MacGregor, James G. *Visions of an Ordered Land: The Story of the Dominion Lands Survey*. Saskatoon: Western Producer Prairie Books, 1981.

Macleod, R. C. *The North-West Mounted Police and Law Enforcement, 1873–1905*. Toronto: University of Toronto Press, 1976.

———. "Crime and Criminals in the North-West Territories, 1873–1905." In *The Mounted Police and Prairie Society, 1873–1919*, ed. William M. Baker, 85–99. Regina: Canadian Plains Research Center, 1998.

———. "Law and Order on the Western Canadian Frontier." In *Law for the Elephant, Law for the Beaver*, eds. John McLaren, Hamar Foster, and Chet Orloff, 90–105. Regina: Canadian Plains Research Center, 1992.

———. "The North-West Mounted Police and Minority Groups." In *The Mounted Police and Prairie Society, 1873–1919*, ed. William M. Baker, 119–35. Regina: Canadian Plains Research Center, 1998.

———. "The North-West Mounted Police as Agents of the National Policy, 1873–1905." In *The Prairie West: Historical Readings*, eds. R. Douglas Francis and Howard Palmer, 225–38. Edmonton: University of Alberta Press, 1992.

———, ed. *Lawful Authority: Readings in the History of Criminal Justice in Canada*. Toronto: Copp Clark Pitman, 1988.

Macleod, R. C., and Heather Rollason Driscoll. "Natives, Newspapers and Crime Rates in the North-West Territories, 1878–1885." In *From Rupert's Land to Canada*, eds. Theodore Binnema, Gerhard Enns, and R. C. Macleod, 249–69. Edmonton: University of Alberta Press, 2001.

Macleod, R. C., and Heather Rollason. "Restrain the Lawless Savages: Native Defendants in the Criminal Courts of the North West Territories, 1878–1885." *Journal of Historical Sociology* (June 1997): 157–83.

Macoun, John. *Manitoba and the Great North West*. Guelph, ON: World Publishing, 1882.

Madis, George. *The Winchester Book*. Lancaster, TX: Art and Reference House, 1971.

Majors, Alexander. *Seventy Years on the Frontier*. Lincoln: University of Nebraska Press, 1989.

Manley, Atwood, and Margaret Manley Mangum. *Frederic Remington and the North Country: An Informal Biography of the Artist in the Old West*. New York: E.P. Dutton, 1988.

Markham, George. *Guns of the Wild West: Firearms of the American Frontier*. New York: Stirling, 1991.

Marriott, Harry. *Cariboo Cowboy*. Sidney, BC: Gray's Publishing, 1966.

Martin, Chester. *Dominion Lands Policy*. Toronto: McClelland & Stewart, 1973.

Martin, Roderick. *The North-West Mounted Police and Frontier Justice, 1874–1898*. PhD diss., University of Calgary, 2006.

Martin, Russell. *Cowboy: The Enduring Myth of the Wild West*. New York: Stewart, Tabori & Chang, 1983.

Mather, Ken. *Frontier Cowboys and the Great Divide: Early Ranching in B.C. and Alberta*. Toronto: Heritage House, 2013.

Mavromichalis, Anna-Maria. "Tar and Feathers: The Mounted Police and Frontier Justice." In *The Mounted Police and Prairie Society, 1873–1919*, ed. William M. Baker, 109–16. Regina: Canadian Plains Research Center, 1998.

McClintock, John S. *Pioneer Days in the Black Hills*. Deadwood, SD: J. S. McClintock, 1939.

McCoy, Joseph G. *Cattle Trade of the West and Southwest*. Ann Arbor, MI: University Microfilms, 1966.

McCracken, Harold. *Frederic Remington: Artist of the Old West*. Philadelphia: J. B. Lippincott, 1947.

———. *The Frederic Remington Book: A Pictorial History of the West*. Garden City, NY: Doubleday, 1966.

McCullough, Alan B. "Not an Old Cow-Hand: Fred Stimson and the Bar U Ranch." In *Cowboys, Ranchers, and the Cattle Business: Cross-Border Perspectives on Ranching History*, eds. in Simon Evans, Sarah Carter, and Bill Yeo, 29–41. Calgary: University of Calgary Press, 2000.

McCullough, David. *Mornings on Horseback: The Story of An Extraordinary Family, a Vanishing Way of Life, and the Unique Child Who Became Theodore Roosevelt*. New York: Simon & Schuster, 1981.

McCumber, David. *The Cowboy Way*. New York: Bard, 1999.

McDermott, John D. *Red Cloud's War: The Bozeman Trail, 1866–1868*. Arthur H. Clark, 2010.

McDowell, R. Bruce. *Evolution of the Winchester*. Tacoma, WA: Armory Publications, 1985.

McGrath, Roger D. *Gunfighters, Highwaymen, and Vigilantes: Violence on the Frontier*. Berkeley: University of California Press, 1984.

McKanna, Clare Jr. *Homicide, Race, and Justice in the American West, 1880–1920*. Tuscon: University of Arizona Press, 1997.

McKinnon, J. Agnes. *The Bow River Range*. Calgary: McAra Printing, 1974.

McLaren, John. "The Early British Columbia Judges, the Rule of Law and the 'Chinese Question': The California and Oregon Connection." In *Law For the Elephant, Law For the Beaver: Essays in the Legal History of the North American West*, eds. John McLaren, Hamar Foster, and Chet Orloff, 237–73. Regina: Great Plains Research Center, 1992.

McLaren, John, Hamar Foster, and Chet Orloff, eds. *Law For the Elephant, Law For the Beaver: Essays in the Legal History of the North American West*. Regina: Canadian Plains Research Center, 1992.

McManus, Sheila. *The Line Which Separates: Race, Gender, and the Making of the Alberta–Montana Borderlands*. Lincoln: University of Nebraska Press, 2005.

McMurtry, Larry. *Custer*. New York: Simon & Schuster, 2012

McWilliams, Mary Ellen. *Fort Phil Kearny, Fetterman Battle, Wagon Box Fight*. Sheridan, WY: Fort Phil Kearny/Bozeman Trail Association, n.d.

Meadows, Anne. *Digging Up Butch and Sundance*. Lincoln: University of Nebraska Press, 1996.

Mercer, A. S. *The Banditti of the Plains: Or the Cattlemen's Invasion of Wyoming in 1892*. Norman: University of Oklahoma Press, 1983.

Meyer, Susan E. *America's Great Illustrators*. New York: Abrams, 1978.

Millard, Candice. *The River of Doubt: Theodore Roosevelt's Darkest Journey*. New York: Broadway, 2005.

Miller, David Harry, and Jerome Steffen, eds. *The Frontier: Comparative Studies*. Vol. 1. Norman: University of Oklahoma Press, 1977.

Miller, David Humphries. *Custer's Fall*. New York: Bantam, 1972.

Miller, J. R. *Skyscrapers Hide the Heavens: A History of Indian-White Relations in Canada*. Toronto: University of Toronto Press, 1989.

———, ed. *Sweet Promises: A Reader on Indian-White Relations in Canada*. Toronto: University of Toronto Press, 1991.

Miller, Nyle H., and Joseph W. Snell. *Great Gunfighters of the Kansas Cowtowns, 1867–1886*. Lincoln: University of Nebraska Press, 1963.

Milner, Clyde A. *The Oxford History of the American West*. New York: Oxford University Press, 1994.

Milner, Clyde A., and Carol O'Connor. *As Big as the West: The Pioneer Life of Granville Stuart*. New York: Oxford University Press, 2009.

Milton, John R. *The Novel of the American West*. Lincoln: University of Nebraska Press, 1980.

Moir, J. S., ed. *Character and Circumstance: Essays in Honour of Donald Grant Creighton*. Toronto: Macmillan, 1970.

Moody, Ralph. *Stagecoach West*. New York: Cromwell, 1967.

Morison, Elting E., ed. *The Letters of Theodore Roosevelt*. 8 vols. Cambridge, MA: Harvard University Press, 1951.

Morris, Edmund. *Colonel Roosevelt*. New York: Random House, 2010.

———. *The Rise of Theodore Roosevelt*. New York: Coward, McCann & Geoghagen, 1979.

Morrison, William R. *Showing the Flag: The Mounted Police and Sovereignty in the North, 1894–1925*. Vancouver: UBC Press, 1985.

Mothershead, Harmon S. *The Swan Land and Cattle Company*. Norman: University of Oklahoma Press, 1971.

Mountain Horse, Mike. *My People the Bloods*. Calgary: Glenbow Alberta Institute, 1979.

Mullins, Reubin B. *Pulling Leather: Being the Early Recollections of a Cowboy on the Wyoming Range, 1884–1889*. Glendo, WY: High Plains Press, 1988.

Murphy, William. "The Forgotten Battalion." *Annals of Wyoming* 7, no. 2 (Oct. 1930): 383–401; 7, no. 3 (Jan. 1931): 441–42.

Murray, Robert A. *The Bozeman Trail: Highway of History*. Boulder, CO: Pruett, 1988.

———. *Johnson County: 175 Years of History at the Foot of the Bighorn Mountains*. Buffalo, NY: Buffalo Chamber of Commerce, 1981.

———. *Military Posts in the Powder River Country of Wyoming, 1865–1894*. Lincoln: University of Nebraska Press, 1968.

———. "The Wagon Box Fight: A Centennial Appraisal." *Annals of Wyoming* 39, no. 1 (April 1967): 105–7.

Myles, Sandra L. *Westering Women: The Frontier Experience, 1800–1915*. Albuquerque: University of New Mexico Press, 1982.

Nesbitt, John D. "Owen Wister's Achievement in Literary Tradition." *Western American Literature* (1983): 199–208.

Nicholas, Liza J. *Becoming Western: Stories of Culture and Identity in a Cowboy State*. Lincoln: University of Nebraska Press, 2006.

O'Neal, Bill. *The Johnson County War*. Austin, TX: Eakin Press, 2004.

Osgood, Ernest Staples. *The Day of the Cattlemen*. Chicago: University of Chicago Press, 1929.

Pal, Leslie A. "Between the Sights: Gun Control in Canada and the United States." In *Canada and the United States: Differences that Count*, ed. David M. Thomas. Peterborough, ON: Broadview Press, 2000.

Palmer, Howard. *Patterns of Prejudice: A History of Nativism in Alberta*. Toronto: McClelland & Stewart, 1982.

Parker, Graham. "Canadian Legal Culture." In *Law and Justice in a New Land*, ed. Louis A. Knafla, 3–29. Toronto: Carswell, 1986.

———. "The Origins of the Canadian Criminal Code" in *Essays in the History of Canadian Law*, ed. David H. Flaherty, 249–80. Toronto: Osgoode Society, 1981.

Parker, Watson. *Deadwood: The Golden Years*. Lincoln: University of Nebraska Press, 1981.

Parkman, Francis. *The Oregon Trail*. New York: Lancer Books, 1968.

Parsons, John E., and John S. DuMont. *Firearms in the Custer Battle*. Harrisburg, PA: Stackpole, 1954.

Patterson, Richard. *Butch Cassidy: A Biography*. Lincoln: University of Nebraska Press, 1998.

Patterson, R. M. *The Emperor's Horsemen*. Calgary: private printing, 2007.

Payne, Darwin. *Owen Wister: Chronicler of the West, Gentleman of the East*. Dallas, TX: Southern Methodist University Press, 1985.

———. "Owen Wister Discovers Wyoming." *Persimmon Hill* 12, no. 1 (1982): 23–33.

Peake, Ora B. *The Colorado Range Cattle Industry*. Glendale, CA: Arthur H. Clark, 1937.

Pelzer, Louis. *The Cattleman's Frontier: A Record of the Trans-Mississippi Cattle Industry, 1850–1890*. Glendale, CA: Arthur H. Clark, 1937.

Penrose, Charles Bingham. *Rustler Business*. Buffalo, NY: Jim Gatchell Memorial Museum Press, 2007.

Pense, Mary Lou. *Boswell: The Story of a Frontier Lawman*. Cheyenne: Pioneer Printing, 1978.

Perry, K. E. *Barbed Wire, Barbed Wire Everywhere: The Evolution of Barbed Wire and the Closure of the Great Western Plains*. Kamloops, BC: Goss Publishing, 1997.

Pettipas, Katherine. *Severing the Ties That Bind: Government Repression of Religious Ceremonies on the Prairies*. Winnipeg: University of Manitoba Press, 1994.

Pfeifer, Michael J. *Rough Justice: Lynching and American Society, 1874–1947*. Urbana: University of Illinois Press, 2004.

Philbrick, Nathaniel. *The Last Stand: Custer, Sitting Bull, and the Battle of the Little Bighorn*. New York: Viking, 2010.

Phillips, Jim, Tina Loo, and Susan Lewthwaite, eds. *Crime and Criminal Justice: Essays in the History of Canadian Law*. Toronto: University of Toronto Press for the Osgoode Society for Canadian Legal History, 1994.

Phillips, Paul C. *Granville Stuart, Pioneering in Montana*. Lincoln: University of Nebraska Press, 1977.

Pointer, Larry. *In Search of Butch Cassidy*. Norman: University of Oklahoma Press, 1977.

Post, C. C. *Ten Years a Cowboy*. Chicago: Rhodes & McLure, 1898.

Powder River Heritage Committee. *Our Powder River Heritage*. Cheyenne: Frontier Printing, 1982.

Prassel, Frank Richard. *The Western Peace Officer*. Norman: University of Oklahoma Press, 1972.

Raine, William M. *Guns of the Frontier*. Boston: Houghton Mifflin, 1940.

Rainbolt, Jo. *The Last Cowboy: Twilight Era of the Horseback Cowhand, 1900-1940*. Helena, MT: America and World Graphic Publications, 1992.

Raper, Arthur F. *The Tragedy of Lynching*. New York: Dover, 1970.

Rasporich, A. W., and Henry Klassen, eds. *Frontier Calgary, 1875-1914*. Calgary: McClelland & Stewart West, 1975.

Reasoner, James. *Draw: The Greatest Gunfights of the American West*. New York: Berkley, 2003.

Rees, Tony. *Polo, The Galloping Game: An Illustrated History of Polo in Western Canada*. Cochrane, AB: Western Heritage Centre Society, 2000.

Remington, Frederic. *Pony Tracks*. New York: Harper & Brothers, 1895.

———. *Crooked Trails*. New York: Harper & Brothers, 1898.

———. *Sundown Laflare*. New York: Harper, 1899.

———. *Men With the Bark On*. New York: Harper & Brothers, 1900.

———. *John Ermine of the Yellowstone*. New York: Macmillan, 1902.

———. *The Way of the Indian*. London: Gay and Bird, 1906.

———. *Frederic Remington's Own West*. Ed. Harold McCracken. London, UK: Failsham, 1960.

———. *The Collected Writings of Frederic Remington*. Eds. Peggy Samuels and Harold Samuels. Garden City, NY: Doubleday, 1979.

Rhodes, Eugene Manlove. *Stepsons of the Light*. Norman: University of Oklahoma Press, 1969.

Richtofen, Walter, Baron von. *Cattle Raising on the Plains of North America*. New York: Appleton, 1885.

Ricketts, W. P. *50 Years in the Saddle*. Sheridan, WY: Star Publishing, 1942.

Rickey, Don Jr. *Forty Miles a Day on Beans and Hay: The Enlisted Soldier Fighting the Indian Wars*. Norman: University of Oklahoma Press, 1963.

Rifkin, Jeremy. *Beyond Beef: The Rise and Fall of the Cattle Culture*. New York: Dutton, 1992.

Riley, Glenda. *Wild Women of the Old West*. Golden, CO: Fulcrum, 2003.

Robbins, Roy M. "Preemption – a Frontier Triumph." In *Essays on the History of the American West*, ed. Stephen Salsbury, 327–41. New York: Holt Rinehart, 1975.

Robinson, Forrester G. "The Roosevelt-Wister Connection: Some Notes on the West and the Uses of History." *Western American Literature* 14 (1979): 95–114.

Rodham, Paul. *The Far West and the Great Plains in Transition, 1859–1900*. Norman: University of Oklahoma Press, 1998.

Rollins, Philip A. *The Cowboy: His Character, His Equipment and His Part in the Development of the West*. New York: Scribner, 1922.

Roosevelt, Theodore. *Ranch Life and the Hunting Trail*. Lincoln: University of Nebraska Press, 1983. First published 1888.

———. *The Winning of the West*. 2 vols. New York: Scribner's, 1926.

———. "Ranch Life in the Far West: In the Cattle Country." *The Century*, Feb. 1888.

———. "Ranch Life in the Far West: The Home Ranch." *The Century*, March 1888.

———. "Ranch Life in the Far West: The Round-Up." *The Century*, April 1888.

———. "Buffalo Hunting." *St. Nicholas Magazine*, Dec. 1889.

———. "Hunting on the Little Missouri." *Saturday Evening Post*, April 2, 1898.

———. "An Appreciation of Frederic Remington." *Pearson's Magazine*, Oct. 1907.

Rosa, Joseph G. *The Gunfighter: Man or Myth*. Norman: University of Oklahoma Press, 1969.

Rosenbaum, H. Jon, and Peter S. Sederberg, eds. *Vigilante Politics*. Philadelphia: University of Pennsylvania Press, 1976.

Rosenburg, Bruce A. *The Code of the West*. Bloomington: Indiana University Press, 1982.

———. *Custer and the Epic of Defeat*. State College: Penn State University Press, 1974.

Ross, J. I., ed. *Violence in Canada: Sociopolitical Perspectives*. Oxford, UK: Oxford University Press, 1995.

Roth, Mitchell. *Reading the American West: Primary Source Readings in American History*. New York: Longman, 1999.

Rubottom, Helena Thomas. *Red Walls and Homesteads*. Kaycee, WY: Margaret Brock Hanson, 1987.

Rush, N. Orwin. *Frederic Remington and Owen Wister: The Story of a Friendship, 1893–1909*. Tallahassee: Florida State University Press, 1961.

Rushdy, Ashraf H. A. *American Lynching*. New Haven: Yale University Press, 2012.

Russell, Andy. *The Canadian Cowboy*. Toronto: McClelland & Stewart, 1993.

Russell, Charles M. *Trails Plowed Under: Stories of the Old West*. New York: Doubleday, 1927.

Russell, Don. *The Life of Hon. William F. Cody, Known as Buffalo Bill*. Lincoln: University of Nebraska Press, 1978.

———. *The Lives and Legends of Buffalo Bill*. Norman: University of Oklahoma Press, 1960.

———. "Captain Charles King." *The Westerners New York Brand Book* 4, no. 2 (1957): 39–40.

Russell, Martin. *Cowboy: The Enduring Myth of the Wild West*. New York: Stewart, Tabori & Chang, 1983.

Salsbury, Stephen, ed. *Essays on the History of the American West*. New York: Holt Rinehart, 1975.

Samuels, Peggy, and Harold Samuels. *Frederic Remington: A Biography*. Austin: University of Texas Press, 1982.

———, eds. *The Collected Writings of Frederic Remington*. Garden City, NY: Doubleday, 1979.

Sandoz, Mari. *The Battle of the Little Big Horn*. Lincoln: University of Nebraska Press, 1978.

———. *The Buffalo Hunters*. Lincoln: University of Nebraska Press, 1954.

———. *The Cattlemen: From the Rio Grande Across the Far Marias*. New York: Hastings House, 1958.

———. *Love Song To the Plains: A Salute to the Earth and Sky and People Who Made the History of the Great Plains*. New York: Harper and Brothers, 1961.

———. "Captain Charles King as Portrayer of the West." *The Westerners New York Posse Brand Book* 2, no. 4 (1955): 84.

Savage, William W. Jr. *The Cowboy Hero: His Image in American History and Culture*. Norman: University of Oklahoma Press, 1979.

———, ed. *Cowboy Life: Reconstructing an American Myth*. Norman: University of Oklahoma Press, 1975.

Schama, Simon. *The American Future: A History*. Toronto: Penguin, 2008.

Scheiber, Harry N. *Abbot-Downing and the Concord Coach*. Concord: New Hampshire Historical Society, 1989.

Schoenberger, Dale T. *The Gunfighters*. Caldwell, ID: Caxton Printers, 1971.

Scott, Douglas D., and Richard A. Fox Jr. *Archeological Insights into the Custer Battle*. Norman: University of Oklahoma Press, 1987.

Scott, Douglas D., Richard A. Fox, Melissa A. Connor, and Dick Harmon. *Archeological Perspectives on the Battle of the Little Bighorn*. Norman: University of Oklahoma Press, 1989.

Seelye, John. "When West Was Wister." *New Republic*, September 2, 1972.

Seidman, Laurence Ivan. *Once in the Saddle: The Cowboy's Frontier, 1866–1896*. New York: Knopf, 1973.

Sharp, Paul F. *Whoop-Up Country: The Canadian–American West, 1865–1885*. Norman: University of Oklahoma Press, 1973.

Sheppard, Bert. *Just About Nothing*. Calgary: McAra Printing, 1977.

———. "The Cattle and the Cowmen." In *Leaves From the Medicine Tree*, ed. High River Pioneers' and Old Timers' Association, 249–79. Lethbridge, AB: *Lethbridge Herald*, 1960.

Sheridan, Clare. *Naked Truth*. New York: Blue Ribbon Books, 1928.

Shirley, Glen. *Law West of Fort Smith: Frontier Justice in the Indian Territory, 1834–1896*. New York: Collier, 1961.

Silva, Lee A. *Wyatt Earp: A Biography of a Legend: The Cowtown Years*. Santa Ana, CA: Graphic Publishers, 2002.

Siringo, Charles A. *A Texas Cowboy*. Lincoln: University of Nebraska Press, 1966.

Slatta, Richard W. *Comparing Cowboys and Frontiers*. Norman: University of Oklahoma Press, 1997.

———. *Cowboys of the Americas*. New Haven, CT: Yale University Press, 1990.

Slotkin, Richard. *The Fatal Environment: The Myth of the Frontier in the Age of Industrialization, 1800–1892*. New York: Atheneum, 1985.

———. *Gunfighter Nation: The Myth of the Frontier in Twentieth-Century America*. Norman: University of Oklahoma Press, 1998.

———. *Regeneration Through Violence: The Mythology of the American Frontier, 1600–1860*. Middletown, CT: Wesleyan University Press, 1973.

Smith, Helena Huntington. *The War on Powder River: The History of an Insurrection*. Lincoln: University of Nebraska Press, 1967.

Smith, Henry Nash. *Virgin Land: The American West as Symbol and Myth*. New York: Vintage, 1957.

Smith, Winston. *The Sharps Rifle: Its History, Development and Operation*. New York: Morrow, 1943.

Sprague, Marshall. *A Gallery of Dudes*. Boston: Little, Brown, 1967.

Spring, Agnes Wright. *The Cheyenne and Black Hills Stage and Express Routes*. Lincoln: University of Nebraska Press, 1948.

———. *The Cheyenne Club: Mecca of the Aristocrats of the Old Time Cattle Range*. Kansas City: Ornduff, 1961.

———. *Seventy Years: A Panoramic History of the Wyoming Stock Growers Association*. Cheyenne: Wyoming Stock Growers Association, 1943.

Springett, Evelyn Galt. *For My Children's Children*. Montreal: Unity Press, 1937.

Starrs, Paul F. *Let the Cowboy Ride: Cattle Ranching in the West*. Baltimore: Johns Hopkins University Press, 1998.

Steckmesser, Kent L. *The Western Hero in History and Legend*. Norman: University of Oklahoma Press, 1965.

Steffen, Jerome O. *The American West: New Perspectives, New Dimensions*. Norman: University of Oklahoma Press, 1979.

Stegner, Wallace. *Beyond the Hundredth Meridian: John Wesley Powell and the Second Opening of the American West*. Boston: Houghton Mifflin, 1954.

———. *Wolf Willow: A History, Story, and a Memory of the Last Plains Frontier*. New York: Viking, 1955.

———. "Owen Wister: Creator of the Cowboy Myth." *American West* 21, no. 1 (Jan./Feb. 1984): 48–52.

Steiner, Stan. *The Ranchers: A Book of Generations*. Norman: University of Oklahoma Press, 1980.

Stocken, H. W. Gibbon. *Among the Blackfoot and Sarcee*. Calgary: Glenbow Museum, 1976.

Stokes, Fanny Kemble Wister. *My Father Owen Wister: And Ten Letters Written by Owen Wister to his Mother during his First Trip to Wyoming in 1885*. Laramie: Wyoming Literary Association, 1952.

———. *Owen Wister Out West: His Journals and Letters*. Lincoln: University of Nebraska Press, 1972.

Strahorn, Robert. *The Handbook of Wyoming and Guide to the Black Hills and the Big Horn Region for Citizen, Immigrant and Tourist*. Cheyenne, 1887.

Strange, T. B. *Gunner Jingo's Jubilee*. Toronto: J. McQueen, 1893.

Stuart, Granville. *Forty Years on the Frontier*. Lincoln: University of Nebraska Press, 2004.

———. *Pioneering in Montana: The Making of a State, 1864–1887*. Lincoln: University of Nebraska Press, 1977.

Symons, R. D. *Where the Wagon Led: One Man's Memories of the Cowboy's Life in the Old West*. Toronto: Doubleday, 1973.

Talent, Annie. *The Black Hills or Last Hunting Grounds of the Dakotahs*. Sioux Falls, SD: Brevett Press, 1974.

Taylor, L., and Ingrid Maar. *The American Cowboy*. Washington, DC: Library of Congress, 1983.

Tefertiller, Casey. *Wyatt Earp: The Life Behind the Legend*. New York: John Wiley, 1997.

Thomas, David M., ed. *Canada and the United States: Differences that Count*. Peterborough, ON: Broadview Press, 2000.

Thomas, Evan. *The War Lovers: Roosevelt, Lodge, Hearst, and the Rush to Empire, 1898*. New York: Little, Brown, 2010.

Thomas, Lewis G. *Ranchers' Legacy: Alberta Essays by Lewis G. Thomas*. Ed. Patrick A. Dunae. Edmonton: University of Alberta Press, 1986.

Thomas, Lewis Herbert. *The Struggle for Responsible Government in the North-West Territories, 1870-1897*. Toronto: University of Toronto Press, 1978.

Thompson, Bob. *Born on a Mountaintop: On the Road with Davy Crockett and the Ghosts of the Wild Frontier*. New York: Crown Trade Group, 2012.

Thompson, John Herd. *Forging the Prairie West*. Toronto: Oxford University Press, 1998.

Thorner, Thomas. "The Incidence of Crime in Southern Alberta." In *Law and Society in Canada in Historical Perspective*, eds. D. J. Bercuson and L. A. Knafla, 53-88. University of Calgary Studies in History, no. 2. Calgary: University of Calgary, 1979.

———. "The Not-So-Peaceable Kingdom – Crime and Criminal Justice in Frontier Calgary." In *Frontier Calgary: Town, City and Region, 1875-1914*, eds. A. W. Rasporich and Henry Klassen, 100-13. Calgary: McClelland and Stewart West, 1975.

Thorner, T., and N. Watson. "Patterns of Prairie Crime: Calgary, 1875-1939." In *Crime and Criminal Justice in Europe and Canada*, ed. Louis A. Knafla, 219-55. Waterloo, ON: Wilfrid Laurier University Press, 1981.

Tompkins, Jane. *West of Everything: The Inner Life of the Western*. New York: Oxford University Press, 1992.

Trachtman, Paul. *The Gunfighters*. New York: Time-Life Books, 1974.

Turner, Frederick Jackson. "The Significance of the Frontier in American History." In *Annual Report of the American Historical Association for the Year 1893*, 199-277. Washington, DC: Government Printing Office, 1894.

Unrah, John D. *The Plains Across: The Overland Emigrants and the Trans-Mississippi West, 1840-1860*. Urbana: University of Illinois Press, 1979.

Utley, Robert M. *Cavalier in Buckskin: George Armstrong Custer and the Western Military Frontier*. Norman: University of Oklahoma Press, 1988.

———. *High Noon in Lincoln*. Norman: University of Oklahoma Press, 1991.

———. *The Indian Frontier of the American West, 1846-1890*. Albuquerque: University of New Mexico Press, 1984.

———. *The Lance and the Shield: The Life and Times of Sitting Bull*. New York: Ballantine, 1993.

———. *Lone Star Justice: The First Century of the Texas Rangers*. New York: Berkley, 2002.

Valentine, A. C. *Vigilante Justice*. New York: Reynal, 1956.

Vestal, Stanley. *Dodge City: Queen of the Cowtowns*. London: Nevill, 1955.

Vorpahl, Ben Merchant. *Frederic Remington and the West*. Austin: University of Texas Press, 1978.

———. *My Dear Wister: The Frederic Remington–Owen Wister Letters*. Palo Alto, CA: American West Publishing, 1973.

———. "Henry James and Owen Wister: A Note On the Western." *American Quarterly* 12 (Fall 1960): 358–66.

Walden, Keith. *Visions of Order*. Toronto: Butterworth, 1982.

Waldman, Michael. *The Second Amendment: A Biography*. New York: Simon & Schuster, 2014.

Walker, Don D., ed. *Clio's Cowboy: Studies in the Historiography of the Cattle Trade*. Lincoln: University of Nebraska Press, 1981.

———. "Wister, Roosevelt and James: A Note on the Western." *American Quarterly* 12 (1960): 358–66.

Wallace, Jim. *Double Duty: The Decisive First Decade of the North West Mounted Police*. Winnipeg: Bunker to Bunker, 1997.

Warkentin, John, ed. *The Western Interior of Canada*. Toronto: McClelland & Stewart, 1964.

Warren, Louis S. *Buffalo Bill's America: William Cody and the Wild West Show*. New York: Knopf, 2005.

Watson, John. *The Real Virginian*. Tucson, AZ: Western Lore Press, 1989.

Webb, Walter Prescott. *The Great Plains*. Boston: Ginn, 1931.

———. *The Texas Rangers*. Austin: University of Texas Press, 1993.

Wells-Barnett, Ida B. *On Lynchings*. Amherst, NY: Humanity Books, 2002.

Werner, Fred H. *The Dull Knife Battle*. Greeley, CO: Werner Publications, 1981.

West, Trevor. *Horace Plunkett: Co-operation and Politics, an Irish Biography*. Washington, DC: Catholic University of America Press, 1986.

White, G. Edward. *The Eastern Establishment and the Western Experience: The West of Frederic Remington, Theodore Roosevelt, and Owen Wister*. New Haven, CT: Yale University Press, 1968.

White, Richard. *"It's Your Misfortune and None of My Own": A New History of the American West*. Norman: University of Oklahoma Press, 1991.

———. "Frederick Jackson Turner and Buffalo Bill." In *The Frontier in American Culture*, ed. James R. Grossman, 7–65. Berkeley: University of California Press, 1994.

Williamson, Joel. *A Rage For Order: Black/White Relations in the American South Since Emancipation*. New York: Oxford University Press, 1986.

Winkler, Adam. *Gunfight: The Battle over the Right to Bear Arms in America*. New York: Norton, 2011.

Wister, Owen. *Owen Wister Out West: His Journals and Letters*. Ed. Fanny Kemble Wister. Chicago: University of Chicago Press, 1958.

———. *Owen Wister's West: Selected Articles*. Ed. Robert Murray Davis. Albuquerque: University of New Mexico Press, 1987.

———. *The West of Owen Wister: Selected Short Stories*. Ed. Robert L. Hough. Lincoln: University of Nebraska Press, 1972.

———. *Roosevelt: The Story of a Friendship, 1880–1919*. New York: Macmillan, 1930.

———. "Chalkeye." *American West* 21 (January–February 1984): 37–52. Wister's unfinished manuscript published posthumously.

Wister, Fanny Kemble. *That I May Tell You: Journals and Letters of the Owen Wister Family*. Wayne, PA: Haverford House, 1979.

Woods, Lawrence Milton. *British Gentlemen in the Wild West: The Era of the Intensely English Cowboy*. New York: Free Press, 1989.

———. *Horace Plunkett in America: An Irish Aristocrat on the Wyoming Range*. Norman, OK: Arthur H. Clark, 2010.

———. *Moreton Frewen's Western Adventures*. Boulder, CO: Roberts Rinehart, 1993.

———. *The Wyoming Country before Statehood*. Worland, WY: Worland Press, 1971.

Woodward, Art. "More of Captain Charles King – A Defense." *The Westerners New York Posse Brand Book* 3, no. 1 (1956): 13–14.

Woolcott, Alexander. "Wisteria." *The New Yorker* 6 (Aug. 30, 1930): 30.

Worcester, Don. *The Chisholm Trail: High Road of the Cattle Kingdom*. Lincoln: University of Nebraska Press, 1981.

Wunder, John R. "Anti-Chinese Violence in the American West." In *Law For the Elephant, Law For the Beaver: Essays in the Legal History of the North American West*, eds. John McLaren, Hamar Foster, and Chet Orloff, 212–36. Regina: Canadian Plains Research Center, 1992.

Wyatt-Brown, Bertram. *Honor and Violence in the Old South*. New York: Oxford University Press, 1986.

Wylder, Delbert E. *Emerson Hough*. Twayne United States Authors' Series, no. 397. Boston: Twayne, 1981.

Index

A

A Decent, Orderly Lynching, 141, 144
A Straight Deal, 310
A Wise Man's Son, 70
Adams, Andy, 112, 309, 311
Age of Reform, The, 281
Alberta, English settlers in, 254
Alden, Henry Mills, 275, 277
Alexis, Grand Duke, visit to the West, 65, 100
Allen, Frederick, 141, 144–45
Allison Commission (1875), 50
American Gun, 16
American Historical Review, 310
Andrews, D.H., 202
Angus, Red, 135, 139–40, 177
Annie Get Your Gun, 77
Archeological Insights into the Custer Battle, 105
As For Me and My House, 256
Atlantic Monthly, 277
Autry, Gene, Cowboy Commandments, 304
Averell, James, 166

B

Bailyn, Bernard, 18
Bar U and Canadian Ranching History, The, 236
Bar U ranch, 201–3
Barber, Amos, 147, 148
Bard, Floyd, 220
Barsh, Russell, 64
Bass, Harry, 132
Bass, Sam, 50, 324
Battle of Adobe Walls, 39

Battle of Rosebud Creek, 100
Battle of the Little Big Horn, 68
Beach, Sumner, 163, 164
Beahen, William, 246
Bear River Massacre, 95
Beaver Heart, 75
Beef Bonanza: or How to Get Rich on the Plains, 120
Behan, Johnny, 146
Bell, William, 245
Belmont, August, 65
Bennett, James Gordon, Jr., 65
Benton, Thomas Hart, 285
Betke, Carl, 223
Big Horn Sentinel, 137
Big Nose George, 86
Bill C-68 (Canada), 27
Bill, Persimmon, 50
Billy the Kid, xiii, 11, 289
birch bark, range in Canada, significance of, 211
Black Hills or Last Hunting Grounds of the Dakotahs, The, 47
Black Hills, discovery of gold (1875), 45–48
Blackburn, Dunc, 51
Bleeding Kansas, 62
Boer War, demand for horses in, 260
Bonheur, Rosa, 81
Boone and Crockett Club, 281, 285
Boone, Daniel, 58, 179, 282
Boswell, Nat, xvi, 86
Bozeman Trail, 94, 100–101, 110, 140
Bozeman, John, 94
Brado, Edward, 263

Brannan, 164
Bray, Kingsley, 97
Breen, David, 222, 234–36
Brinkley, Douglas, 283
Brisbin, J. S., 120
British North American Act, Canada (1867), 25
Brooks, Billy, 41
Brown, Dee, 98
Brown, R. Blake, 222
Brown, Richard Maxwell, 10, 11, 14
Bryan, Pete, 184
Buck, Dan, 133
Buffalo Bill: The King of the Border Men, 67
Buffalo Bill's Wild West and Congress of Rough Riders of the World, xii, 61, 63, 65, 68, 72, 76–81, 83–84, 119, 187, 220, 257, 259, 267, 288–89
buffalo
   extermination of in Canada, 3
   extermination of in USA, 64
   hides, demand for, 63
   hunt, 64
   hunt, at Dodge City, 41
Bull, Frank (White Clay George), 173
Bunch, Willow, 248
Buntline, Ned. *See* Edward Zane Carroll Judson
Burt, Struthers, 306
Butch Cassidy and the Sundance Kid, 133
Butler, Pierce, 267
Butters, Donna, xiv

C

Calgary Herald, 238–39, 244, 248–50
Calgary Stampede, American influence in, 257
Campaigning with Crook, 74
Campbell, Malcolm, 162
Canadian Cowboy, The, 92
Canadian
   frontier, not lawless, 25
   National Policy, Western settlement, 214
   ranching frontier, British presence in, 209
   ranching policy, 230
Cannary, Jane "Calamity," 53
Canton, Frank (Joe Horner), 139
Carey, Senator Joseph M., 147
Carlyle, Frank, 247

Carmack, George, 227
Carr, General, 75, 76
Carrington, Colonel Henry B., 95, 97, 100
Carson, Kit, 61
Casey, Robert, 222
Cassidy, Butch (George Leroy Parker), xii, 12, 128, 133–34
Cather, Willa, 311
cattle
   drives, 36–37
   rustling, epidemic of by 1887, 135
   stampedes, 37
Cattle Grower's Association of America, 136
Caven, Henry, 220
Cawelti, John, 14
Century Magazine, 279–80
Century of Criminal Law, 221
Chadbourn, J.H., 13
Chambers, Lou, 256
Champion, Nate, 148
Chapman, John Jay, 156
Chapman, Tommy, 316
Cheyenne Club, 125, 154, 165
Cheyenne Daily Leader, 53, 74
Cheyenne Daily Sun, 86
Cheyenne–Black Hills Trail, 49
Chicago Evening Herald, 65
Chicago Tribune, 171
Chisholm Trail, 40
Chivington, Colonel John M., 95
Choate, Julian E., 55
Civil War
   effect on settlement of the West, 9
   influence on Johnson family, 32
Clark, Walter Van Tilburg, 145, 171, 311
Clarkson, Bob, 333
Claus, Frederic, 107
Clay, John, 118, 120–21, 132, 137–38, 140, 147, 149, 162
Cleveland, President Grover, 136
Coates, Ken, 228
Cochrane, Dave, 235
Cochrane, Matthew H., 230, 231, 234
Code of Honour, 14
Code of the West, 4, 9, 24, 55
Cody, William F (Buffalo Bill), xii, xv–xvi, 38, 59, 61–84, 98–99, 119, 257, 259, 288–90
   "first scalp for Custer," 71–72, 81
   "inverterate liar," 73

Congressional Medal of Honor, awarded to, 63
   Pony Express, riding for, 63
   Springfield rifle "Lucretia Borgia," 64
Cody, Wyoming, 83
Cole, Thad, 139
Common Sense, 170
Comstock, William, 64, 76
Concord coaches, 51
Connor, General Patrick, 95
Connor, Ralph, 15
Cook, James, 38
Cooper, Gary, xii, 304
Cosmopolitan, 277
Cowan, Roy, 198, 200
cowboys
   "America's hope for the future," 184
   Anglo-Saxon racial characteristics of, 281
   frontier image of, 112
Cowboys of the Americas, 110, 297
Cowboys, Gentlemen, and Cattle Thieves, 242, 243
Crazy Horse, 96, 101
Creighton, Donald, 212
criminal law, American, 5
Critchley, Harry, 260
Crook, General George, 100, 109, 159
Cross, A. E., 198
Cross, Jim, 321
Crown land, concept of, 231
Cunningham, Monte, 174, 200
Cunninghame Graham, Robert, 316
Custer, George Armstrong, 46, 66, 76
   at Little Bighorn, 101
   Battle of Gettysburg, in, 76
   Democratic National Convention, influence of, 76
   overconfidence of, 101

D

d'Eyncourt, Captain, 260
Dalton gang, 139
Dangerous River, 328
Darwin, Charles, 297
   social Darwinism, 286
Davis, John W., 147
Dawson City, crime in, 227
de Winton, Sir Francis, 234
Deadwood Dick dime novels, 57
Deadwood, South Dakota, 52–55, 324
   lynchings in, 54

Dean-Freeman, Billy, 323
Deane, R. Burton, 245
DeArment, Robert, 56
DeBarthe, Joe, 137
Dempsey, Hugh, 222, 236, 242, 246
Desert Land Act (1877), 123, 163–64
Dimsdale, Thomas J., 166
Dobie, J. Frank, 40
Dodge City
   crime in, 42
   Johnson's arrival in, 40
   southern cowboys and violence in, 43
Dodge, Col. Richard, 41
Dodge, Theodore, 316
Donahue, Cornelius "Lame Johnny," 53
Donahue, Deborah, 122
Donaldson, James, 245
Done in the Open, 308
Drago, Harry Sinclair, 10
Driscoll, Heather Rollason, 238, 239, 240, 241
Drummond, Jim, 182, 190, 275
Duggan, Sam, 86
Duke, Dean, 183
Dull Knife Battle, 110
Dutch Charley, 54, 57, 86–87
Duty to Retreat, 2, 4. *See also* No Duty to Retreat
Dyer, Gwynne, 22
Dykstra, Robert, 10

E

Early Days, 309
Earp, Virgil, 146
Earp, Wyatt, xii, 11, 42, 55, 134
Economist, and gun control, 21
Effingham, 92
Eisenhower, President Dwight, 55
Elofson, Warren, 144–45, 237, 242, 243, 244, 246
English, Tom, 7
Erickson, Lesley, 238, 240, 241
Ernst, Donna, 132
Evans, Simon, 232, 236

F

Fares, W. H., 198, 207, 265
Federenko, Nicolai, xii
Fetterman massacre, 110

Fetterman, Captain W.J., 96
Fifty Years on the Old Frontier, 38
Firearms Freedom Act, Montana, 19
Flyspeck Billy. *See* Fowler, James
folk mythology, western, 77
Foran, Max, 232, 236
Forgey, George, 318, 319
Fort C.F. Smith, 101
Fort Hood killings, 20
Fort Phil Kearny, 101
Forty Years on the Frontier, 144
Foster, Martha Lucretia, 31
Fowler, James "Flyspeck Billy," 56–57
Fox, Richard A. Jr., 105
Franz, Joe B., 10, 55
Freifeld, Sidney, xi
Fremont, John C., 146, 285
Frewen
   76 Ranch, 110, 126–27
   Moreton, 89–90, 113, 168–69, 195, 197
   Richard, 89–90, 196
Friedland, Martin, 27, 221
Frink, Maurice, 112
Frontier in American History, The, 288
frontier law, influence on United States development, 28
Fuller, G. J., 265
Furlow, Will, 34
Furness, Walter, 273

G

Gall, 101
Garrett, Pat, 129
Gavigan, Shelley, 240, 241
George, White Clay (Bull, Frank), 173, 175, 179, 191
Ghost Dance, 82, 224
Gibson, Guy, 325
Gibson, Samuel, 103, 107
Gilje, Paul, 171
Gillies, Charles, 245
Glafcke, Herman, 53
Globe and Mail, 21
Glock, handgun of choice, 19
Goddard, G. E., 319
Gohmert, Congressman Louie, 22
Golden Age of the Canadian Cowboy, The, 222, 236, 246
Goodnight, Charles, 35, 114
Gordon, Charles W. *See* Connor, Ralph

Gordon, J. T., 207
government authority, dislike of in America, 6
Graburn, Marmaduke, 243
Grant, President Ulysses S., 98
Graybill, Andrew, 253
Great American Desert, 91
Great Plains, destruction of by over grazing, 124
Great Plains, The, 23
Green, Helen Clark, 184
Green, Lorne, xi
Grimes, Leon "Curly," 58
Gromyko, Andrei, xii
guns
   control of, in Canada, 27
   Firearms Freedom Act, Montana, 19
   Glock, handgun of choice, 19
   gun culture, American, 2, 17
   gun culture, Canadian, 2
   gun culture, media manipulation of, 19
   gun laws, in Britain, Australia, South Africa and Canada, and murder rate, 22
   gun ownership, in United States, rate of, 9, 16
   handgun legislation, in Canada, 26, 222
   handgun murder rate, United States, 16
   handgun registry, national, in Canada, 26
Gunfighter Nation, 14
Gunfighters, Highwaymen and Vigilantes: Violence on the Frontier, 10
gunfighters, professional, 11

H

Hadsell, Donell, 165
Hamilton, Thomas, 22
Hardisty, Richard, 315
Hare, Sergeant, 245
Harney, William S., 159
Harper's New Monthly Magazine, 275, 277–80, 291, 300
Harris, Dr. William, 148
Harrison, Dick, 14
Harrison, President Benjamin, 82, 149
Harvard University, 153, 184, 269–70, 301–2
Hat Creek Gang, 51
Hatfield, H. M., 224
Helena Daily Herald, 142

Heller vs. District of Columbia, Supreme Court, 18
Henry, Catharine, 92
Henry, Mike, 159
Herchmer, Commissioner Lawrence, 225, 245
Hesse, Fred, 89, 113, 118, 127, 134, 189, 195, 198, 263
Hickok, "Wild" Bill, xi, 11, 55, 61, 63, 67, 68
High Noon, xii
Hill, Alexander Stavely, 234
Hindman, Jesse, 222
Historical World of Frederick Jackson Turner, The, 288
Hofstadter, Richard, 10, 17, 281
Hole-in-the-Wall Gang, 128–29, 134
Holliday, Alexander, 31
Holliday, John Henry "Doc," 42, 146
Holliday, Patricia Quarles, 31
Hollon, Eugene, 10, 55
Holmes, James Eagan, 20
Homestead Act (1862), 122, 137
Hopkins, Monica, 256, 257
Horn, Tom, 151
Horrall, Stan, 246
Horse Creek Treaty, 94
horse
    key to cowboy life, 112
    stealing, in Canadian West, 224
Horses of the Conquest, 316
Hosmer, Hezekiah, 142
Hough, Emerson, 138
Howells, William Dean, 270
Hudson's Bay Company, 213
Hunger, Horses, and Government Men, 240
hunting
    culture, in the West, 219
    culture, United States, 17
Hunting Trips of a Ranchman, 283, 284

I

immigrants
    Chinese, mistreatment of, 7, 8
    treatment of, in American West, 7
import duty, on cattle brought into Canada, 196
In Search of Butch Cassidy, 134
Indian Removal Act of 1830, 6
Ingraham, Prentiss, 63, 67
Ings, Fred, 220

Invaders of Johnson County, members of, 150
Ironside, Robert, 207
Irvine, W.C., 148
Irving, Washington, 155

J

Jackson, President Andrew, 6
Jacobs, Wilbur, 288
James, Henry, 158, 267, 294, 303, 311
James, Jesse, 127, 289, 315
Jerome, Clara, 116–117
Jimmyjohn Boss and Other Stories, The, 301
Johnson County War, 14, 121, 134–40, 170, 290, 322
Johnson, Elizabeth Hunter, 31
Johnson, Everett Cyril, xi–xiii, xiv, xvi, 1–3, 12, 28, 29, 31, 33–43, 45, 48–52, 54–59, 61–62, 67–68, 72–74, 77, 84–87, 89–92, 98–100, 110, 113, 116, 119, 127–29, 131–32, 134–36, 151, 153–54, 156, 158–61, 166–69, 172–75, 177–80, 182, 189–93, 195–202, 204–5, 207–9, 221, 229, 235–36, 242, 253, 259–65, 272, 275, 278–79, 290, 301, 309, 312–34
    and Wister, 193
    as horse trainer, 262
    copy of *The Virginian* inscribed to, 265
    early education, 33
    establishes butcher shop, 315
    family settlement in Minnesota, 32
    forebears, 31–32
    grandmother's influence on, 34
    in Alberta, 195
    Indian wars, and Johnson's father, 33
    in Europe, 260
    last years, 331–34
    life in Rochester, Minnesota, 45
    opinion of Billy the Kid, 129
Johnson, George Poindexter, 31, 48
Johnson, Jean, xiv, xv, 92, 100, 109, 132, 135, 166–67, 193, 199–201, 208, 265, 278, 313, 315, 318, 320–34
Johnson, Laurie, xiv, 199–201, 232, 260–63, 265, 313, 316, 318–26, 328, 330
Johnson, Mary, 260
Johnson, Thomas William, 31
Johnson, William, 31
Jones, Frank, 247

Jordan, Philip, 10, 220
Jordan, Terry, 111
Judson, Edward Zane Carroll (Ned Buntline), 67

K

Kelly, L.V., 264
Kemble, Fanny, 267
Kerfoot, Archie, 321, 323
Kincaid Act (1912), 122
King, Charles, 73
Kipling, Rudyard, 277, 286
    "white man's burden," 296
gold rush, 226
Knafla, Louis, 237
Ku Klux Klan, xiii, 14
Kyle, Chris, 16

L

L'Amour, Louis, 304
LaDow, Beth, 247
Lady Baltimore, 186–87, 299, 305–6, 310
Lake, Stuart, 55–56
Lane, George, 202
Langtry, Lillie, 114
Lanza, Adam, 21
LaPierre, Wayne, 21
Laurier, Sir Wilfrid, 264
Lawrence, John, 174
Laycock, Joe, 205
Laycock, Maggie, 259
Legacy of Conquest, The, 289
Legare, Jean Louis, 248
Legend of Sleepy Hollow, The, 155
Leuch, Dutch Henry, 247
Limerick, Patricia Nelson, 289
Lin McLean, 301
Lister-Kaye, Sir John, 198
Liszt, Franz, 270
Little Bighorn, 101
Little Wolf, 101
Littman, Corporal Max, 107
Llewellyn, William, 58
Locker, Bill, 163
Lodge, Henry Cabot, 286, 309
Londale, Claude, 323
Longabaugh, Harry (Sundance Kid), xii, xv, 12, 128–29, 131–34, 205
Longly, Bill, 52

Lougheed, James, 315
Lougheed, Peter, 315
Lucas, Alexander, 7
Lukacs, John, 305
Lusk, Tom, 198
Lynch, Tom, 204
lynching, 13, 300, 306
    beginnings of, 171
    in Johnson Country, 138–40
    in Montana, 145
    in West and South, 171
    lack of in Canadian West, 222
    recorded between 1889–1927, 171

M

Macdonald, Sir John A., 196, 214, 229, 230, 251, 255
    "one body of criminal law," 25
Macdonell, Inspector A. R. (RCMP), 143
Mackay, Marion, 329
Mackenzie, Col. Ranald, 39
Macleod Gazette, 229, 238, 239, 246, 248, 249, 250
Macleod, James F., 217, 256, 321
Macleod, R.C., 238, 240, 241
Madden, Bill, 132
Madsen, Chris, 73
Major, Alexander, 63
manifest destiny, 230, 255, 285, 288
Mark Twain, 276
Marriages of Scipio, The, 310
Marshall, Chief Justice John, 6
Marshall, Ed, 260
Marshall, Tom, 260
Martin, Trayvon,, 15
Masterson, Bat, 42, 114
Maunsell, E.H., 243
May, Daniel Boone, 58
McCall, Jack, 55
McCook, James, 335
McEachran, Duncan, 235
McGath, Roger, 10
McKinnon, Lachlin, 202
McLaughlin, James, 82
McLean, Lin (Jim Drummond), 275
McMurtry, Larry, 304
McNaught, Kenneth, 4
Meadows, Anne, 132, 133
Members of the Family, 309
Merritt, General Wesley, 68, 75

Metis Rebellion (1885), 3, 243, 249, 251, 252
Mickelson, Ole, 245
Mickle, Wheeler, 319
Miles, General Nelson, 82
Miller, Jack, 316
Minto, Lord and Lady, 264
Mitchell, S. Weir, 271–275
Moonlight, Thomas, 138
Morrison, William, 228
Mosby, General John Singleton, 106
Moses, Phoebe Ann (Annie Oakley), 77, 80
Munch, Edvard, 81
Murphy, E. W., 113, 126, 196–97
Murray, Robert, 98, 104
My Life on the Plains, 76, 149
Myrick, Andrew, 33

N

National Rifle Association (NRA), 8, 18–19, 21, 23–25, 27–28
Native incarceration, frequency of in West, 239
Native rights, suppression of in Canada, 3
Neighbours Henceforth, 310
Neil, Jim, 160
Nelson, Charles "Red," 247
Nelson, Thomas, 162
New York Herald, 65, 74
New York Times, 65
Niar, Shorty, 259, 260
No Duty to Retreat, 2, 9, 15, 23. *See* Duty to Retreat
North American Cattle Ranching Frontiers, 111
North West Mounted Police (NWMP), 2, 212, 214–19, 223–24, 253–54
  pass system, 250, 251, 252
  patrol routs, 223, 225
North-West Territories Act (1875), 218
North, Major Frank, 38
Northwest Ordinance (1787), 5, 93

O

O.K. Corral, 146
Oakley, Annie. *See* Moses, Phoebe Ann
Obama, President Barrack, 18
Oliver, Frank, 232
Oregon Trail, 94
Osborne, Blue, 198, 259

Osborne, John, 87
Outing Magazine, 280, 285
Ox-Bow Incident, The, 145, 171

P

Padre Ignazio, 301
Paine, Thomas, 170
Palin, Sarah, 23, 24
Parker, Watson, 52
Parks, Gentleman Charlie, 320
Parrott, George "Big Nose," 54, 87
Parslow, Kathleen, 264
Patterson, R. M., 328
Patterson, Richard, 132, 134
Payne, Darwin, 180–81, 185, 190, 272
Peach, Tucker, 244
Penrose, Dr. Charles, 148
Pentecost of Calamity, The, 310
Perry, Charlie, 201
Pfaelzer, Jean, 7
Pfouts, Paris, 141
Phillips, John "Portuguese," 61, 98–99, 110
Phillips, William T. *See* Butch Cassidy
Philosophy 4, 302
Piercy, Inspector William, 245
Pinkerton agents, 53, 133, 227
Pizantia, Jose "The Greaser," 142
Plummer, Henry, 141
Plunkett, Horace, 196
Pocaterra, Norma Piper, 327
Poindexter, Sarah Quarles, 31
Pointer, Larry, 132, 134
Policing the Great Plains, 253
Powder River country, 89
Powell, Captain James, 103, 105
Powell, John Wesley, 122
Prassel, Frank, 10

R

Ranch Life and the Hunting Trail, 280, 285, 287
ranching, removal of impediments to, 90
Ray, Nick, 148
Red Cloud, 98, 101, 109
Red Men and White, 290
Red Sash gang, 177
Reed, Tom, 57
Reid, Bill, xiv, 67, 92, 99–100, 104, 109, 329
Reid, Jack, xiv, 67, 330

Remington, Frederic, 37, 39, 41–42, 62, 83, 96, 215, 258, 261, 273, 277, 279, 280–82, 285–86, 290–91, 293–299, 301–2, 306, 308, 331
  importance of, 96
Rhodes, B. F., 321
Rice-Jones, Cecil, 263
Ricks, Frank, 264, 315
Riel, Louis, 82
rifle
  Federal Assault Ban on, 18
  Henry repeating, quality of, 106
  improvements in, legacy of Civil War, 109
  Spencer repeating, performance of, 107
  Springfield, performance of, 105
  Winchester repeating, value of, 105
Road to Mobocracy, 171
Robertson, Sgt. Frank, 103
Rock Springs, Wyoming, 7
rodeo
  beginnings of, 77
  heritage of, 258
Rogers, Magnus, 244
Romney, 310
Roosevelt, Theodore, xii, 12–13, 24, 83, 109, 143, 168, 181, 269, 273, 276, 280–81, 283–90, 294–97, 299, 302, 306–10, 312, 331–33
  "What Americanism Means," 294
  influence on Wister, 283
Roosevelt: The Story of a Friendship, 181, 273
Rosa, Joseph, 10
Ross, Charley, 57
Ross, Sinclair, 256
Russell, Andy, 92
Russell, Charlie, 197, 247, 316
Russell, Don, 62, 75

S

Sand Creek Massacre, 95
Sandoz, Mari, 118, 139
Sandy Hook Elementary School, 21
Saufley, Judge Micah C., 138
Saxon, Alexander, 7
Scott, Douglas D., 105
Scott, Sir Walter, 296
  popularity in the South, 187
Searight, G.A., 155

Semple, Robert, 213
Seven Ages of Washington, The, 309
Seven Oaks Massacre, 213
Shackleton, Ernest, 297
Sharp, Paul, 237, 246
sheep
  introduction in Wyoming, 125
  ranching, Canadian federal policy, 231
  wars, in Wyoming, 151
Sheppard, Burt, 317
Sheridan, General Philip, 46, 65, 98, 114
Sifton, Clifford, 232
Simpson, George, 213
Siringo, Charlie, 227
Sitting Bull, 72, 78, 82–83, 101, 110
Six Gun Mystique, 14
Skagway, Alaska, 227
Skirdin, Charles D., 180, 181, 185, 309, 312
Skrine, Walter, 198
Slade, Joseph A., 142
Slatta, Richard, 110, 297, 316
Slaughter, John, 89, 324
Slotkin, Richard, 10, 14
Smith, "Black" Henry, 172–73, 175–76, 178
Smith, Helena Huntington, 138
Smith, Jefferson "Soapy," 227
Smith, Lorenzo, 200, 265
Smith, Major B.F., 105
Smith, Mary Greeley, 205
Snow, Clyde, 133
Snyder, Harry, 330
Spirit-of-Iron, 14
Spotted Tail, 66
Spring, Agnes, 112–13
Stark, General John, 173, 305
Stark, Molly, 173
Steele, Harwood, 14
Stegner, Wallace, 38, 216, 220, 232, 250, 311
Stein, Gertrude, 157
Steinbeck, John, 311
Stephens, Doug, 258
Stimson, Fred, 202, 205, 208
Storey, Milton S., 184
Story of Chalkeye, The, 275
Strange, Thomas Bland, 205
Stuart, Granville, 143
Sturgis, Thomas, 123, 136
Summit Springs, battle of, 67
Sundance Kid. *See* Longabaugh, Harry

410 THE COWBOY LEGEND

T

Tallent, Annie, 47
Taylor Grazing Act, 123
Teschemacher, Hubert, 147
Texas Rangers, 253, 254
Texas
    violent culture of, 35
    Wister's opinion of, 186
Thomas, L. G., 234, 236
Thompson, Ed (Boney), 318, 319
Thompson, Phatty, 58
Thorner, Tom, 239
Timber Culture Act (1873), 122
Tisdale, Bob, 148, 276
Tombstone, Arizona, 146
Towle, Frank, 57–58
Treaty of Medicine Lodge (1867), 40
Treaty of Washington (1866), 248
Trollinger, Joe, 195
Turner, Frederick Jackson, 83, 157, 254, 280, 288–89
    "The Significance of the Frontier in American History," 83

U

U.S. Army, condition of post–Civil War, 96
Undiplomatic Notes: Tales from the Canadian Foreign Service, xi
Union Pacific Railroad, 64, 94
United Empire Loyalists, 2
Unnamed Country: The Struggle for a Canadian Prairie Fiction, 14
Utley, Robert, 97, 104, 210

V

Van Devanter, Willis, 147
Van Tassel, Van Rensselaer Schuyler, 155
vigilante
    action, in Canada, 252
    Bannack vigilantes, 142
    committee, in Dodge City, 41
    honoured as heroes in Montana, 145
    in California and the Carolinas, 289
    law, 165
    Stuart's Stranglers, 144–47
    tradition, 14
    tradition, not in Canadian West, 25
Vigilantes of Montana, The, 166
vigilantism

"one of the greatest curses of the United States," 143
    and Sara Palin, 23
    and television, 14
    emergence of, 1
    in Canadian West, 245
    origin of, 12
    racial background, 12
    reasons for, 12
violence
    American history, causes of, 4
    in American West, 10
    in Canadian history, 4
    in movies, 21
Virginia Tech killings, 20
Virginian, The, xi–xii, xvi, 57, 85, 119, 129, 155, 158–60, 163, 165, 168–69, 172–73, 176, 178–83, 185–88, 193, 265, 267, 272, 277, 279, 287, 296–97, 299–300, 302–12, 317, 332
    as play and movie, 304
    first publication of, 303
    most popular folk hero, 189
    synopsis of, xviii–xxxv
Virginian, the, character of and inspiration for, 14, 15, 158–59, 165, 168–69, 173, 176–77, 179–86, 189–92, 200, 265, 272–73, 276–79, 283, 300–301, 303–5, 308, 334

W

Wagon Box Fight, xiv, 92, 100–110, 329–30,
Wallace, Michael, 10, 17
Walrond-Walrond, Sir John, 234
Ware, John, 190, 201, 204, 264
Waring, George, 184, 301
Warner, William D., 92
Warren, Louis, 63–64
Warren, Senator Francis, 147
Washakee, Chief, 100
Watson, Ella, 166
Weadick, Guy, 257
Webb, Walter Prescott, 23, 24
Wellman, George, 177, 320
Wells-Barnett, Ida, 13
West
    America's destiny, 121
    attitude toward Native people in, 84–85
    British view of American, 79
    Manifest Destiny, 285, 288

racial decay, fear of, in American, 79
testing ground for Anglo-Saxon qualities, 293
West, George, 181, 183, 190, 200, 273, 309, 312
Western Range Revisited, The, 122
Western Trail, 40
Westward Bound, 238
Wheeler, Edward, 57
When West Was West, 311
White, Jonathan, 73
Whoop-Up Country, 237
Wibaux, Pierre, 198
Wild Bunch, members of, 132
Wild West Show. *See Buffalo Bill's Wild West*
Wilde, Sargent, 242
Wilderness Hunter, 285
Wilderness Warrior, The, 283
Wills, Gary, 17
Winder, William, 234
Winning of the West, The, 283, 286–88, 296
Wister, Fanny Kemble, 180
Wister, Mary Channing, 301
Wister, Owen, xi–xii, xv–xvi, 1, 12–15, 40, 63, 79, 83, 85, 111, 114, 116–17, 119, 129, 132, 140, 148, 150, 153–63, 165–93, 195, 199–200, 255–56, 258, 265, 267–83, 285–87, 290–91, 293–97, 299–312, 315–16, 320–21, 330, 332, 335
    American South, opinion of, 187
    Charlestown, S.C., spiritual home of, 305
    decision to write about the West, 273
    education of, 269–72
    stories
        "Baalam and Pedro," 181, 276–77, 290
        "Destiny at Drybones," 300
        "Dragon of Wantley, The," 276
        "Evolution of the Cow-Puncher, The," 192, 276, 287, 290–91, 293, 297, 299, 301
        "Game and the Nation, The," 301
        "Grandmother Stark," 300
        "Hank's Woman," 177, 181, 274–75
        "Horses of the Plains," 295
        "How Lin McLean Went East," 181, 275

        "National Guard of Pennsylvania, The," 295
        "Right Honorable the Strawberries, The," 184
        "Separ's Vigilante," 300
        "Story of Chalkeye: A Wind River Romance, The," 178
        "Winning of the Biscuit-Shooter, The," 279
    upbringing and early life, 267–69
Wister, Owen Jones, 269, 270
Wister, Sarah Butler, 267, 303
Wolcott, Frank, 140, 147, 149, 153, 158, 161–63, 272
Wood, Gordon, 18
Wood, Zachary Taylor, 227
Woods, Lawrence, 112
Wooly-Dod, Bill, 321
World's Columbian Exposition (1893), 73, 288
Wounded Knee, battle of, 83
Writings of Owen Wister: The Virginian, The, 186
Wyoming Farmers and Stock Growers Association, 148
Wyoming Range War, 147
Wyoming Stock Growers' Association (WSGA), 123, 132, 138–40, 148–r49, 151, 163, 165
Wyoming
    British capital investment in, 119
    British economic presence in, 164
    census of 1880, 91
    Great Die Up (1886–87), 115, 138, 148, 153, 265
    importance of water in, 122
    Maverick Law (1884), 139

Y

Yellow Hand (Yellow Hair), 69–70, 77, 80–81, 289, 321
York, Duke and Duchess of, 264

Z

Zimmerman, George, 15
Zimmerman, John, 58